The Tack Buyer's Guide

The
Tack
Buyer's
Guide

The Horseman's Complete Handbook on the Purchase and Use of Equestrian Equipment of All Kinds

by

CHARLENE STRICKLAND

Drawings by HEATHER J. LOWE

For information address:

Breakthrough Publications, Inc.
Scarborough Station Plaza
Briarcliff, New York 10510

International Standard Book Number: 0-914327-22-4

Designed by Jacques Chazaud
Manufactured in the United States of America
Second Printing: November, 1990

The following products mentioned in this book are Registered in the U.S. Patent and Trademark Office:
Absorbine, Adams Equipment, Alprima, Atherstone, Baker Balanced Ride, Balding, Barnsby, Battle, Betadine, Bickmore, Bienenwachs, Billy Cook, Biothane, Bixton, Blivens, Borks of Pendleton, Blue Ribbon, Campbell, Canterbury, Caprilli, Capriola, Champion, Circle Y, Cliff-Barnsby, Continental, Conway, Cordura, Corfa, Corona, Cotton Craft, Courts, Craigmyle, Crates, Crosby, Crosby Collegiate, Crump, Cutter Animal Health, Dave Scott, Duraglit, Dural, Dutton, Dyo Chemical Company, Easy Entry, Ectrin, Ed Sims, Elmer Miller, Ensolite, Eskadron, Exhibitor Labs, Farnam, Fiebing's, Fillis, Garcia, Gold Cup, Gore-Tex, Hamilton, Hampa, Hartley, Hermes, Hinshaw, Hollofil, Horseman's Dream, Houghton, Hufgrip, Hydrophane, IPS, Jeffries, Jerald, Jimmy's, Josey, Keyston, Kieffer, Kineton, Kodel, Lampwick, Lederfit, Ledersbalsam, Lexol, Lexol Ph, Liverpool, Lysol, Mac Pherson, Meadowbrook, Miller's, Mother Hubbard, Monel, Never-Rust, Oster, Parrant, Passier, Partrade, Peacock, Peakes, Permectrin, Permethrin, Pessoa, Plexiglas, Potts Longhorn, Quick, Rawhide Manufacturing, Resmethrin, Rios, Ritter, Roy Martin, Saddle King, Sanforized, Scotchguard, Sid Hill and Sons, Simco, Sliester, Slym-Line, Stanhope, Stockmen's, Sunbeam, Superior, SuperSweats, Telfa, Tex Tan, Thinsulate, Tilbury, Toklat, Toowoomba, Trammel, Trevor James, Triple Crown, Trivera, Ulster, Ultra Grooming Products, Uxeter, Valhoma, Vaseline, Vetrap, Victor Leather Goods, Victor Supreme, Wayne Walker, Whitman, Wilform, Winner's Circle, Wonder Whip, Woof, Wright Bernet, Wrip Wrap.

To Jill-Marie Jones, for launching and supporting the "Tackline" series.

CONTENTS

Introduction

In horsemanship, your goal is to establish a harmonious partnership. You and your horse should move with artistry—with light, confident movements.

You will utilize a variety of saddlery and accessories in your interactions. This equipment, which is in contact with your horse, influences it by exerting unnatural pressure on its body.

You cannot achieve your goal if your equipment irritates, distracts, or hinders your horse. Therefore, to reduce discomfort and interference, any tack or accessories you use must exert as little pressure as possible. Proper equipment can enhance your partnership with your horse; improper equipment can adversely affect both of you. The horse will be uncomfortable and unresponsive, and you will not enjoy your sport. Improper equipment can even lead to an accident.

Selecting the proper, least irritating equipment is a complex equestrian activity. Like equitation and training, it combines art and science.

The art aspect consists of achieving your goal of artistry. The scientific includes both equine behavior and dynamics, the branch of mechanics which involves forces that affect motion. Equipment must be engineered in order to function properly.

It also involves a third aspect: economics. Ideally, the cost of equipment should be your final consideration, after you have weighed its artistic and scientific merits. However, the reality is that most people concentrate on price.

Experts estimate horse owners spend up to $2,000 for equipment in their first two years of horse ownership. After they have established their basic collections, replacement and new additions will average from $100 to $700 annually, depending on tastes and needs. Horse owners who switch disciplines can expect to buy at almost the start-up rate.

This book will enhance your knowledge of the art, science, and economics of equipment selection. It will help educate you to make the right decisions and purchase the appropriate equipment, while receiving the best value for your money. You will understand how to evaluate products in order to identify quality. Background information surveys the horse equipment industry, the basic materials used in tack and accessories, and what factors determine quality. You will learn quality factors in the design, materials, fit, and craftsmanship of over forty product types. And, you will discover how to work your way through the marketplace to arrive at the best buying decisions.

1

Although the book surveys the thousands of choices among products, it focuses chiefly on equipment selection. It does not cover specific uses of saddlery, which you can learn from other sources.

This book is based on the series, "Tackline," originally published in *Horse Illustrated* magazine from 1985 to 1987. Information has been expanded with input from dozens of professionals associated with the horse equipment industry—manufacturers, importers, artisans, and retailers. These industry experts represent horse tack and accessories produced worldwide—in the United States, Canada, Mexico, Latin America, Europe, Asia, and Australia. Also contributing were tack connoisseurs and officials from trade associations. Each firm or individual contributed information through personal interview, a survey by mail, and by sharing product catalogs, and brochures.

To aid you in working your way through the multitude of individual products on the market, the book's chapters are arranged to duplicate the layout of the average tack shop. Each item includes a brief description of its design, plus specific buying guidelines and recommendations.

To assist you in your tack purchasing, the "Quality Recommendations" summarize the brands most often mentioned by the contributing experts. Added are "Insiders' Preferences," which are candid quotes from sellers and a few experienced consumers. These opinions are based on the contributors' individual experiences; therefore, they are attributed only to the person's industry affiliation.

Please remember that brand-name comments are only guidelines. As explained later in this book, the saddlery industry differs from other industries in the lack of clear brand identification. Unlike a washing machine or even a sweater, many products do not carry any labels. Even brand-name items are often made by other firms and later stamped with the brand name.

Before you shop, you must clearly understand your needs. After each chapter is a summary of questions you might ask yourself and the seller. In addition to product-specific questions, the following apply to any item:

- Do you really need this product?
- Do you know how to use this product safely and humanely?
- Does it match your style of horsemanship?
- Does it fit your horse comfortably?
- Does it fit you?
- Will you receive value for your money?
- How much care does the item require?
- Do you require any special features, or will the basic model suffice?
- If this is a show item, will it meet current requirements and remain in fashion?
- Do you like high-tech materials and designs, or should you stick with the tried-and-true?

Quality tack enhances the partnership between horse and rider, without hindering either's performance. David Wilson on Academy Award.

PART I: INDUSTRY BACKGROUND

Chapter 1

THE TACK INDUSTRY

The horse-equipment industry actually encompasses four groups of firms: manufacturers, importers, distributors, and retailers. Manufacturers consist of large firms that produce horse tack in factories, companies who produce horse equipment as part of a line of goods, smaller cottage industries specializing in one type of equipment, and the one-person custom shop. There are approximately three to four hundred manufacturers in the United States.

Importers may bring items into the United States to sell directly to consumers, or they may sell to distributors, who wholesale goods to retailers. Distributors purchase items directly from manufacturers or importers, and some also manufacture certain products in their line. Distributors can influence importers by selecting which items and models to import, and some control distribution of imported goods by acquiring exclusive rights. For example, a prominent saddle line may offer only a few models to U.S. buyers through a distributor agreement. If you visit a European saddle shop, you may see a totally different product line.

Retailers acquire items either from manufacturers or distributors, or by manufacturing or importing goods themselves. They sell goods through a permanent shop, through mail order, or a combination of both. In the United States there are six to seven thousand retail operations, many of them small shops.

In many ways, the horse equipment industry resembles the apparel industry. Many items fall into the "cut-and-sewn" category. Before the Industrial Revolution, craftsmen used hand tools to cut items from cloth or leather, then stitched the pieces with needle and thread.

As it affected the clothing industry, the Industrial Revolution also altered the production of horse equipment. A factory could produce a greater number of machine-sewn saddles than could a crew of workers using hand tools. However, most horsemen still consider a handcrafted piece of tack superior to a mass-produced one.

In the United States, the entrepreneurial tack industry functions as a part of the free-enterprise system, at the same time reflecting the rugged individualism among horsepeople. Even though organizations exist, only a certain percentage of

Renowned trainers set trends in showing and training gear. Linda Baker schools Astro Chex at home.

firms participate. The industry is comprised of individuals holding their own opinions, each focusing on specific viewpoints. Numerous differences of opinion often lead to representatives jealously criticizing others' products, motivations, and marketing tactics.

The industry's disorganization is reflected in the variety of standards. The major manufacturers tend to establish their own individual sizes, grades, or even definitions of equipment. This conflicting information can confuse buyers of similar products.

However, the industry does generate substantial dollar volume. According to the *1987 Membership Survey of the American Quarter Horse Association*, members' expenditures for equipment totalled $108,440,000. The 160,000 members and their families spent almost half this amount on Western saddles alone.

As riding increases in popularity, the equipment industry will grow to meet consumer demands. Continued profits depend on the sport attracting consumers' disposable income. Riding competes in this regard with tennis, golf, and skiing, all individual pursuits which fall into the "elite" sport category.

Industry spokesmen express concern about riding's image. To attract more riders, especially young people, many representatives strive to popularize riding. They feel it should a be more accessible sport, not one confined to the rich, and contend that the up-front costs should not discourage the entry-level rider.

Research and Development

Manufacturers are constantly designing and producing new products, as well as using new materials to improve existing items. Riders are similarly seeking equipment that will offer them a competitive edge.

Ideally, manufacturers should be actively involved in the equestrian sporting scene. In order to produce and market the best products, they should be practitioners as well as businesspeople. Knowing how a product functions under field conditions gives insight into its eventual success or failure. However, some manufacturers complain that opinionated riders should not attempt to design saddles. What works for one talented competitor may not function correctly for the average rider.

As the sport becomes more scientific, progressive firms are striving to improve their products. Generally, firms new to the field seem most interested in designing new products or making variations on existing models.

The horse show industry greatly affects equipment design. Experts request modifications from manufacturers and manufacturers seek input from renowned exhibitors. The two often collaborate on new models. For example, Jimmy Williams has developed and tested many bit designs produced by Quick Bits. Lynn MacKenzie and Martha Josey actively participate in perfecting games equipment, and Billy Cook, Monte Foreman, Tad Coffin, and Nelson Pessoa have lent their names to saddle designs.

To ensure a new product's success, the designer and manufacturer must test prototypes thoroughly. Some new bit designs undergo testing for as long as five years before they enter the market. The firm can guarantee the product's satisfaction and maintain its reputation by such extended field testing.

There will always be traditionalists, however, who criticize new developments. They consider the modern inventions travesties compared to the tried-and-true equipment. Even hide-bound purists, though, recognize the influence of fashion, which is seen especially in Western saddlery. Riders at all levels will buy equipment in order to follow trends, and changes in fashion keep many companies solvent. American buyers are conditioned to accept product changes, and they expect new choices each season.

Fashions can begin through a user-suggested or manufacturer-designed model. Because show riders are most concerned with being in style, fashions are usually initiated and copied in the show ring. A manufacturer may convince a winning rider to display a new saddle pad, hoping that the rider's imitators will want one, too.

Fashions usually begin on the East or West Coasts. They generally progress in five-year cycles, with slight modifications developing gradually into a takeover. The Quarter Horse leaders set the pace in Western saddlery, Saddlebred trainers in saddle-seat equipment and the East Coast hunter/jumper celebrities in hunt-seat styles.

Manufacturers realize that even the most fashion-conscious riders will be hesitant to accept a radically different innovation. Some admit that they aim fashions at the woman rider, whose tastes, they believe, dominate fashion. Research indicates that men who purchase items for women will usually choose those preferred by women.

Manufacturers try to stay ahead of the market, hoping that a new design will succeed in setting a trend. If a new saddle decoration attracts attention, the saddlemaker can sell more product. However, when a new design becomes popular, competing firms commonly copy it. This can in-

At trade shows, manufacturers and distributors exhibit their product lines to retailers.

undate the market with so many look-alikes that the trendsetter must look for a new, unique design.

Like apparel manufacturers, saddlery firms routinely resurrect old designs. Recently the basket-stamped Western saddle has made a comeback. Popular in the early years of this century, it practically disappeared for decades. The thousands of riders who bought saddles with white buckstitching must be eagerly hoping for *its* return to the show ring.

Marketing

Manufacturers and distributors market products to retailers through print media and personal contacts. The industry's trade magazine, *Tack and Togs*, serves as both a communication and marketing tool. Sales representatives contact buyers both at retail outlets and at trade shows, which are held throughout the year. Manufacturers and distributors exhibit at shows across the United States, displaying product lines exclusively "to the trade" and inviting other distributors and retailers to inspect both established and new goods.

Marketing outlets also allow communication within the four industry groups. Retailers can convey customers' responses and product requests directly to manufacturers. Manufacturers can promote products and explain technological advances in materials and construction.

All segments of the industry advertise in popular equestrian magazines. Larger firms often hire an advertising agency or public relations firm to produce attractive ads. Companies also submit product announcements to magazines' "new products" features.

Advertising promotes new fashions and keeps brand names familiar to consumers. Also, paid ads support most horse magazines. Without this income, many publishers could not continue to produce attractive magazines with a large percentage of editorial matter.

The advertising of brand names in horse equipment is very different from that of more familiar sporting goods, such as footballs. Because the manufacturer sells to a much smaller market, it is not cost-efficient to advertise in a mass-market magazine whose riding readers total a possible 1 percent.

Many firms choose not to advertise their brands nationally in equestrian publications, especially if they distribute only within a region. Therefore, their quality products do not receive national coverage, and you do not hear about many excellent choices.

Retailers market their wares either locally or through mail order. Usually, retailers benefit from manufacturers' print advertising and through word of mouth. For example, a riding instructor will advise her students to acquire a certain bridle style, or a brand-name saddle pad.

Current Trends

Five factors affect the tack industry in the United States: offshore production, fluctuation of the dollar, the availability of leather, consumer education, and manufacturer responsibility.

OFFSHORE PRODUCTION As with all manufactured goods, companies have discovered that some products can be made more cheaply by foreign workers, primarily those in Asia and Latin America. Some firms, known worldwide for excellence, now contract out production and import finished goods. Offshore production quality varies according to the skill of the work force, the materials used, and the onsite management.

Some firms concentrate on offshore assembly. The importer provides materials and components to these firms, then receives back the finished products.

Offshore production offers advantages and disadvantages. Proponents argue that information and technology are not exclusive to Europe or

North America. Foreign workers can learn to imitate quality methods, and some countries are renowned for certain products. Why should tack be so difficult?

Those critical of offshore production maintain that foreign workers may produce goods that cannot function properly. A poor copy of a handmade bit can be greatly inferior, with incorrect balance and even an ill-fitting mouthpiece. Foreign workers may not fully understand what is needed in a bit for an American horse.

Also, shipping costs and import duties may limit availability of some items.

FLUCTUATION OF THE DOLLAR Imported goods vary in price due to the world economic situation. Currently, fluctuations of the value of the dollar affect the cost of saddlery imported from the respected European names. One saddle shop owner notes that a distributor marked up a popular line of German saddles 200 to 300 dollars each in a month. Therefore, when you compare models among shops, you might pay less for a saddle that has been on the floor before the new models arrived after the price increase.

However, if you select an Australian import, you might save money by waiting another month or two. Currently the value of the Australian dollar has lowered prices of goods from that country.

LEATHER The demand for beef has affected the U.S. leather market. Cattle go to market earlier, which results in younger animals producing hides of lesser quality. Recently, some major tanneries have closed their doors, reducing the number of hides available to saddlery manufacturers. In addition, foreign investors have purchased large quantities of the hides on the market.

These factors have caused a 30 percent increase in the price of leather from 1986 to 1987, and thirty-day price quotes indicate frequent increases. The consumer will undoubtedly notice the increase in costs of leather tack, and many may switch to similar products constructed of formerly unconventional materials.

CONSUMER EDUCATION Industry experts realize that the influx of new riders and owners means more buyers—and that these novices lack knowledge about the products they purchase. Experts agree that the major errors consumer, make are to buy on impulse and to buy on price alone.

Manufacturers want consumers to buy wisely, to be satisfied with their purchases and not to learn by trial and error. When equipment fulfills the buyer's expectations, he or she will become a repeat customer. If the customer buys an inferior bit, which breaks and causes an accident, she may decide to quit riding and spend her leisure time (and dollars) playing tennis.

Sellers face a dilemma: they want you to be pleased with their merchandise yet buy more. Quality-conscious manufacturers aim for long-lasting, durable products. However, they also want you to continue buying their products, too. The way they can maintain or increase sales is to satisfy your needs.

Many firms do attempt to educate consumers. Their print advertising contains useful product information, to aid you in comparisons. Mail-order firms often indicate proper fitting and use in catalog copy.

Other firms contend that the consumer should not attempt to make decisions. They feel that a little knowledge can be dangerous, and they recommend that you rely only on expert advice.

Like consumers, many retailers lack knowledge. They may have opened a shop because they like horses and enjoy one riding style, but they need help in matching the customer to the appropriate product. They learn by consulting manufacturers and attending trade shows and seminars. Major manufacturers and distributors educate their dealers. For example, Miller's, County Saddlery, Foxwood, and B. T. Crump present frequent dealers' seminars.

Manufacturer Responsibility

In this era of widespread litigation, tack manufacturers have been challenged for equipment failure. One firm recently defended its product in a six-figure lawsuit.

Obviously this trend concerns all segments of the industry. Insiders claim the major factor in equipment failure is consumer misuse of their products, subsequently leading to a lawsuit. They emphasize that the buyer must realize the product's intended purpose, and that it is unrealistic to expect a product to function beyond reasonable expectations. For example, one firm reported a claim by a customer who broke a lead rope while attempting to tow a loaded boat trailer out of water.

Proper care of equipment is also an issue in manufacturer responsibility. One customer threatened a retailer with a lawsuit over an injury caused by a broken girth. The exhibited article showed dried leather that had never been oiled since its purchase.

Many manufacturers now attach care-and-use tags to their products. As with any other purchased item, the buyer must assume the responsibility of regular maintenance. A court of law would not consider a case against an automobile manufacturer sued for equipment failure because the buyer forgot to add oil to the engine.

The Western and English Manufacturers' Association (WAEMA) has produced a videotape to illustrate the importance of tack inspection and maintenance. Many shops purchase the tape, "Pre-Ride Checklist," to help educate their customers about the rider's safety responsibilities.

Chapter 2

—

MATERIALS

Manufacturers construct horse tack and accessories from six basic forms of materials: leather, rubber, flexible fibers, metals, plastics, and fiberglass. Before you compare products of various materials, it helps to understand the properties of each type.

Leather

Traditionally, saddlery is composed of leather pieces stitched together. Leather is treated animal skin, usually cow hides. Beginning with a piece of skin covered with hair, the leatherworker produces a hide with a smooth, "grain" side, and a rougher, "flesh" side.

The leather tanner cures hides by a series of mechanical and chemical processes. How leather is tanned affects its future use. Today tanneries choose one of two proven methods: vegetable or mineral tanning. In the first, tannins—acids obtained primarily from tree barks—soak into the hides over several weeks or even months. Mineral tanning involves treating hides for a few days in a chromium salt solution.

In general, saddlers consider oak-bark tanned leather superior to chrome-tanned. Vegetable tanning seems to result in a plumper and firmer leather, with what tanners consider more temper or stand (firmness). It will absorb oils better, while resisting water. One tanner affirms that you should choose a vegetable-tanned leather for any product that is intended for direct exposure to animal or human skin, since chrome-tanned leather can cause an allergic reaction.

Chrome-tanned leather feels softer and more flexible. It is more heat-resistant than other leathers, and it retains strength, although it will stretch more than oak-bark tanned leather.

After tanning, leather is soaked with penetrating oils and fats, such as tallow or fish oil. Oiling and rolling prevents the preserved hide from drying out and hardening.

The final step, currying, dresses the leather. Hides are run through splitting and shaving machines, which produce an evenly thick surface. Because leather's fibers create what is called a homogenized weave, its weight can be decreased without sacrificing strength.

Finished leather can be defined by its eventual purpose. For strap goods, saddlers differentiate between two types of finished leather: strap and harness. Strap leather, weighing from eight to ten ounces per square foot, is flattened and compressed by rolling; it is then buffed for a smoother finish. The heavier harness leather weighs from sixteen to eighteen ounces per square foot. Because it has been impregnated with dressings for increased flexibility and resilience, its surface feels oily or greasy. This workmanlike leather will repel sweat better than strap leather; it is com-

monly used in working tack. Today harness leather is the most expensive type.

Excellent leather is marketed as full-grain. Other leathers are cut horizontally, to produce split leather. Top-grain leather consists of the top or outside layer of the hide, usually considered the best section because the fibers are close together. Soft glove leather is also made from top-grain leather; it is formed by removing layers of the flesh side. The characteristic reddish brown Western latigo is the result of an oil tanning and splitting process.

Western saddlery also utilizes rawhide, a split leather treated by simply removing the hair and soaking the leather. Rawhide is known for its toughness and elasticity. You will see it cut into straps and plaited, or covering parts of a saddle.

Tanners color leather either by soaking or spraying dye onto the surface. English leather traditionally appears in three stains: London, a golden shade; Havana, a brown reminiscent of a havana cigar; and Warwick, an almost black shade. Undyed harness leather is russet color; it is dyed either black or a deep, rich brown. Leather found in Western saddlery may be russet or latigo.

Finishing handwork can improve the quality of the final product. The time a currier spends scraping and rubbing both sides of the leather, then working in more tallow, will result in a supe-

Look for fine finish in a top quality leather.

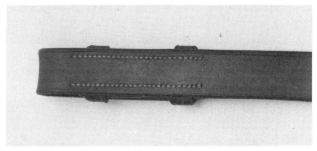

rior piece. Machinework can disguise poorer leather, by imprinting an embossed, textured surface, or buffing the leather to add a polish or remove blemishes. However, excess buffing can weaken leather by reducing its weight and its future durability.

Patent leather features a glossy surface, which may crack over time. Many patent leathers today are finished with a plastic coating.

Although processing affects leather's fineness, the source of the hide itself also contributes to the quality of the final product. Most saddlery is made of cowhide. The size and thickness of the hide varies according to the cow's age, diet, and environment. A feed-lot steer butchered at two years of age may not produce a hide that is large enough for seven-foot reins, or thick enough for the stirrup leathers of a western saddle. Quality-conscious saddlers prefer to choose tougher, larger hides from range-fed animals butchered in the prime of life.

Hides also show surface defects after hairs are removed. Many are scarred by barbed wire cuts or damaged by external parasites. A currier can buff some scars or dimples from the leather's surface, but this weakens the hide by reducing its thickness.

Saddlers also utilize leather from animals other than adult cattle. Calfskin is softer and thinner than an adult's hide. Pigskin provides an elastic, tough leather covering often used for the seat of an English saddle. Doeskin, or deerhide, produces a suede leather with a dense fiber structure.

You will also see leather from two distant continents: buffalo and kangaroo. The domesticated water buffalo produces a heavy, coarse-grained leather, used in some stirrup leathers and in tack manufactured in India. Buffalo leather has an extremely strong tensile strength, but the tanning process limits its shine. The rarer Australian kangaroo leather makes strong, supple, and durable bridles and reins.

Because cowhide comprises most saddlery, saddlers define leathers by the section of the animal. A half hide, or side, is the piece most saddlers receive from the tannery. This flat section is a hide split down the length of the animal's backbone.

Butt leather, from the animal's back from tail to shoulder, is considered the thickest and strongest. Shoulder leather is also thick, but is not as as pliable and smooth as butt leather. Neck leather will be thinner than either, and belly leather is the thinnest, most porous, and weakest leather.

Quality

Test leather for quality by learning its origin and how it was tanned. Also check its thickness. Thicker leather holds more fat and retains the greatest strength.

To gauge leather's thickness, ask about its weight, as tanners grade leather by its weight per square foot. Leather ranges from three to twenty ounces, with the heaviest weight butts—about one-quarter inch thick—best for saddles, bridles, and reins. Strap and skirting leather, often seen in the skirts of Western saddles and some bridles, are about one-eighth inch thick.

Leather should feel smooth and substantial. Realize that oiling can make a difference in the feel of new leather goods. Two identical straps, one dark and oiled, the other the lighter London color, will not feel the same. The amount of oil absorbed in the darker strap will make it feel smoother.

Feel the pliability of leather by stroking both sides, searching for a warm, vibrant touch. Bend leather in both directions to see that both grain and flesh sides feel supple and flexible. Leather will wrinkle when you bend it, but the wrinkles should vanish as soon as you flatten the piece. Poor-quality leather will remain creased or bubbled.

New leather should feel slightly greasy, but never spongy or limp. Avoid leather that feels papery, stiff, or rough.

The flesh side should show tightly packed fibers. You should not see or feel loose threads.

Like coffee, leather should smell rich and full-bodied. One tanner even claims that good leather tastes good, too.

Leather's origin can indicate its quality. For English saddlery and strap goods, professionals usually prefer leather that has been tanned in Europe.

Argentine leather, for years considered vastly inferior, has improved over the past two decades. Tannage and surface appearance are good, probably due to a strong European influence on the Argentine saddle industry. Untanned hides however, are a drier leather, which still does not measure up to European standards.

Some industry experts blame importers for the reputation of Argentine leather. Importers continually search for inexpensive lines of tack as alternatives to the high-priced European goods. Therefore, the Argentine products imported have not been the best, but the lower grades.

Some leather sold as "English" is actually imported from Argentina. There is also Argentine tack available that does not use Argentine leather —certain Argentina saddlery firms import their leather from England and France.

High-quality domestic leathers may closely resemble European varieties. For example, the grade and strength of the harness leather used in Amish products compares favorably to English harness leather. The primary difference is in the details of finish—the waxing and rubbing—which still separates Pennsylvanian products from those of the famed Walsall shops.

Currently, the level of exchange has made European leathers even higher in price than domestic counterparts. As you compare similar products of different origins, weigh your desire to own a product "Made in England" against the cost of inflation.

The Western saddlemaker requires a leather suitable for carving the traditional designs. Certain domestic tanneries are considered outstanding in the production of tooling leather. Across the United States, industry insiders rate the Hermann Oak Leather Company the best current source of leather for quality Western saddles. According to saddlemakers, this brand tools the best and retains its shape. Many companies attach a tag to their products to label the leather as Hermann Oak leather.

Rubber

A gum resin extracted from the rubber tree, rubber can be used alone or as a coating; items can be dipped into rubber's liquid form, latex. This stretchy material appears in several forms: molded into hard, solid rubber; as a spongy foam or latex rubber; and in a flat sheet. The last version is usually bonded to other fabrics to serve as a waterproof layer.

Plantation rubber, which is natural and untreated, can be formed into gum rubber, a golden-brown material used to make bell boots and bit guards. Also, natural rubber can be vulcanized, a process in which it is treated with heat and pressure to become highly elastic, firmer, and more heat-resistant. Rubber products should be checked routinely; all rubber will age due to the effects of oxygen and exposure to a strong light source.

Textiles

In horse equipment, manufacturers utilize textiles in three basic forms: fabrics, twisted cordage, and clumps of loose fibers. Both natural and synthetic fibers compose a wide variety of horse tack and apparel—parts of saddles, pads, strap goods, lead shanks, clothing, bandages, and boots. Natural textiles and cordage include wool, cotton,

You can choose from natural or synthetic fleeces. On the right, a sheepskin saddle pad has a denser, more resilient pile than the polyester fleece style.

linen, jute, hemp, and sisal.

Wool

Wool fibers, from sheep, can be used as fleece or woven into fabrics. Wool is prized for its excellent insulation properties; its surface traps air between the naturally flexible fibers. Used as a covering, it permits skin to breathe; it also absorbs moisture, which serves to wick wetness away from a horse's body.

Fleece, also called sheepskin, creates a naturally soft cushion. The fluffy wool tufts remain attached to the hide, which is oak-bark tanned to preserve it as a backing. Removed from the hide, tufts of wool or pulverized wool fibers produce flocking. This loose material is used for padding and stuffing saddlery.

Wool yarn can be woven by hand, as in a Navajo blanket, or by machine, which produces woolen fabrics like flannel, kersey, and serge. The first two are soft, napped cloth. Flannel is loosely woven, while the heavier kersey is a nonwoven, sometimes prickly material. Serge is a heavy cloth, a type of wool worsted. Closely woven with a smooth surface, it is a traditional lining fabric in English saddlery.

Processors create wool felt, thicker than plain fabric, by matting fibers together with heat and pressure. Felt may also contain hair or fur from other animals. The resulting material is dense, smooth, and resilient. Needled felt consists of interlocked fibers, which may or may not be pressed together.

Animal Hair

Animal hair is used in other fabrics and cordage. The most familiar hair used is horsehair itself. Long hairs from manes and tails can be twisted into cordage, and short body hairs from cattle or horses can be intertwined with fabrics to produce a thick felt.

Cotton

Cotton is used in tack in several different forms. Plain cotton, which is a woven fabric, is light in weight, and creates a porous covering. Cotton will shrink and rot, but its durability will extend if it is mercerized or Sanforized.

Cotton fabrics range from heavy to light, the heaviest being canvas or duck, two interchangeable terms. This tightly woven fabric is known for strength and durability.

Cotton yarns can be woven into twill or drill fabrics. This durable weave produces a heavy fabric, with its interlaced yarns forming diagonal ridges.

Cotton terrycloth consists of short loops of fabric which protrude from the basic weave. The nonslip texture is also comfortable against the horse's skin.

Heavy cotton can also be woven into an open mesh, forming scrim. (Scrim is also sometimes made from threads of jute or hemp.)

You will also see cotton woven into lengths of webbing. Made in various widths, webbing can be used to make girths, lead ropes, surcingles, and longe lines.

Linen

Linen yarn results from processed flax. It may resemble cotton, but it is stronger, more lustrous, and rot-resistant. Many saddlers prefer linen thread to cotton or synthetics.

Burlap

Rarely seen in today's apparel, burlap lined many inexpensive blankets in the past. This plain woven-jute fabric is a strong material, but it tends to rot and tear easily when exposed to moisture.

Hemp and Sisal

Hemp fibers, from the stalk of the hemp plant, are twisted to produce cordage. This coarse material is stronger than cotton, but it has become difficult to obtain. Manila hemp is used to produce Manila ropes. Ropes are also made from sisal, fibers from the leaves of the agave plant. However, sisal is not as strong or moisture-resistant as Manila hemp.

Synthetic Fibers

Chemists have created a multitude of synthetic fibers, primarily spun from filaments of plastic liquid, or polymers. These man-made fabrics can be woven, knitted, or utilized in loose-fiber form.

Nylon is the most popular synthetic. Bright and smooth, it has proven to be the strongest fiber created. Its easy care is due to its absorbent-resistance surface. Nylon will not soil easily, and it dries quickly after washing.

Nylon fabric can be categorized by measuring its denier and thread count. Denier indicates weight in relation to length, with one denier equalling .05 grams. The denier varies according

to the number and size of the yarn's filaments, which influence the fabric's weight. You will see deniers ranging from 200 to 1000.

Thread count is measured by counting the number of threads woven per inch. A more tightly woven nylon is generally less porous, with higher resistance to air circulation and insulation leakage.

You can buy nylon fabrics in several varieties. The lightweight ripstop nylon features a characteristic weave, with reinforcing threads creating a checkerboard pattern on the surface. A heavier nylon is taffeta, which has a smooth, crisp surface. Tafetta can be either matte or slick surfaced.

Packcloth is a medium-weight durable nylon. Its weave appears finer than the heavy-duty Cordura, a tough, coarse fabric with a canvaslike appearance. Abrasion tests prove that 1000 denier Cordura is the toughest fabric tested available for tack manufacturers.

Tricot is a form of finely knitted nylon. This fabric is often seen in a double-knit construction, in which two narrow ribs are interlocked to create a stretchy material.

To improve its durability and water resistance, nylon's exterior surface may be laminated with other synthetics. Heat treatment is used to bond the surfaces so they adhere to one another. The

Manufacturers offer many items made of fabric webbing. Above is a longe line of cotton; below, one of nylon.

plastic polyurethane coats some nylons. It protects best when bonded to finer yarns of low denier.

Another synthetic coating popular today is Gore-Tex. This film laminates to fabric to create a waterproof surface, yet it still allows the fabric to breathe.

Nylon is also used in narrower widths to create belting and webbing. You will see nylon webbing in a variety of widths and thicknesses. The thicker the webbing, the stronger the material. Some manufacturers use seat-belt webbing for extra strength. Although most horse equipment is sewn from flat webbing, the tubular form is considered stronger and more flexible.

Nylon strands can form cordage of any size. Narrow cords are often machine-braided to create a flat-braided strapping, and thicker cords are twisted into nylon rope. Rope can also be formed from another synthetic—polyethylene. This petroleum by-product is a resin material that is tough and chemical-resistant.

Another fiber, polypropylene, closely resembles nylon in its webbing and rope forms. This lightweight synthetic has a similar tensile strength, greater than 50,000 pounds per square inch. Some experts consider its strength inferior to nylon, however.

Polyester, another textile created from petrochemicals, is used to create woven and knitted fabrics. Resilient, durable, and shrink-resistant, this familiar material is easy to care for. A popular brand is Trevira (TM), known for its softness.

Polyester is often formed into a pile, with tufted fibers woven into a knitted cloth backing. This manmade fleece has proven to be a popular replacement for natural wool fleece, and is seen in sherpa and Kodel fleeces, with the latter considered superior. Either will provide a dense insulating nap in saddle pads, girths, breastcollars, and blanket linings. Kodel is tightly knit, while the tufts of cheaper fleeces can be separated easily to see the fabric backing. Polyester also appears as polyester felt, sometimes called hospital felt due to its nonallergenic properties.

Acrylic is another popular synthetic; it is produced from mineral sources. Like polyester, it is soft, warm, and lightweight. It will not shrink, stretch, or absorb moisture. When formed into fleece, however, its straight, slick fibers are not as dense as polyester, and are more likely to slip. However, acrylic fleece absorbs dye more consistently than polyester, resulting in deeper colors.

Manufacturers often combine polyesters and acrylics with cotton. This textile blends the best properties of each. It is claimed to be more durable and washable than natural fabrics, yet it still breathes and absorbs moisture. It can be used as either a smooth fabric or a felt.

Hollofil, also called polyfill, is a form of loose polyester fibers. Resembling goose down, this lightweight material is used for insulation in horse clothing. The soft, fluffy fibers are tubular shaped, and they loft together without forming clumps. The resulting air pockets create a barrier between the horse's body and its environment.

Textile Quality

Manufacturers weigh various factors in the selection of textiles. You can evaluate a material's quality by considering the following:

• **Strength**. Can the material resist physical forces? Will it withstand impact, and can it hold weight? Does it tear or fracture? With fabrics, you can estimate strength by weight, usually measured in ounces per yard. For example, a sixteen-ounce cotton duck weighs one pound per yard, in contrast to a ten- or twelve-ounce duck.

• **Resilience**. Is the material elastic under stress? Does it resume its original shape when you remove the stress?

• **Abrasion resistance**. Does the material resist friction without showing any weakening of the fibers? In general, synthetics resist wear better than natural materials.

• **Shrinkage**. When the material becomes wet, does it shrink? Fabrics of natural or loosely woven fibers tend to shrink more than others.

• **Waterproofing**. Some items should resist moisture. Test the material's absorbency by sprinkling water droplets onto its surface. If the droplets remain after a few minutes, the material is water repellant. Nylon and polyester resist absorbency.

• **Colorfastness**. The product's dye should be permanent. It should not change due to the weather or laundering, although fabrics will fade and deteriorate after years of exposure to sunlight.

• **Comfort**. People pick clothing for comfort, searching for softness and smoothness. You must estimate how a product feels against a horse's skin. After use, does it create irritation? Does it create a temperature too hot or cold? Some synthetics, such as nylon and polyester, may create a clammy feeling.

Metals

Metal is used both for individual products and for fasteners attached to larger products. Today, most metals are alloys, in which pure metals are blended for superior properties.

Steel is the most common alloy used in horse equipment. Known for its strength, it is processed from an iron which contains carbon. One version, mild or sweet steel, is made from a low-carbon steel.

Stainless steel is iron alloyed with chromium or chromium and nickel. This metal has a long-lasting, bright, silvery gloss, and it resists wear.

When alloyed with chromium alone, stainless steel usually includes 11 to 26 percent chromium for toughness and hardness. Nickel adds strength and elasticity; when nickel is combined with iron and chromium, the ratio can be 18 percent chromium and 8 percent nickel—often described as the superior "18–8" type.

Nickel can be alloyed with steel to produce nickel steel. This metal will not rust, break, or turn yellow. By itself, pure nickel can bend and break easily, and it will yellow with age.

One successful alloy of galvanized steel and nickel is Never-Rust. Popular in England and Germany, this metal has a rich luster that will not peel. It will not shine as brightly as stainless steel, however, and over time the surface will pit.

Copper, a pure metal, is fairly strong and resists corrosion. It can be plated over other metals, or blended to produce superior alloys.

Brass results from a blend of copper and zinc. Solid brass will not rust. Alloyed with zinc and silver, copper produces the ornamental nickel silver, also called German or alpaca silver. This tough metal closely resembles silver, yet it will not tarnish or scratch as easily.

Other copper alloys include Monel, a corrosion-resistant copper-and-nickel alloy, and Dural, a lightweight aluminum alloy hardened with some copper. Both can be formed into bits. Bronze is a copper and tin alloy that will not rust. Solid bronze hardware is stronger than brass.

Zinc is alloyed with aluminum to produce cast

Above is a twenty-year old eggbutt snaffle made of Never-Rust; below, a newer full-cheek model of stainless steel.

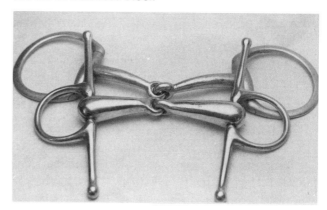

You will also see cadmium hardware, usually plated over iron or steel. This silvery-white metal is denser than zinc.

The highly reflective silver can be used in pure or sterling form. Pure or fine silver must be at least 99 percent silver; the sterling silver alloy contains as much as 7.5 percent copper as a hardener, but must be a minimum of 92.5 percent silver.

A malleable metal, silver is frequently bonded onto metal surfaces as decoration. Often, silver tack decorations are neither pure nor sterling, but German silver. You can easily learn to discern German silver from sterling. Real silver has a certain sparkle under lights, a light feel, and finer, deeper engraving. Manufacturers shape metal into products by a variety of methods, all involving heat and pressure. The five most common processes are casting, rolling, forging, extrusion, and cutting.

Cast metal is shaped by pouring molten metal into a mold. Depending on the process, the result can vary from poor to excellent quality.

To produce quantities of identical items, most metals are cast in permanent molds. Molten metal is poured or injected into the mold, and the mold is later opened to remove the completed product.

Sand casting produces good results. The interior of a mold is lined with sand to insulate and form fine surfaces. Lost-wax casting generally produces higher quality items of great precision and smooth surfaces. A wax mold forms the metal. When the shape hardens, the mold is broken to remove the item.

Rolling shapes metal by pressure, making it hard and stiff. Heavy rollers flatten the material into the desired sheet or bar, as in cold-rolled steel.

Forging can be performed by machines or by hand. Impact or pressure shapes a hot metal. In drop forging, sometimes called stamping, two dies squeeze metal into shape. Usually forged metal is stronger than cast, with fewer defects.

A smith forges rolled metal by hammering it into the desired shape. The metal may need to be heated in a forge. Or, if it is a malleable metal such as copper, silver, or gold, it can be bent and hammered without heating. A silversmith hammers silver to shape it, or to raise it into a three-dimensional piece such as a concho.

Cutting is another method for shaping metals. A craftsman working in a small shop will use hand tools to cut metal from sheets. In a factory, machines stamp forms, usually from sheets of aluminum alloy.

A metalworker joins sections of metal components in four basic ways. Separate rivets or pins connect pieces together, either firmly or loosely. Or heat can be used to form a more permanent bond, by soldering, brazing, or welding. Molten metal is used to fuse pieces at desired angles, or overlay one piece onto another. Soldering is used to join metals with a molten filler, without melting the metals themselves. Brazing involves using an alloy, usually brass, to bond metals.

Metal can be decorated with a raised design by machine embossing or by stamping with hammer and chisel. Metal can also be engraved, in which the craftsperson uses a sharp-pointed tool to incise lines of a design into the surface. Engraving with hand tools produces the most detailed, defined, and sharp decoration, resembling sculptural relief.

Metal can be coated to strengthen or color its surface. With electroplating, a metalworker fuses a coating to protect iron or steel; however, plating can chip or wear. Some steel is blued, which involves coating it with a solution to turn it a deep blue color.

Plating can make it difficult for you to discern between a solid or plated metal. When you wish to tell whether a product is solid brass or brass plated, try holding a magnet next to the hardware —it will attract the brass-plated steel but not the solid brass.

The rough edges on any metal product are

trimmed and smoothed by hand or machine work. Abrasives are then used to buff and polish the metal for a final shine.

Metal Quality

Metal must be able to resist stress. It should have a high level of tensile strength and not weaken under pressure, which is known as metal fatigue. The tempering process reduces a metal's brittleness, while maintaining its hardness.

Some metal must be resilient, flexing slightly without bending out of shape. For example, you should be able to form a spur to fit around your boot.

Study a metal item carefully. Look for an even, smooth surface. Finishing work is the most time-consuming, expensive task in metal production. A hand-polished piece displays the manufacturer's pride.

Feel all joints, looking at how pieces meet. Test any movable parts by working them back and forth. Do all parts meet smoothly, and are fastenings secure?

A metal's surface should also resist corrosion. Air and moisture attack iron and copper to cause rust or a greenish coating. Alloys and plating help protect against corrosion.

Study the design of individual pieces of hardware. On a buckle, look for either a depression for the tongue, or a roller. Either will prolong the buckle's life, for without this protection, the tongue will protrude to snag other objects.

Some buckles are wire-formed, or welded from a piece of heavy wire. Check that the weld does not fit under the roller, for the tongue pressure could break the weld.

Today almost all metal hardware—buckles, rings, and snaps—is imported from Korea and

Cast steel snaps vary in finish and durability. From left, two cadmium-plated bull snaps show more wear than the chrome-plated trigger snaps on the right.

Japan. Even the long-established firms in the United States and Europe market Orient-manufactured metal goods. You can assume any hardware to be an import unless it bears a stamp noting its country of origin.

Plastics

Plastics include polymers, which may be formed into shapes other than textiles or cordage, and expanded foam plastics, such as the open-cell polyfoam and the newer closed-cell foams. Polyvinyl chloride (PVC,) polyethylene, and polystyrene are used to form many products, including buckets, feeders, and horse boots.

Synthetic rubbers such as neoprene and butyl resemble natural rubbers but are also polymers. Neoprene is elastic yet durable, and it features outstanding resistance to the effects of sweat, chemicals, and weather.

Plastics are shaped by molding, casting, or suction. Many products are formed by injection molding, in which a liquid plastic is pressed into solid form in a mold.

Polyurethane coats many synthetics, especially nylon. The easy-to-clean plastic increases durability, abrasion resistance, and flexibility. When used in synthetic strap goods, it can increase comfort.

The above polymers produce a product of a uniform composition. They are lightweight, strong, and chemical resistant. Although synthetics are strong, you should test them for resistance to physical forces. Flexible materials may tear. Hard surfaces may shatter under stress.

Fiberglass

Another synthetic is fiberglass, which is formed from fibers of melted glass. This strong, lightweight material can form a fabric or a solid of any shape. It is often mixed with plastic to form a glass-fiber–reinforced plastic.

Chapter 3

QUALITY CONSIDERATIONS

Quality is a product's degree of excellence. In horse tack and accessories, quality results from a knowledgeable craftsman applying his skill to the best materials.

Manufacturers offer different levels of quality to serve three basic levels of users: the professional, the intermediate, and the casual or pleasure rider. The professional needs hard-working, top-quality gear to withstand daily use. On the other hand, casual buyers are more likely to select the cheapest items, which offer a limited lifespan. If a product fails, they toss it out and replace it with another. This seems to be a uniquely American concept, fitting the country's image as a society of disposable products.

As a consumer, you determine which standard of quality you will purchase.

When you select good or excellent quality, you buy for value, not price. A product's value is determined by its long-term cost-efficiency.

Quality will prevail over the initial price you pay. An excellent item can last for decades, while you might have to buy two or three lesser-quality items over the same period. As prices increase on all products, you will save money over the long term by buying quality merchandise.

Quality tack is a wise investment because it actually appreciates in value. You can usually resell it at a profit, while ordinary or poor equipment will depreciate.

Industry experts applaud the consumer's desire for quality. They note that many purchasers expect and will pay the price for high-quality goods, especially in the English riding styles.

Research

Before buying a product, you should do certain research. First, investigate the product's history. The brand name can help you determine quality; you can expect a major manufacturer or distributor to handle products of value. However, you cannot assume that a European firm really manufactured its bit in its own shop. Your "English" tack can include a bit from Korea, a saddle from Spain, a pad from Taiwan, and a bridle from India.

Ask about the country of origin, if it is not printed on the item or sales tag. The words "Made in England" offer a clue to the quality of English saddlery, usually indicating superior goods. However, Japan and Korea also produce quality goods, often under the auspices of a European parent company.

Beware of counterfeits or look-alikes of unknown origin. As one brand gains a major share of the market, competing firms will attempt to copy the original. The copy can be equal or superior, but sometimes it results in a less expensive, poorer quality item.

You may choose to "Buy American" and support domestic industries. Some manufacturers note that the unique conformation of American breeds is matched best by U.S.-made products.

Or, you may consider European craftsmen superior because of their long tradition of excellence. The snob appeal of certain German, French, and Italian designs has created a profitable export market for European firms.

Be aware that a local manufacturer can produce only a limited amount of quality items. Lack of distribution or advertising does not indicate a marginal product.

Inspection of Form

Basic tests should be performed on all equestrian equipment. You can "kick the tires" of an item by rating its quality factors. Study its form and function, then compare versions of the same product.

To judge quality of form means to evaluate a product according to your design standards. Consider the following: do you consider the product safe and attractive? Is it in style?

Do all materials appear appropriate for the product's function? Does the material quality seem to imply safety and durability? For example, the type of thread used to stitch pieces of leather or fabric can affect an item's performance. Some craftsmen consider nylon thread best; others rely on silk or waxed linen.

Study the craftsmanship carefully, looking for strength and quality of finish. All edges should feel smooth, and joined layers should appear perfectly aligned and secure.

Find out how much handwork a product includes. Generally, the more handwork, the higher the quality. A good quality saddle is about 80 percent handmade. Handwork implies pride of craftsmanship, superior materials, and greater attention to detail.

On a stitched product, avoid large needle holes, uneven stitches, or puckers in the fabric. Count the number of stitches per inch to gauge the stitching's strength. For example, on a nylon blanket, expect to see six to twelve stitches per inch.

The amount of stitches will vary, depending on the material, the item, and the specific area of the item. Overly close stitching can weaken some materials because it cuts too many needle holes. But long stitches can also pose hazards; they can snag, as the thread forms large loops.

Ideally, the craftsman should reinforce stress points by doubling the lines of stitching, or by adding bar-tacked stitching, a bar-shaped line of stitches sewn across the original line of stitching. If you notice loose threads at the end of a row, you should be wary.

Look at the fasteners to check that all are securely attached. If a fastener fails, the item will not function. An opened buckle may appear to be a minor malfunction, but it could lead to a serious accident.

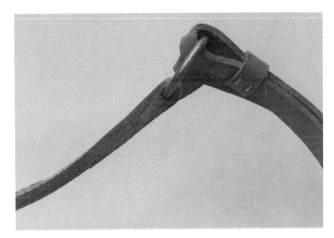

Look carefully at details of craftsmanship. The maker of this halter has shaved the leather where layers join, but edges appear rough.

Estimate of Function

Form influences the product's fit and function. Any item of tack must fit the horse in order to be effective, comfortable, and safe. Fit can be determined by an integral part of the design, such as the tree of a saddle, or you can adjust fit through fasteners. Strap goods should feature sufficient fasteners in the right places for optimum fit.

In addition to correct fit, a product must be easy to use off the horse. Predict the amount of care you will need to maintain an item. Will you be able to devote the time necessary? Where will you store the item?

Does a product fit you? Test it at the shop as much as you can. You can sit in a saddle, hold reins, or handle a brush or bucket.

Evaluate the quality of fabric goods by checking stitching and finish. A nylon web cavesson shows attention to detail by the finishing of holes on the noseband; each has been melted to prevent fraying.

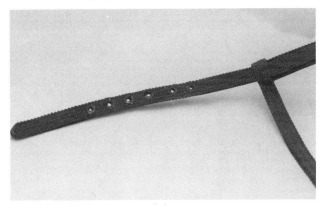

A quality leather product combines excellent materials and detailed craftsmanship. This boot of baghide leather should last for many years.

Last, estimate durability. With proper care, a quality item should last for years. But don't forget to consider your horse's impact. Even a small horse can exert a great deal of pressure on any object it touches. The best saddle can fracture under a horse's weight. Not all buckets can withstand the power of a horse's kick.

Remember that when two forces impact, one will weaken more than the other. When you or your horse are concerned, it is better to replace a broken piece of equipment rather than risk serious injury or even death. If a blanket tears, you can repair it or buy another—but your horse's broken leg is another story.

Note to Parents:

Parents who purchase riding equipment for their children face a dilemma. Why invest a substantial amount of money for quality tack if you cannot predict the child's continuing interest?

Some experts agree that you can start with a lower grade, and trade up to quality equipment when your child proves that riding is not a passing fancy. However, most manufacturers and retailers urge parents not to scrimp on quality. A child's safety depends on quality materials and craftsmanship. If you buy a cheap girth that breaks, your child could sustain serious injury. You can resell quality tack to recoup your investment if your child switches sports.

Also, poor equipment can cause a beginner unnecessary frustration. Having quality, equipment at the outset can increase enjoyment and introduce a youngster to a lifelong hobby. A good saddle actually helps the rider maintain correct position and can ease the learning process. A poorly balanced model can cause misalignment and undue pain.

Safety is especially vital with a child rider.
Quality tack will not fail under stress.

PART II: SADDLES

Chapter 4

—

ENGLISH SADDLES

In the United States the saddle used for English riding is called an "English" saddle. Around the world, it is considered the standard model for international horse sports.

The English saddle gained its name because it was first manufactured in English shops. Actually, saddlemakers the world over build this style, based on the traditions of classical horsemanship.

Basic Design

All English saddles are built on a simple tree of pommel, seat, and cantle. Onto this frame are added a seat, skirts, and flaps. Panels line the underside to lift the saddle above the horse's spine and to protect it from the pressure of the

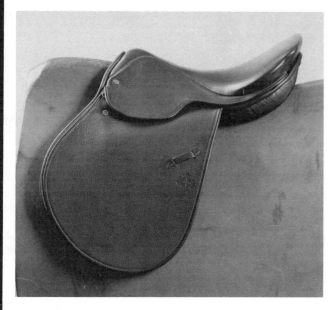

The close contact saddle provides a balanced seat for jumping. Courtesy of Courbette Saddlery Co.

A dressage saddle has a deeper seat and straight-cut flaps. Courtesy of Courbette Saddlery Co.

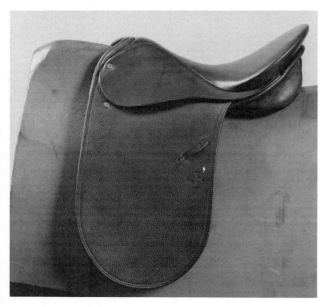

tree. Three straps, or billets, buckle onto a separate girth, and bars on the tree support stirrup leathers and irons.

The dynamics of movement are crucial to saddle design. The saddle distributes weight evenly over the broadest surface of the horse's back without restricting the horse's free movement. It acts as a shock absorber, protecting the horse from the rider's shifting weight.

Different saddle styles match specialized horse sports. The shape of the tree and the cut of the flaps distinguish the various types.

Most familiar today is the jumping or forward-seat style. Its design places you over the horse's center of balance. The dip of the seat holds you close to the horse's back.

The jumping saddle's flaps match the angle of your thighs when you are seated. For jumping, you shorten the stirrup leathers to place your knee further forward as your leg angle closes.

You can choose from two types of jumping saddles: the German and the close-contact models. The German style holds you in position with a deep seat and high cantle. Continental panels, lining the entire undersides of the flaps, hold padded knee and thigh rolls for secure, comfortable support ahead of and behind your legs.

A recent development is the close-contact or "flat" jumping saddle. Some riders felt the heavier German style caused them to grip too tightly with their knees, and the padding obstructed their closeness with the horse.

The close-contact saddle, also called the French, Olympic, or Hermes style (the Hermes saddle, manufactured in France, was the first of this style.) It has a flat seat and narrow French panels for minimum bulk under the legs. This athletic saddle is the most popular seller in the United States. European saddlers developed it to American specifications in the early 1970s, but the conservative Old World artisans still prefer the German style. Importers feel that the saddle-makers consider the close-contact saddle a fad, even after the design has aided U.S. riders to win the highest honors.

Most advanced competitors choose the close-contact model for today's hunter and jumper classes. However, the style does not provide sufficient security to steady an unbalanced rider. Most experts do not recommend it for a beginner.

The dressage saddle differs from the jumping saddle in its seat and flap design. The seat is deeper, the cantle is usually round and high, and the thickly stuffed panels help you to sit vertically.

A dressage model should allow you close contact with the horse while maintaining a classical seat. Most styles feature narrow knee rolls, slightly padded to hold your leg in place. The flaps hang straight down, angled slightly to match the natural bend of your knees.

The stirrup bars are set farther back than on a jumping saddle so that the leathers hang straight down from the centers of the flaps. Dressage riders usually ride with long stirrups so that they can move their legs freely.

The "all-purpose" saddle is a compromise between the dressage and jumping saddles. The flaps are cut slightly forward for a balanced seat. Most all-purpose saddles feature knee rolls, and some add thigh rolls. This extra padding can be stitched to the flap, under the flap, or in both locations.

This style gives you a comfortable, secure seat for pleasure riding, hunting, and casual showing. The all-purpose design will satisfy many riders, and it is the most popular design sold in England. However, some saddle designers complain that the compromised design does not succeed in any discipline.

Another innovation from saddlemakers is the adjustable flap, on which a fastener is provided to allow you to adjust the angle of the saddle's flaps. Some permit two adjustments, for dressage or jumping, while others provide three separate angles for dressage, eventing, or jumping. On some models you can also add or remove the amount of padding in the knee rolls.

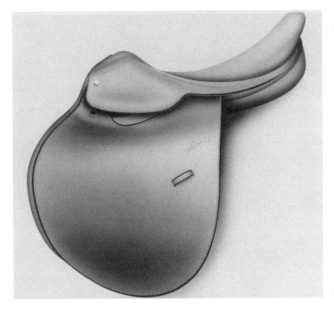

Compare close contact saddle design by looking at the depth of the seat and cut of the flaps. Nelson Pessoa saddle courtesy of Gardiner Imports.

The panels of a close contact saddle affect its fit. Courtesy of Courbette Saddlery Co.

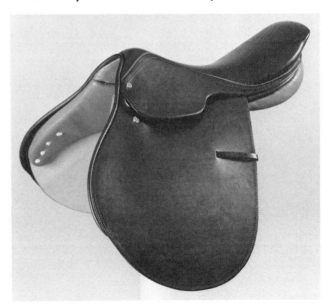

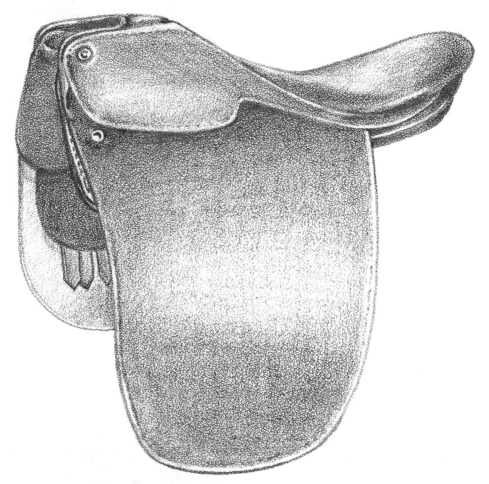

The show saddle places the rider in a vertical position.

Riders of breeds like the Saddlebred, Arabian, Morgan, and Tennessee Walking Horse usually select a saddle known as a show saddle, (sometimes called the Lane Fox style). This saddle helps present the high-stepping horse at its best. You sit back with your legs positioned behind the horse's shoulders, so that you do not interfere with the flashy action of the horse's forehand.

The seat is very flat, with the center closer to the cantle than the pommel. Thin half-panels allow the saddle to rest flat on the horse's back. The straight flaps encourage you to sit with your legs almost vertical. Stirrup bars are set back, to assist your leg position.

A quality show saddle will have four billets on each side. You can place the girth on any two to adjust to the horse and your riding position. This also spreads the wear among four locations rather than the usual three.

For two sports—racing and polo—riders select very specialized saddles. Jockeys and exercise riders use lightweight race saddles. With flaps cut far forward, the jockey can ride with very short stirrups. Polo players naturally prefer the polo saddle. Similar to the all-purpose model, its design promotes maximum flexibility, grip, and security. It features a short, wide, secure seat and often adds knee rolls.

Selecting Materials

The traditional saddle is built from wood, metal, cloth, and leather. In recent decades, some manufacturers have developed synthetic materials to replace the standard choices. Opinions vary as to which produces the superior saddle. High-tech proponents scoff at the "eighteenth-century" approach and claim that they are committed to improving the sport; conventional saddlers condemn any deviation from time-proven methods.

Except for some race saddles, all English saddles are built on either a rigid or spring tree. The

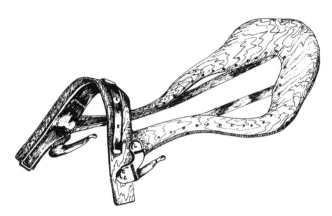

The tree forms a framework for leather and fabric.

traditional rigid tree is made of solid beechwood, which is strong but limited in flexibility. Most of today's models feature the spring tree of laminated wood veneers or molded from synthetics.

Wood will allow the tree to flex with the horse's movement. Its supple character helps avoid shock, yet it will not rebound too far above the horse's backbone.

The laminated tree consists of wood pieces crisscrossed at ninety-degree angles, glued, and heated under vacuum pressure on a mold. This bonds the wood into one unit. The saddler then covers the wood with canvas or fiberglass for added durability.

The synthetic tree is molded into an unbreakable, standardized product. Both right and left sides duplicate uniform angles and heights, which is difficult to achieve in a wood tree. Wood's flexibility may cause near and off sides to vary slightly, and it can warp or twist.

For synthetic trees, treemakers use either high-density polypropylene or fiberglass blended with other polymers. The lightweight trees are still considered revolutionary by many traditionalists. Actually, one European firm has utilized this material since 1963. Two disadvantages may be the tree's inflexibility compared to wood and a tendency to spread with age.

Underneath the tree, flat steel strips stretch from the head to the cantle. These metal "springs" add support and make the seat feel more resilient.

Steel or aluminum plates are riveted onto the tree as reinforcement. The pommel can be the tree's weakest point, so metal plates help brace its top. A quality saddle will feature hand-forged, heavy-gauge steel reinforcements both above and below the saddle's gullet, and around the cantle.

The polo saddle, built on a rigid tree, must contain this reinforcement. Some saddlemakers describe the reinforced head as "keyed," noting that it will prevent the tree from spreading.

The saddler strains the seat, adding layers of material to build a suspension system. Usually seat stringers of webbing are nailed or tacked to "crosstension" the tree in both directions. These durable, flexible straps help to suspend you over the horse's back.

One high-tech design adds nylon bands strung crosswise between the seat and the head of the pommel. These create a tension that keeps you suspended, preventing your weight from affecting the saddle's position over high fences. The design inhibits the saddle from rising from the horse's back.

Next the saddler adds a layer of foam, either the conventional sponge rubber or polyfoam. When you sit in the saddle, foam improves the comfort. It should spring back into shape when you rise, not remain compressed or collapsed. Sponge rubber is often preferred because polyfoam may break down after a year's wear, while sponge rubber usually retains its shape longer.

The saddler blocks the completed padding with a section of wet leather. Stretching it over the seat, he nails it in place. When it dries, it remains shaped over the tree.

The traditional seat material is pigskin, a long-wearing, large-pored leather that adds texture for a more secure seat. Today, some seats consist of cowhide embossed to resemble pigskin. Some saddlers promote a softer, less durable seat of glove or bridle leather.

Leather covers the rest of the tree. Most quality saddles are made from thick cowhide—a tough yet supple material. You will see other variations, such as a preshrunk cowhide with a raised grain for better grip. If you prefer a rarer leather, you might purchase a saddle crafted of elephant hide. Saddles originating in India are made of water buffalo leather.

Flaps endure great wear, and the top-grade saddle's flaps are cut from butt leather. A lesser grade saddle may use back leather for its flaps; the most inexpensive models are sometimes constructed of the coarser shoulder leather.

Most flaps match the rest of the saddle, but many forward-seat models feature padded inserts for better grip. You will see suede, doeskin, or elkhide—all nonslip leathers to help your leg adhere to the saddle. Inner padding can be foam or rubber.

Certain forward-seat or dressage saddles add smooth leather under your leg, usually a thinner, softer leather, such as calfskin or glove or bridle leather. Or, you might prefer a rare leather like the pliable, stretchy sella, or an embossed variety produced from specially treated shoulder leather.

The saddler next adds skirts and possibly an inner sweat flap. He attaches billets to the webbing that crosses the tree. Always study these carefully, as they hold the saddle on the horse. You will see chrome-tanned leather, of a single layer, or two-layer billets, doubled and stitched or lined and stitched. Added between the layers may be an extra reinforcing strap of webbing.

Opinions vary on this construction. Advocates

claim an inner layer increases the billets' strength and prevents stretching. Others note that over time, the stitching will fray or tear due to abrasion, perspiration, and oiling the leather, and the straps will separate.

For where the saddle rests on the horse's back the saddlemaker crafts leather panels filled with various inner materials. With a long rod, he stuffs the panels with wool batting (also called flocking) or felt, then pounds them onto a form that simulates the horse's back.

Purists claim that only wool flocking can create a durable, well-stuffed panel. Wool felt can become hard or ball up, pressing against the leather to cause excess wear. If flocking does settle, or if the horse gains or loses weight, a saddler can easily shift, add, or remove the stuffing.

Contemporary designers have fabricated panels filled with synthetic materials. The traditionalists object to synthetic flocking, noting that it compresses and expands improperly. Inexpensive foam stuffing will deteriorate, and it will not allow readjustment.

One superior solution might be the laminated panel. Here layers of felt, closed-cell urethane foam, and open-cell polyfoam form a durable, unified mass. Against the horse's back, the spongy foam helps mold the panel to the animal's conformation. The high-density closed-cell foam retains its shape and prevents the panel from crushing, denting, or becoming compressed. Manufacturers claim that filling of this design remains uniform, never varying as flocking will, and it does not create any pressure points.

Saddle-repair specialists contend that the laminated panel is irreparable, that the foam will not hold up and that the felt's molecular composition will break down over time. Ultimately, it is not cost-effective to attempt to rebuild the laminated panels.

Finally, saddles feature metal fittings: stirrup bars, nails, rings, and rivets. You will see forged-steel or brass stirrup bars on quality models.

Other fittings should be of brass or stainless steel.

In recent years, several manufacturers have challenged the establishment with a major departure: the synthetic saddle. This wash-and-wear model duplicates the standard designs in manmade materials.

Synthetic saddles are built on a wood, nylon, or injection-molded plastic tree. Fabric replaces leather in the seat, skirts, and flaps. You can choose from a tough neoprene covering, or a PVC imprinted to resemble pigskin suede. All edges should be bound for a smooth feel, and panels are stuffed with foam.

The materials make the saddle extremely comfortable and lightweight. Models range in weight from six to twelve pounds, depending on the tree's weight. Fabric should resist tearing and be completely waterproof. Neoprene will stain, so spray it with Scotchguard for protection.

Look for a material that does not feel slippery. A tacky feel, especially on flaps, will give you a more secure seat, almost like the feeling of riding a leather saddle while wearing chaps. The texture will attract loose horsehair, too.

Features include plastic or leather billets or removable knee rolls, attached with Velcro closures. Most manufacturers recommend matching plastic stirrup leathers.

Surprisingly, the industry has accepted synthetic saddles as a positive trend. Some traditionalists remain suspicious about the models' durability, but most applaud the durable fabrics as a good value. This may be due to the saddler's philosophy of "Less is more," always seeking to reduce bulk and weight for improved performance.

Manufacturers continue to improve the quality of synthetic saddles. One new design, to be marketed in late 1988, features a molded polymer foam on a synthetic tree. This quality saddle will weigh only three pounds!

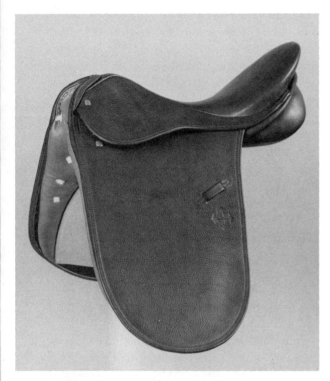

Look for well-stuffed panels to conform to the horse. Dressage saddle courtesy of Courbette Saddlery Co.

Selecting Fit

No matter what your riding style, you can maximize fit for both you and your horse. Comfort will make a difference in your enjoyment and success, and a correctly fitted saddle will last longer.

The model you choose must fit your horse first, then you. For the horse, the tree must conform to its withers and back. It sits forward over the withers, with the pommel clearing the withers by at least two inches, or three fingers.

The points of the tree, reaching downward from the pommel, rest just behind the tops of the horse's shoulder blades. They must mold to the shoulders without crowding the muscles below the withers. A saddle that is too narrow can injure the horse, as the points dig into its shoulder.

A saddle that is too wide will press on the horse's back and withers, and it will shift back and forth. Ideally, the panels should form a wide, high channel to keep all pressure away from the horse's spine and loin. By following the curve of the horse's back, the panels distribute pressure evenly along the back muscles. Stuffing lifts the pressure away from the withers. Panels should not be overstuffed, however, as they can become are too firm and cause the saddle to shift.

The saddle compresses weight onto a comparatively small area, so panels must maintain equal pressure. If they bind at the wither or shoulder, they can inhibit the horse's free movement. When their pressure is uneven, you will see dry and wet areas on your horse's back when you remove the saddle. A dry spot indicates excess pressure.

The size and length of panels also affect fit. A saddle might fit better along a horse's shoulders with shorter or longer panels. You will need to fit the saddle on your horse to evaluate this area.

One expert describes saddle fitting as "a bit of art and a lot of science." It is essential that the saddle's tree and panels fit the horse without impeding the animal's movements. Yet, knowledgeable saddlers agree that over half of today's horses wear ill-fitting saddles. Even many outstanding, FEI-level competitors can choose the wrong saddles for their horses.

Choices available from manufacturers include from three to eleven tree widths, which can be measured in inches or centimeters. A production-line saddle is usually available in fewer sizes than a custom-saddler's line.

Today, saddle trees are shaped to fit horses of popular breeds. Forward-seat and dressage styles feature trees of various widths. A medium (31 cm) tree will fit most horses. Narrower (28–30 cm) trees generally fit horses of Thoroughbred background, who tend to have high withers and narrow backs. Wide (32 cm) trees fit best on flat-withered breeds. Saddles made in England are sized by number, with narrow sized "2," average a "3," and wide a "4."

As you search for a saddle for your horse, you may note that some companies do not import a range of sizes to the United States. In order to maintain a manageable inventory, distributors limit the sizes to three or even only one choice. This may be better business, but it works against you and your horse.

Choosing which saddle to use on a warmblood will depend on the animal's predominant ancestry. Some warmbloods have high withers and a deep back. This hard-to-fit conformation requires a tree narrow in front, but well stuffed in the panel. Another difficult shape to fit is the Thoroughbred with heavy withers.

For wider horses, manufacturers adapt tree widths. For example, the show saddle must be wide enough across the panel and cutback. Morgans, which are wide across the withers, require additional tree width to allow free action without any constriction. A wider pommel generally forms a wider seat, which forces the rider to adjust to the needs of the horse.

A well-fitted dressage saddle rests properly on the horse's back, without impeding free movement.

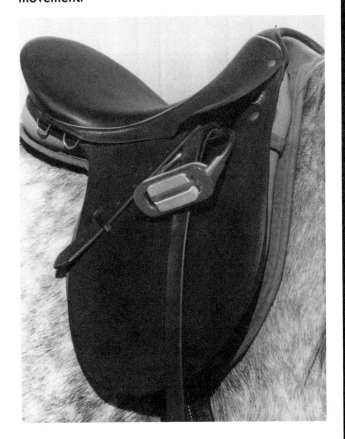

The pony saddle should be scaled down in size. Be sure the tree is wide enough to fit properly. Many pony saddles feature a metal crupper ring at the cantle, so you can attach a crupper to keep the saddle in place.

After considering all the factors that affect saddle fit, realize that you must test models on the horse. Avoid relying on the "coat hanger" test, where you mold a flexible wire over your horse's withers to estimate fit. This test will not indicate the horse's true width, which varies according to the firmness or softness of the horse's shoulder muscling.

Some manufacturers offer an adjustable tree, on which molded plastic shifts to accommodate different wither slopes. On another model you can change the gullet plate to alter the tree's width. A wool-stuffed saddle can be restuffed to adjust the panels, but not the tree itself.

The head of the tree also affects its fit. A straight head requires sufficient clearance over the withers. A cutback head will fit more horses, as the open area permits a closer fit. This places the pommel lower on the horse's back while preventing it from pressing against the withers. You can position the saddle further forward, over the horse's center of gravity. Saddle-seat models feature a full cutback head; many forward-seat styles have a semi-cutback head.

With a saddle on your horse, test that the gullet completely clears the horse's backbone. You can check this by inserting a long whip through the gullet, from the withers toward the croup. The whip should slip easily through this channel between the saddle's panels.

Lastly, check the saddle's length. Never use a long saddle on a short-backed horse. If the bars press onto the loins, you can cause serious injury.

Once you have chosen models that fit your horse, select the one that fits you. A saddle is like a shoe. It should mold to you and feel comfortable, yet be functional as well.

First determine which size seat you need. On forward-seat, dressage, and polo saddles, adult sizes vary from 16 to 19 inches. The size measures the length of the seat from the nailhead at the pommel to the center of the cantle. A very large man would choose the 19, while the average women needs a 16-1/2. A child may feel comfortable in a size 16—or may need a special child-size saddle.

A show saddle, with its flatter seat, runs from 19 to 22 inches. An average-sized woman would choose a 20- to 21-inch seat.

Fit the saddle on your horse with only a thin pad or towel, and look for the seat to sit level from back to front. The deepest part should remain in the saddle's center, and the pommel and cantle should measure the same height.

You will have to determine what area encompasses the seat. A deep seat may include a higher cantle, so subtract an inch or two from the cantle's height. Although the cantle may appear to be higher than the pommel, the seat is level if its center is the deepest part of the saddle. The pommel must never sit higher than the cantle, as this will shift your weight too far back.

Sit in the saddle to test if you feel perfectly centered. You can check the seat size by placing your hand behind your seat. See if you can fit four fingers between you and the cantle; more or less room may indicate a poor fit.

You should be able to sense immediately if the saddle feels right for you. The seat angle should make you feel balanced. Avoid a saddle that feels too high in front and flat in the back, even if it appeared level on the horse.

The depth of the seat affects the saddle's feel and security. A deeper one allows you to sink your weight to drive the horse forward, which will aid you in jumping and schooling green horses. With a flatter seat, you must possess good control of your body so you won't lost your balance or slide forward.

The waist or twist of the seat (the portion behind the pommel where you sit) should not hinder your leg movement. Avoid one that feels too narrow or wide. Some saddles come in different seat widths; on one model, you can choose either 9 or 10 1/8 inches.

Does the saddle's head feel comfortable for your riding style? The semi-cutback seems to please most riders. If you choose a full cutback head, look for a gentle slope so you won't hit it when posting or in the two-point position.

Check the placement of the stirrups. In a well-designed saddle of the right size, the bars will suspend the stirrups in the proper position for your leg angle.

The shape and size of the flaps should help you maintain your center of gravity. Press your legs against the flaps. When you adjust the leathers, does the flap conform to your leg? Will the leathers pinch?

Also, you should check to see if the flap is the right length for you. A too-long or too-short flap will make you look and feel awkward. In general, long-legged women need a small seat with long flaps. Many women buy saddles with flaps that are too short, and they find that their boot tops catch against the flaps.

Very short and very tall riders encounter unique fitting problems. If you are short, a saddle's flaps may feel too long and its seat too small. But a six-foot-four rider has to search for a saddle with a long enough flap.

If you switch riding styles, you must adjust to different flap angles, or buy an adjustable-flap saddle. If you are changing to dressage, you will find that the straighter leg position required stretches your thigh. You might ease the transition by choosing a saddle with a more forward-shaped flap.

The show saddle features a wide flap to protect your clothing from the horse's sweat. A typical size would be sixteen inches wide at the skirt, tapering down to twelve inches at the lower edge.

The amount of padding under flaps is a matter of personal preference. You can choose from the soft, padded rolls or firmly stuffed blocks for solid support.

The close-contact saddle usually doesn't feel as comfortable as one with knee and thigh rolls. Decide which is more important to you: feeling the horse and developing a tight leg, or relying on the padded flaps to hold your legs in place. You can compromise with a saddle with slight padding under the flaps.

Features

Forward-seat, dressage, and all-purpose saddles usually have keepers—loops at the rear edge of each flap—for the stirrup leathers. Most also feature D-rings below the pommel, to attach a breastplate, and on the offside panel, for a sandwich case.

Safety stirrup bars, standard on most saddles, allow you to adjust the bar from closed to open. When the bar is open, stirrup leathers can be removed easily from the saddle. The bar is designed to open under pressure, so that the stirrup leathers can slide free in case of emergency. (Or you can leave the bar open if the closed bar does not open easily under pressure.)

Many saddles feature recessed stirrup bars. Attached to the inside or outside of the tree, these do not protrude or interfere with your leg. However, they do make it difficult to remove or attach stirrup leathers.

The more advanced you become, the more specifics you seek. Dressage riders want flaps to remain immobile, so designers offer a flap strap. An extra strap, attached to the flap, buckles onto the girth and ties down the flap.

The long billets on some dressage saddles allow you to use a short girth. This reduces bulk under your inner thigh. However, it is difficult to tighten from the saddle, and the saddle may shift from side to side. As a compromise, one model features a unique third billet, a nylon strap that reaches from under the seat down to the middle buckle of the short girth. Another design offers an extra billet in front of the regular three, to strap onto a foregirth.

Another design feature seen in dressage saddles is the extended stirrup bar. It is set further back on the tree to aid you in keeping your leg under your body.

Quality show saddles feature adjustable stirrup bars, which permit you to hang the leathers at one of four different positions. You pull a pin, slide the bar forward or back, and reinsert the pin.

This best-selling feature benefits beginners and riders with short or long legs. You can set the leather at the position which lets you balance your legs and feet under you. This discourages you from balancing on the reins.

Color choices in most English saddles are limited to light, medium, and dark leathers. Generally, dressage saddles are made in dark colors, polo saddles in the lighter London color. Panels may contrast or match in color.

Quality Craftsmanship

Saddle-repair specialists note that many saddles are built for point-of-sale appeal, not long-range durability and ease of repair. Carefully examine a saddle's craftsmanship to evaluate how it is put together and how it will withstand your type of riding.

In examining the craftsmanship of a saddle, look for meticulous construction with attention to detail. On a quality saddle, all leather should be thick and strong, yet not too stiff or bulky. Study the underside, or flesh side, for smoothness. You should see no blemishes on the leather. Feel the flaps, which must be durable to resist wear. Flaps that are uneven in thickness or thinner near the top will shift as you post.

Check the quality of the leather in the flaps by bending the lower part of each flap under itself, toward the sweat flap. Look closely for any break-down—do narrow lines appear in the leather as the fibers spread apart? Examine the entire surface of the flap in a medium light. As light reflects off the leather, do you see layers of horizontal lines on the surface? These are stretch marks in the hide, which stain unevenly. Any breakdown or lines indicate a lesser-quality leather.

Check all sides to see that the skirts and flaps match in material, size, and placement. If the saddle is embossed, compare all parts to be sure the pattern matches.

Observe how the pommel is stitched along the head, and how it attaches to the front of the seat. Look at the welting of the gullet. (The welting is a narrow edge of leather, doubled to appear rolled.) It should be sewn down, as this padding protects the horse from the metal plates reinforcing the tree. Check that the D-rings are nailed into the tree, not just sewn.

You don't have to be an expert to test the quality of a saddle's finishing. The back of the cantle, where it meets the panels, often indicates the overall quality. If the seat leather is attached neatly, you can expect the rest of the saddle to match in craftsmanship. This is a difficult area to stretch flat.

The seat should never contain any wrinkles. Feel the piping between the skirt and the seat. It should begin at the pommel and end close to the cantle. The skirt must meet the cantle smoothly, again at equal distances on both sides.

Look closely at the stitching. It should be inlaid at the piping, for hidden stitching reduces wear. Note the amount of stitching on the flaps and the top of the skirts. Abrasion will fray the threads.

An internally turned seam will reduce wear. On a show saddle, look for this type of seam under the skirt. It will keep threads from wearing and the seat from loosening.

You won't be able to study the tree, but you can

expect a quality saddle to feature a durable tree. Flip the saddle over to survey the panels. They should feel firm and well-stuffed. You should not be able to squeeze the panels or feel the padding shift under the leather. The panels of a well-made saddle, stitched securely and stuffed with wool, should withstand years of pounding. They provide no space for the wool to shift from its original position.

Look at the quality of the billets and stirrup bars. Lift the flap to look at the point pockets. These pockets of leather cushion the points of the tree so that they do not press against the horse or rider. They should be sewn to leather and reinforced for greatest durability.

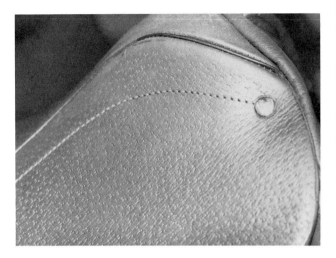

Most English saddles feature embossed leather, to resemble the pigskin of the seat. Note the evenness of the stitching along the skirt.

Quality Recommendations

Because your saddle is a major investment, shop for the best quality you can afford. Most well-made saddles are manufactured in four European nations: England, France, Germany, and Italy. You can expect a saddle from one of these countries to be solidly constructed from quality materials.

Saddles from Argentina and India are less expensive, but experts disagree about their quality. In general, their leather has improved in quality. However, the trees may tend to spread with use.

Prices of English saddles have just about tripled in the last two decades. As with many products, market fluctuations affect saddlery value. When you see a price, it will be for a saddle without fittings, since traditionally you are expected to select these separately.

A respected brand reassures you that the saddle's groundwork (the tree and layers of material under the seat) will be good. Look for a lifetime guarantee on the best quality saddles.

Look at the quality of stitching where skirts meet the cantle.

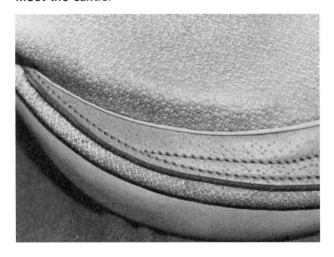

Preferred Brands

In hunt-seat and dressage saddles: Cliff-Barnsby, County, Courbette, Crosby (Miller's brand name), Crump, Hartley, Hermes, Jeffries, Kieffer, Pariani, Passier, Pessoa, Stubben.

Show saddles: Blue Ribbon, Cliff-Barnsby, Crump, Whitman.

Polo saddles: Cliff-Barnsby, Crosby.

Good buys: Campbell, Caprilli, Crosby Collegiate.

A few saddle-buying tips: Realize that there is no magic saddle that will make you a champion. If you are a good rider, better tack will help. The best equipment will not make a bad rider good, however.

If you buy an inexpensive saddle, choose a synthetic saddle rather than a leather one from India or Pakistan. In general, the synthetics are better made on better trees.

Store your saddle at an even temperature.

Avoid leaving your saddle in the hot sun when you are not riding. Intense sunlight deteriorates stitching and dries out the leather. On a hot day, place the saddle in the shade before and after your ride.

In the tack room, hang your saddle on a secure rack so it will not fall, and be sure it sits evenly to avoid denting the panels. Remove the girth so the buckles do not wear into billets any more than necessary.

Cover your saddle to keep it clean, or keep it in a saddle case. If dust settles on the seat and flaps, your weight will press the dirt deeper into the leather.

You may need to have your saddle's stuffing adjusted after two years of average (daily) use. Restuffing or reflocking helps the panels maintain proper shape, and it lengthens the life of the saddle. Restuffing also helps if you wish your saddle to fit on a different horse, or your horse's confor-mation has been altered due to a change in weight or muscling.

Consult a specialist to perform restuffing on a wool-flocked saddle. The specialist has the skill to measure your horse and saddle, and to move the correct amount of material within the proper areas.

Saddle Questions

Does the flap angle match your sport?
Do you need this particular brand, or would a less popular saddle meet your needs?
Would a synthetic saddle substitute?

Insider's Preferences

• "County is one of the few saddle manufacturers you can talk to with a problem. I find it unusual that Gene Freeze [the president of County] will sit down and help you. He understands problems and can correct them. In contrast, most United States distributors of imported saddles won't deal with problems after the sale." (Saddle-shop owner)

• "You can usually rely on Crosby, Eiser, and Crump." (Saddle-shop owner)

• "I wouldn't buy a Stubben or a Passier, but a lot of people swear by them. I find them irreparable." (Saddle-repair specialist)

• "The Kieffer synthetic tree adjusts to fit different horses. It's been an all-fiberglass tree since 1963, so it must be okay. Courbette is also made on a synthetic tree." (Sales representative)

• "The Stubben V.S.D. is good for American women. It has a small seat and a longer flap. The Siegfried flaps are too short." (Saddle-shop owner)

- "The Hermes and most of the Crosby line don't offer tree sizes. They come in average or one-size-fits-all." (Saddle-shop owner)

- "Stubben takes an old-world approach to saddlemaking. They aim for the long-term buyer, and they're not supersensitive to fad changes. They still use wool and wool/felt panels." (Sales manager)

- "Miller's is using more Argentine products. Their Collegiate line is out of Argentina. It looks decent compared to the Cortinas and Borellis. They wear pretty well—I only had a problem with one, where the stitching came loose at the panel. Miller's fixed it at no cost." (Saddle-shop owner)

- "The Campbell saddle is actually made in Spain." (Saddle-shop owner)

- "The Courbette saddles are eminently affordable for any student who wants quality tack. You get what you pay for, and the company stands behind their product. Their quality control is second to none—I have never once found anything wrong that they have shipped. And I have never had a Courbette gall a horse." (Riding-school manager)

- "The Pariani is flatter in the back, and it causes the rider to slide backwards." (Saddle-repair specialist)

- "Kieffer sells more dressage saddles, because trainers recommend them to students. They do give you a deep seat. They only come in three sizes and have a fiberglass tree, which I consider a cheap trick. With that tree, they can use only loose wool flocking to avoid pressure points. It moves around and can cause a sore back." (Saddle-shop owner)

- "Whitman is the only cutback [show saddle] made in the United States. Its tree has a better design for the modern horse breeds." (Sales representative)

- "Stubben, Passier, and Kieffer are fine saddles, made in the old style." (Saddle-shop owner)

- "The Passier lasts forever, but it's unforgiving to a rider. It's so uncomfortable it's like sitting on concrete." (Saddle-repair specialist)

- "The Barnsby polo saddle has felt panels for better fit and closer contact." (Sales representative)

- "The German, Austrian, and Swiss-made saddles hold up best, except for the Kieffers. My Passiers and Stubbens last, with some going strong after twenty years. I wouldn't have an English-made saddle." (Riding-school manager)

- "The main advantage of the Crosby is that you have Miller's reputation behind them—that's what you're buying. If there's a problem, Miller's stands behind them. They guarantee the tree. They seem to be pretty responsive to people's needs. They redesigned the Prix de Nations, so it has a deeper seat than [it did] eight to ten years ago, and the Hunterdon has the deeper seat. They're not necessarily a better quality saddle." (Saddle-shop owner)

- "It's difficult to work on the Kieffer's fiberglass tree. It tends to spread with age. You can't nail into it, and you can't fix it if it breaks." (Saddle-repair specialist)

- "Jeffries is a major English saddlery with a higher quality standard—they take great pride in craftsmanship." (Sales representative)

- "I find a snooty show stable will not buy the top of the line for its school saddles. But rather than go with a Wintec [synthetic], they buy a lower-grade model like the Crosby Collegiate, or an older used saddle." (Saddle-shop owner)

• "The Ainsley saddle is made in England. It's not a well-known brand, but it's affordable. The workmanship and quality is pretty good, similar to the other companies out of England. They're about $100 less than a comparable Crosby. It offers the "Made in England" quality for a little less." (Saddle-shop owner)

• "The Whitman Equithane panel will shape to the horse. It will never vary as a flocked panel will, and it has a memory—it will reform its proper shape without crushing." (Sales representative)

• "We had problems with the stirrup bars breaking on Kieffer saddles. Kieffer took them back and replaced them." (Saddle-shop owner)

• "The Stalker Parisienne saddle is from the same maker who produces the County Competitor —it's an identical saddle selling at a lower price with a lifetime guarantee. The firm of Stalker-Naffey (in business since 1876) brought Barnsby to the United States and later formed its own company when Barnsby changed hands. Barnsby quality has since gone down, and they've lost 100 years of prestige." (Saddle-shop owner)

• "The County Drespri is a moderately deep saddle that is unbelievable." (Sales representative)

• "I find the Kieffers to be bad saddles. They're expensive, have a good reputation, and people like to ride in them, but they have inferior interior workmanship. Two screws and hooks hold the plastic parts of the tree together, and the plastic components break inside. You can't take the saddle apart to fix it. There are only two holes for

a small stuffing stick, so they're difficult to restuff." (Saddle-repair specialist)

• "Caprilli is a great bargain. It's well made and the Aussie dollar is down." (Sales representative)

• "Goodwood manufactures several synthetic saddles for Imperial, Ulster, and Jack's. I saw a horse fall and stomp on one for five minutes, with no tears or breakage!" (Saddle-shop owner)

• "A new trend is the Pessoa-type close-contact saddle, with hidden knee rolls and a suede knee pad." (Sales representative)

• "There is one Kieffer [dressage] model, the Wien, with a better long-billet design. A unique nylon third billet buckles around the girth for greater security." (Saddle-shop owner)

• "County is good, but depending on the amount of use and the type of horse, it breaks down easily. I get new County's, only one or two years old, to restuff. They need only a quick restuff, and they hold up after repair very well." (Saddle-repair specialist)

• "Courbette and Stubben are very similar in style. Courbette imports saddles from two different countries. The German ones are a higher quality, equal to the Stubbens. They offer different tree widths, from a narrow 28 to a wide 32. The Swiss-made models have a narrow tree of synthetic Lemetex, and it sits a little high on the wider horses. The leather seems of good quality, and they've had no problems with the tree breaking or spreading." (Saddle-shop owner)

• "The Pessoa close-contact saddle features a deep seat and a discreet pommel to give the rider the best possible seating efficiency." (Sales representative)

• "Kent Leather's Olympic Competitor has a sensible design for the rider's leg position, and it's extremely well stuffed. The Crosby stuffing is reasonably good, and it holds up well." (Saddle-repair specialist)

• "Don't start out with a specific saddle, like the Ahlerich model made by Hoepfner in Germany. You don't need that if you're just doing simple movements like leg yields." (Saddle-shop owner)

• "The Klimke is an excellent model that sits well on the horse and puts you in the right place with the right seat angle. However, it's hard to find because it's ordered through exclusive dealers, and it's not kept in stock for immediate shipment." (Saddle-shop owner)

• "There's no need to break in the Klimke Ahlerich. It molds immediately to you. It's like a bedroom slipper compared to a leather shoe." (Riding-school manager)

Maintenance

Handle your saddle with care. Clean it regularly, and condition leather as needed.

A new saddle will feel "perched" before it settles. It takes time for the leather to adapt to your body, but it will feel better with use. When you break in a new saddle, realize that there is probably air in the panels. Girth it snugly so there is less distance between the girth buckles and the tree. This will create less friction and movement between the saddle and the horse's back. To allow panels to mold to the horse's back, avoid using a pad for the first twenty to forty hours.

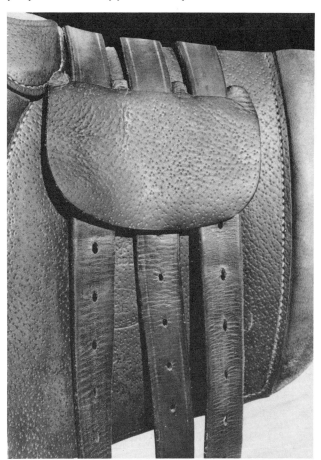

After eight years' use, the billets of an all-purpose model appear worn yet still durable.

Chapter 5

—

WESTERN SADDLES

Most saddles in the United States are Western, or stock, saddles. A 1987 survey by the Future Farmers of America showed that 87 percent of horse-owning families chose Western saddles. This style is popular because it's comfortable. You can relax and feel secure between the high pommel and the high cantle. It's versatile, too, allowing you to use it for trail riding, showing, events, or ranch work.

Riding Western gives you a feeling of kinship with the horsemen of the past. Today's saddle models trace to the tack of the Spanish horsemen who colonized Mexico. Cowhands of the West modified the Mexican saddle to fit their needs.

All Western saddles feature a horn on the pommel. This well-fitted model adds silver lacing around the gullet. Courtesy D. R. Brittain Custom Saddlery.

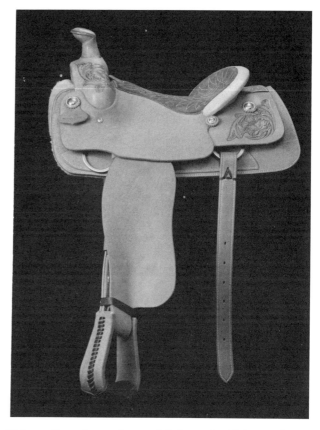

This well-made roping saddle's seat, skirts, and fenders are made of roughout lether. Designed for competition roping, it has a low cantle. Courtesy of D. R. Brittain Custom Saddlery.

Basic Design

Cowboys' saddles were made with a wide pommel featuring a distinctive horn, which served as a post for roping. The high cantle held the rider snugly in the seat. Wide skirts spread the weight around the horse, and the fenders over the stirrup leathers helped protect the rider's legs.

The saddle's horn still distinguishes a Western saddle from any other. Under the pommel is the fork, or swells, with the gullet the curved arch on the fork's underside. The leather that forms the seat extends over the wide skirts as the front and rear jockeys. These sections cover the saddle's groundwork, or layers of leather over the tree. One or two girths, or cinches, fasten the saddle onto the horse.

You can choose from several different types of Western saddle, depending on your favorite sport. Most popular is the pleasure model, which has a deep seat and small horn. The swells can be either wide, medium, or a slick fork. The cantle is usually medium or high, and the saddle weighs from thirty to thirty-five pounds.

Show riders often use deep-seated equitation saddles. The pommel is often the slick fork style, with modified swells and silver decorations to attract the judge's eye.

If you compete in events, you'll need the appropriate saddle. The tough team-roping saddle

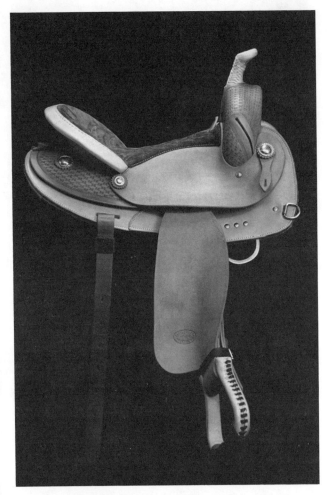

A lightweight barrel racing saddle features a tall, rawhide-braided horn. In-skirt rigging gives it a snug fit. Courtesy of D. R. Brittain Custom Saddlery.

will sustain the stress of stopping a steer. It features a tall, vertical horn, often called a post horn, to dally the rope. Wide swells give you support when you stand up to rope. A roping saddle weighs from thirty-eight to fifty-five pounds.

The calf-roping saddle differs slightly, with a shorter horn for tying the rope. The swells and cantle are lower for a quick dismount, and the seat is not as deep.

Cutting-horse riders prefer saddles made with a low, flat seat. This design lets you sit over the horse's center of gravity and does not restrict your movement. Wide swells help the rider maintain position during the fast action in the arena, and a tall horn provides enough room for a secure handhold.

Barrel racers and other contest riders prefer lightweight saddles. These feature wide, upright swells, a tall horn, and a high cantle, all to increase rider balance around the turns. Many current styles also feature the popular flat cutters' seat. To reduce weight, some styles have rounded skirts.

A popular all-around saddle is the forward-seat type, the Balanced ride saddle. Originally designed by the late trainer Monte Foreman, several firms now manufacture this style. A flat seat and forward-hung stirrups put you over the center of gravity, so your weight does not inhibit the horse's forward or lateral motion. Stirrup leathers attach to the tree on a swivel rather than over the bars of the tree as in most saddles.

Staging a comeback is the cowhand's saddle, today called a ranch or buckaroo saddle. This plain style has a high pommel and horn, with an upright seat.

Every Western saddle secures onto the horse through rigging, or straps that connect cinch and tree. You will find two rigging styles: tree and skirt. The first type, standard on the roping saddle, features large D-rings suspended on straps fastened over and into the tree. The cinch attaches to the ring by billets called cinch straps or latigos.

This show saddle is decorated with silver trim.

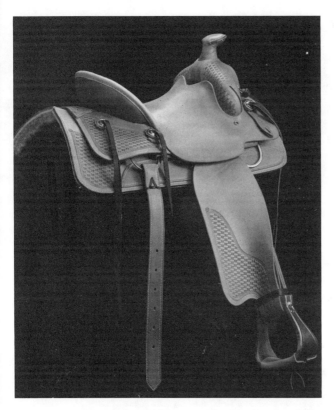

For work or pleasure, you can choose a saddle based on the old-time styling. This model has a smooth leather seat with basket weave stamping on the corners. Courtesy D. R. Brittain Custom Saddlery.

Most of today's saddles feature skirt rigging. The saddlemaker either secures a metal plate onto the skirt or builds it into the skirt. Generally, the built-in type is stronger; it features a leather reinforcement sandwiched between the plate and the skirt.

A recent rigging innovation is the balanced-ride style, in which an extra leather section holds the rigging plate lower than the skirt to reduce bulk under your leg. The latigo pulls from the back and the center, wrapping low around the horse to keep the saddle flat.

Variations in rigging placements affect the position and security of the saddle relative to the horse's center of balance. Full rigging places the billets in the most forward position, under the swells. Ropers prefer this style because it keeps the saddle from sliding forward.

You can add a back cinch to a full rigging for greater security. Both cinches hold the roping saddle in place without stressing the horse unnecessarily. This combination is called a full double rigging.

The three-quarters rigging places the cinch farther back on the saddle. This and the seven-eights rigging, a compromise between full and three-quarters, are seen on pleasure and equitation saddles. Most saddles today feature the seven-eighths, as it pulls the saddle down on the horse's back. The bulk of the rigging rests forward so it does not interfere with your leg position.

Two other riggings, center-fire and five-eighths, are uncommon today. On a center-fire rigging, the cinch attaches midway between pommel and cantle. The five-eighths sits farther forward than the center-fire, but not as far forward as the seven-eighths.

Some saddlemakers offer a three-way skirt rigging. Two slots in the plate allow three locations for the latigos: the forward slot for full rigging, the second for three-quarters, or both for seven-eighths.

Many saddles have additional rigging in the

A full double-rigged saddle is constructed on skirting leather in a smooth finish.

rear skirts for the attachment of a back or rear cinch. You'd only need a rear cinch if you rope or ride steep trails, because its purpose is to keep the saddle flat on the horse's back under stress.

Using two cinches does not make your saddle double rigged. Only a full-rigged model is correctly termed double, since the complete definition is full double rigging.

Other design variations are available, depending on your personal preferences. For example, you can choose from various horn shapes and slopes. You will see two basic styles of skirts: square and round. Popular on many show saddles is the Mother Hubbard skirt, in which no rear jockeys cover the skirts. This style eliminates some bulk and allows closer contact with the horse's back.

Selecting Materials

Like an English saddle, a Western model is built from wood, leather, and metal—or synthetic substitutes. Again, the visible sections of the saddle fit over a rigid tree.

Traditionalists prefer the wooden rawhide-covered tree. A fork, cantle, and two side bars are cut from cottonwood or pine, either lodgepole or ponderosa. Pieces are securely glued and screwed together. Metal reinforcements are placed between the bars, and the bare metal is covered with leather.

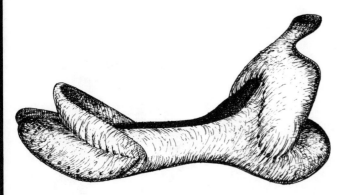

A wooden tree, covered with rawhide, forms the basis for top-quality Western saddles.

Most modern Western saddles are built on a molded plastic tree.

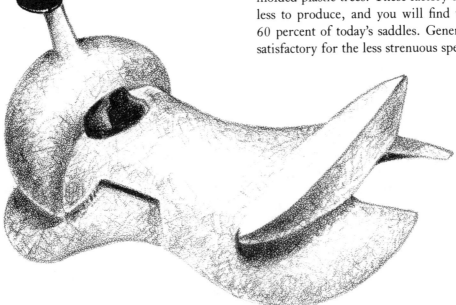

A quality tree will be cut, joined, and finished by hand. It must be sanded as smooth as a piece of furniture to prevent irriation of the horse's back. If even a small bump protrudes from the wood, eventually it will work through the padding to exert uneven pressure.

The tree builder strengthens the tree by stretching the wet hide of a bull, cow, or steer over the wood (strength is due to the animal's age, not its sex). The rawhide sections are stitched together with lacing, and as the hide dries, it shrinks to encase the wood.

The resulting combination provides a durable, safe foundation for the saddle's leather components. Wood bars and cantle will flex, rock, and twist as the horse moves. The swells should not give or spring. The rawhide increases the wood's tensile strength. One saddlemaker notes, "Rawhide is the toughest stuff known to man—it shrinks from the day it's put on the tree."

The two bars allow air circulation along the horse's backbone, by holding the seat above the spine. They also support the stirrup leathers and sometimes the rigging.

Modern scientists have developed injection-molded plastic trees. These factory-made trees cost less to produce, and you will find them in about 60 percent of today's saddles. Generally, these are satisfactory for the less strenuous specialties.

Most experts recommend wooden trees for roping saddles. Saddlemakers note that in the long run, rawhide-covered trees prove more durable. Manufacturers claim molded trees will resist breakage, but some repair professionals claim that molded trees are brittle, especially during the colder months. Plastic trees may also warp. Fiberglass can develop a hairline crack in a nailhole, which will fracture overtime.

The saddle horn—bolted, screwed, or riveted through the gullet—is made of steel, brass, or bronze. It is usually covered with leather or rawhide, and the cap is protected with a metal plate. On a plastic tree, the horn's base is totally encapsulated by the plastic.

The most visible parts of a saddle are the leather sections that compose every saddle. Saddlemakers choose thick skirting leather for the skirts and fenders. Weights vary through light, medium, or heavy, with sixteen ounces per square foot a desirable weight.

The Western saddle is composed of cowhide sections. One full-grown cow or steer, or one and one-half medium-sized animals, will provide enough leather for a saddle.

Generally, the saddler will cut out the seat and jockeys from the butt and hips, the skirts and fenders from the back, and the cantle from the belly. The swells require one large piece of leather, which is fitted over the curves by welting.

The saddlemaker attaches leather to the tree with screws and nails. Six saddle strings are threaded through all of the leather layers and into the tree to secure all parts. Fenders are stitched or riveted to the stirrup leathers.

Leather is stretched over the seat and tacked in place over the seat strainer. In a padded seat, the builder adds a layer of foam or sponge rubber over a piece of felt. Although this cushions the seat, most working cowboys choose a smooth leather seat, which requires a large section of exposed, premium-quality leather. Padding can conceal lesser-quality materials. Underneath many padded seats are two pieces of leather, seamed down the center to result in a weaker construction.

Most saddles feature the grain side on the outside. Some riders prefer a roughout surface, with the flesh side out. The texture on seat and fenders can give you a better grab on a cutting, roping, or games saddle. The half-breed saddle combines both roughout and smooth surfaces.

Smooth leather is usually decorated in traditional designs. In addition to adding to the saddle's beauty, the imprinted leather creates texture to improve your grip.

The saddler adds the design by embossing, carving, or both, usually before he puts the saddle together. An embossed design is created by stamping the leather, either by hand or machine. Stamping beats down the leather, compressing the fibers. Carving or tooling, which results in a raised relief, is performed by hand. Tooled leather will be tougher and last longer than smooth.

Handwork is an art, as the craftsman usually plans the pattern before building the saddle. He can stamp a background for tooled floral motifs. The saddle can be fully tooled, spot tooled, or just corner tooled, with tooling on only the corners of skirts, fenders, and front jockeys.

Swells are tooled after the saddle is built. This allows the craftsman to place designs in the proper location after he has stretched the leather over the pommel.

The saddle's underside is padded with either sheepskin or polyester fleece. Quality saddles feature the traditional one-inch-thick woolskin to help keep the horse's back cool; the saddlemaker stretches and tacks the leather backing over the bars. Wool's dense, plush fibers hold the saddle in position on the saddle blanket or pad.

Woolskin prices continue to escalate, and the supply to shrink. Lesser-quality saddles are lined with the more affordable polyester fleece. This material resembles woolskin when a saddle is new, but over the years tends to mat and pack down. It will not cushion as well as woolskin and keeps the

Look for a saddle to fit well, setting evenly on the horse's back to equalize pressure. The rear skirts should conform to the back, not lying above the pad. This ranch saddle features a high pommel, with no Cheyenne roll. Courtesy D. R. Brittain Custom Saddlery.

horse's back hotter. Also, the polyester fibers sometimes slip.

On the rigging hardware, look for stainless steel, cast bronze, or brass. Avoid aluminum or welded-steel D-rings.

Selecting Fit

A saddle's design affects its fit and comfort. Always consider the fit of the tree and skirts on the horse first, before you choose a saddle that fits you.

A tree's fit varies by the width, angle, flare of the bars, and length of the bars. In all its parts, the tree must distribute weight evenly.

First, evaluate your horse's conformation to gauge which tree best matches its back and withers. Standard trees are the Quarter Horse, semi-Quarter Horse, regular, Arabian, and pony. A regular saddle best fits a Thoroughbred type—with higher withers and a narrower back. Never use this saddle on a broad-backed horse, or a wide tree on a horse with high withers. One that's too narrow will pinch as the edges of the bars press into the skin. One that's too wide will create excess pressure on the withers and the back along the top edges of the bars.

Measure the width across the gullet and the spread of the bars. The gullet of the semi-Quarter Horse tree usually runs from about 6 to 6 1/2 inches wide and from 7 1/2 to 8 inches high. Quarter Horse bars (also known as full Quarter Horse bars) are spread about 7 inches apart. Regular bars are spread from 5 1/2 to 6 inches apart. Arabians and Morgans may require wider bars than the Quarter Horse.

Correctly fitted, the gullet should sit high enough to clear the horse's withers. Check the clearance by fitting your fingers between the bottom of the gullet and the top of the saddle pad. Two fingers are the minimum clearance for comfort.

The spread and flare of the bars should allow the entire length of the saddle to lie flat with even pressure. Bars should cup the muscles of the horse's shoulder blades and back.

One way to see which tree fits your horse is to try on a bare tree to scrutinize how the bars press onto the back. Be sure that the contact remains even on all areas.

On a completed saddle, look at the length of the tree. Long bars on a short-backed horse can dig into its loins. The fronts of the bars should fit into the horse's back just behind and below the withers. When you shake the front of the saddle, it should naturally slide into this area.

Look at the length of the skirts. Most measure about 27 inches. Choose round or shorter ones, about 25 inches, for a short-backed horse.

When you select a saddle to fit yourself, your first consideration should be the size of the seat. Standard sizes range from 12 to 17 inches, measured from the base of the fork to the base of the cantle. A youth or pony saddle will usually have a 12- to 14-inch seat and shorter fenders.

You will have to sit in different saddles to select the right size seat. The size can vary according to your body type and weight. No one can claim that all women require a 15-inch seat, or men a 16-inch size.

In a well-fitted saddle, you will feel secure at any speed.

The padded seat of an equitation model features a built-up front.

The seat must feel long enough so you can shift your weight when necessary; it should not be so big that you slide back and forth. If you are loose in the saddle, you can't remain seated forward over your horse's center of balance.

The seat's slope, or rise, affects its size and fit. Look at the slope from the base of the cantle to the gullet. A higher rise will shorten the size of the seat, making a 16-inch seat with a high rise slightly smaller than a flat seat of the same measurement. The angle of the swells can also shorten seat size.

Experts disagree on the ideal seat shape and angle. Some feel it should be flat from pommel to cantle so that you may lean forward. Currently popular is the Buster Welch tree, with a flat seat preferred by cutters. Many women complain that seat is uncomfortable, and they prefer a built-up seat, with extra padding against the pommel. This design helps keep you in place, with the deepest part of the seat against the cantle.

When you are trying out a saddle in a saddle shop, an expert can tell if the seat fits you by your body language. If you fidget, the seat isn't right. If you look content, the saddle probably feels comfortable and the seat is right for you.

Whichever type you choose, the saddle's deepest part should place you near the center of the seat. Where you sit should be the narrowest, most comfortable part of the seat.

A saddle's throat, or its width at the front part of the seat, varies according to the width of the fork. This can measure from 10 1/2 to 14 inches; it is generally wider in a longer seat.

Generally, a better saddle will feature a narrow waist. The spread and angle of well-designed bars will result in less width between your legs, and longer-lasting comfort. Remember that the bars still need to fit the horse. Narrow bars might irritate the horse and weaken the tree.

Test the width of the waist by placing your palm on the seat ahead of your crotch. The waist, directly beneath your crotch, must not spread your legs too far apart.

If you choose a padded seat, be sure it does not feel too thick. Layers should not add excess bulk between you and your horse. A custom saddle can feature a full-, half-, or three-quarter-sized padded seat.

Lean back to see how the cantle fits you. Its slope, or dish, should touch you at the proper angle for greatest comfort. Most cantles measure three or four inches high from the seat.

Press your legs against the saddle to check how the rigging and stirrup leathers feel. You should not feel any bulk or metal rubbing your knee or thigh.

How do the stirrups' position affect your seat in relation to your horse's center of balance? When you sit in the saddle, you should be able to swing your legs in the stirrups. Some riders prefer stirrups that are hung slightly forward, which allows freer movement. Ropers, for example, do not want their stirrups to swing back to overbalance them while roping.

Check the shape and width of fenders. Most measure about eight inches wide, with the teardrop style narrower at the top for greater swing. Stirrup-leather buckles at the bottom of the fenders allow you to adjust the stirrup length up or down.

Features

Swells range in width from the 9-inch slick fork to the wide 15 inches. Most saddles feature 12- or 13-inch swells.

You can choose from two cantle styles: the plain roll or the Cheyenne roll. A plain cantle should feature upright binding, with a separate section of leather or rawhide stitched along its edge from one skirt to the other.

Most saddles today have the Cheyenne roll. This can be plain, tooled, rope edge, or trimmed with silver.

Most saddles today include a near-side cinch-strap holder, also called a latigo carrier. After you secure the cinch, you thread the end of the latigo through the slot of the carrier.

On the offside of the pommel may be a rope strap. This looped thong can carry a coiled rope, or serve as a hanger for the cinch when you store your saddle.

At the forward edge of the skirts will be attached metal D-rings. These connect to the snaps or straps of a breastcollar.

The team roper's saddle can feature a roper's-style rear cinch. An extra strap laced to the cinch

helps both to anchor it and to balance the saddle on the horse's back.

Before you buy a show saddle, investigate the current styles. Silver trim is still almost a necessity, but today silver should be refined and elegant, not gaudy or massive. You will see many saddles with silver lacing on gullet and cantle, but other new models feature rawhide lacing.

The quick-change buckle allows simple adjustment of stirrup length.

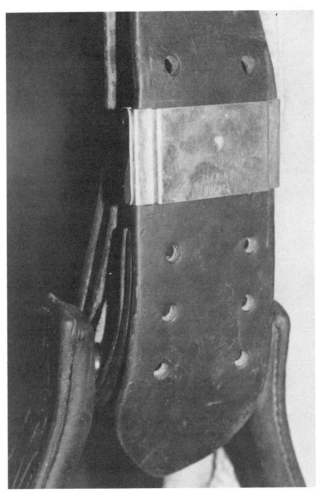

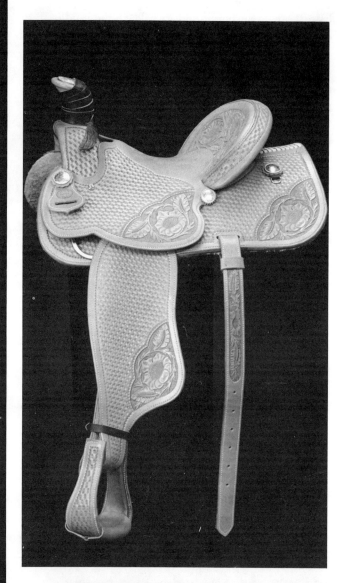

A custom model shows a high cantle with a Cheyenne roll. The craftsman has added full basket stamping with Oregon poppy tooling on skirts, fenders, seat, and billets. Courtesy D. R. Brittain Custom Saddlery.

Today's show saddles feature silver conchos added to swells, horn cap, and over the saddle screws. Saddlemakers also add silver trim, called plates, on the front corners of the jockeys and the rear corners of the skirts. Quality trim will be sterling silver overlaid (soldered) onto nickel. The nickel base gives conchos and plates greater strength. Before you invest in silver, remember that you can always buy a plain saddle and add your own choice of silver later.

Recently the basket-weave stamp has become popular. A current pattern combines the basket-weave with the acorn motif.

Remember that if you show West Coast-style, AHSA rules require that you add a reata and hobbles to your saddle. The show reata is a long rope of braided rawhide or leather. Coil it and attach it to the saddle's rope strap. See Chapter 20 for descriptions of show hobbles.

Rawhide trim is now fashionable on barrel-racing and cutting saddles. This durable material can prevent fraying on the horn cap and cantle, but it will become slick when wet.

Ropers and trainers often choose a saddle with rawhide swells. The tough leather will withstand the abuse of a rope dragging against the swells, or a rank colt trying to rub off the saddle.

Most saddles today are made in a light brown leather. You can also choose from the reddish russet, or the dark-stained chocolate. With lighter colors you can choose either to darken the leather, by oiling it, or to keep the light shade.

Quality Craftsmanship

In general, the more handwork, the better the saddle. Expect a quality saddle to contain 80 or 90 percent handwork.

Even a custom builder will utilize machines for some tasks, mostly in concealed areas of the saddle. Some parts may be stitched by machine, while others are better sewn by hand. Hand stitching may prevent leather from tearing.

Power tools such as the air gun will save time in punching holes and stapling or tacking layers, and other machines can cut, sand, and polish. However, experts agree that the more time spent in handwork improves the craftsmanship.

As you examine a saddle's craftsmanship, find out which parts were sewn by hand, and which by machine. Usually the skirts are machine-sewn— but ask about the horn cap and Cheyenne roll. Many saddlemakers sew the horn by machine and the Cheyenne roll by hand. Look closely at several saddles to see the difference.

A well-crafted saddle is usually made from quality materials.

Look for thick, flexible leather of thirteen to sixteen ounces per square foot in all of the layers. Ask about its origin. Expect the finest saddles to be made from top-quality domestic leather, most often from the Hermann Oak tannery. A lesser-quality saddle may be built from imported leather in order to be priced competitively, but softer leather will not hold tooling well.

Feel the edges of layers for smoothness and uniform thickness. Look at the front edges of the skirts. All edges should appear as one, with no visible lines separating them. The edges should be beveled to produce an even, finely bonded surface. You should not be able to insert a fingernail between edges.

Face the gullet and visually compare the skirts. Do both measure the same? Move to the side to check that the lengths are the same from front to rear. When the saddler blocks the saddle, or stretches wet leather to secure the fleece lining, the leather often stretches out of shape. After it dries and shrinks, its size can alter. Look for heavy skirting leather, most visible on skirts and fenders. It should be rich in natural color and have a dense body. When you squeeze this leather, you should not feel a squishy or cardboardlike texture. The leather should flex back and forth

while still holding its shape. The various leather sections should fit together well, blending into an attractive product.

Leather's imprinting can conceal a saddle's craftsmanship. For example, machine embossing can cover defects in leather, such as scars and wire marks. You can expect a lesser-quality saddle to be made of lower-grade hides, and not of the choice parts of that hide.

A saddle of high quality should feature hand-tooled leather. Feel the tooling for its artistry and depth. Examine the detail for intricacy and lack of errors. Look on the flesh side of the fenders, which may show the outline of the tooling. Quality work on good leather will withstand abrasion for decades, without change in the depth of the design.

Although a quality saddle might have no tooling at all, generally more hand tooling indicates a higher proportion of handwork. When you see a saddle that features tooling under the cantle and swells, you can expect it to be of high quality.

A hand stamped basket weave pattern combines with the acorn design to display outstanding craftsmanship.

On a quality saddle, look for fine detail at the pommel.

Study the seams where the saddlemaker has attached one piece to another. For example, look at the leather covering the swells. It should be stretched tight and solid. You will see a stitched, welted, or laced seam. Run your finger along the area to feel for a smooth, even seam. Some swells feature a hidden seam, with a section attached over the seam to assure a smooth surface. Compare both sides to see if the seams or welts match.

Look at the gullet to see the leather of the swells is folded and seamed under the fork. A quality saddle will feature smooth layers, tacked by a welt, topstitching, or brass nails.

Feel the edge of the horn cap for a firm, smooth surface. Study any exposed stitching. If hand-sewn, the seam will be placed close to the edge for a solid construction. The farther from the edge the stitching, the greater the chance that the layers will peel apart.

How do the jockeys lie in place over the fenders and skirts? They should not protrude, but lie flat. Also check that the rear skirts fit tightly underneath the cantle. They can be laced, stitched, or sewn by a back jockey-connector plate stitched over the skirts.

The seat should fit tightly against swells and cantle. Feel the top and sides of the cantle, especially the Cheyenne roll. Can you move or bend it? If it feels thick and solid, the builder has fastened an extra layer of leather between tree and seat.

Pull on the billets to see if the rigging feels secure. Look at the rigging itself; you should not see any fibrous leather, which can tear under pressure.

How is the rigging attached, by stitching or with copper rivets? Look at the saddle from the front to verify that the rigging is attached at the same location on each side. The cinch must pull evenly on both near and off sides. If you plan to attach a rear cinch, check that rigging, too. Look for strong reinforcement on skirt rigging to prevent the slot from tearing.

Study the exposed stitching on the seat and skirts. Check the seat for sturdy handstitching; this area must endure the heaviest wear. Look for stitching that is uniformly five to six stitches per inch, tightly holding parts together.

Examine the underside for the dense, firm woolskin. Fibers should face down and toward the rear to "grip" the pad or blanket. Some saddlers taper the length of fleece at the front edges. Fleece should feel evenly thick throughout, with no thin spots.

Although the seat's groundwork is not visible, it contributes greatly to the saddle's quality. All layers should be lined and contoured to provide a smooth foundation. When you sit in a well-made seat, you will feel how the quality differs from a lesser model. The quality seat feels firm, not as though it is stretching under your weight.

You won't be able to scrutinize the tree unless you buy a custom-made saddle. Ask about its construction and guarantee. Top-of-the-line saddles often carry lifetime guarantees against breakage. More common is a five-year guarantee.

Even small details can exhibit a saddle's overall quality. Look at the leather rosettes or metal conchos over the screws or strings that hold the saddle together. Are the rosettes or conchos centered, or are they slightly off center?

Lift several models to compare their weight and heft. A well-made custom saddle will probably weigh more than a similar factory-produced model, indicating greater durability and quality of materials.

Finally, on an inexpensive saddle, look at the size of the various parts. Some unscrupulous manufacturers reduce leather costs by scaling down the fenders, jockeys, and skirts. Check the sizing by comparing these components to those of a more expensive saddle made by a quality manufacturer.

Quality Recommendations

Realize that a saddle is a major purchase, similar to buying a horse. A good saddle can last you a lifetime, outlasting several horses. A poor one will constantly irritate you. Only a professional will wear out a quality saddle, and a pro can invest in another.

Do not complain when a good saddle costs more than you paid for your horse. One custom saddle-maker comments, "Horse prices go up and down. I have never seen leather, trees, or hardware prices go down since I've been making saddles."

You can order a custom-made design from a saddlemaker or choose among many manufacturers. Either choice can provide you with a durable piece of equipment.

Custom saddlemakers claim higher quality than comparably priced production-line saddles. You can receive the exact fit and features you desire, and you can rely on the quality of the product. The builder relies on customer satisfaction to maintain his reputation. Also, you have the opportunity to evaluate the interior components during the process.

A custom model is a major investment, however. If you're new to riding, anxious to saddle up

An inexpensive saddle of cheaper leather will show the effects of use. Instead of one piece of skirting leather, the manufacturer stitched together several pieces of lighter weight leather to form seat, jockeys, and fenders. As stitching deteriorates, saddle parts will not hold their shape. CourtesyD. R. Brittain Custom Saddlery.

immediately, or short of funds, you'd probably choose a factory-made saddle. Most top manufacturers will do custom work, substituting features on regular models in their lines. One expert compares saddles to tires—retreads provide basic transportation, but choose radials for quality. You should buy as much saddle as you can afford.

Recommended saddlemakers are Rios, Crates, Court's, Saddle King, Potts Longhorn, Victor Leather Goods, Circle Y, Tex Tan, Champion, MacPherson, Keyston, Billy Cook, and Simco. Many lesser-known firms also produce excellent equipment. Ask your local retailer for suggestions, because most custom shops serve walk-in customers only.

Because a saddle is only as good as its tree, inquire which firm produced your saddle's tree. Three recommended tree builders are Dave Scott, Superior, and Ritter.

Insiders' Preferences

• "Your better factory-made saddles come from the West Coast—Victor Leather Goods, Champion, and MacPherson. They're all close to custom-made." (Custom saddlemaker)

• "The Rios Brothers of Phoenix make the best saddles." (Saddle-shop owner)

• "As a rule, Circle Y makes nicely finished saddles. They aim at the fast-track riders, using rodeo stars and famous trainers in their marketing. They have a high profile, they're up-to-date in their designs, and they use glitzy trim. But, this attractive product is priced higher than comparable brands, which may not be as highly marketed. They're made in the same plant as Billy Royal and Silver Royal brands, interchangeable models priced as much as 15 percent less." (Saddle-shop owner)

• "Look at the D-rings on the rigging. For example, on this Saddle King, they use Korean stainless steel D's, costing about $1 apiece. On our saddle, the D's are marked 'Roy,' made by the Roy Bit Company [Texas]. They cost $9 apiece and are much stronger for roping." (Custom saddlemaker)

• "The best saddles—Crates, Longhorn, and Courts—use Hermann Oak leather." (Sales representative)

• "I recommend the rawhide-covered trees made by Kenny Haas of the Tennco Manufacturing Company in Midway, Utah. They have a smooth surface and are finely finished." (Custom saddlemaker)

• "Victor Leather Goods is known for beautiful handwork. They use the same leather as other makes, but they have the best tooling." (Saddle-shop owner)

• "I've seen Ralide trees break easily, especially in winter, but today their quality is improving." (Custom saddlemaker)

• "Montana Silversmiths provide excellent conchos." (Sales representative)

• "One Texas company makes all the kids' saddles that they job out to Tex Tan, Circle Y, etcetera. You'll see the same model sold in all the catalogs. I recommend the kids' roping saddle from the Wofford Leather Company [Colorado] as one of the best buys I've seen in that size." (Saddle-shop owner)

• "Earlier Circle Y saddle models are better than the current ones." (Saddle-repair specialist)

• "Crates Leather produces quality Western saddles and strapwork with fine craftmanship." (Custom saddlemaker)

- "On any saddle, a certain percentage has to be machine-sewn. For example, an old-time saddle like Vancore is a custom saddle about 80 percent handmade. One like Tex Tan's Hereford Billy Lewis Roper [a quality factory-made saddle] is roughly 50 percent hand, 50 percent machine." (Custom saddlemaker)

- "Courts is a family-owned business catering to professional ropers and barrel racers. Saddles retain a high resale value." (Sales representative)

- "In a medium-priced saddle, I prefer Tex Tan, Longhorn, Veach, Circle Y, and Colorado Saddlery." (Custom saddlemaker)

- "Champion is a good brand in a manufactured saddle." (Saddle-shop owner)

- "The Rios saddles aren't built for roping. They're built to ride for thirty minutes in the show ring. They use split leather, not full-grain, on their saddle's seats." (Custom saddlemaker)

- "We have good luck buying at Broken Horn. I think the best equitation saddle I have I bought off the floor new from Broken Horn [a California manufacturer and shop]." (Trainer)

- "Courts makes the best Western pony saddle." (Saddle-shop owner)

- "Next to our product, two good custom saddlemakers are Jim Lathrop [Montana] and Scott Denzer [Arizona]." (Custom saddlemaker)

Maintenance

Take care of your investment. Clean your saddle often with a high-quality saddle soap (see chapter 33). Brush off dirt and dust from tooled leather. Unfasten straps and remove stirrups, and clean all areas of fenders and stirrup leathers. Use leather oil to help break in new leather, and re-oil at least twice yearly to preserve the leather. Avoid over-oiling the saddle, and never oil a padded seat. Oil can soak into the padding.

If your saddle is equipped with silver trim, polish it regularly with a product like Duraglit, and avoid letting polish contact the surrounding leather. Clean lacing with a cotton swab.

Saddle-repair professionals advise that you should handle your saddle carefully. Never toss it into the bed of a pickup, which can break the tree where the cantle joins the seat. Carry it off the ground; do not let it drag in the dirt.

Store your saddle on a saddle rack or stand at least two and a half feet from the floor. Keep the stirrups up off the ground; if the saddle rests too low, the fenders can become folded out of shape.

Chapter 6

—

AUSTRALIAN SADDLES

Australian saddles have been in existence for over two hundred years, but only in the 1980s have they become popular in the United States. Market-wise Aussies introduced their tack here after the success of Australian action movies, notably "The Man From Snowy River" (1982).

U.S. distributors market the Australian saddle primarily to pleasure and trail riders. It has also gained popularity with Western trainers, trainers of green horses, and beginners. The saddle's unique appearance, light weight, and emphasis on comfort and security attract riders looking for alternatives to the traditional English and Western models.

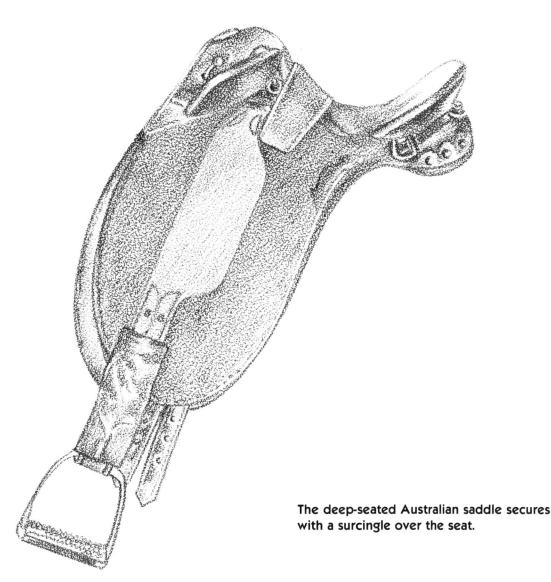

The deep-seated Australian saddle secures with a surcingle over the seat.

Basic Design

The saddle resembles an English saddle at first glance. The most obvious difference is the addition of knee pads, sometimes called "poleys." These padded leather crescents are attached to the skirts, below the pommel. Stationed immediately in front of your upper thighs, the pads allow you to lock your legs in position. You can follow every movement of the horse, no matter which direction it goes.

The tree features a deep, level seat with a narrow twist. Panels include up to three inches of stuffing to create a comfortable fit. They create a generous air channel to allow circulation along the spine to keep the horse's back cool. Long flaps protect your legs, and wide stirrup leathers prevent pinching of your lower legs.

The shape and the height of the cantle spreads weight across the horse's back. Distributing the pressure over a broader area contributes to the horse's comfort.

The saddle secures onto the horse with a double system—both a girth and a surcingle. A girth buckles to a forward billet, attached to the tree. The surcingle straps around the belly, and it threads through slots to wrap over the seat. This extra strap locks the saddle into position.

Both straps must be used in order to obtain a safe, comfortable fit. If you connect only the girth, the forward position of the billet could allow the saddle to slip.

English-style stirrups attach to leathers that hang under the seat, over the tree. The placement of the leathers allows them to swing far forward or back. This enhances your security on hills and makes it easier for you to apply leg aids.

Clever manufacturers have produced various designs for specific American equestrian sports. Some Australian saddles add a Western flavor, sporting a stock-saddle horn, stock-saddle rigging, and even a Cheyenne roll.

Selection of Materials

Australian manufacturers claim the saddle's leather is superior to other saddle leathers. The tough-hided cattle the leather is made from feed on range vegetation, and their hides show few scars due to the scarcity of barbed-wire fences in Australia. The unique "cold-climate" leather, from New Zealand, is extremely thick because the cattle there live in colder weather and thus develop thicker hides.

The highest quality handmade saddles feature thick flaps of roughout leather. The leather has been sized, or buffed, for an even thickness, so the flesh side feels smooth but slightly tacky. This provides more grip and is easier to maintain. Slight scratches will not mar the flesh side permanently, as they will the grain side.

Look at the seat of the Australian saddle. In this critical area, the leather should be of top quality, without any weak spots, to stretch. On a handmade saddle, the maker will select back leather for the seat.

Trees can be made of laminated wood or molded synthetics. Either type features a steel plate to reinforce the gullet.

The panels are stuffed with synthetic flocking, loose wool, or doehair. Doehair is considered the best; it is steamed, washed, and tossed before use. This natural material dissipates heat from the horse's back upward through the saddle's air channel. The heat exchange helps the horse's back stay cooler on long rides.

Lining the panels is heavy-duty wool serge. Unlike leather panels, this fabric breathes. If sweat soaks into the panels, the stuffing and lining will air dry. Leather-lined panels would hold water, damaging the saddle's underside.

Selecting Fit

The Australian saddle sits well forward over the withers. At first it may appear to be too high, but this placement puts weight over the horse's center of gravity. The horse can carry your weight most effectively with the saddle balanced forward. The position also benefits the short-backed horse by preventing pressure on the loins.

Because this saddle fits differently from Western and English styles, many shops prefer to assist customers in selection. They recommend on-site fitting to insure that you understand how the saddle should be correctly placed.

Like any other saddle, the Australian saddle fits the horse without creating excess pressure. Manufacturers have developed standard, narrow, and wide trees to fit popular American breeds. They have designed the angle of the panels to feel comfortable along the horse's back. If necessary, you can adjust the ample stuffing to fine-tune the saddle's fit. Simply insert a nail through the serge lining to pull the doehair from one side to another.

You should use only a light pad with this saddle. Buckle the girth as low as possible, near the forward edge of each flap.

In the saddle, you will notice its balance, comfort, and secure feeling. Because the panels contain so much stuffing, you may also realize that the saddle places you higher than an English or Western model.

Seat sizes range from 15-1/2 to 18-1/2 inches. The seat is measured straight back from the leading seam on the gullet to the inside of the cantle.

For maximum comfort and control, the seat must fit properly. You can measure the fit by sitting in the saddle and sliding your palm between your thigh and the knee pad. If you lose or gain weight, you may need to switch saddles in order to maintain the correct fit.

The saddle should fit you as correctly as a shoe on your foot. You may wish to sit in several models to find the one that best fits you and your riding style. The placement of the knee pads and the shape of the seat varies. Some pads are placed low, which aids the endurance rider to post and stand in the irons. High, wide pads define the traditional saddle used for breaking horses.

Features

Many models feature extra pads, placed to support the backs of the thighs. These can vary from a raised leather piece to a smaller version of the knee pad, protruding from the flap directly below the seat.

All Australian saddles attach metal hardware at pommel and cantle. Foot staples are screwed into the tree at the pommel for attachment of breastplate and canteen. Four D-rings, two on each side of the cantle, allow you to snap or tie on other accessories.

You can also attach a crupper to the D-ring at the center back of the cantle. This accessory can help hold a new saddle in place during the breaking-in period. It also maintains the saddle's position during steep downhill runs.

Fancy stitching decorates the flaps and exposed panels on many styles. Although the stitching is mainly cosmetic, its amount and style can indicate the quality level of the saddle.

Quality Craftsmanship

Look for the same details as those you would inspect on an English saddle. Ask about the tree, verifying that it is steel-reinforced. Fittings should be solid brass.

Quality Recommendations

With the popularity of this style, domestic manufacturers have begun to produce Australian look-alikes. Investigate the saddle's origin carefully to buy an authentic import. Look for these respected Australian firms: Trevor James, Wayne Walker, Toowoomba, and Sid Hill and Sons.

Insiders' Preferences

• "A factory-produced Australian stock saddle is factory-quality. They buy leather in bulk, not individual hides. We import and sell quality handmade saddles, made by individual saddlers only." (Saddle-shop owner)

• "The Trevor James saddle tree and knee pads carry a lifetime guarantee against breakage." (Saddlemaker)

Maintenance

Treat the leather as you would any other saddle. Clean the serge lining with a stiff brush to remove any dried sweat and to prevent deterioration of the fabric.

Chapter 7

—

ENDURANCE SADDLES

Specialized saddles for distance riding have developed from this growing sport. As more riders enter the field of competitive trail and endurance riding, they demand a saddle that is comfortable to both horse and rider for long hours.

Manufacturers advise that although these saddles are designed for distance riding, they are appropriate for field trials and all types of pleasure riding. However, they would not be acceptable in most show rings.

Basic Design and Materials

With improved function as the goal, designers have adapted features from both Western and English saddles into the lightweight endurance saddle. In all aspects, they attempt to adapt the saddle to the horse's movement.

Some riders have performed exhaustive studies of the dynamics of the interaction between horse and saddle. The primary problem is that a saddle remains static, while the horse's back moves constantly—as much as eighteen inches up and down in the course of a long ride.

All design factors in endurance saddles improve the saddle's efficiency. Briefly, the saddle can feature a high pommel with or without a horn. The hornless style developed because many riders post or stand in the stirrups while trotting. A horn can interfere when you shift your weight forward over the horse's center of gravity.

The seat does not include the added padding usual on most modern Western saddles. Swells on the pommel help support the rider. Rigging is usually Western style, although some manufacturers have developed unique designs to eliminate weight and bulk.

Manufacturers have used modern materials in their high-tech saddles. On cinches, you will see neoprene and Biothane. Stirrup leathers may be constructed of Biothane, and stirrups themselves are often formed of a magnesium alloy with neoprene treads.

The saddle is usually built on a wood tree, wrapped with fiberglass. The leather of the seat, skirts, jockeys, and fenders is the same as that used in Western saddles, although it may be of a lighter, softer, and more comfortable weight.

Synthetic saddles have not proven successful for endurance riding. Riders have encountered problems with breastplates or cruppers pulling hardware loose from the fabric. Also, the endurance saddle must not substitute acrylic for wool lining. Wool provides maximum comfort over long miles.

You can choose an endurance saddle in an English or Australian style. One version of the English type features flaps that are cut out to allow for oversized knee and thigh blocks. A new Austra-

This endurance saddle is based on Western saddle design, without a horn. It features skirt rigging and an almost flat seat. Courtesy of Sharon Saare Endurance Saddles.

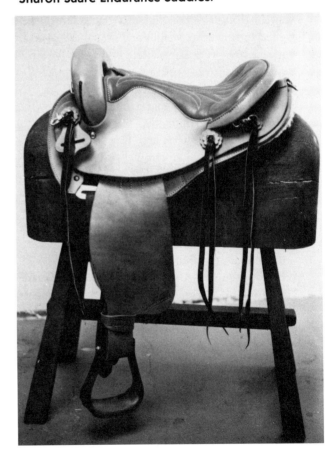

lian model, still in development, will enable the rider to readjust the channel to conform to the horse's changing body shape during conditioning or an arduous competition.

Selecting Fit

With function the primary goal, endurance saddle designers and riders conscientiously study the details of saddle fit. Manufacturers have learned to look closely at the horse's movement to understand what happens when pressure is added.

The tree remains crucial to the design of any saddle, especially one designed to be used for hundreds of miles of competitive riding. To prevent bruising the horse's back, the saddle is designed to spread its weight and the rider's over as wide an area as possible. Therefore, the Western design has proven superior, as it fits around the horse, not just along the back.

Designers try to avoid bars that contact the horse's back intermittently. They try to build a tree whose bars curve and flare properly. Bars should form a wide channel to permit unobstructed air flow along the horse's back.

Because fit is so important, many competitive riders select a specific saddle for each horse. Some riders even stock multiple saddles per horse, which they can switch as necessary.

One manufacturer combines flexible skirts to refine adjustment. An inner layer of plastic, available in four thicknesses matched to the rider's weight, helps spread the weight beyond the shape of the bars of the tree.

After seeing to the horse's comfort, you can concentrate on the feel of the saddle's seat and fenders over those long hours. A saddle that feels comfortable to you can allow you to relax more, avoiding fatigue.

Understand your conformation type and riding style. Do you know if one leg is shorter, and

which one? Do you tend to sit more to one side? When you feel tired, do you slump?

In your experience, have you found a seat style that fits you best? Can you assume different positions depending on the terrain and the stage of the ride? The seat should allow you to sit or stand. Some manufacturers claim a rise helps support you in a standing position. A flat seat can force you to bend to maintain your forward balance, which causes fatigue.

Three-way in-skirt rigging increases comfort. Changing the rigging shifts your leg and seat position to combat fatigue. Obviously, the rigging should never press against your leg, especially not on your knees.

Features

Padded stirrups—an optional feature—ease the shock on the soles of your feet. They also make it easier for you to stand in the stirrups for a longer period of time.

A trail-riding saddle should feature D-rings at front and back to enable you to add a breastcollar or crupper. These also permit you to attach a canteen, jacket, or saddle bags.

Quality Craftsmanship

Evaluate this saddle as you would any other model. Avoid one that displays obvious shortcuts in construction; search for functional quality.

Quality Recommendations

Buy a saddle that has been researched and tested by active riders. Saddles such as Brown's, Gorencheck, and Sharon Saare meet the unusual demands of the sport.

Avoid less-expensive saddles from companies that do not specialize in meeting the needs of distance riders. A copy will not incorporate all the design features of the rider-tested model.

Insiders' Preferences

• "The Brown's rigging holds the saddle down like glue. The saddle is anchored equally from front to back, not just from the front." (Saddlemaker about a girth that combines both front and rear cinches into one, joined at the belly.)

• "The Courbette endurance saddle is similar to the Australian style. It has blocks at the front and back of the rider's thighs, and a very wide channel for better air flow." (Sales representative)

• "The Sharon Saare saddle's three-way in-skirt rigging offers 7/8, 3/4, and 5/8 options that accommodate horses of various sizes and weights, and eliminates bulk between the rider and horse." (Saddlemaker)

Chapter 8

—

SPECIALTY SADDLES

Certain saddle styles meet specialized requirements for pleasure and show riding. These include the sidesaddle, Buena Vista Saddle, Peruvian Saddle, and Spanish Saddle.

Sidesaddle

Women of past centuries were expected to ride aside. Today, the nostalgia of sidesaddle riding offers women a challenge, a different riding style.

The sidesaddle consists of a large, flat seat with two pommels, called horns or heads. (Some Victorian versions held three pommels.) Wide panels distribute the weight of this heavy saddle.

You can choose from two styles: hunting and Western. In both, a pommel holds each leg in position. Your left leg fits over the leaping horn or head, also called the hunting horn. An upper horn holds your right leg parallel to the horse's spine.

The saddle secures with a girth, and a balance strap helps maintain the saddle's position. This strap runs from the seat to connect to the girth.

Fit is crucial on a side .ddle. It should fit the horse's back like any other saddle, not pressing on the backbone at any point. The wool-stuffed panels should contact the back muscles smoothly so that the seat is parallel to the ground. If the seat rests at an angle, either the stuffing of the panels needs adjustment or the tree is too narrow. Check that both near and off sides rest level.

Both girth and balance strap adjust on the off side. The girth should be tight. Adjust the balance strap so that it is snug, but not as tight as the girth.

The seat should feel comfortable and secure. You should sit in the middle of the seat, with your body following the contour of the seam of the saddle. Seat sizes usually measure 18 inches. Check that the seat size is correct by looking for only a few inches of saddle behind you.

The horn positions have to fit your legs comfortably, especially the right one. You carry most of your weight on your right thigh. Fit your leg over the upper pommel so that your thigh parallels the horse's spine. Your left leg fits against the curve of the leaping horn.

Some saddles feature a movable leaping horn. Screws permit it to swivel as you mount. It should not move as you ride, and your leg pressure tightens its position.

Only a few English firms, such as Eldonian, still manufacture hunting sidesaddles, and you may have to wait for months after you order one. Most riders purchase used saddles; some recommended brands are Whippy and Champion and Wilton.

The Western sidesaddle differs primarily in the square skirts, Western rigging, and fancy decora-

tion. It may feature carved leather on the flaps. The padded seat is covered with suede, stitched in ornamental designs. The stirrup can be any Western style.

Western sidesaddles are made by some custom shops, such as the Rios brothers.

A handmade Peruvian saddle shows exquisite tooling on the pommel.

Buena Vista Saddle

Riders involved in field trials often choose the Buena Vista or plantation saddle. This modified flat saddle is built for long days of hunting game. The quilted leather seat is well padded, with a supportive cantle. The bars of the tree extend ahead of the pommel and behind the cantle for extra support. This saddle also features metal rings on both sides of pommel and cantle for attachment of game bags, dog leads, and other necessary items.

Peruvian Saddle

The Peruvian saddle, or "montura", is designed for the Peruvian Paso breed. Developed from the Moorish-style saddle ridden in by the Conquistadors, it features a high pommel and cantle.

All Peruvian saddles are handmade. The working saddle consists of a simple wooden tree, covered with rawhide and trimmed in leather on the pommel and cantle. Wool pads the tree under the pommel in the "basto de lana" style.

The show saddle adds handtooled leather to the tree. The seat is not padded, but riders often cover it with a piece of leather or sheepskin, or the traditional pellon of black wool strands. In shows, the pellon is used only on a fully trained horse, shown in the bit rather than the bozal.

Metal rings of a cord cinch attach to leather billets with latigos. Stirrup leathers hold the pyramid-shaped stirrups, or "estribos." Carved from wood, these feature a metal loop at the top of the pyramid. A short leather strap attaches the stirrup to the leather.

Show saddles feature hand-stamped silver trim on pommel and cantle. Silver also adorns the stirrups.

Owners of Peruvian horses prize their magnificent tack almost as much as they do their horses. Many wealthy ranch owners gather large collections, and they exhibit their finest saddles in special tack rooms, artfully displayed in a museumlike environment.

Spanish Saddle

Horsemen of the Iberian peninsula still use two traditional saddle styles, the Spanish and the Portuguese. Also developed from saddles of Moorish design, these saddles resemble the Peruvian saddle.

The traditional cowhide Spanish working saddle features a pommel and front shaped like an inverted "V." The saddle secures with a girth, which fits over the seat. A sheepskin pad covers the seat, and a high cantle supports the rider. Some models add a crupper. The saddle's massive solid-steel stirrups are triangular in shape, with an open toe and heel.

The Portuguese model is built for the "rejoneador." It fits the rider closely at pommel and cantle, providing a snug fit for when the horse works the bull. The leather seat can be covered in suede or velvet.

Spanish and Peruvian saddles also appear in sidesaddle styles. The high pommel is replaced by the two horns.

Chapter 9

—

SADDLE PADS

Between most horses and their saddles lies some sort of saddle pad, cloth, or blanket. Each style functions for a variety of purposes—protection, absorbency, breathability, height adjustment for the saddle's seat, adornment, or tradition.

The first three factors are the most important. The pad protects the saddle from sweat and can act as a temporary cushion between the horse's back and the saddle's pressure (To avoid injury, the saddle should fit the back perfectly with or without a pad.) On a sensitive back, the proper pad can prevent irritation of the skin as it absorbs moisture and keeps the back cool.

The Navajo blanket is still popular
with Western riders.

Basic Design

A pad is usually layered fabric of varying thicknesses. A cloth, which is usually thinner than a pad, can be one layer or several. The blanket is one piece of fabric.

Pads match either English or Western saddles. English pads often duplicate the shape of the saddle. Many English and most Western models are square to accommodate various saddle shapes and sizes.

A forward or saddle-seat pad will conform to the saddle's flaps. For dressage, riders traditionally choose either a shaped pad, a square saddle cloth, or a square cloth with forward-curved corners at the front. Eventers also prefer the saddle cloth.

Some pads feature billet straps to keep the pad in position underneath the saddle. Sewn on top of the front sides, the straps lie over the saddle's panels so that you can slide the billets through loops on the strap ends. Another design features a pair of Velcro straps on each side of the pad, which fasten over the panels, underneath the flaps.

Another option is the pocket or slotted pad. Here a section of fabric is sewn to each side of the pad, and the sweat flap of the saddle slides through the slot. A similar design features a loop stitched horizontally above the pad's edge, through which you slide the billets or girth ends.

English riders sometimes choose a half pad or wedge pad, which covers only the withers and top part of the back, not the area underneath the saddle flaps. You can use this pad alone or atop another regular-sized one.

Other smaller adjustment pads are the pommel pad and the seat riser. For years, riders have used the oval pommel pad on horses with prominent withers. Traditionally knitted of yarn, it rests under the pommel to ease wither pressure.

The seat riser, or bump pad, acts in the same fashion under the cantle. It is also called a lollipop or keyhole pad because of its shape: it is a round pad with a short stem attached. The stem fits into the channel between the saddle's panels.

Western riders always use a pad or blanket underneath their saddles. The most traditional is the Navajo blanket, but also popular are a variety of woven blankets, folded to fit under the saddle's skirts.

Usually shaped in a square, a pad can also be rounded to fit under round skirts. The barrel racer's pad is smaller than most pads to conform to the size and shape of the games saddle.

A model used less often is the corona pad. This model frames the saddle's skirts with a rolled edge of black and white stripes.

Selecting Materials

Select material carefully, aiming for protection, absorbency, and ventilation. Today you can choose from natural or synthetic materials, or a combination of the two.

Riders of centuries past chose saddle pads of wool, cotton, or hair simply because these were their only alternatives. Many people still prefer the natural fibers, especially wool. You will see wool pads in several versions: felt, fabric, woven wool, carpet, and fleece, sometimes called a "numnah" (the Hindustani word for felt) in England. Some pads combine wool with jute, the wool yarn spun around a treated jute core for increased durability.

Naturally springy wool fibers will absorb sweat under the saddle. They draw moisture away from the horse's back and breathe to help keep the horse's back cool. Wool is less likely to slip than other fibers.

In general, wool felt is denser than fleece. You can test the density of a pad by compressing the pad between your hands. The denser the pad, the more room it has to absorb warm air. This allows the horse's back to remain cooler and more comfortable.

A dense pad also protects the horse by absorbing the shock of sudden weight shifts of rider and saddle. The denser the pad, the more it will support weight. However, avoid a pad that is too dense; it might be too hard and unyielding against your horse's back.

Many Western riders consider the Navajo blanket superior to all other blankets or pads. Made of thick wool, these products have been marketed since the 1880s. Traditionally, the Navajo weave these rugs in a tapestry weave with bound edges. They color the yarns with vegetable dyes.

Expect these durable blankets to help absorb sweat and protect the horse's back. You can choose from a striped design or a twill weave. Expect today's blankets to be machine woven, probably in Mexico.

Cotton is another natural material used to make saddle cloths. A cotton saddle cloth with a terry-cloth lining will hold its position against the horse's back. Many styles are quilted to maintain the fabric's shape. One version, of cotton velvet pile, is currently popular in dressage competition and with some Western riders, too.

A standard pad for Western saddles is the hair pad. This thick felt pad is made from animal hair interlaced through burlap. A typical mix is 80 percent cattle hair and 20 percent manmade fibers.

Many riders use one material in combination with another, layering them to perform different functions. For instance, you can place an absorbent wool, cotton, or felt pad next to the skin, then cover it with a fancier cloth or pad. This can save a showy, expensive pad from getting dirty.

Although pads made of natural materials are considered superior, pads of manmade materials are more popular. You will see many styles of polyester or acrylic fibers, often made into pads that simulate wool fleece or felt.

Synthetics offer the advantage of easy care and durability. They do not mold or mildew: however, they may cause your horse's back to become hotter without drawing away the extra moisture they create.

Manufacturers use polyester and acrylic fleece in many pads, with Kodel considered the best polyester. Extremely popular in hunt-seat riding, these pads are sometimes called "orthopedic" pads. Some manufacturers describe fleece as "hospital-tested," implying comfort and washability.

Look for a heavyweight polyester, with a twenty-four-ounce fiber creating a thick fleece. Short pile can reduce the synthetic's tendency to mat after use.

Although attractive when new, the fibers of a fleece pad will eventually become lumpy and flattened. Fleece tends to collect hair, and it is difficult to remove hairs intertwined in the fibers. If you use a double-sided pad, with fleece on both sides, always place the same side down to preserve the unmatted appearance of the top side.

Synthetic felts either combine cotton or wool with polyesters, or are entirely polyester. "Miracle" or "hospital" felt is considered to be nonallergenic, porous, moisture absorbent, and said to "breathe." Kodel felt will not gall or mildew.

Felt may be used as an inner layer on a pad. It can add body and padding. One pad version, a needle-hair felt, is said to dry better than most. This material will not remain saturated with moisture.

Another synthetic material used in pads is polyfoam, which is available in thicknesses from one to two inches. These resilient, nonslip pads are available either in smooth or textured surfaces, called waffle, egg-crate, or eggshell foam. Polyfoam will absorb moisture, however, and it tends to stay wet against the horse's back, which adds extra weight. Also, it is not good at dispersing weight evenly, and it can tear or gouge easily.

The sealed air chambers of closed-cell foam create a denser surface and better insulation than open-cell polyfoam. This material will not compress as flat as polyfoam, so it does not have to be as thick. It also resists water absorption. Designers claim that this high-tech material can absorb shock and protect the horse's back regardless of saddle fit. One version is made of the PVC material Ensolite.

A similar material is the synthetic rubber that is sometimes used as a lining in an antisweat pad. It has a textured "honeycomb" surface which grips the horse and creates air pockets for good air circulation. It causes the horse to sweat less and prevents it from absorbing sweat.

Manufacturers often combine both natural and synthetic materials in one pad, aiming for a pad with the benefits of both. Because wool is still considered superior as a backing, some designs feature a wool lining stitched to a synthetic cover. You will see pads combining both wool and cotton with a variety of synthetics, or a combination of synthetics with varied functions. For example, one manufacturer offers a pad made of a hospital-designed fabric. The quilted material features a polyester lining, a porous polyfoam inner layer, and a felt top. The layers pull moisture off the horse's back and hold it away from his body. The moisture dissipates through the material rather than remaining on the underside of the pad.

Among the synthetic pads available in Western styles are woven blankets, polyester or acrylic fleeces, and miracle felts. Again, many models will combine one or more materials. Some of the choices you have are a hair pad covered by cotton duck fabric, a blanket lined with acrylic fleece, and an upholstery fabric lined with felt or Kodel fleece.

The upholstery fabrics are currently fashionable in Western pads. Available in a variety of colors and patterns, some are of durable, Scotchguarded material, either smooth or with a velveteen nap. Others are of a nubby weave in classic tweeds or plaids.

Some Western show riders prefer the nylon

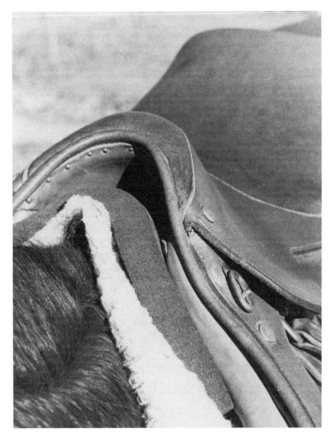

A wedge pad of closed-cell foam fits between this saddle and a polyester fleece pad.

This pad combines two materials—a Navajo-type blanket stitched to a fleece underside.

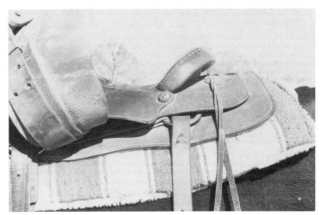

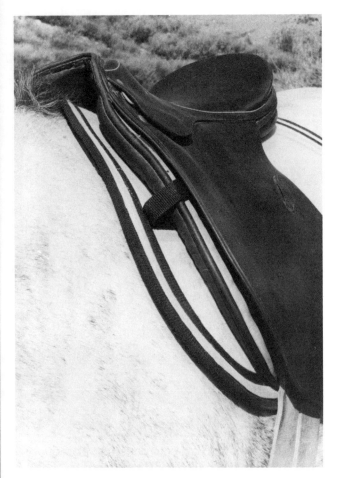

With a well-fitted saddle, a thin felt pad protects the leather from the horse's sweat.

carpet pad. Made of looped carpet material, this pad comes in a wide variety of colors and patterns. Edges should be bound with leather for greater durability. Some styles contain an inner pad of closed-cell foam to increase shock absorbency.

Because any pad must withstand stress, manufacturers usually stitch layers with tough nylon thread.

Selecting Fit

All pads are not alike, although many brands may appear the same except for price. You can't expect one pad style to fit all horses and saddles.

The pad should provide the necessary buffer between the horse's back and the saddle. You need to choose the proper size in thickness, length, and breadth.

With a well-fitted saddle, a pad functions primarily to protect the saddle's lining from sweat. It can be as thin as 1/4 inch under an English saddle, to provide a closer contact. Western pads are traditionally thicker, with a folded Navajo blanket about 1/2 inch thick.

Realizing the variations that exist in saddle fit, manufacturers offer a choice of pad thicknesses. In synthetic fleeces, you can pick single-ply or double-ply models. Western pads can measure from 3/4 to 1 inch thick.

If its material is dense, a thicker pad sometimes can act as a cushion. The saddle settles into the pad. However, a thicker pad can actually increase the pain a horse feels from an ill-fitting saddle. No cushion can alter pressure points, and the added width can intensify the pressure by compressing the withers between pads as it makes the saddle narrower. Most experts advise against both using a thick pad and layering pads to build up thickness. Two or three pads will create friction, which will irritate the horse.

You can compromise by using a pad that is

thicker in one section. In English pads, liftback and padded-seat models feature two layers of material, or foam padding under the seat or back. Some types include zipper or Velcro closures, which allow you to add or remove foam to adjust the thickness. You can even try an inflatable air pillow for variable adjustment.

Some pads are designed with extra cushioning at the withers to protect high withers from the pressure of the saddle's bars. Many felt and fleece pads provide wither rails or rail cushions, primarily to allow a wider saddle to fit a horse with high withers.

The seat riser is condemned by most experts. They feel this pad increases pressure by concentrating weight directly on the horse's spine in the area where the pad lifts the saddle. Also, tilting the saddle forward may increase the rider's security, but it exerts pressure onto the horse's withers.

The seat riser also slips and slides, creating friction for the horse and insecurity for the rider. Models cut from lightweight foam will lack density; these usually mash down so much that they actually fail to lift the saddle.

You can substitute a wedge pad for the seat riser. This pad may help improve the fit of a slightly narrow saddle or a saddle on a horse that has gained extra flesh. Because it is less bulky against a horse's shoulder, the wedge pad may help a horse that resists moving its shoulder.

The wedge lifts the saddle and still provides even distribution of pressure. Unlike a thicker full-sized pad, it does not increase bulk between horse and rider. Another alternative is to try a pad with a section removed. One design features a built-in air channel to eliminate any spine pressure.

If your horse has a minor abrasion on its withers or back, you can try cutting a hole out of a felt pad where it would rub against the injury. When you ride, there should be no pressure in this area.

The cutback pad is designed to be used with a cutback saddle. The Western version features a six-inch cutout at the front of the pad.

When you are selecting an English pad, be sure that the edges fit your saddle. A pad that is too small will slip. For appearance's sake, the hunt-seat pad should not extend more than one inch from your saddle. When the horse is tacked up, the edges of the pad should frame the saddle evenly all the way around. Quality brands are sized to fit specific models and sizes of saddles.

Conversely, a pad used under the flat, saddle-seat saddle should not show at all. Traditionally Saddlebreds, Tennessee Walking Horses, Arabians, and Morgans never appeared in the show ring with a pad under the saddle. Some exhibitors, however, are now using pads on these show horses.

In hunt-seat riding, pads also used to be considered improper. Experts claimed that with a correctly fitted saddle, a pad was not required. Their contention was that a pad could overheat the horse's back and lead to soreness, as well as inhibit the rider's contact with the horse. Today pads are standard equipment.

The Western pad should fit about two inches ahead of the saddle's front skirts. If you use a full-sized blanket, measuring thirty by sixty inches, fold it in half and place the fold over the withers. The two edges should always fit over the loins. Some blankets feature fringe or tassels on the back edges or corners. When the saddle is in place, these will lie behind the rear skirts.

If you ride in a balanced-ride saddle with the bulkless rigging, you can buy a special pad. It features a cutout area to fit under the rigging. This permits the rigging to rest close to the horse, reducing any bulk.

A pad must never irritate the horse's skin or pull against the hairs. When you place a pad in position, pull it up against the saddle's gullet to leave room over the withers for air circulation. Smooth any wrinkles before saddling.

A pad should not slide under the saddle, and it

should remain poised over, not on, the withers. Quality styles are contoured, shaped from two panels with the center seam curved to conform the pad to the horse's spine. This design helps keep the center of the pad aligned over the horse's backbone.

Polyester fleece pads may slip. If your English pad tends to slide around or bunch up, try one that you can secure to the saddle. Or switch to a pad lined in a nonslip fabric, such as terrycloth.

Western pads can be contoured to shape to the horse's back. Those models that are arched over the withers stay in place the best.

Features

A useful feature in many Western pads is the addition of wear leathers. Pieces of vinyl or smooth or suede leather are sewn on the top side of the pad at the withers and along the sides, where the saddle rubs. Without these reinforcements, a pad may begin to tear over the withers or wear out on the edges.

Wear leathers can be either rectangular or of the L-shaped "dog leg" style. The latter will protect the pad's front edge as well as the sides. Suede leather is considered more durable than top grain, which might dry out sooner.

You can choose a Western pad colors to coordinate with your horse or tack. The West has a colorful tradition, and your choice is unlimited by any rules.

As you might expect, the colors of English pads are much more conservative. For show, almost all riders choose white fleece pads. The creamy "sheepskin" yellow is now rare in hunter-jumper classes. When schooling, English riders often use a Western pad, either alone or underneath an English pad.

Dressage riders often choose a square white saddle cloth. Some feature colored borders or

Jumper riders can use any style pad. A pile of fleece and foam makes this close contact saddle perch far above the horse's back.

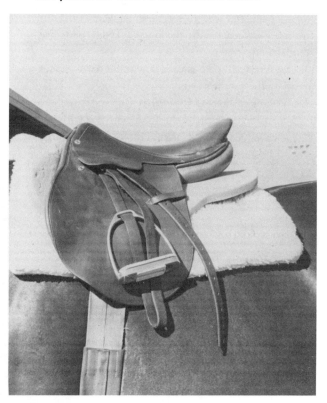

binding, and many also have a monogram or appropriate breed symbol (only if you are riding a warmblood). New in the dressage arena are the black pad and the black pad bordered in white, which complement a light-colored horse.

Some event pads feature built-in pockets for weights. These are attached in front of the pommel and at the rear edges, under the cantle.

Quality Craftsmanship

Feel a saddle pad for its density and resilience. On a stitched pad, press down to observe how the edges and stitching flex. If the body of the pad is covered in another material, look for smoothness on both sides.

Look for durable construction. Many fleece pads are stitched on the knit underside, then turned to expose the fleece. You cannot study the quality of the stitching, so you must rely on a recognized brand name. Look at any exposed stitching, such as reinforcements on billet straps or the center seam.

Feel the pad's edges. Binding or rolled edges should be smooth and even. If seams edge the pad, study that the rows of stitching appear sturdy. Pads often tear at the withers, so look for solid construction or extra reinforcement there.

If a pad is stitched through its layers, look at the pattern. Stitching should support the whole pad, while preventing the inner material from shifting or matting. An average stitch length would be five per inch; closer stitches can tear many fabrics.

In a blanket, stroke the weave to search for any bumps or unravellings. Is the weave heavy or fine? The finer the weave, the smoother the texture of the blanket's surface—and the less friction on the horse's back.

When selecting an uncovered open-cell foam pad, look for a separate piece of fabric bonded to

Rough-out wear leathers protect a pad from the rubbing of tie straps and fenders. This blanket's stitched but unbound edges have unravelled after years of use.

the top, over the withers. This will extend the lifespan of the foam, as it will be less likely to tear.

Quality Recommendations

The great variety of materials and styles makes it difficult to recommend specific brand names. In English pads, good brands are Toklat, Canterbury, and Eskadron.

Insiders' Preferences

• "Canterbury does very well. They make different pads for different saddles, and they have turned the saddle-pad industry into a complete industry by itself. We have no complaints about their products." (Saddle-shop owner)

• "The Eskadron pad acts like an air pillow and eliminates problems. It lifts the saddle and allows more freedom of movement." (Saddle-shop owner)

• "Peakes makes excellent Western pads. They have a shorter nap of fleece that seems to trap less heat than the Coolback, and they hold up real well. To me, the Coolback is a misnomer. It's from two to three inches thick of very heat-producing fleece. It's comfortable, resilient, and shock-absorbing, but not cool." (Saddle-shop owner)

• "The Lemetex cotton quilted pad, sold by Courbette, is outstanding. It stays soft and pliable, and it washes beautifully. The girth slot and billet straps are strong and don't pull out. I've used some for a year and they show no use. They do have to be washed frequently, and every now and then the quilted stitching pulls out. But you can easily mend it on your home sewing machine." (Riding-school manager)

• "The Ulster pads and boots are good on thin-skinned horses. The material is less irritating, it dissipates heat better, and it doesn't absorb moisture. You can hose it off, so it's easier to clean than fleece. A fleece pad gets wet and stays wet. However, it's synthetic; if you like natural next to your horse, first put on a Stubben cotton pad, then the Ulster. Ulster also makes the best quilted-velvet show pad, backed with a brushed cotton." (Saddle-shop owner)

• "The Ulster synthetic pad is rubber-lined and antisweat. It gives good air circulation." (Saddle-shop owner)

• "The Canterbury Backsaver fits the saddle well." (Sales representative)

• "Royal Riders makes English and Western wool pads that are machine-washable." (Saddle-shop owner)

• "Toklat distributes a nice fleece pad." (Saddle-shop owner)

• "Eskadron pads are too absorbent, like a wet sponge, and they slip." (Sales representative)

• "The Ulster pads work great in our desert climate, because everything gets so sweat-soaked. It's got to make the horse sweat more to wear a piece of plastic, but you don't have all that washing. Professionals go from horse to horse with the same pad. With a cotton pad, they'd wash five or six pads a day." (Saddle-shop owner)

• "Toklat's Coolback Medallion pad allows you to insert a foam wedge, so you can customize one pad for several horses." (Saddle-shop owner)

Maintenance

Separate your saddle and pad after each ride. Allow the pad to dry by turning it upside down. Some riders place the upside-down pad on top of the saddle.

Pads collect sweat and dirt. To prevent your horse from getting a sore back, you must clean your pad regularly. A pad made of synthetic fibers can be cleaned in the washer and dryer (some manufacturers recommend using a tumble washer rather than an agitator). Wool usually requires either hand washing or dry cleaning, but most cotton pads can be machine washed. Check manufacturer's instructions to be sure.

When washing wool fleece, wring it as dry as you can, and then allow it to drip dry in the shade. When the leather side feels about halfway dry, spray it with liquid glycerine saddle soap. Flex the damp leather to work in the soap.

Hand wash a wool-felt pad with a cold-water detergent. Brush off loose hair first, then rinse the pad by hosing. Air dry it in the shade. If a felt pad separates or curls you can rejuvenate it with a wire dog brush.

Soak polyfoam in soapy water for an hour or two, then rinse and squeeze out excess water without wringing.

Some pads should not be laundered. You can wipe or brush clean felt and hair pads; shaking them first will loosen dried dirt and hair. If a felt or hair pad becomes very stiff and hard, replace it before it causes back problems. For closed-cell foam, wipe the material with a damp sponge.

You will probably acquire a collection of pads, using some for everyday riding and others for shows. If your favorite sheepskin takes a while to air dry, having a spare on hand won't stop you from riding.

Questions

Does the pad's density place minimum bulk under the saddle?

Is the shape appropriate?

Chapter 10

—

GIRTHS

No saddle is complete without a girth. This strap attaches to the underside of the saddle's skirts to encircle the horse's heartgirth. Wrapped ahead of the belly, the girth keeps the saddle securely positioned.

A girth is crucial to your safety. It must withstand pressure as the horse's body expands and contracts while breathing, moving, and bending. Your shifting weight also stresses the girth. The pressure of the girth is probably unpleasant to most horses, but you can ease the discomfort by selecting the right size, shape, and material.

Basic Design

Any girth is a wide, flat strap with metal buckles or rings on both ends. The hardware connects to the saddle's billets.

Most models are identical on both ends, to connect to either the near or off side of the saddle. They are made in two basic styles: English and Western. The Western girth is called the "cinch." or "cincha."

The English girth holds four buckles, two stitched to each end. The tongues of the flat, rectangular-shaped buckles fit through holes in the billets. You adjust the girth by sliding the buckles up or down the billets.

The basic English model is a plain strap, measuring the same width throughout its length. However, this plain style is rare today, and most girths are now shaped to fit more comfortably. A variation of this outdated style is the three-fold girth, which is one section of leather that is folded into thirds along its length.

Hunt-seat riders usually pick the Atherstone girth. Also called the chafeless or antichafe girth, it is contoured to fit around the horse's elbows. The padded strap features narrower ends that prevent the girth from rubbing the skin behind the elbows. One or both ends are fitted with straps of elastic webbing to allow the horse to breathe more comfortably. A split end, with each elastic strap separated, adds more comfort.

Another antichafe design is that of the Balding girth, also called a ribbon girth. The leather is divided into three strips, with the two outer strips plaited over one another, once on each side. This shape also protects the skin behind the elbows.

Two specialized girths are available to augment your primary one: the overgirth and the foregirth.

The contours of the Atherstone style protect the horse's elbows from chafing.

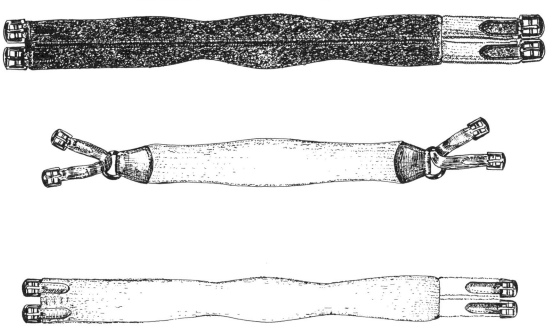

Cords of this rayon cinch wrap over the cinch ring, and a woven crossbar secures two D rings.

The overgirth is a web surcingle that wraps over the entire saddle for extra security. Competitors in racing, polo, and eventing often add this accessory because the horse's efforts might cause the regular girth to break.

The foregirth helps to keep a saddle in place on a horse with low withers. Used on some European warmbloods, this girth fits ahead of the regular girth, underneath the front of the saddle. Arch-shaped metal rings secure the saddle so that it will not slip.

The above girths fit the sport-horse breeds, with the emphasis on comfort when the horse gallops. Girths designed for saddle-seat riding are designed to be comfortable while the horse moves in more upright gaits.

Most girths fitted to flat show saddles (saddle-seat saddles) feature "humane" buckles. On each side of the girth, the buckles connect to separate straps, which attach onto a metal ring at the end of the girth. This design allows some flexibility, because each of the four buckle straps moves independently. You can fit the two buckles on each side at different heights on the billets—for the horse's comfort and to avoid interference with your knees.

Another English-type girth is the dressage girth. Basically a flat girth, it is made in a shorter length to connect onto longer billets. This places the buckles lower and reduces the bulk under your legs. Some dressage girths feature three buckles on each end or flaps that fit over the tops of the buckles.

The Western cinch is a strap made of a series of cords knotted over two cinch rings. The number of cords can range from fifteen to twenty-nine, with the widest cinches having the greatest number.

Some cinches are of a double-ply, or double-woven, design. In this design the majority of the cords lie in one layer, next to the horse. To strengthen the cinch, a row of additional strands covers the first.

Traditionally, cinches measured the same width along the entire length. Many riders today prefer a cinch in the roper's style, in which extra cords are woven across the middle. The flared center creates a greater width to absorb the strain of a roped calf or steer.

The cinch rings of modern cinches feature buckles to connect to the latigos on each side of the saddle. Most buckles are the sturdier bar-buckle style, with the tongue attached to a center bar. The tongues of the buckles fit through holes on the near-side latigo and off-side billet.

Only older or very inexpensive models are fitted with round rings without buckles; on these you must cinch the saddle by knotting the latigo through the rings. (You can tie any cinch, but the knot can create a bump under your knee.)

To keep the cords spread flat, most cinches feature one or several diamonds and crossbars of cords woven across the length, usually in a contrasting color. Most include two metal D-rings connected to each side of the middle crossbar. These allow you to buckle or snap on a breastcollar, tiedown, or rear cinch connector.

You can add a rear or flank cinch to most Western saddles. Billets thread through the rigging and secure with a lace or loop end. Buckles on the cinch's center body attach to the billets. This optional strap is unnecessary unless you plan to rope stock or ride steep trails. A short connector strap, which fastens both cinches together, runs from the center of the rear cinch to the D-ring in the middle of the front cinch.

Selecting Materials

Leather is the traditional material for English girths intended for sport horses. It can be a single thickness, cut for a Balding girth. Or, leather is folded or stitched over an inner lining, as in a layered girth. English saddlers sometimes add a serge lining between the leather sections.

Fit a rear cinch somewhat loosely. A connecting strap keeps it in place.

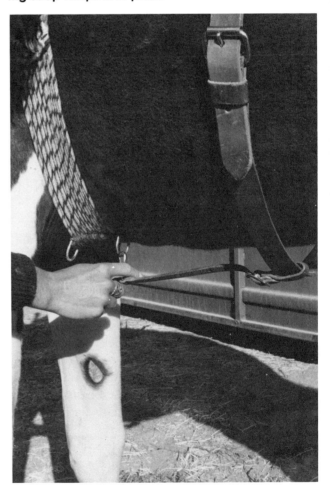

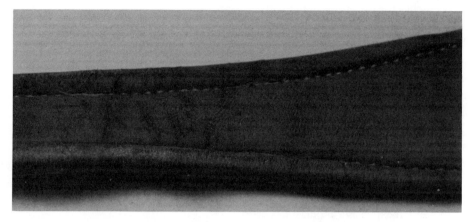

Leather girths require constant care. This model, only two years old, shows cracks in its center.

Because the girth absorbs sweat and receives constant pressure from the horse's movement, you should look for top-quality leather. Older styles were made of baghide, a thick, coarse, yet supple leather embossed with a crosswise grain. Look for smoothness, thickness, and solidity on a leather girth's inner layer, where it contacts the horse's belly.

New on the market is a vinyl girth, textured to resemble leather. You will need to look closely to discern the difference between the two materials. The vinyl material will not require as much care, but it may not feel as comfortable to your horse.

Many riders prefer a durable fabric girth for showing, casual riding, and schooling (hunt-seat riders should show with a leather girth, however). You can pick a natural web material, a tubular fabric such as linen or lampwick, or nylon web, plain or padded with acrylic fleece. Other favorites are the string or cord girth, similar to the Western cinch but fitted with the English buckles. This can be made of polyester, nylon, or wool-mohair cord.

The advantages of fabric girths over those made of leather are their easier care and softness. Some horses react adversely to leather girths and de-velop girth galls. A fabric girth may help you to avoid this problem.

A newer girth material is tubular polyester, padded and shaped to look like an Atherstone girth. Fitted with a cotton lining, this model is a popular everyday girth, easily cleaned and comfortable for the horse. Other synthetic girths, made of neoprene, nylon, or plastic strapping with a felt lining, are also available.

Many girths feature elastic web inserts on one or both ends, between the girth end and the buckles. Check for wide, durable elastic, in doubled or tripled layers.

Saddle-seat girths are traditionally made of white tubular linen. A sponge-rubber lining, textured in a raised "pimpled" pattern, is secured to the center of the girth. This keeps the girth in position.

You can also select this girth in nylon web. Both must be perfectly white in the show ring, which usually requires painting the material with white shoe polish.

To avoid this chore, you can switch to a leather or glossy white vinyl girth. The vinyl will not become stained and is simple to whiten with commercial cleaning products.

In the more flamboyant saddle-seat breeds, colored vinyl or patent leather girths have become popular. The girth can be a solid color or often coordinating shades, with a stripe overlaid onto a basic color. Colored girths can be chosen to match the horse's browband and cavesson to create a uniform appearance.

Look for stainless steel buckles. Compare the sizes of buckles; larger ones often create more bulk under your leg.

The cords of Western girths are made from a variety of fibers. Many old-time horsemen claim that mohair, woven from the wool of the Angora goat, is the best material for strength and comfort. It is said to absorb sweat and remain soft, without rubbing the horse's skin. It also washes well. Unfortunately, genuine mohair is rare and expensive.

Another natural fiber used in Western girths is cotton, which has almost vanished from today's marketplace. Cinches of manmade fibers will outlast cotton models.

You can choose from a variety of rayon and nylon cinches. Some combine rayon, wool, and mohair fibers—you'll see these described as either rayon, wool, or mohair. The proportion of materials determines the description. For example, a "mohair" cinch will contain a major percentage of mohair, probably blended with rayon.

In general, cinches made entirely of rayon do not wear as satisfactorily as the mohair blends. Rayon tends to become crusty when the horse sweats, and you will have to scrub harder to clean the fibers.

Whichever material you choose, feel its texture. The strands should feel thick and soft for greatest comfort.

For extra reinforcement, a heavy-duty cinch sometimes includes a piece of nylon web or leather stitched across the center crossbar. This helps keep the cords lying evenly and provides an anchor for the D-rings. On less-expensive cinches the rings will be woven in, without this reinforcement. Some cinches add nylon web straps stitched lengthwise over the cords. Nylon is superior here to leather because the leather will eventually become stiff and hard, then deteriorate and tear.

Web and leather cinches are two recent Western styles. A wide strap of nylon webbing can be lined with fleece, polyester felt, or Navajo blanket fabric. These designs are popular in the show ring, with many riders considering them more attractive. It is thought these cinches may feel more comfortable for the horse than the separate cords, since they are less likely to pinch the horse's skin.

However, like the fleece saddle pad, the girth's fleece will flatten. Sweat and hairs can mat the fibers, which will never recover the airy, fluffy appearance of new fleece. Fleece also causes the horse to sweat more, and the fibers may remain soggy many hours after your ride. The felt and blanket linings are thought to feel more comfortable for the horse and to be less likely to slip.

The rear cinch can be made of single- or double-ply skirting leather, or web lined with fleece or polyester felt.

Over time, you may need to replace your cinch strap (latigo) on the near or off side. You can choose leather or nylon web straps. Some people feel that as nylon stiffens with absorbed sweat, it can cause a cinch sore. They recommend using nylon only on the shorter, off-side strap. This length only contacts the skin for three to six inches, depending on the length of the cinch and how high the ring fits on the horse's side.

When you compare girth materials, be sure to look at the buckles. On English girths, the buckles should be stainless steel. Look for a groove at the top of the buckle, which helps keep the tongue secure so that the girth will not unbuckle accidentally.

Metal hardware on Western cinches should outlast the fabric. One manufacturer comments, "Cinch hardware can't be strong enough!" A good mohair cinch should be equipped with rings of stainless steel, solid brass, solid bronze, or an alloy of zinc and steel. All will prevent the hard-

A fleece-lined web cinch guards against chafing.

ware from rusting, especially in a humid climate.

Less-expensive cinches feature brass-plated or nickel-plated steel rings. Avoid the cadmium-plated steel rings, which are considered the least durable.

Cinch makers choose different sizes and shapes of rings. You may prefer a squarish ring, which will fit the latigo without making the leather bend. A round ring, however, will produce an even, straight pull, and it prevents the cinch from hanging off center. Ring edges can be flat or rounded; both styles have supporters.

Selecting Fit

You will usually purchase a girth separately from a new saddle, so you can pick a size that matches your horse first by length, then by width.

A girth that is too short can irritate the horse if the metal rubs against sensitive skin. An overly large girth is dangerous, as it prevents you from securing the saddle snugly.

For a hunt or flat show saddle, look for a girth

Although dressage girths are much shorter than other English styles, they should also fit near the middles of both billets. You will find these models in sizes from 22 to 30 inches long.

Western cinches are made in various lengths, averaging 32 inches. You can buy a cinch as short as a 22-inch pony model, up to a 36-inch cinch for a stout horse.

Any girth must be wide enough to prevent the edges from cutting into the horse's skin, but not be so wide that it chafes the elbows. Position the front about one inch behind the elbows.

Most English girths measure about 2 1/2 to 3 1/2 inches wide, but Western cinches vary greatly. The narrowest models, with the fewest number of cords, measure about 4 inches across. Some roping cinches are shaped up to 12 inches wide at the center. Cinches with a greater number of strands, from 27 to 35, distribute the pressure over a larger area. Each cord should be thick in diameter; thin strands will bite into the horse's skin.

The center body of the rear cinch measures from 2 to 6 inches wide. Again, calf ropers prefer the widest models. Some roper-style designs add pockets on each end of the cinch to hold the loose ends of the billets.

Features

Girth accessories can improve a girth's comfort. The most common add-on is the English or Western girth cover. This sleeve of fleece tubing slides over the entire girth to act as a cushion between the girth and the horse's skin. It can help prevent skin irritations.

Covers usually measure about 30 inches long. If you fit a cover over a Western cinch, be sure it is wide enough so that the cinch will slide into the tubing.

Occasionally, horses develop sores from the cinch rings of a Western saddle. To provide added protection for these horses, you can place a fleece pad or leather shield over the metal ring.

Girth guards are standard on most English saddles. These leather flaps fit over the buckles of the girth. They protect the saddle flap and your leg from the pressure of the tongues of the girth's buckles. Some experts recommend a larger guard, as a smaller one may form more of a bump under your leg. A smaller girth guard can also fold upward as you tighten the girth.

Another English girth accessory is the girth extension. This is short section of extra billet buckles that can be added to the saddle's billet to allow you to fit a too-short girth on a larger horse.

Quality Craftsmanship

Because a strong girth is crucial to your riding safety, do not scrimp on quality. Study the girth's construction, looking for even, tight stitching and a smooth surface next to the horse's skin. For example, an Atherstone girth should feature a beveled center strap at both ends. An abrupt edge could dig into the horse's skin. You might wish to flex various girths to gauge which model is the most resilient, since the strap must conform to the shape of your horse in order to be comfortable.

Look at the buckle attachment. Usually the buckles will be stitched in place by leather pieces wrapped over the ends. On a quality girth, the leather should be reinforced on all four buckles.

On a cinch, study the strands. Look for finely woven and tied strands near the rings and the center. Each strand should be wrapped smoothly over the rings, with no lumps to sore the horse. The best cinchmakers tie the strands several times for strength, then wrap the ends vertically over each strand to prevent unraveling.

Cords should hang evenly from the ring, and they should spread slightly wider than the bottom of the ring to help prevent chafing. Off the horse, the outside strands may appear loose. When you fasten the cinch on the horse, however, they adjust to the rounded shape of the horse's underside. You should not see any gaps between the strands, as gaps could collect sweat and hair. All strands should lie at the same tension.

Look for the web reinforcement to be stitched and backstitched. Study the diamond, which should appear smooth and tight so that it maintains flat strands. The diamond should not make the web crinkly or lumpy.

A roper's cinch displays a sophisticated level of engineering. Because the cinch contains so many strands in two levels, the craftsman has to allow for the spread. The overlay hangs loosely when the cinch is unfastened. In place, the strands tighten to rest flat and smoothly against the horse. You should note even pressure on all strands.

Quality Recommendations

Often girths are not labeled with a manufacturer's tag. In English models, you can rely on the major saddlery firms, or the fabric Cottage Craft girth. Western cinches often accompany the saddle; a respected brand is Bork's of Pendleton.

Insiders' Preferences

• "Girths usually aren't marked with brand names. A lot of places make them. In the United States, Whitman is a very good brand, as good as English models. Most English girths are nice, made of strong shoulder leather. They're particular over there, very meticulous. It's an art form. It's important for a girth to be made with English elastic." (Saddle-shop owner)

• "We find that dressage riders who use the short billets like the Stubben Trevira cord girth that won't shrink. It's less bulky and softer under [the rider's] legs. It's a wider girth, and it grips a larger area of the horse so the saddle won't slide around as much." (Saddle-shop owner)

• "Girths aren't marked, but the English and German models are better quality. Crosby makes both lesser and better quality styles in its line. I recommend to go to the expensive end. Stubben or Kieffer don't have a lesser quality, and Crump has a nice girth, too." (Saddle-repair specialist)

• "The Whitman girth is pretty good. They make girths for many companies, and the product is steady and consistent." (Saddle-shop owner)

• "European saddlers usually don't make girths to match their saddles. If they sell girths, they job them out, then put their names on them." (Saddle-shop owner)

• "I find that the Cottage Craft girth is too narrow on a large or broad horse. It concentrates the pull in a smaller area." (Saddle-shop owner)

• "Miller's nylon string girths have wide crossbars to prevent shrinkage, and they don't stretch. They're good in a hot climate, for they breathe in the summer. Crump has a cotton/nylon blend string girth, too." (Saddle-shop owner)

• "The Courbette leather girth has a good stainless steel buckle with a roller, so it won't wreck your billets. The quality is good." (Saddle-shop owner)

- "The Cottage Craft girth is great, although I think the elastic-end version looks ugly." (Saddle-shop owner)

- "Bork makes great cinches." (Saddle-shop owner)

- "Hinshaw makes a two-piece cinch of hospital felt Velcro-ized to a web girth with two-inch-wide Velcro. You can separate the parts to wash either, or replace the felt if it wears." (Sales representative)

- "I liked the Super Cinch till I had to wash one. I recommend using it with a fleece girth cover—it's easier to wash just the cover." (Saddle-shop owner)

- "Peakes makes a wonderful cinch of web and fleece." (Saddle-shop owner)

Maintenance

Keep your girth in good condition for safety. Being in constant contact with the horse, the girth receives hard wear and absorbs heavy sweat. A dirt-encrusted girth can create girth galls.

Soap and oil a leather girth after each use so that it remains soft. A new leather girth will be stiff at first and could gall the horse. If you use a rear cinch, clean it often, too. Although it does not contact the horse as closely as the front cinch, it also collects sweat.

Never allow a fabric girth to become encrusted with sweat and dirt. Fabric will become hard with dried sweat, and the front edge could cut into the horse's skin behind the elbows.

About once a week, wash web, string, cord, and fleece-lined girths in soap and water. Use a scrub brush to remove loose hairs from the fabric. Rinse the fabric thoroughly to remove all traces of soap, and air dry the girth.

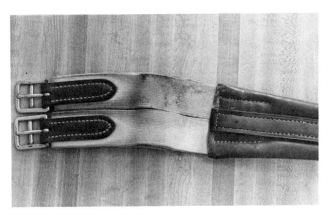

After a year of use, elastic ends stretch and should be replaced.

Keep your girth clean by unbuckling it and placing it over the seat of your saddle when you untack. If you carry your saddle with the sweaty girth dragging across the yard, the fibers will collect more dirt.

Regularly inspect your girth for safety as well as cleanliness. Have your saddler repair any loosened stitching on a leather girth. When elastic ends lose their stretch, replace the webbing.

Leather and even vinyl girths will eventually crack. The cords of a cinch can fray, and cinch rings may rust. Replace the girth when you observe this type of wear, which cannot be repaired.

Questions

- Is the girth strong enough?
- Does the girth rest smoothly against your horse?
- If the girth will attach to a show saddle, does the material and style meet official and current fashion requirements?
- If you add a rear cinch to a Western saddle, will that cinch function correctly?

Chapter 11

—

STIRRUPS

Stirrups serve as a firm foundation for your feet and help you maintain proper balance. They are a handy convenience to make riding more comfortable for you and your horse.

Basic Design

Most stirrups are shaped wider at the bottom than at the top. The broad, flat tread provides a surface for the ball of the foot. For safety, the opening of the stirrup must be slightly wider than the rider's foot—in an emergency bailout, you want to be able to remove your foot quickly.

In both English and Western styles, stirrups are made in oval, three-sided, and four-sided shapes. Models used on English saddles are more correctly termed irons, since they are shaped of metal.

The most familiar iron is the straight or Prussian-sided style. The sides, or branches, are rounded, with a wider section near the tread. Black rubber pads can be fit into the slots of the treads for greater security. These pads have raised parallel ridges to grip the bottom of your boots. Stirrup pads also add some warmth, as they shield your boot soles from the cold metal treads.

Today most riders prefer the cleaner appearance of the Fillis irons. The branches are rounded rather than flat, and they form a curved shape. Fillis irons are distinguished by their white rubber pads, which fit only this style. Instead of ridges, the pads feature a pattern of raised dots for a more secure grip.

Most hunt and saddle seat riders choose Fillis irons, with the distinctive white rubber pads.

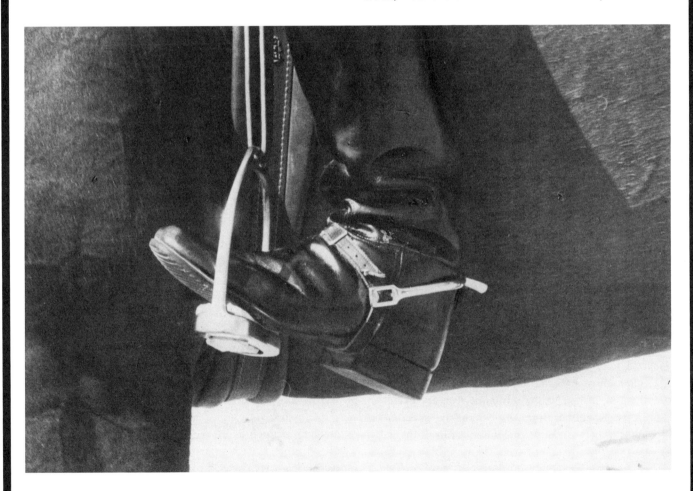

Two popular Western styles, with leather-covered necks and treads: Left, Oxbow; right, Visalis.

A recent development for the Fillis iron only is the security pad. This white rubber pad substitutes a flat abrasive center for the raised dots. With a texture similar to sandpaper, the center grabs the bottom of your boot to help you hold your foot in position.

You can also choose more unusual styles of irons. The offset iron slopes so that the outside edges of both the right and left irons are shorter than the insides. This design forces you to hold your foot with the heel down and ankle in. Though the concept seems viable, most trainers consider these irons to be an unhelpful artificial aid.

The safety iron, also called the Peacock, is another unusual design. Made in a squarish shape, the top, inside, and tread of the iron are made of metal. A rubber ring attaches on the outside. If you fall, the pressure of your foot causes the rubber ring to disconnect from the top of the stirrup, releasing your foot.

Although the safety iron appeals to many riders, it has its drawbacks. Rubber tends to deteriorate, and the ring should be replaced occasionally—before it breaks under normal use. This style is also not necessary if you have safety releases on your saddle's stirrup bars that allow the stirrup leather to slide off in case of emergency (or if you leave the bars open).

Rarely seen except in racing and cross-country irons is the cradle pattern. It features a rounded bottom with a stud grip tread and an optional rubber pad.

Stirrup leathers hold irons in place. These long, narrow straps thread through the slots at the tops of the irons and through the stirrup bars. A metal buckle on one end connects through one of the numbered holes in the strap, forming the doubled leather into a complete loop. The leather hangs with its grain side facing inward and touching the metal of the stirrup. The grain side is considered stronger against the constant downward friction of the stirrup.

English irons and leathers are usually purchased separately from the saddle. Western saddles are equipped with stirrups on permanently attached leathers, covered by fenders.

The traditional Western stirrup shape is the Visalia style, a four-sided shape that flares outward toward the tread. A variation is the bell-bottom stirrup, which features widened sides, or neck, that look similar to bell-bottom pants.

The roper stirrup is similar, except that the wide sides are almost the same width as the tread. This deep stirrup will withstand the weight of a quick dismount.

On cutting and reining saddles you will see the round or oxbow stirrup. Covered with rawhide, this stirrup features wide sides and a narrow tread.

Wide stirrup leathers, attached under the saddle's fenders, hold the stirrups in position. They twist to position the stirrup treads at ninety-degree angles from the horse's flanks.

Today's Western saddles feature the Blivens adjustable stirrup-leather buckle, in which metal prongs fit through double holes in the leathers. The buckles slide up and down the leathers for quick changes in length.

Infrequently used are tapaderos, leather hoods for the stirrups. Prohibited in most show classes, they are often seen on parade saddles. They can protect your feet from the cold and from brush; they also keep your boot from sliding too far into the stirrup. However, they are heavy and cumbersome.

Selecting Materials

Today's English stirrup irons are manufactured of nickel, stainless steel, metal alloy, or chrome-plated steel. The best quality irons are made from heavy stainless steel, forged with the lost wax method. They are also the safest choice. The heavy metal is more likely to drop free of your foot if you start to fall.

English leathers are cut from lengths of cowhide, rawhide, or buffalo hide (which is often called "red" leather). Manufacturers describe leathers by the tanning method utilized. Oak-bar-tanned butt leather is considered the best. "Red" leathers are usually chrome-tanned for softness and pliability.

There are also leathers made that are two layers, or one layer doubled and stitched, for extra strength. One type is made of cowhide backed with latigo or a synthetic webbing.

Traditionalists argue that a two-piece leather, like a two-piece billet, will be weaker than a similar leather of a single thickness. When the stitching wears, the leather separates.

One new style attempts to solve the stitching problem by bonding the straps. In this model the two flesh sides are bonded by a secret process, with the pieces fitted at a ninety-degree angle to

Fillis-style stirrups are made of stainless steel. Two German-made examples: Left, a lightweight, exercise model; right, a regular model. Photo courtesy of Hartmeyer Saddlery.

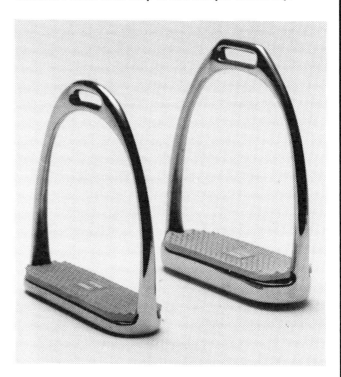

prevent any weak areas. Leathers of this design are less expensive to craft than the traditional one-piece strap because they use less leather.

You can also buy leathers made of brown nylon webbing.

Variations from the single leather do not stretch as much, but their extra thickness can make them difficult to fit onto the stirrup bars.

Buckles on stirrup leathers should be stainless steel.

Western stirrups are usually shaped of wood, with a wooden or metal hanger to space the sides. Oak is a traditional, strong wood used for these stirrups.

Most Western stirrups are covered by leather or rawhide, which is stitched or laced into place with latigo leather or heavy doubled-thread laces through holes punched in the leather covering. Only the cheapest models are bare wood or wood bound with metal.

Many newer saddles feature a molded stirrup, made of heavy-duty nylon or plastic. Manufacturers claim that this model will not break under 2,000 pounds of pull, which no wooden stirrup could withstand. When covered with leather, you cannot distinguish the plastic stirrup from one made of wood.

You can also buy all-metal stirrups, choosing from lightweight models of cast aluminum or heavier ones of nickel, brass, iron, or nickel with silver overlays. While the first three materials are fine for everyday use, reserve your silver-plated stirrups for the show ring. Some metal stirrups add a leather-covered tread for greater comfort.

Selecting Fit

Irons come in a limited number of sizes—from 4 to 4-3/4 inches wide across the tread. Most riders choose the 4-1/4 or 4-1/2 inch size. Look for the tread to give you about 1/2 inch clearance on each side of your boot.

Regular-length stirrup leathers measure 54 to 56 inches long when new. Children's sizes can be as short as 36 and up to 52 inches. Leathers also come in 60- or 62-inch extra-long lengths.

All leathers will stretch. Some may stretch up to twelve inches over years of use, with the rawhide and buffalo models stretching the most.

You should ride with your leathers even on both sides. The hole numbers marked on the flesh sides will help you fasten the irons at equal distances. You may need to punch extra holes above or below the ones provided. With new leathers, allow both to stretch the same amount by switching them from side to side.

You can choose from a range of leather widths. The narrowest—3/4 inch—look best on a show saddle. The widest, up to 1 1/2 inches, are recommended for hunting, polo, or eventing. Most riders choose the 1 or 1 1/8 inch width. Make sure the leather corresponds to the eye of the stirrup iron. A narrow leather in a wide eye can slip from side to side and cause the iron to hang unevenly.

Western stirrups vary in size by the width of the tread and the neck. A common size is a 3-inch neck with a 2- or 3-inch tread. A youth stirrup might have a 2 1/2-inch neck and a 1 1/2-inch tread. An oxbow stirrup, popular in cutting, features a 3-inch neck and a narrow 1-inch tread.

Western stirrup leathers are usually 2 1/2 to 3 inches wide. The leather should be thick, to support the rider's weight.

Features

You can equip English stirrups with two unique accessories: foot warmers and extension leathers. Foot warmers are fleece-lined covers that fit over the irons; they protect your feet from winter chills.

The near-side extension leather helps you to mount more easily. It features an elastic section that you can let down to make the leather six to eight inches longer.

Western stirrup leathers should feature hobble straps. These are narrow leather straps that encircle the base of each fender to hold together the leather and fender. These keep the stirrup in place and help to twist the leathers and fenders forward so that your feet can rest comfortably in the stirrups.

Quality Craftsmanship

Irons must appear solid, with no rough or sharp edges. Metal polished by hand indicates the highest quality product.

Check leathers for the quality of the finishing. Flex the leather to study its resiliency and durability, and feel the edges for smoothness. Beveled edges indicate higher quality.

Look for the buckles to be fastened with a triple row of straight, even stitches. Buckles should be made of stainless steel, and they should lie flat under the saddle flap for greatest comfort.

On Western stirrups, study the way the outside layer of leather or rawhide fits over the base. Look for precise stitching and secure lacing on the neck and tread. If the stirrup is laced with leather, count the number of holes. Usually a better-quality stirrup features more lacing with a narrower strap. Because the tread must endure abrasion from your boot soles, check for extra layers of material between the wood and the outer covering.

Quality Recommendations

To match an English saddle, choose the best leathers you can afford. If a leather fails while you are jumping or eventing, it could cause a serious fall. You can rely on leathers made by the major saddle manufacturers.

Insiders' Preferences

- "Barnsby makes a two-piece stirrup leather, bonded under heat and pressure. It will take over 1,200 pounds of pressure, so it's good for eventing." (Sales representative.)

- "Most irons are made in Korea. Stubben irons seem better finished than some other types. I think they may be Korean steel." (Saddle-shop owner)

- "The Miller's Imperial iron is better finished, with a uniform consistency. It is cast in the lost wax method." (Saddle-shop owner)

- "Stubben has created a two-piece stirrup leather. Two leather straps are split, and the two flesh sides are bonded at 90-degree angles so there is no weak spot. This uses only 20 percent of the hide you'd normally use for a one-piece leather." (Sales representative)

- "Stubben and Korsteel irons are both made in Korea. Stubbens are better finished with higher quality control—you won't find any flaws, and

On a quality English leather, check for three rows of stitching. The buckle should be made of stainless steel, with a depression under the tongue.

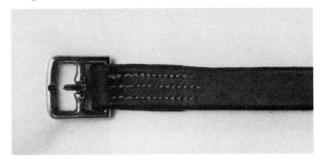

they're more highly polished. There's no difference in the quality of the stainless steel itself." (Saddle-shop owner)

• "Courbette rawhide leathers are a luxury leather. They're popular because they're very supple and don't stretch as much as regular ones. They're also not as thick as buffalo leathers." (Saddle-shop owner)

Maintenance

Metal stirrups require little maintenance other than occasional polishing. Leather-covered stirrups should be soaped and oiled as regularly as the rest of your saddle.

Routinely inspect the condition of your leathers. Replace a cracked leather, and have any frayed stitching repaired promptly. Oil leathers regularly and clean sweat and metal marks.

Switching leathers from side to side will help distribute the weight of the iron onto varied locations, helping the leathers last longer. The wear of the eye of the iron causes great strain on the leather fibers, which shows up as a black mark worn into the leather. You can obtain longer wear from leathers by asking a saddler to move the buckle a few inches lower on the leather. This will shift the weight onto an unmarked section.

English leathers are simple to inspect, as they rest on the outside of the saddle. However, you should not ignore Western leathers just because they are concealed by the saddle's fenders. Resting against the horse, the leathers absorb a great deal of sweat. Unless you scrub away the crusty dried sweat and renew the leather's natural oils, your leathers can break under stress.

Leathers become drier around the buckle holes and at the top. On many saddles, the maker may have attached the leathers without oiling their entire length. The raw, untreated leather is more likely to break. When you clean your saddle, pull the leathers down to apply treatments to their entire surface.

Questions

• Do the stirrups match the leathers?
• Does your foot feel comfortable in the stirrup?
• Do the stirrups feel secure, not slipping from the bottom of your boot?

PART III:
STRAP GOODS

Chapter 12

—

BRIDLES AND REINS

Ever since humans first handled horses, the bridle has been the primary means of control. This arrangement of adjustable straps secures onto the horse's head to hold a controlling device in or around the animal's mouth. Reins attach to this device, allowing you to communicate with the horse.

Basic Design

A bridle can be a simple strap encircling the horse's head to hold the bit in place. To allow adjustments, the one strap is usually three: the crownpiece, which lies across the poll and ends midway down the cheeks, and two cheekpieces, which connect the crownpiece and the bit.

While such a simple bridle allows adjustment, it may not stay on the horse's head. To keep it in place, the bridlemaker can add a browband or earpiece and a throatlatch.

The browband rests across the horse's brow, in front of both ears. Many Western bridles secure onto the head with an earpiece, a short strap or loop that fits over the ear. Two earpieces are also common. The split-ear bridle's crownpiece has a long split in the leather through which the horse's right ear fits. Other variations include the shaped-ear and sliding ear bridles.

All English and many Western bridles also have a throatlatch, sometimes called a "throatlash." This strap runs from the off side of the crownpiece below the ear and under the jowls to just below the opposite ear, where it attaches with a buckle. When secured with a throatlatch, a bridle has little chance of being pulled off a horse's head accidentally.

Most English bridles are made of a series of connecting straps. Hunt and saddle-seat styles are similar, with variations in the straps' shape and

width. The ends of the cheekpieces are attached to the bit and held in place with a hook, or stud, fitting into a slot on the inner side, although some models feature outside buckles. English bridles add keepers—short leather loops on the cheekpieces and throatlatch that hold down the ends of straps. Keepers may be fixed or sliding, to adjust to varying strap lengths.

In the traditional hunt bridle, flat leather straps buckle together. For show riding, bridles are also available in rounded or raised patterns. The leather on a rounded, or "rolled," bridle is sewn into round straps; these straps are flat only where the buckles are stitched into the leather. Recently this style of bridle has become less popular, as many people pick the raised bridle. On raised bridles certain parts—usually the browband, noseband, and reins—are sewn from two straps, the top one of which has a half-round shape. These styles can be used on both snaffle and Pelham bridles; the bridle name depends on the bit attached.

The double or Weymouth bridle, which carries two bits, is used in all styles of English riding—hunt seat, saddle seat, and dressage. It adds a separate crownpiece called the "bradoon carrier." This holds the small snaffle bit in place above the curb bit.

Although hunter riders customarily use a plain browband with a double bridle, saddle-seat riders add fancy browbands and sometimes matching nosebands to their show bridles. The browband can be of any color, pattern, or texture, and some exhibitors use leather browbands with brass or silver inlays.

Popular in dressage is the continental browband, made of a pattern of raised colored squares. Dressage riders also prefer the continental bridle, which is lined with white leather for an attractive two-tone look. A newer design features tone-on-tone padded leather, which combines two layers of brown or black leather.

Other styles of English bridles are the racing bridle and the gag. Horses on the track are

Look for large stud hooks on an English bridle, which prevent cheek pieces or reins from detaching unexpectedly. The hook on the top cheekpiece is undersized compared to the lower straps.

equipped with a durable snaffle bridle, simply constructed with buckled attachments at the bit. The reins are short and feature rubber hand grips for security.

The gag bridle is a modification of the snaffle; it is used only with a gag bit. The gag's rounded cheekpieces connect directly to the reins, through slots in the bit, for precise control.

Your reins should match the style of your bridle. Plain reins are flat straps, while laced reins have thin leather lacing wrapped through and around the hand parts of the reins for better grip. The plaited rein has been split into five to seven strands and then braided. A rounded rein matches the rounded bridle, with the leather the first eighteen to twenty-four inches from the bit round and the rest flat, plaited, or laced.

Historically, English reins to be used with a snaffle bit are two separate reins connected by a buckle. This design permits you to unbuckle the snaffle reins to slide them through the rings of a running martingale. Curb reins, which are not used with this device, are usually sewn together at the center.

Avoid an English bridle of softer, thinner leather, which is usually made from lower on the hide. This belly leather will stretch more. Test straps by pulling them. If you can see them stretch, the leather is not the denser butt leather.

Western riders can also choose from a variety of bridles, often called "headstalls." Western cheekpieces and browbands may be flared instead of straight. The cheeks attach to the bit with either Chicago screws, buckles, or leather thongs.

A Western browband can be one or two pieces. The latter, called the Spanish or crossover style, features two sections laced or tied with a woven knot.

The Western throatlatch may split off from the crownpiece, English style. Or, a separate strap may connect to the crown on metal rings or through loops. As in all bridles, the throatlatch buckles on the near side.

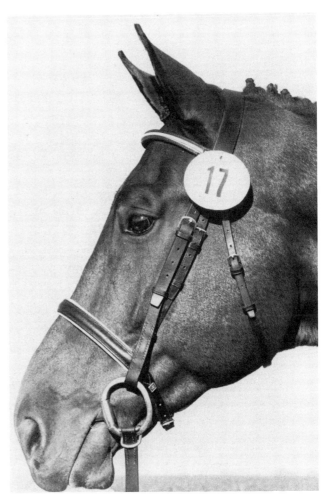

A dressage-style snaffle bridle includes a slotted cavesson. This model features white leather lining and loop ends on the reins.

English snaffle reins always features a buckle to connect the two straps. Her fine stitching and plaiting are evident.

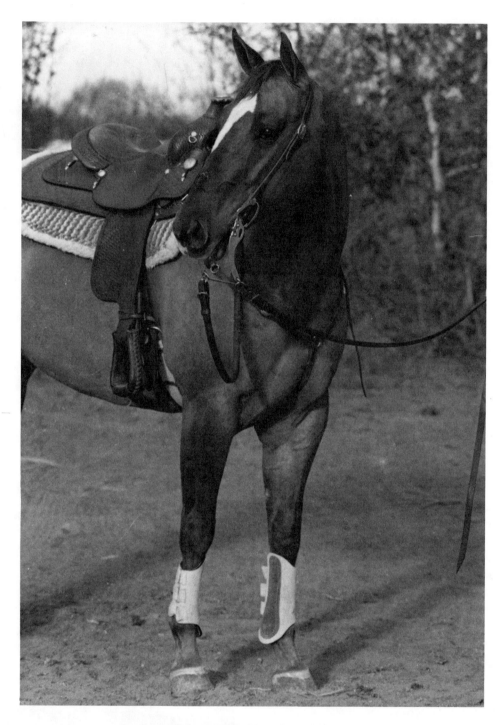

An entrant in the Working Cow Horse event
models a simple headstall with split reins.

For pleasure and schooling, you can use any style of bridle. In competition, cutters use the ear bridle, while those competing in other Western events use show bridles that can be as flashy desired. Leather can be rounded, flat, or braided; it is often decorated with contrasting designs.

Western reins are available in three types: open, closed, and roping. The open or split rein is the most common, consisting of two separate straps. The closed rein is actually three parts—two reins connected to each other by a long flexible quirt, called a "romal." This style is also called the California rein, since it originated with the vaqueros of that state. It is still most often used by West Coast riders.

Contest riders often use the roping rein, which is one continuous strap. Because the rein has no loose ends, you can't drop it while working.

To match a flashy show bridle, you'll need the right reins. Leather reins for show bridles are either flat or rounded. Fancier reins are decorated on the first eighteen to twenty-four inches from the top and on the romal if they are attached.

Selecting Materials

Leather is the standard material for tack for the formal atmosphere of the show ring. The best English bridles are constructed of full-weight English butt leather. Look for eight to ten ounce leather, rolled and treated to feel smooth and luxurious.

On the finest bridles, a craftsman cuts off measured strips by hand with a draw gauge, which cuts lengths evenly. He or she then uses an edging tool to rounds the edges and gives the reins a smooth feel. Another tool is used to vein the bridle, marking a slight indentation along the strap's length, close to the edging. On some straps, this veining serves as a guideline for stitching. Finally, the edges are finished with wax and dye.

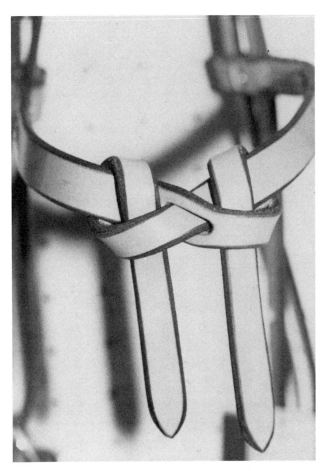

This Spanish browband is stained the popular light tan color, with hand-dyed edges in a darker hue.

A recent development is a more durable nylon strapping coated with polyurethane. This material resists deterioration; it will not crack, fade, or stretch. Smooth to the touch, it does not create friction and thus prevents chafing. This material is made into all types of strap goods.

Cord and rubber reins are popular for eventers, jumpers, and for schooling. Cord reins are made of plaited linen or nylon cord, while rubber ones add lengths of dimpled rubber to leather or web reins. The textured surface provides a secure hand grip, which is useful with a strong horse and in wet weather.

The rubber grips made in England remain superior over other imports. The English models usually consist of a higher density rubber; they resist cracking along the edges, which must endure constant abrasion.

A new rein combines the lightweight comfort of cotton with the flexibility and strength of rubber. The rein is made of cotton web with rubber threads woven through it—a design that eliminates the bulk of rubber hand parts.

All bridles contain metal hardware—buckles and studs. Look for solid brass, Never-Rust, or stainless steel on quality tack. Plated hardware is not as durable; the protective plating will eventually chip or peel. Also, buckles tend to catch on other objects, and cheap ones will break more easily.

Western bridles are made of both leather and synthetic fibers. For schooling, you can choose from harness, latigo, or russet skirting leather. About half the bridles you see are made of harness leather. Reins of this material are heavy and strong, which is useful when you are training a colt to neck rein.

Most Western bridle parts are cut out with a clicker, a machine that punches out the varied shapes. Quality leather will be hand-rubbed and dyed, with the edges evenly dyed darker than the flat surface. Reins will be beveled to appear wider on the flesh side.

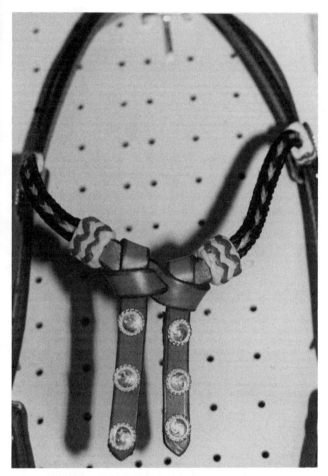

Miniature silver conchos decorate this Spanish browband.

For schooling, eventing, and casual showing, English riders can select bridles and reins of synthetic materials. Nylon webbing creates a strong bridle, but the fabric loses its crisp appearance over time. Sunlight fades its color, and its edges will fray. Nylon reins will feel slippery when wet, hard and stiff after they dry out.

Cotton or lampwick webbing produces superior reins. Leather stops, are stitched at intervals on the hand parts to make the webbing less slippery.

Except for those made of thick skirting leather, most straps are doubled and stitched. Some are lined with the thinner latigo leather to reduce bulk while adding strength.

Western show bridles are usually made of ten ounce bridle leather. It should feel strong, but not be too thick or wide. The flat leather cheeks may be scalloped or flared. Cheeks and browband are customarily adorned with a variety of decorative materials and designs.

Common silver ornaments that may be attached to leather bridles include cylindrical ferrules, conchos, tips, and brow or ear plates. Some may attach with Chicago screws, so you can easily remove the silver for cleaning. Silver can replace the usual metals in buckles, keepers, and Chicago screws. Some bridlemakers offer the ornamental jewelers bronze as a substitute for silver.

Artisans also embellish western bridles with leather lacing and horsehair designs of contrasting colors. Leather and rawhide laces can be plaited over the straps or inlaid into holes punched in the cheeks or brow. Horsehair, plaited into various designs, can also be overlaid or inlaid.

You may prefer the authentic appearance of braided leather headgear. Here the craftsperson plaits lengths of smooth leather, latigo, or rawhide to form rounded headstalls and reins. Cylindrical barrels and spherical buttons decorate the straps, and some craftsmen add silver ferrules. A latigo headstall may feature rawhide barrels and buttons. Latigo reins should be braided over a nylon core for greater strength.

For top-level showing you should choose a leather headstall; however, for roping, games, and pleasure riding, you can pick from a variety of materials. Most tack shops display a rainbow of bridles in nylon and polypropylene, both in flat web and braided cord. These headstalls are durable and easy to clean. They may be either doubled and stitched, or doubled and stitched with an overlay of contrasting web trim or plaited cords. You can choose from hand- or machine-braided polypropylene. A new option in headstall material is a nylon web coated with clear vinyl to resemble plastic.

Reins can be selected to mix or match your bridle. You can choose from flat or braided leather, braided mohair or rayon, plaited cord, or webbing. When you choose a lightweight rein, realize that the strap may not lie straight against your horse's neck.

Pleasure and games riders often prefer the easy care of the machine-braided polypropylene bridle.

Schooling for reining, this rider chooses split
reins of plaited cord.

Look at the fasteners on bridles and reins. Usually you will choose metal buckles, either the prong type or the Conway buckle, which features a short nub that fits over two holes on the strap end. Bit ends can also be fastened with Chicago screws.

If you prefer leather fasteners, you can buy reins that have been slot cut so that the rein fastens to itself through a slot. Or, you can thread leather thongs through holes on the reins or cheeks as fasteners. Braided leather tack features self-locking ends, with a button fitting through a loop. An extra reinforcement protects the cheeks from the wear of the metal bit loops.

Selecting Fit

Because bridles adjust to fit different head sizes, manufacturers offer a limited choice of sizes. The selection usually includes pony, cob or Arab, and horse or full size. As a guide, a cob cheek should measure 10 inches, a full-size cheek 11 inches. The cob brow band will run 11-1/2 inches, a full-size one, 12-1/2 inches. A cob crown will measure 26 inches total: cheek section each 7 inches, and the main crown section 12 inches. A full-size crown will add another inch on each side to total 28 inches.

If your horse's head seems to be an in-between size, measure the distance from the corner of one lip, over the poll, and to the other lip corner. Compare this measurement with the bridle you are considering; this will ensure that it will fit your horse.

If your horse has an unusually large jaw, measure that area so that you can be positive the throatlatch will fit. A properly adjusted throatlatch will allow you to slide four fingers between it and the horse's throat. This allows room for the horse to breathe and flex its poll.

Check that the browband is not too short; an overly short browband can pinch the horse's ears.

On a Western bridle with a separate throatlatch, the buckle is traditionally placed close to the ear.

Match the width of the straps to the horse's head. A hunt bridle can measure from 3/4 to 7/8 inches in width; show versions will be 3/8 to 5/8 inches wide. English reins can measure from 3/8 to 1 inch.

When you use a double bridle, the snaffle reins should be slightly wider than the curb. A typical combination would be a 5/8-inch snaffle with a 1/2-inch curb. This allows you to discriminate between the two reins in each hand.

If you are choosing an English bridle for schooling, avoid a model with narrow straps. A practical, imported bridle with thick, heavy cheekpieces will last longer than a beautifully finished 1/2-inch-wide bridle.

Western headstalls and reins can measure from 1/2 to 1 inch wide. Braided straps vary in diameter according to the number of strips. Four wide strands will produce a slim, pencil-like rein or headstall. Twelve will result in a cigarlike length, about 3/8 inch wide. The thicker the rein, the less flexible it is.

Also, be sure that the bridle you select will connect onto the bit that you use. A wide snaffle bridle won't fit through the loops of a curb or Pelham bit. There's no problem, however, with using a narrow bridle with a large-ringed bit. If you use a hackamore bit, you should choose a bridle with short cheeks to place the hackamore in the proper position.

Reins range in length from 5 to 7 foot English reins to 7 1/2-foot Western split reins. A roping rein may total from 6 to 8 feet.

Certain bridles can complement or detract from the look of your horse's head. A bridle of wide leather looks out of place on a horse with a delicate face. Use that style on a large-headed hunter. If your horse has a large head, you're wiser to avoid a narrower or rounded bridle. A wider bridle will not accentuate the largeness so strongly.

You don't want the bridle you select to distort

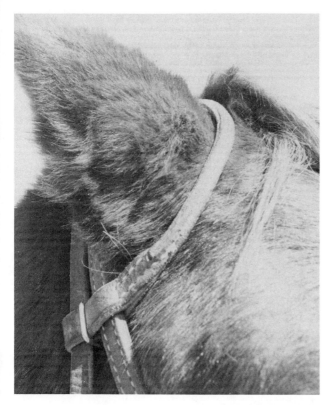

The ear loop of a sliding ear headstall encircles the offside ear without pinching or binding.

You can pick rein widths to fit your hands comfortably. Top, Western split reins of plain leather, Conway buckle ends; Middle, English laced snaffle reins; Below, English plaited reins. Note the fine veining on the English models.

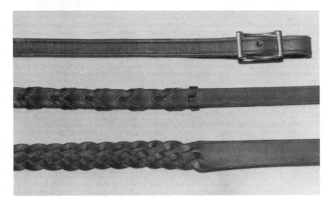

the length of your horse's head or the depth of his jowls. Vertical lines of browband and throatlatch can help to shorten the look of a long head. With Western bridles, strategically placed silver ornaments can attract the eye away from certain areas. Silver can make a short head look longer, or a long one appear shorter.

When buying a bridle and reins, you usually have the option of putting together the set you prefer. Most bridles are sold without bits, and some are sold one piece at a time. Many shops will allow you to purchase a bridle and change one part; for example, you might substitute laced reins for flat reins on a hunt snaffle bridle.

Features

If you choose braided leather show reins, you will probably want to connect rein chains between the bit and the reins. These protect valuable reins from being chewed or dunked into water when the horse drinks.

With rope reins on a snaffle bit, you may wish to add slobber straps. These leather sections function as a lightweight version of rein chains.

English show bridles look best in dark brown or black. Hunter riders prefer a medium reddish-brown bridle; dressage riders like dark brown or black. Few riders enter the show ring with a London-colored (light tan) bridle. In dressage and saddle-seat events, you can add a colored browband.

Western show bridles can be dark oiled or the newer light finish. Many feature a variety of colors overlaid on the cheekpiecess and the browband. You will see traditional shades of red, white, black, brown, and tan, as well as such newer colors as pastels, pink, and blue. Braided tack comes in chocolate brown, the reddish latigo, and the characteristic rawhide.

Quality Craftsmanship

Test the bridle both for how it looks and how it feels. Leather should feel supple, firm, smooth, and silken. Look for a fine finish on all edges. Study areas where one section of leather joins another. At first glance, the two layers should appear as one, skived so that thin layers meet to form a consistently thick surface. Seams and edges should be so smooth that the division is almost imperceptible. Avoid flimsy leather with straight, unbeveled edges.

Stitching should appear straight and even, with the stitches closely spaced. A bridle made with long stitches—only five or six per inch—demonstrates poor craftsmanship. One with nine to ten stitches per inch will last much longer, and a thirteen- to fourteen-inch model shows the skill of a true craftsperson stitching by hand. Study the stitching at stress points to see if the bridlemaker increased the number of stitches per inch.

On the bit ends of a Western bridle, lines of stitching that form an "M" add reinforcement. When you buy reins with rubber hand parts, check that stitches are not too close—they can tear through the rubber.

Some bridlemakers feel that silk thread is superior; others claim nylon is more durable. Thread should hold leather straps together without tearing the holes larger.

Look for reinforcements in areas that receive extra stress. On a quality English bridle, you should see an extra length of strap lining the inner ends of the cheekpieces and reins: the turn backs. This reduces the amount of wear from the bit rings rubbing into the leather. (Be sure the turn backs fit into their keepers.)

Are stationary keepers attached securely, with sufficient leather folded under the stitching? Are English bridle keepers veined to match the bridle? How does the throathlatch split off from the

An Arabian models a classic show bridle for Western classes, trimmed with silver bars, tips, hearts, and clovers.

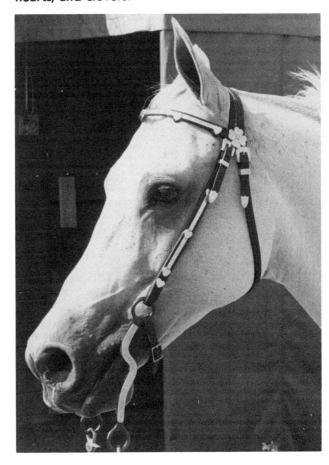

crown? This weak area should be strengthened by a round hole punched at the split, to reduce tearing.

When selecting braided or plaited leather, study the workmanship. Look at how the pattern begins and ends, and note any rough edges. Feel the sides for smoothness throughout. You should not feel any protrusions. If the item has multicolored lacing, look closely to see if the colors are plaited in, or painted on after plaiting. Flex the tack to check its durability and resiliency.

Look at metal hardware. Are buckles strong? Do they lie flat, with the prong pressing against the bar, not sticking out from the strap's surface?

If silver adorns a bridle or reins, study its quality and be sure all pieces match. Silver on a bridle

Handbraided headstalls and reins display fine craftsmanship. From left: flat braid over doubled and stitched leather; plaited rawhide with overlaid buttons, barrels, and knots; plaited leather with overlaid barrels and knots and silver ferrules; plaited leather with overlaid barrels, buttons, and knots.

does not necessarily indicate top quality. You can always buy a plain bridle and add silver in your own choice of design.

Bridles of synthetic materials should display careful construction. Look for smooth edges and no loose threads. Nylon fabric and thread should be heat sealed, with raw edges melted to prevent delamination. Holes for adjustment of cheekpieces and throatlatch should also be sealed.

Quality Recommendations

As with girths and stirrup leathers, quality bridles are produced by respected saddlery firms. A few brands to look for include Barnsby, Crump, Gold Cup, Jeffries, Jimmy's, and Stubben. However, many experts feel that bridles crafted in the U.S. are equal in value to English or German products.

The "Made in England" stamp helps label bridles, but it is not the only criterion to use. Argentine bridles are improving in quality; experts still differ about the durability of strap goods manufactured in India.

For Western bridles, again rely on well-known brands. These companies are known for excellent bridles and reins: Circle Y, Roy Martin, Rawhide Manufacturing, Victor Leather Goods, and Victor Supreme.

Insiders' Preferences

• "Crosby is only Miller's trade name. They go to various bridle shops for the product, so there is a variation in quality. Other English manufacturers do the same thing." (Saddle-shop owner)

• "English 'full-size' strap goods are often too large. Blue Ribbon and Crosby are sized down, but full-size in every brand is a different size." (Saddle-shop owner)

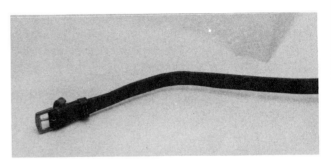

Check keepers for sturdy attachment. Strain often causes the leather to pull free if the keeper was not stitched securely on both ends.

• "Stubben has a new web rein with plastic straps embedded inside the web, which prevents stretching. Plastic rein stops are screwed through the rein—they're colored black or brown to match the web." (Saddle-shop owner)

• "Jimmy [Wiebe] is known as a craftsman and an innovator in bridlery." (Custom saddlemaker)

• "The bridles from New Cavalry Saddlery are our top of the line for someone who wants a fancy raised, almost a half-rounded raised, bridle. They're sewn very fine, from eleven to thirteen stitches per inch, everywhere on the bridle. The quality is good and they're made here in the United States from American hides, which is amazing. They're similar in quality to Jimmy's, and they're sized right for our horses. With the devaluation of the dollar, they're a good buy." (Saddle-shop owner)

• "English bridlemakers, such as Eldonian and Blue Ribbon, are consistently fine, if you buy those [bridles] made by the master saddlers.

Some, made by apprentices, are a lower grade, with less hand-rubbing. There's a lot of jobbing out in England, so you need to develop an eye for the goods." (Saddle-shop owner)

• "Bullion is an English import company that brings in a quality oak-bark-tanned bridle. It's a thicker, heavier grade that resists stretching." (Saddle-shop owner)

• "The better companies also make a range of quality. For example, Crosby makes a range of lesser-quality tack. I find the better end of the Crosby line and the German bridles usually good quality." (Saddle-repair specialist)
"You go to Walsall, England, and there are all these little shops—there is no County Saddlery or Crosby there. They send out the labor to farm ladies who do piecework. The importers are responsible for the quality control in which pieces they select." (Saddle-shop owner)

• "Any Courbette strap goods are of top quality." (Riding-school manager.)

• "Kieffer has its own tanning method and produces sturdy leather that feels supple. The British are known for better hand-finishing and more beautiful workmanship. For feel more than looks, go with the German bridle." (Saddle-shop owner)

• "In my school, I use school-quality bridles for durability, suitability for many horses and riders, and ease of maintenance and care. They survive daily use, and they're presentable for show. I like Foxwood's Number 91, a raised snaffle bridle. If cared for properly, it holds up. We clean bridles immediately after riding." (Riding-school manager)

• "Dressage riders prefer the Courbette, Stubben, and Kieffer lines. We find the German bridles more durable, but the leather feels stiffer and denser, so people choose a softer English bridle. A lot of the English are cut of such soft, thin leather that they stretch badly. It's better to go with the thicker hide. That takes oil and work, but it lasts longer." (Saddle-shop owner)

• "Victor Leather Goods makes one of the best headstalls and halters. Champion and MacPherson are also top quality. Double R show bridles aren't as finely finished." (Saddle-shop owner)

• "Circle Y bridles are made by another firm; the saddlemakers job out strap goods." (Saddle-shop owner)

• "For working equipment, Cowhorse Supply [Fort Worth, Texas] makes the best harness-leather bridles and reins. Dennis Moreland is really good, and Morgan's is very good. Champion Turf Equipment does an excellent job of finishing their product; they're very dependable and they deliver well. In the show tack, we use Vogt Western Silver and Diablo." (Saddle-shop owner)

• "Kathy's Show Equipment employs two braiders, who tan their own hides. We have some braided reins made by Israel Medina, the finest braider, who's now out of the business." (Bridle-maker)

• "Victor Leather Goods makes excellent doubled and stitched bridles and reins [Western style]." (Saddle-shop owner)

Maintenance

Keep your leather bridle in good condition by cleaning it both inside and outside after each use. Sweat, saliva, and the rubbing of metal parts can damage leather. If you notice cracks, have the bridle repaired or replace that section. A saddler can replace worn rubber hand parts on reins, too.

Clean white stitching by scrubbing with a soaped toothbrush. Rinse with water from a clean toothbrush.

Castile soap will clean dirt from white leather padding. The white leather will turn yellow as it absorbs oils from the horse's skin. Look for white padding that has been coated to prevent stains. However, realize that even the coating will eventually peel and crack.

Watch for wear on metal parts, too, especially where the cheeks secure onto the bit. A hook-stud attachment may have slipped out of its slot, or the threads of a Chicago screw might have loosened. It's quite a shock to have the bit suddenly fall from your horse's mouth, so be careful to inspect the parts.

Store your bridle on a rounded hanger; a nail can crease the leather. Let the reins hang down or loop loosely. Since your bridle is your primary control device, keep it in top condition for safety.

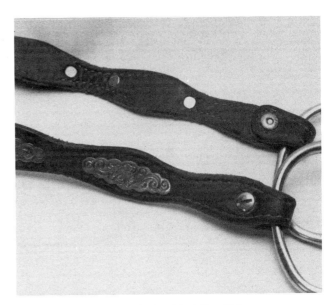

On a doubled and stitched bridle, Chicago screws attach cheekpieces to the bit. Check these fasteners frequently for tightness.

Questions

- Will the bridle fit your horse's head?
- Do the style and color match your other tack?
- Do the sizes of bit ends and reins match the intended bit?
- Do the reins feel comfortable in your hands?
- If this will be a show bridle, is it the current style?

Chapter 13

—

NOSEBANDS

As part of a bridle, the noseband can dress up a horse or augment the bit by increasing pressure. This accesssory encircles the horse's nose in dressage, hunt, and saddle-seat riding, and it is used on many Western horses as well.

Basic Design

The cavesson is the most familiar English noseband. With a cavesson, one strap wraps around the horse's nose and a two-part crownpiece holds the band in place. A cavesson can decorate the horse's head, prevent it from opening its mouth, and connect to a standing martingale.

Traditionally, you could choose only the regular, or slotted, cavesson. Slots in the band, sometimes described as slotted straps, hold the crown and maintain the cavesson's shape.

Saddlers have refined the style of the cavesson over the years and created a variety of alternatives. Although many riders continue to prefer the regular cavesson's classic look, others are attracted by a different shape or decoration.

You can select a cavesson with a brass overlay on the noseband, or a noseband that flares wider above the horse's nostrils. If you wanted to match the style of your hunt or dressage show bridle, you might want to select a rounded, stitched, raised, white-lined, or padded cavesson. Saddle-seat riders have the option of choosing from a variety of fancy show cavessons to mix or match with the browbands on their show bridles.

In some show rings, the spike-ring cavesson is more popular than the regular model. With this style, the crownpiece connects to two rings—one on each side of the band—instead of fitting through slots. The band itself consists of three pieces of leather instead of one. This hunt-seat style dresses up the horse's head and complements the rest of the bridle. It may be used as a controlling device if you adjust it snugly or connect it to a martingale.

A number of other cavessons are specifically intended to increase control. The flash cavesson is designed to keep the horse's mouth closed. Available in either a plain or padded style, it features a second noseband, attached to the first noseband at the top of the horse's nose and buckled lower around the horse's muzzle and just below the bit. This cavesson acts both above the snaffle, to keep the horse from opening its jaw, and below, to prevent the animal from opening its mouth and evading the action of the bit.

Some riders prefer using a flash attachment with a regular cavesson rather than the permanently-connected flash cavesson. The flash attachment can be unbuckled when it is not needed—or when it is prohibited by show regulations, such as in hunter or hunt-seat equitation classes. The flash

attachment is sometimes called a hinged dropped noseband.

Four other cavessons—the curb, spiked, rope front, and chain—should be used by experts only. Each can bruise the horse's nose. The curb model, used on horses shown in saddle-seat classes, corrects the animal that pulls on the bit. Chains under the jaw connect to a curb bit's hooks to transfer pressure onto the nose. Check the A.H.S.A. rules before using these cavessons, as

Dressage and jumper riders often choose the flash noseband.

some may be prohibited in certain classes.

The spiked or spike-nose cavesson, not to be confused with the spike-ring style, includes small metal cone-shaped studs in its lining. These abrasive spikes increase control of the horse's head. However, they can also damage the nose, particularly if the horse should fall.

Both the rope-front and the chain cavesson replace the smooth noseband with stronger textures. In each, the rope or chain is wrapped with leather, but the effect is rough.

Other more conventional devices are often seen in competition. The figure-eight noseband is a favorite of eventers. Flat straps crisscross over the nose in the shape of an eight, wrapping under the horse's chin to keep its mouth closed. Most feature a sliding disc across the nose for adjustment, which is usually cushioned with sheepskin so it won't rub the bone. The noseband usually buckles in two places under the chin and jaw, with one model featuring six adjustments for exact fit.

The figure-eight noseband adds to your control by putting pressure on part of the nasal bone and on the jaw above and below the snaffle bit. Unlike the flash and the dropped noseband, the figure-eight noseband cannot interfere with the horse's breathing since it is placed far above the nostrils.

The dropped noseband, which encircles the horse's nose below the bit, is also designed to control the horse's mouth. With its mouth pressed shut, the horse cannot work its tongue over the snaffle bit and is less likely to pull. The dropped noseband also is believed to encourage a lower head.

The dropped noseband looks similar to the spike-ring cavesson, with a wide, shaped noseband attached to a crownpiece. However, its design allows it to be placed lower on the horse's face, below the bit.

Infrequently seen in this country is the Kineton, an English noseband. With this noseband, metal sections fit on the sides of the muzzle, through the snaffle bit rings. The combined pressure on both nose and mouth provides strong control for a horse that pulls.

Western trainers use nosebands for the same reasons as English ones: to keep the horse's mouth closed and to attach a tiedown. Nosebands are prohibited in most Western classes, but trainers, ropers, games contestants, and pleasure riders use these accessories.

For schooling, Western trainers often use the English cavesson to help the horse to accept the bit (most often the snaffle). Western riders also use the dropped and figure-eight styles for the same reason.

A few pleasure bridles are equipped with a noseband shaped as a single strap. With no crownpiece, this band fits through loops on the bridle's cheekpieces, above the bit ends.

The parade horse's silver-mounted bridle features a decorative noseband. The leather of the noseband is almost completely covered with plain or engraved silver. It fits around the nose, held in place by loops through the cheekpieces.

The noseband is usually connected to the top of the parade bridle's crownpiece by a faceplate, which is a string of silver conchos connected by a double row of fine link chain.

The pencil bosal and cable noseband are popular for connecting to a tiedown, especially among rodeo and gymkhana contestants. These nosebands feature a ring at the bottom to which you can snap the tiedown. They also prevent the horse from opening its mouth wide or crossing its jaw. Some trainers claim that the pressure action of these nosebands is superior to that of the dropped noseband, since their oval shape enables them to avoid contact with the horse's chin groove.

Sometimes called a bosalillo, the pencil bosal is held in place by a separate crownpiece. It can also fit onto the bit ends of a fork-cheeked headstall, a bridle in which the cheekpieces split into four ends rather than two. One version of the pencil bosal is a rounded leather ring, which slips over the nose without a crownpiece.

Selecting Materials

Traditional English-style nosebands are made from the same leather as the bridles they augment. For hunt-seat showing, your noseband should match your bridle and reins as closely as possible.

Saddle-seat riders often choose a colorful cavesson to enhance their flashy appearance. Cavessons are available in leather, patent leather, or plastic in a rainbow of shades and patterns; some are even silver-mounted.

For schooling, a nylon web noseband can be used. Manufacturers offer all traditional styles in this durable material.

Pencil bosals are available in plaited rawhide, similar to the larger bosals used in hackamores. Many contestants prefer a lariat noseband. Made from a length of nylon rope, it fits more snugly than a bosal and exerts stronger pressure.

Some rodeo competitors like the stronger cable noseband. With this noseband, a core of flexible spring steel wire is clamped to form an oval shape, similar to the bosal. It is covered in vinyl, rubber, or leather. Ropers may prefer a plain steel noseband.

Western nosebands made of metal are not resilient and can cause a noticeable dent on the horse's nasal bone. Some contestants feel the leather noseband is more humane. Attached to a narrow crown, it consists of a flat band of doubled and stitched leather.

Selecting Fit

Changing or adding a noseband may improve your horse's responses, but it could cause harm if it is incorrectly fitted. Any noseband must be adjusted to fit the horse's head, combining comfort and effectiveness. To fit a cavesson, place it under the crownpiece and cheekpieces of the bridle, threading the crown through the loops of the browband.

The crown adjusts on the near side, with a buckle connecting the two straps. Be sure that you place the longer strap on the off side, fitting it behind the horse's ears to buckle to the shorter strap. The buckle will rest below and usually a few inches ahead of the horse's near eye.

Fit a drop noseband snugly, on the tip of the nasal bone.

The crownpiece length affects the noseband's placement. The cavesson should fit on the nasal bone, approximately halfway between the mouth corners and cheekbones, or close to the cheekbones.

When the cavesson is in position, buckle the noseband underneath the horse's jaw. On most models, you will find keepers to hold any extra strap length in place. Tighten the buckle so that you can slip two fingers either between the bottom of the cavesson and the horse's jaw, or between the top of the band and the horse's face.

When you use a noseband to keep your horse's mouth closed, position the noseband slightly lower, on the more sensitive area of the nasal bone, where the bone meets the cartilage. On most horses, this area will be about one inch below the cheekbones. You may wish to tighten the cavesson so that only one finger fits between the strap and the horse's jaw.

Some horses have such narrow muzzles that the cavesson cannot be adjusted snugly. You will find that many English-made models are too large around the muzzle for horses in the United States. On a spike-ring cavesson, you can have a saddler shorten the bottom strap where it is attached on the off side.

A flash cavesson or dropped noseband should be placed so that the top of the band rests on the tip of the nasal bone, not the cartilage. Be careful the device does not obstruct the horse's breathing or pinch its lips. The edge of the noseband should rest directly below the bit, just touching the corners of the horse's mouth. The dropped noseband's rings must not interfere with the bit rings.

The width of the dropped noseband affects its pressure, with a wider strap distributing pressure more evenly across a broader area. You should be able to slip one finger between the band, so that it will help keep the bit in place.

A dropped noseband that features three adjustment buckles is less likely to cut off the horse's wind than the one-buckle model. With the three-

buckle style you can adjust one buckle at the chin groove and two others on each side of the nose.

Adjust a flash cavesson so that the buckle rests in the curb groove under the horse's chin. A figure-eight noseband can be more complicated to adjust. Experts suggest keeping the upper strap snug so that the bottom one doesn't pull the noseband out of position.

You cannot attach a standing martingale to either a dropped or figure-eight noseband. If you need to connect this device, use either a regular or flash cavesson, and attach the martingale strap to the regular cavesson.

Consider the appearance of the noseband when you select fit. The band's width should both complement your horse and conform to current fashion. The regular cavesson ranges in width from 1 1/8 to 1 1/2 inches, with its crown measuring 1/2 to 3/4 inch wide.

Spike-ring cavessons are narrower in width, from 1/2 to 1 inch. Their crowns measure 3/8 to 1/2 inch wide.

A flash section is narrower than its regular noseband. It will measure from 5/8 to 7/8 inches wide.

Pencil bosals and cable nosebands are less than 1/2 inch wide. The tiedown snaps to the bottom ring of the bosal, or to the lower loop of a cable noseband. If you use a noseband with your mechanical hackamore, place it about one inch above the hackamore's noseband.

The lengths of noseband crownpieces match bridle sizes. You can choose from pony, cob, and horse.

Features

Some models of dropped noseband add leather quarter pieces over the rings. These cushion the sensitive skin of the muzzle against the rubbing of the metal rings.

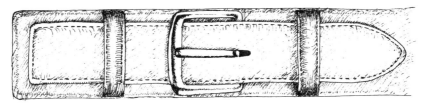

On a cavesson, look at the craftsmanship to gauge durability. This design features two keepers and solid stitching at the noseband.

You can pad almost any noseband with a fleece cover. Or, try wrapping a soft piece of leather over the band.

Quality Craftsmanship

In a noseband made of leather or webbing look for the same standards of craftsmanship as you would in a bridle. A noseband receives a great deal of wear, so it must be constructed durably. Stitching should resist the effects of sweat and saliva.

Quality Recommendations

See bridle recommendations.

Maintenance

Keep any noseband clean so that it won't irritate your horse's skin. Soap it regularly so that it stays soft and flexible and does not crack. Avoid over-oiling leather, however, or it will absorb so much that it becomes spongy.

A dropped or flash noseband is liable to collect dried saliva, which will rot the stitching over time. Be particularly sure to clean these nosebands frequently.

Nosebands will stretch beneath the horse's chin due to the constant pressure the horse exerts as it breathes and moves its jaw. Also, every time you tack up, you stretch the leather around the horse's jaw. You may have to ask a saddler to shorten the band.

If you use a noseband with metal rings around the muzzle, inspect the rings while you clean the leather. The sharp ends that hold the rings in place can extend through leather or stitching to abrade the horse's skin.

Questions

- Does the noseband match your bridle?
- Will it attach to a martingale or tiedown?

Chapter 14

—

HALTERS AND LEAD SHANKS

The halter and lead shank are essential items for daily horse handling. They allow you to influence the horse's movements by tying it in one place or moving it from one location to another.

Basic Design

Halters fall into two broad categories: the functional stable halter and the fancier show halter. The most familiar style is the stable halter, called a head collar in Great Britain. The straps are separate pieces that are stitched onto metal rings.

A crownpiece fits behind the horse's ears, and two cheekpieces or cheeks, rest along the sides of the horse's head. The noseband is made of three straps—

one that goes over the top of the nose and two that form the chinstrap—surrounding the jaw area above the muzzle. A throatlatch holds the halter in place and a bottom connector runs from the middle of the throatlatch to a ring between the two sections of the chin strap.

When brushing or clipping a horse's head, some people switch to a grooming halter, which consists of a narrow crown and cheekpieces and a noseband. There is no throatlatch or bottom connector.

The grooming halter allows limited control over a lively horse. For a strong animal, you might instead choose the stud-handling halter, also called the iron halter. With this halter an oval ring of iron or steel replaces the straps of the noseband. Crown and cheekpieces hold the ring in position. A powerful tool for the rank horse, the ring exerts pressure on the nasal bones and jawbones when you pull the lead shank.

Show halters highlight the beauty of the horse's head. Popular in many of today's show rings are two basic styles: an elegant, decorated stable halter, and the streamlined Arabian style.

At first glance, the Western show halter resembles the stable halter, but subtle variations in the straps' shape and length enhance the horse's head. To highlight the prominent jaw of the Quarter Horse and other Western breeds, the halter features a longer throatlatch that places the cheekpieces directly on the cheekbones. Cheekpieces, throatlatch, and noseband frame the jawbones.

The shapes of the straps may also attract the eye of the observer to certain areas of the horse's face. You will see halters with flared or scalloped nosebands and cheekpieces, and rolled throatlatches.

In contrast to the Western halter and its thick straps, the Arabian style appears delicate. On most, the straps are as narrow as possible, sometimes as slim as a pencil. In place of a chinstrap, many Arabian halters substitute the fine-link chain of the lead shank.

Many Arabian halters also feature an added

An Arabian models a nylon web stable halter, fitted with a fleece noseband.

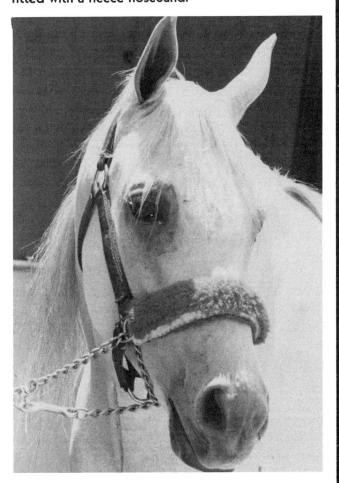

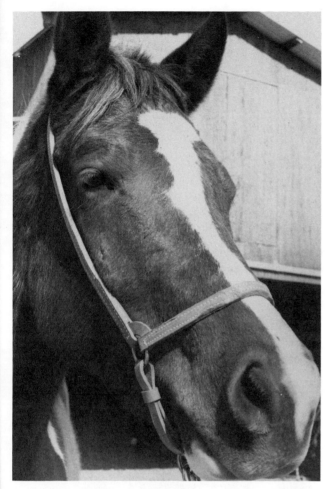

Use a grooming halter for minimum control during clipping and facial grooming.

browband. Some styles are flared, and others have decorations added to the browband and noseband.

Exhibitors of several breeds use the Arabian-style halter. You will see Morgans, Pintos, Pasos, Saddlebreds, and Welsh Ponies showing in this more elegant style.

In one type of showing, the stable halter is acceptable. Hunters shown on the line may wear a well-fitted halter, usually of the track style, or a snaffle or Pelham bridle.

Every halter should include an attached lead shank, consisting of a long strap snapped to or through the halter's center ring. Except in the show ring, the shank does not need to match the halter. Strength and easy handling are more important than appearance.

Selecting Materials

Traditionally, all halters were made of durable bridle leather, usually doubled and stitched. Heavy-duty models usually consist of three layers of leather which are tripled and stitched. Natural or synthetic fibers are inexpensive substitutes for leather. Rope halters—an old standby—are made either of cotton, polypropylene, or nylon. Sections may be fused together or held by metal clamps.

Nylon and polypropylene web are the most common materials used for modern stable halters. Nylon is stronger and more expensive, with the heavier, thicker nylon slightly stronger than the more lighter-weight version.

Because the straps will not break, avoid leaving a nylon halter (other than a safety halter) on an unattended horse. Your horse could snag its halter on a fence post, tree branch, or even its hind foot; and when it struggles to free itself, your horse could break its neck.

While many people leave halters off their horses when they are unattended, a haltered horse can be handled more easily in an emergency. If

·you leave your horse in a halter while it is in its stall or paddock, be sure that the halter's fastener will separate under pressure. You can choose a lightweight leather halter or a nylon safety halter, which is equipped with a leather crownpiece, Velcro closing, or special breakaway buckle.

For showing always use a leather halter. A Western show halter should be constructed with quality leather. The straps are of doubled leather, stained a rich, dark brown. Most are stitched on the edges, with silver decorations riveted or screwed into the unstitched areas.

Silver trim is standard on the Western show halter. Silver bars, conchos, hearts, or other shapes decorate the cheekpieces, noseband, and even part of the throatlatch. Some halters are covered with silver on all visible areas except the chinstrap and the bottom connector. The silver can be plain or engraved, and some models even feature gold, bronze, or gemstones in addition to the silver. You will also see silver tips decorating the ends of the crownpiece, and silver buckles instead of the usual brass or steel.

Like Western show bridles, halters display colorful decorations other than silver. You can choose from different overlays on the cheekpieces and nosebands: designs of braided horsehair, flat braided rawhide or leather, or inlaid lacing.

In Arabian halters, you can choose from a variety of materials on browbands and nosebands, ranging from plain leather to patent leather to plastic. Today's narrower crown and cheekpieces demand a strong material. A strip of leather narrower than 1/2 inch will flatter an elegant head, but it will not control 1,000 pounds of prancing stallion.

Some leather Arabian halters are only 1/8-inch wide, but the plastic or leather noseband is lined with a steel cable. This creates an unbreakable device with a tougher "bite."

One current Arabian fashion is a thin halter with no browband. A throatlatch is required according to AHSA rules, but it can be a threadlike

The Arabian show halter enhances a fine head.

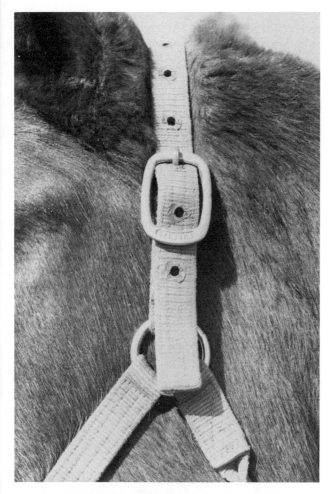

This nylon halter features a brass-plated swedge buckle. The edges of the holes have been melted to prevent the fabric from fraying.

strip of leather, or even a thin gold or silver chain.

On any halter of leather, fabric, or vinyl, study the hardware. Solid brass or stainless steel are the strongest metals for buckles and rings. Cheaper substitutes are brass-plated zinc and chrome-plated steel. You can test hardware by scratching it to see if it has been plated.

Many quality halters feature the swedge buckle. This buckle features oval ends that curve upward. The shape simplifies threading the strap into the buckle.

Some new halters feature a double-bar buckle, in which two bars run across a swedge buckle, one to hold the tongue and the other to hold the short strap of the crownpiece. This design will not weaken nylon.

While the above two three-dimensional styles add to a halter's appearance, some manufacturers question their durability. They contend that a buckle stamped from flat steel will outlast one cast into a raised shape. Consider whether you would prefer greater durability or added style.

Another new development in halters is the all-metal Arabian show halter, which eliminates hardware. This halter is constructed of one fine metal piece, which slips over the horse's head. Some models feature a cable core, threaded through a brass pipe. Exhibitors usually choose shiny brass for bays and chestnuts, and nickel for grays.

On a metal halter, the metal encircles the horse's muzzle to form a "control bar." This device encourages the horse to carry its nose upward and outward, and not dropped. As the metal can bump hard against the nasal bone, experts advise that this style be used only on a well-schooled horse.

For lead shanks, old favorites are ropes of cotton, nylon, or polypropylene. A rope is easy to handle, and it will tie and untie easily.

You can also buy shanks of flat webbing. These may look neater than rope, but they are not as comfortable to hold. They are also difficult to knot. If your horse pulls the knot tight, you'll have a hard time loosening it.

Certain firms offer nylon webbing braided into a round lead rope. Some feature four lengths of webbing forming two contrasting colors in the braid; these can complement a fabric halter.

To match a show halter, select a leather shank of round or flat leather. Most attach to a metal chain, which snaps to the halter ring. On the opposite end may be a leather stop, a circular leather piece that prevents the lead from being pulled through your hand.

Hardware is crucial on any lead shank. The metal snap that attaches the lead or chain to the halter must absorb stress, and it often proves to be the first segment of tack to fracture under pressure. Look for a large, solid, heavy snap. In a trigger snap, the mechanism should feel springy and quick. You may prefer a bull snap for a more secure closing.

Many horse owners prefer to fabricate their own lead ropes. You can buy a length of rope or webbing, select a strong snap, and connect the two with stitching or clamps. Metal clamps can be hammered in place over two rope ends. Or, you can try the new plastic rope clamps. Two molded sections close around the ropes, and you thread six screws through holes in the clamps. These secure the clamp tightly around the ropes, as prongs slip between the strands.

Selecting Fit

To function properly, both stable and show halters must fit the horse's head. Leather and fabric halters range in size from foal or small pony, weanling or pony, yearling or large pony, cob, horse, and large horse. Arabian metal styles are manufactured in three sizes: yearling, two-year-old, and full-size. If you are unsure which size to buy, measure around your horse's head, from the corner of one lip over to the corner of the opposite up.

The halter should not be too tight or too loose. A stable halter should fit so that the horse can open its mouth comfortably; the noseband should rest about two inches below the point of the horse's cheekbone. You should be able to place your palm in the gap between the horse's head and the throatlatch. Cheekpieces should hang parallel to the cheekbones. A show halter should fit more snugly to conform to the shape of the horse's head.

Adjustments can help you to fit a halter onto your horse's head. The basic stable halter features only one; a buckle on the nearside crownpiece. Better models add another buckle on the offside crownpiece, and some feature a buckle or snap on the nearside throatlatch. Some styles have five buckles: two at the crownpiece, two on the top and bottom of the noseband, and one at the bottom connector. Adjustable straps are especially useful on a foal halter, as they allow you to alter the halter's size to fit a foal's growing head.

Look at the width of the halter's straps. Usually, stable halters feature the widest straps—about 1 inch. A track halter can be narrower. The Western show halter varies from 3/4 to 1 inch.

Lead ropes and shanks measure from six to twelve feet long. Choose one that you feel is long enough for safety, but not so long that it is always underfoot. On a show halter, you would want a long lead so that you can step back from the horse to allow the judge an unobstructed view.

If your lead shank includes a metal chain, you can use this to increase control. It may be attached in a variety of ways: doubled through the halter ring and snapped to itself, threaded across the nose or under the jaw, or encircling the muzzle.

Avoid abusing your horse with the chain. Use pressure and release to establish control; never jerk roughly. Never tie a horse so that it could pull against a chain shank.

Features

A new feature on nylon halters is black metal hardware. At first glance, the metal resembles plastic, but actually it is coated with black paint.

A release snap on the throatlatch of a stable halter can allow you to slip the halter off the bottom of the horse's head, rather than reaching up to unbuckle the crownpiece.

An additional buckle on the halter noseband can make it possible for you to bridle a haltered horse. After you place the bridle over the halter, you can unbuckle the noseband and crownpiece and slide off the halter. This permits you to retain control over a rambunctious horse during bridling. This style is common on many halters made in England.

You can dress up a stable halter by adding fleece tubes. Made of natural or synthetic fleece, these slip onto straps to cushion the crown, nose, and cheeks. They are particularly popular for shipping.

Quality Craftsmanship

Evaluate a halter's construction as you would a bridle's. Study the way straps are attached to the hardware at the rings. Cheaper leather halters often substitute rivets for stitching at the ends. Or, the stiching can form a "V" shape, with no backtacking (doubled stitches) at the ends of the rows; this should be avoided.

On a decorated show halter, check the attachment of any overlays. Are lines evenly centered or parallel with the straps? Does the overlay lie smoothly, without inhibiting the flexion of the leather? Are the edges smooth? Is the overlay attached permanently, or can you remove it for cleaning?

Because a silver-trimmed halter accentuates facial bones, be sure to fit cheeks parallel to the jaw bones.

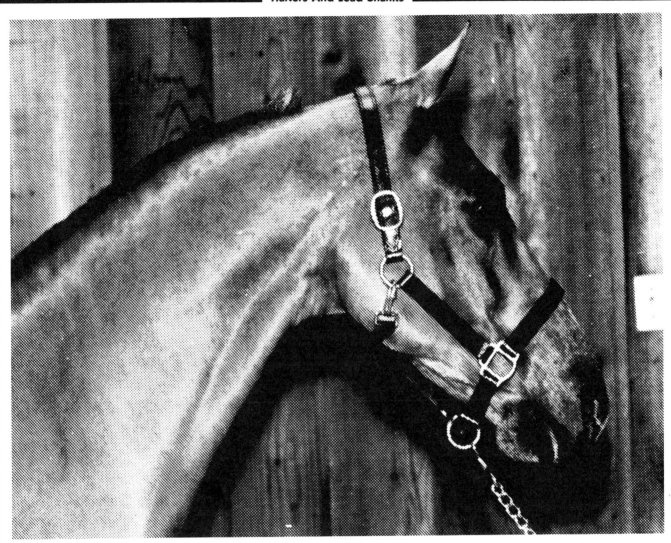

A leather stable halter features a release snap on the throatlatch. Unsnapping allows you to slip the halter over the horse's head, without unbuckling the crownpiece. Photo courtesy of Hartmeyer Saddlery.

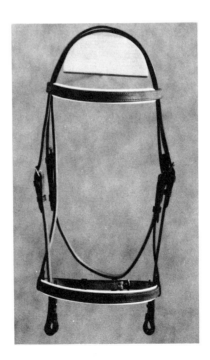

Features that indicate better quality are a rolled throatlatch, additional buckles for adjustment, and an added leather lining on the crownpiece. On a web halter, this lining can prevent chafing.

A top-quality stable, track, or Western show halter will feature triple thick cheekpieces. If you buy a leather halter with cheekpieces of only two layers, after use and oiling the leather can collapse and not maintain the halter's shape.

Always study the metal hardware, because it is often the first part to break under stress. Feel the rings for smoothness, especially where one piece joins another. Although some people like the convenience of the throatlatch release snap, it often proves to be the weakest link on an otherwise strong halter.

On a nylon halter, look for clean, neat, and strong construction. Check for molded holes through the fibers for easier buckling and resistance to fraying. Brass-plated grommets indicate a better quality product. Check for tack-box stitching where straps overlap on the noseband and bottom connector. Look for edges that are overlapped on the outside, so that they will not rub the horse.

A metal show halter should be one integral piece, not sections brazed together.

Quality Recommendations

You can expect a halter made by a reputable bridlemaker to be of high quality. Preferred brands of web halters are Craigmyle, Hamilton, and Valhoma.

Insiders' Preferences

• "Champion Turf Equipment is style conscious and a consistent supplier. They make nice halters and other strap goods.

However, they do cost more, and I consider them a 'luxury company.'" (Saddle-shop owner)

• "Craigmyle makes the best nylon halter, with solid brass hardware." (Saddle-shop owner)

• "In nylon halters, Stockmen's makes a nice model. It's jazzy, with woven-in stripes and bronze hardware. However, I find the BMB the best in the industry. It shows consistent workmanship and the best stitching. Hamilton, Valhoma, and BMB are all equally good, but I think the BMB is the best buy, dollarwise. It does not have the stronger solid-brass hardware, which the Walsh does. Walsh also has a different weave, a tighter nylon, and a leather-lined crown." (Saddle-shop owner)

• "The Hamilton halter is good. It has strong hardware." (Saddle-shop owner)

• "I like the Corway leads [Arizona.] They use a smaller-diameter nylon rope, which won't stiffen as much as the larger ones. The inexpensive snap will give if your horse pulls back, which prevents a dislocated neck. I think it's better for the rope to let go." (Saddle-shop owner)

Maintenance

Keep the halter clean. Treat leather halters as you do your other leather tack. Wash fabric halters often, as web becomes stiff and hard. Polish a metal show halter before each use.

Questions

• Does the halter seem strong enough to hold your horse?
• Will the halter rub your horse?
• Does the lead shank feel comfortable in your hand, not slippery or rough?
• Can you tie and untie the lead rope easily?

Chapter 15

MARTINGALES/
TIEDOWNS

This strap or series of straps acts to hold down the horse's head. For both English and Western riding, there are two basic martingale types: standing and running.

Basic Design

An English-style standing martingale connects to the noseband, under the horse's jaw, and to the girth. The pressure of the strap limits the height of the horse's head. A neck strap holds the main strap in place, ahead of the horse's neck, so that the horse won't catch a foot in that strap.

Western riders also use standing martingales, called tiedowns. These are often seen on horses contesting in timed events; they are used to provide extra control.

A standing martingale restricts the height of this hunter's head.

The tiedown strap attaches to the bottom of a noseband, not to the curb strap or chain. You can connect it directly to the center ring of the cinch or run it through a ring on a breastcollar. A short tiedown could snap to a breastcollar, but for security, the breastcollar should also fasten to the cinch.

The second type of martingale is the running model, used by trainers in all styles of riding. Western trainers often call it a training fork. It resembles the standing martingale, but the one main strap divides into two, with rings at each end. Reins are run through these rings.

This martingale acts as a pulley when the horse raises its head too high. It does allow the horse some freedom to balance its head, as the rings slide back and forth along the reins.

A variation of the running martingale is the German Olympic martingale. Instead of the two short straps ending in rings, it features two longer straps that thread through the rings of a snaffle bit and snap onto D-rings that are attached along the reins. When you take up contact, the martingale applies pressure to teach the horse to give to the bit. You can adjust the connection for greater or lesser pressure.

A rarer martingale is the Irish style, a short leather strap with rings on each end. It fits between the reins to hold them together. It acts as a safety device by preventing the horse from flipping the reins over its neck.

Draw reins are another device that trains a horse to flex to the pressure of the bit. These powerful tools also produce a pulley effect. The reins thread through bit rings and connect to the girth or cinch, or to the D-rings of a Western saddle. They force the horse's head down toward its chest.

Use draw reins with care because they exert

Trainers often use the running martingale with both Western and English tack.

strong pressure and can make a horse overflex. They are usually attached to a snaffle bit, but you'll see some trainers using them with a curb for maximum pressure. You can also connect them under your regular reins to fashion a double bridle.

The above training tools are accepted by many horsemen for schooling, but they are not allowed in many show classes. You will see many martingales and draw reins in the warm-up ring.

More controversial variations on martingales are two stronger restraints, the chambon and the gogue, which may be custom-made gimmicks or European imports. The chambon is a training martingale that applies pressure to the horse's poll to pull its head down. It is most often used for longeing.

The gogue, also called the De Gogue, is considered an extension of the chambon. It also lowers the horse's head by forcing the horse to bring in its nose and flex at the poll. It is usually used under saddle with a snaffle bridle. Both the chambon and the gogue are suitable only for experts, and they are condemned by many horsemen as being too forceful.

One new device combines the functions of the German martingale, gogue, and chambon. By refastening straps, you can easily convert this martingale to any of the three styles.

Selecting Materials

Any martingale will have to sustain strong pressure as the horse pushes against the straps. Select a durable material that will not break. If your martingale gave way, your horse's head could smack you in the nose or forehead.

English martingales are made in the same grades of leather as English bridles. Match your bridle with a flat, raised, or rounded martingale.

The German elastic martingale features a strap of elastic webbing from chest to noseband, for stretch instead of pull. Expert riders sometimes connect this to bit rings for direct downward pressure.

Tiedown and training-fork materials also match Western bridles. You can choose from flat leather, doubled and stitched leather, braided leather or rawhide, nylon web, steel cable, or braided nylon or polypropylene cord. Some Western riders prefer a stretchy tiedown, which has an insert of doubled elastic webbing or surgical rubber tubing.

Draw reins are available in both leather and nylon webbing.

Selecting Fit

English-style martingales are available in three sizes: pony, cob, and horse. The width of the leather can measure from 1/2 to 7/8 inch. On some models, the strap running between the forelegs to the girth measures an inch wide. The extra-strong polo martingale is made of 1 1/4-inch-wide leather, with a extra buckle above the chest strap.

Tiedowns measure from 40 to 57 inches long. They range in width from 5/8 to 1 inch.

On a standing martingale with one long strap running from noseband to girth, always add a rubber stop to hold the strap to the neck strap. This keeps the slack of the long strap ahead of the neck strap, so that the horse will not catch its forelegs by accident. You will not need a stop if your main strap connects at the chest instead of at the girth.

With a running martingale, always attach rein stops. These rubber or leather loops slide onto each snaffle rein, fitting a few inches below the bit ends. They prevent the martingale rings from catching on the bit.

Connect the loop end of a standing martingale to your cavesson. A tiedown snaps to the ring on a noseband or bosal. Tiedowns fasten to the breast-

Ready to enter the roping box, this buckskin wears a tiedown.

Rubber rein stops prevent martingale rings from catching on the hook studs of the reins.

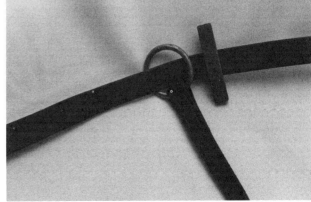

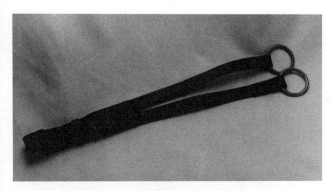

The rings of this running martingale attachment are securely attached to the straps.

plate with a Conway buckle, and many models add another buckle for length adjustment.

A martingale or tiedown should exert sufficient pressure—not too much or too little. Check your standing martingale by lifting it to the horse's throatlatch. It should be long enough to lie flat against the jawbone, throatlatch, and neck. Watch that a tiedown strap does not hit against the bottom bar of a Western bit, which can affect its action.

Adjust a running martingale so that the rings stand at the level of your horse's withers. Hold the straps straight up to measure. Look for no pressure on the reins when the horse holds its head in a natural position. Many trainers ride with the

straps too short, which exerts constant, severe pressure.

Draw reins connect to girth or saddle D-rings by a loop or snap.

Quality Craftsmanship and Recommendations

Evaluate martingales by the same standards as for bridles and reins. Remember that durability is a crucial factor. Bridlery firms often manufacture martingales as well, so refer to listings in Chapter 12.

Maintenance

Care for leather straps as described in Chapter 33. Because a martingale strap rubs against the horse's chest and belly, you should scrub off sweat after a ride. Dried sweat will seep into the fibers and weaken the leather, and it will irritate the horse's skin.

Questions

Do you need to control the height of your horse's head?

Is the martingale strong enough?

Chapter 16

—

BREASTPLATES

Breastplates are designed to match either English or Western saddles. Primarily used to hold the saddle in place, the breastplate can serve as an ornamentation as well.

Basic Design

Western breastplates are one of two styles: the breast strap or the breast collar. Each consists of one long strap that stretches across the chest. At each end of this strap is buckled a narrow strap, which connects to the saddle's cinch rings or D-rings. A third, optional strap across the withers holds the strap in place.

Some straps rest straight across the chest; others are angled to fit around the base of the horse's neck. The latter design prevents the strap from pressing against the horse's windpipe.

A decorated breast strap rests straight
across the chest.

The breastcollar, also called a ring breast-collar, is made of two straps, with a large metal ring at the center of the horse's chest. Each section can move independently with the shoulders, and you can snap a tiedown to the metal ring.

The breastcollar should feature girth straps, to connect it to the front of the saddle or the cinch. It usually features as well a third strap that goes between the horse's legs rather than across the withers. This strap, which is tapered with its widest section forming a protective tab under the ring, connects to the middle of the cinch.

The English breastplate is plainer and more conservative than its Western counterpart. It, too, appears in both a strap and a collar design.

The breast strap is often called a breastgirth, or a polo breastplate. Both polo ponies and jumpers wear this style. Placed straight across the chest, the wide strap is usually lined and padded for comfort. A neck strap fits over the withers to hold the strap in place. A narrower version of this breast strap, often seen on Tennessee Walking Horses, is designed to hold the saddle in place while the horse moves with an elevated forehand.

This jumper wears a polo breastplate.

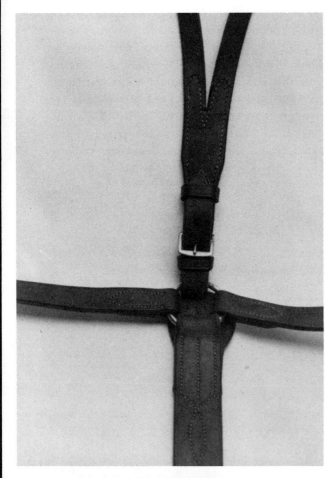

On a hunting breastplate, neck straps and chest strap meet at a large ring. A tab protects against rubbing.

Hunters are more properly tacked with the hunt breastplate. It is made of six leather straps: one encircling each side of the neck, a chest strap that connects to a ring where the neck straps meet, a short wither strap, and two narrow straps that attach the breastplate to the saddle's rings with a buckle. The chest strap secures to the center of the girth. You can substitute a hunt breastplate for a martingale by buckling either a running or standing martingale attachment to the breastplate's center ring.

You should usually avoid using a breastplate when showing in hunter classes, unless it serves as a martingale in classes over fences. Alone, it implies that your horse has such poor withers the saddle might slip on level ground. If your horse needs a breastplate, however, you should not jeopardize his back for the sake of style.

The crupper is a piece of equipment that also serves to secure the saddle, keeping it from sliding forward. This strap attaches to the back of the cantle and loops around the base of the horse's tail. It is secured with two buckles—one at the saddle end and one to buckle the loop around the tail. Cruppers are commonly seen on ponies with low withers.

Selecting Materials

Breastplates are made of different materials for show, pleasure, and event riders. Western show riders usually pick doubled-and-stitched or harness-leather styles, which are often scalloped along the straps. Western show breastplates are decorated to match the saddle or bridle. Designs include silver conchos, plates, or lacing; braided horsehair; and plaited leather or rawhide. Remember that a flashy breastplate will draw attention to your horse's forehand. Avoid this ornament if your horse is narrow-chested.

Western working equipment uses strap leather. Stamped patterns increase the leather's strength by packing the fibers.

In hunter classes, the leather straps should match the width and finish of the bridle: plain, round, raised, or even white-lined. Polo breastplates are usually made of layers of leather, although some players prefer webbing.

Pleasure riders pick models for durability as well as appearance. Besides leather, popular materials for breastplates are nylon web (often lined in fleece or felt) and the cinch style, made of woven strands of mohair and rayon.

Ropers and barrel racers require sturdy equipment. The steer roper's breastcollar is made of strong, heavy leather, securely stitched. The breastcollar ring is often cushioned with wool lining or leather padding. The "turn back" style adds strength and decoration. With this style, petal-shaped strap ends fold over rings to the outside and are stitched in place.

Breastplate hardware must sustain strong pressure. Stainless steel performs best. In Western models, look for thick, flat rings at the center and girth straps.

ing to a narrower width at each end. Ropers may pick a strap over 3 inches wide. For the show ring, some straps are as narrow as 3/4 inch. Wither straps measure from 1/2 to 3/4 inch.

The hunt breastplate measures from 5/8 to 1 inch wide. You can select a model in pony, cob, or horse sizes. Most are adjustable at the neck strap, with better models fitted with buckles on both sides.

The polo breastplate measures from 1 to 1 1/2 inches wide. Like the Western model, it can be adjusted at the rigging and wither straps.

Adjust the breastplate so that the ring fits in the middle of the chest. Be sure the chest strap does not hang so low that it could catch your horse's foot. (Remember that a horse's feet are quite close to its chest when it jumps.)

You can increase the comfort of a breastplate by padding it. One long or two shorter fleece tubes can wrap over the chest strap to prevent chafing.

Selecting Fit

The breastplate should not fit too tightly or loosely. A tight fit will cause discomfort and interfere with breathing; a loose one will bounce up and down as the horse moves. Adjust the wither or neck straps to position the breastplate at the correct height, just above the point of the shoulder so that the breastplate does not impede movement.

Western breastplates are made in one standard size. You adjust the length by shortening or lengthening the rigging straps.

On a Western breastplate, you should match the strap's width to your horse. Most straps measure from 1 to 2 inches wide, with some designs taper-

A quality breastcollar of skirting leather displays ornate hand carving.

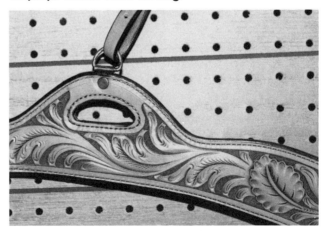

Quality Craftsmanship and Recommendations

In general, apply the same standards to breastplates as you would for bridles. Look for hand-rubbed, hand-dyed edges on leather models.

A breastplate must withstand great pressure as the horse gallops, jumps, and stops. The stitching endures the most wear at the center of the breastplate, where straps pull from three or four directions. Look for secure stitching at the ends of the straps.

The strongest breastplate construction adds a separate, skived leather piece between the doubled end of the strap. Beveled at the ends, all three layers meet smoothly and solidly.

Maintenance

Clean your breastplate regularly. Sweat collects at horses' chests and bellies, and over time this sweat can cause leather straps to deteriorate if not cleaned off.

Questions

- Does your horse need a breastplate to keep the saddle from sliding back?
- Is the breastplate strong enough for your sport?
- Does the breastplate connect to the saddle without any extra straps—or do you need to buy straps separately?

Chapter 17

—

HARNESS
AND CARTS

As both a pastime and a sport, driving is making a comeback. To join the nostalgia boom with your pony, donkey, mule, or horse, outfit the animal with a suitable harness and hitch it to a simple vehicle.

Harness Design

A harness attaches a horse to a load by fastening around the horse and connecting to the vehicle's shafts. When the horse moves forward, the harness allows the animal to use its weight to drag the rig.

For the light horse, two basic harness styles are available. The most familiar is one modified from heavy harness, featuring a neck collar. Sometimes called the English harness, this pleasure and show tack has an efficient and practical design,

You can add breeching to a pleasure harness.

constructed for strength in the pulling sections. The bridle usually holds a curb bit.

The second type of harness is lighter in weight and more elegant, with narrower straps. A breastcollar fits around the horse or pony's chest, and the bridle features a snaffle bit.

The construction of both types of harness is similar. Every harness is built with certain parts: a collar, traces, bridle, and saddle.

The source of power for the vehicle is the horse which pushes its weight against the collar to begin moving its load. The lighter harness utilizes a breastcollar, a wide strap embracing the horse's chest. A neck strap over the withers holds the padded band in the most efficient, comfortable position. In the heavier style of harness, an oval neck collar is shaped to rest at the base of the horse's neck, above the shoulders.

Either collar connects to traces, thick straps stretching back to connect to the vehicle. Snapped to or wrapped around the shafts of the cart or carriage, traces transmit the pulling power of the horse to the vehicle.

On a neck collar, traces clip to rings on the hames. Hames are pieces of metal and wood that join both sides of the collar, and they serve to distribute the pressure of the load evenly around the horse's neck.

The bridle consists of a crownpiece, cheekpieces, browband, reins (called lines), and throatlatch. A noseband is optional. Almost all driving bridles have blinders, also called blinkers, attached to the cheekpieces. Traditionally used for safety, these rigid pieces prevent the horse from being distracted and focus its attention on the road ahead.

To increase control, you can equip the bridle with one or two check reins, which run from the bit to the saddle. You can choose between the single overcheck or pair of side checks, one on each side of the horse's neck.

If you pick side checks, you can use them with either the snaffle or curb bridle. Drivers who prefer these to the overcheck feel that they are more comfortable for the horse, which can easier flex its neck.

The narrow saddle, sometimes called the backpad, consists of two padded panels, which rest on each side of the horse's backbone and are secured by a girth. Atop each panel is mounted a ring, or terret. You thread the lines through the terrets so that they remain in place along the horse's back.

On the saddle is also a backband, which secures the shafts to the saddle, and a bellyband which buckles over the saddle's girth. Connected on each side of the bellyband are tugs, loops that wrap around the ends of the shafts.

The crupper fastens to the back of the saddle with a back strap which follows the horse's backbone and connects the crupper and the saddle. Encircling the tail, the crupper helps distribute the pressure and keeps the saddle from pulling forward.

You can add other straps to help the horse to slow the rolling of the vehicle. Breeching consists of a strap that fits around the base of the horse's rump. The strap wraps around the cart's shafts on each side of the horse's flanks. A loin strap holds breeching in place over the croup. These permit the horse to shift its weight onto its haunches against the weight of the vehicle, which is useful on downhill slopes.

Lightweight pleasure and show harnesses can also include a pair of "thimbles" in place of breeching. With this design, two straps run from each side of the saddle and end in a leather thimble. Cupping the tip of each shaft, the thimbles help to bear the pressure of the load and aid the horse to slow a lightweight rig.

Selecting Materials

You can choose harness of either leather or synthetic materials. Your choice depends on what type of driving you plan.

If ease of care is more important to you than tradition, you would probably prefer the durability of a nylon-web harness. For schooling and pleasure driving, nylon has proven a durable substitute for leather.

However, nylon has two disadvantages: its failure to release in an emergency and the friction it creates when rubbing against a horse's skin. You can solve the first problem by adding breakaway sections in three places: where the traces attach to the vehicle's singletree, at the shaft loops, and at the breeching. Connect the harness straps in these locations with either a shoelace, a leather thong, or a homemade wire hook and eye. The release mechanism should sustain about a hundred pounds of pressure but give way in a wreck.

Nylon should not rub a horse so much that it causes a sore unless you use it for a long, hard drive. You can easily protect your horse from this abrasion by fitting the harness with a fleece cover, especially on the breastplate, or by placing a towel or fleece section under the saddle.

If you prefer the traditional look of leather, you can buy a reasonably priced set of imported or domestic materials. Or you can choose a Corfam harness, which looks like leather but requires little care.

For show, black leather is traditional. Styles vary according to the breed and discipline, with the fanciest styles of fine harness used on Saddlebreds, Arabians, Morgans, and Andalusians.

A show harness is often trimmed with black patent leather on the blinders, browband, cavesson, breastcollar, martingale, saddle, and girth. If you buy a show harness, ask if the patent leather is not liable to crack, warranted not to wrinkle and split with age.

Metal hardware on pleasure harness is usually nickel. You will usually see solid brass only on the most expensive show harness, made in England.

Selecting Fit

Match the width of the harness straps to your activity. On a pleasure harness, the straps will be slightly wider than on a fine harness. Most harness straps measure from 5/8 to 1 inch wide, although the saddle should be at least 2 1/2 inches wide and breeching 1 3/4 inches wide.

Safety is a vital concern when fitting harness. Riding behind a horse can be more hazardous than sitting on its back, because you have fewer aids and must help the horse control the direction and speed of the vehicle.

If you are unfamiliar with fitting harness, have an expert demonstrate the proper adjustment. Most drivers recommend that you follow a regular routine for tacking up, so that you check each component and connect all straps. In most instances, an assistant should help you tack up and position the horse in the shafts.

Be sure that the bridle fits snugly. In a pleasure harness, you can fit the lighter-weight bridle with a half-cheek snaffle with either a smooth, rubber, or twisted-wire mouthpiece.

For the wider straps of the heavier harness, choose a traditional curb bit like the Liverpool or Buxton. Both provide several slots for attachment of the reins, which allow you to adjust the severity of the bit to your situation.

In either bridle, you must adjust the blinder stay straps for the horse's comfort. Usually the blinders should rest about one inch from the eyes.

Check reins are not designed for abuse, as described in *Black Beauty*; they increase your safety by controlling the height of the horse's head. Adjusting the rein or reins so that they maintain the horse's head at a comfortable, efficient height can prevent a runaway.

With a snaffle bridle, use the overcheck only.

The overcheck strap ends in a headpiece, which fits flat against the horse's head and splits into two ends. You connect each end to a separate overcheck bit, which is placed above the snaffle. You can select this bit with either a straight or jointed mouthpiece.

The fine harness usually includes a running martingale. You connect its strap to the girth and up through the breastcollar. The lines thread through the martingale's rings.

If you use a harness with a stuffed collar, be sure that it fits your horse. It must conform to the size and angle of your horse's neck and shoulders in order to prevent soring.

Quality Craftsmanship

Look for strong straps that also feel flexible. Both leather and nylon straps should be doubled and stitched for greatest durability.

Quality Recommendations

If you demand the top of the line, for competitive driving or breed shows, expect to pay $ 1000 or more. English harnesses are considered the best.

In the lower price range, harnesses from India can be a good value. Look for a fairly heavy leather.

For a better quality, Amish harnessmakers produce excellent pleasure harness for the money. These models will cost about double to three times that of Indian harnesses.

Maintenance

To avoid chafing and prevent accidents, clean and inspect the harness after every use. The com-

A high-stepping Saddlebred wears a fine
harness and pulls a show buggy.

bined weight of the vehicle and passengers exerts great strain upon a harness, so examine your tack carefully, especially any single-ply leather straps.

Oil a leather harness regularly to maintain its durability. (Expect to absorb dye when you clean a black harness.) Keep the harness out of the sun to avoid drying the leather.

Replace or repair any worn parts or loose stitching immediately. Your harness will last longer if stored and transported in a ventilated bag.

Carts

For driving a single horse or pony, you can choose either a two-wheeled cart or a four-wheeled buggy. Experts recommend a cart for the beginner driver or green horse. You will find a sensible two-wheeled rig safer, more stable, and easier to turn and back.

Most drivers choose a pleasure cart. The pleasure cart, which is also called a roadster, a road cart, or a jog cart, is a simple rig constructed of a chassis, shafts, wheels, and seat with footboard and dashboard. Inexpensive models for everyday use are made of welded steel, with rubber tires and a spring seat.

The basic model is built around the shafts, which support the cart's body. Although this design is durable, it forces you to step over a shaft to step in or out of the cart. This can be a minor irritation, or a safety hazard for children or elderly passengers. It can also force the trainer to drive hanging one leg out over the shaft to prepare for a faster bailout in case of emergency.

Because the shafts are integrated into the body, the cart will sway from side to side. A superior design adds a singletree, a crosspiece at the shafts. This separates the shafts from the cart, improving the ride while easing the load on the horse's shoulders. The singletree keeps the shafts ahead of the cart's body, allowing easier entry.

In a pleasure cart, look for an all-steel construction of the floorboard and basket, and a cover around the floorboard. A metal backrest provides better support than a low rail. Metal is stronger than pine for the floor, dashboard, and seat. Wood will deteriorate faster, and wood seats have collapsed under the combined weight of two hefty adults.

Also, check if the wheels attach to an axle or fit into forks. The latter construction is weaker, with all of the cart's weight resting on the wheels.

A showier, more expensive cart may feature a hardwood frame and shafts, with a basket and wire wheels. Some manufacturers offer a conversion kit to substitute sleigh runners for the wheels.

Several styles of road cart are available, both contemporary reproductions and restored antiques. They are generally heavier and more elaborate than the previously discussed models, and they are more difficult to locate and purchase. For pleasure driving and showing in hunter-style driving or dressage driving classes, look for the Meadowbrook and East Williston Long Island carts, and the Stanhope and Tilbury gig. For a pony, an old favorite is the governess or tub cart, with a body of wicker that can seat four to six passengers.

In road carts, look for a model that has a low center of balance. The lower the cart, the less likely it is to tip over. A high-seated gig may appear more elegant, but this impractically designed cart can flip during a sharp turn at a brisk trot.

The heavier breaking cart is recommended for training. Built low to the ground and with longer shafts, this wooden model is safest to use with a green horse. Most types allow you to step in and out of the cart so that you can control the horse from either on or off the ground.

For a trained horse and driver, the four-wheeled buggy is the most popular choice. The show-ring style, used in fine-harness classes, offers only a single seat, with side rails and wire wheels. Other versions of buggies and surreys hold from two to four passengers.

Selecting Fit

To select the right size of cart, consider the size of your animal and the number of passengers you may want to transport. Generally, a pleasure cart will hold two adults or an adult and possibly two small children.

Pleasure carts are manufactured in three main sizes: miniature, small pony, and horse. A fourth size—Arabian—is sometimes available. For the greatest versatility, choose the horse size, unless your pony measures less than 13.2 hands. Check that the cart pulls level, and don't worry if the shafts appear slightly longer than necessary. This will increase the distance between horse and cart but should not pose a problem while pleasure driving.

Safety should be your foremost concern in driving, so be sure that all moving parts are securely attached. Avoid any sharp edges on metal surfaces.

Quality Recommendations

A few manufacturers offer a small selection of inexpensive mass-produced models. Other show and pleasure carts are restored antiques or custom-made by specialty carriagemakers.

The Easy Entry cart is the pleasure cart of choice. For show, choose Houghton, Jerald, or Wilform.

Maintenance

Again, safety is more important than appearance. Grease the wheels regularly. If you venture on drives far from home, it's wise to carry a tool kit for on-the-road repairs of vehicle or harness.

You can avoid an embarrassing flat tire by installing tire liners, or by adding a foam sealer to the tires. Especially in the West, tires can pick up burrs as you drive along country roads.

To forestall deterioration, store a cart with its tires off the ground. Clean the rubber with a product like Armor All if you do not plan to use the cart for some months.

With a wood cart, store it out of the sun, indoors or covered with a tarpaulin. Prevent the shafts from warping by propping them up so that they do not rest on the ground.

Questions

- Do you need leather harness—or will another material suit your needs?
- Can your horse pull the vehicle safely and comfortably?

PART IV:

CONTROL DEVICES

Chapter 18

ENGLISH BITS

Bits mystify riders, which is why most tack collections contain a variety of discarded bits. Realize that there is no magic bit. Many factors apply in selecting bits—you, your experience, your horse's level of training, and your immediate goals.

English bits fall into three major categories: the snaffle, the curb, or a combination of the two. The snaffle is a direct action bit; the curb operates as a lever in the horse's mouth and under its chin. Combination bits aim to blend both actions.

Basic Design

The snaffle, which is considered the basic bit, is used in all forms of horsemanship throughout the world. It is considered by most to be the ideal training bit for a young horse, although riders use it at all levels of schooling and showing.

The mildest, straight-bar snaffle is formed of a mouthpiece and two rings, one at each end of the mouthpiece. The bridle's cheeks and reins attach to the bit rings. When you pull the reins, the bit pulls mostly on the corners of the horse's mouth.

Most snaffles are jointed, with the mouthpiece composed of two sections, or cannons. These produce a nutcracker action, pulling the lips, pressing on the tongue, and pinching the thin skin at the corners of the mouth. If you pull one rein, the bit acts on only one side of the mouth.

The snaffle can encourage a horse to drop its head and flex to the pressure of the reins. When the horse flexes at the poll, the snaffle also works on the bars of the mouth.

Snaffles are defined by the style of rings and mouthpiece. In the loose-ring snaffle, the rings slide freely on the mouthpiece. This allows some play in the bit so that the horse can relax its lower jaw, although some riders complain that the rings can pinch the lips.

More popular in the show ring are the D-ring and eggbutt snaffles, whose rings are fixed in place to avoid pinching. The D-ring features rings shaped like the letter D. The rings of the eggbutt are egg-shaped.

Many riders prefer the cheeked snaffles. The straight cheek pieces of the full- or half-cheek snaffle are thought to help the horse respond. When you pull one rein, the metal piece presses against the side of the mouth. On the fulmer snaffle, the cheeks are attached to the mouthpiece and loose rings are on the outside of the cheekpieces.

Snaffle mouthpieces vary in severity. In general thicker mouthpieces are milder. Wide cannons distribute pressure over a broader area than thinner ones.

A more severe snaffle would be one with a thin mouthpiece, such as the small-ringed bridoon

A double-twisted wire snaffle features a copper mouthpiece.

This polo pony wears a gag bit.

(also called bradoon) used with a curb bit in a double bridle. Another sharp mouthpiece is the twisted-mouth or twished snaffle, which is molded to simulate the texture of wire. The roughened surface creates a stronger, intermittent contact.

In the twisted-wire snaffle, the cannons are strands of twisted heavy-gauge wire. This powerful bit can damage a horse's mouth if used roughly. It can be made of either two cannons (single twisted wire) or four (double twisted wire.) Some people feel that the double-twisted-

For an English pleasure class, an Arabian wears a double bridle.

wire snaffle is less severe than the single, since it distributes pressure over a larger area of the mouth.

When you look at snaffles in your tack shop, you'll notice additional styles of mouthpieces. One mild unconventional bit is the breaking bit, which features dangling keys on the mouthpiece. These encourage a colt to chew on the bit and develop a sensitive mouth.

Two moderately severe snaffles are the French and the Dr. Bristol. Both are double-jointed mouthpieces, with three-parts: a flat middle piece and two cannons. The flat piece presses on the horse's tongue, the cannons on its lips.

Very severe snaffles include the Dexter, bicycle chain, Springsteen, and four ring. These designs provide sharp control for extreme situations.

Experienced riders sometimes use the gag bit on problem horses. Gags are also commonly used on polo ponies. With gags, rounded cheekpieces slide through the bit rings to create a pulley effect. The bit and headstall combine to act on the corners of the horse's mouth and pull downward on the poll to raise the head. This helps lift the horse off its forehand so it will feel lighter and more responsive.

In contrast to the snaffle, there are few varieties of the English curb. This leverage bit consists of a mouthpiece attached to straight shanks. At the tops of the shanks are loops for connecting the bit to the bridle, and hooks for attachment of a curb chain. Below the mouthpiece are smaller loops for an optional lip strap. Reins connect to the bit through rings at the ends of the shanks.

The cheeks of the curb bit form a lever, which presses on the horse's bars and tongue. A curb chain acts as a fulcrum against the chin groove. The bridle not only exerts pressure on the mouth and chin, but its crownpiece also pulls down at the poll.

The severity of the curb varies according to the design of its cheeks and mouthpiece. The longer the cheek, the more leverage you can apply. Se-

Two Pelhams: left, Tom Thumb, right, Hartwell.

verity also varies according to the bit's ratio, which compares the length of the cheek's shank below the mouthpiece to the length above. A 6:1 ratio means that there are six inches of shank below and one inch above the mouthpiece.

The curb is often called a Weymouth. Its cheeks can either be fixed to the mouthpiece, or attached loosely so that they swing to the sides. Other varieties exist, such as the Ward Union, in which the movable cheeks slide a short way up or down the mouthpiece; the Banbury, with the cheeks revolving around the mouthpiece; and the Tom Bass, with fixed cheeks. Curbs with sliding cheeks are considered stronger, although they allow the horse to play with the bit without pulling on the reins.

The mouthpiece of the curb also affects its severity. As in the snaffle, the thicker the mouthpiece, the milder the effect.

Most curbs feature a port, or slight arch in the middle of the mouthpiece. This helps the bit fit over the horse's tongue. A wide, low port is acceptable to most horses. A high port can press against the palate.

The curb chain helps direct the action of the bit. It lies in the groove of the horse's lower jaw behind its lips. A ring in its center serves to hold an optional lip strap. This narrow strap attaches to the loops on the shanks and threads through the ring of the curb chain. It holds the shanks parallel to the horse's mouth, to prevent the horse from grabbing or "lipping" the shank. In English riding, a single curb is properly used only on a Walking Horse bridle. The Tennessee Walking Horse is trained with a special curb with long, curved shanks.

The curb combines with the bridoon in a double bridle. In the double bridle, you can use the two bits independently. The action of the curb and the snaffle both help to position the horse's head, with the snaffle raising the head and the curb lowering it.

The Pelham and the Kimberwick are considered combination bits. The Pelham features four rings, to combine the curb and snaffle into one mouthpiece. You hold four reins, as you would with a double bridle. The curb reins affect the bars of the mouth; the snaffle reins raise the bit in the mouth. Purists complain that neither action succeeds, because the effects are not as precise as those of the two separate bits. However, the bits are widely used.

Use a Pelham with a curb chain and lip strap. You can choose mild mouthpieces, such as the straight or mullen mouth, or one with a port, which is more severe.

Other variations on the Pelham include the S-M, in which the mouthpiece works on a swivel for control with less pressure, and the Hartwell, in which a port creates pressure on the bars. The jointed Pelham, also called the Argentina-style bit, combines a snaffle mouthpiece with curb shanks. Many horsemen believe that this bit is too severe, as its effect is both a lever and a nutcracker.

The Kimberwick looks like a Pelham with the curb shanks removed. Its mouthpiece is either mullen, with a port, or jointed, and its rings are D-shaped. A curb chain applies leverage as it presses the horse's chin groove, and the mouthpiece presses on the bars and tongue.

Again, some trainers complain that this bit isn't very effective. They feel that it may deaden the horse's mouth and cause the jaw to become stiff. The Uxeter model seems to provide more consistent control. The Uxeter features four slots for the reins, which makes them less likely to slip. If you attach reins to the bottom slot, the bit acts more like a curb.

Selecting Materials

Most of today's bits are constructed of steel alloys. Today the 18-8 stainless steel bits, produced in Germany and Korea, are the most popular.

Other common bit materials are aluminum, nickel, and chrome-plated steel. The latter two materials are not noted for their durability, as nickel may bend and chrome will chip. Although few makers today manufacture solid nickel bits, nickel gained popularity because horses preferred the flavor over other metals.

Mouthpieces of any style can be made of copper, a tradition on many Western bits. This material is said to encourage the horse to salivate, and a moist mouth is more responsive than a dry one. You can choose both copper mouthpieces and mouthpieces featuring small copper rollers or copper wire wrapping.

For a milder effect, manufacturers offer mouthpieces of hard or soft rubber or nylon. Or, you can wrap a mouthpiece in a stretchy, self-adhesive latex tape.

A curb chain is usually a length of interconnected links. You can soften its effect by replacing the chain with a leather strap, or by sliding a rubber or sheepskin cover over the chain.

Lip straps can be made of flat or rounded leather. You can also fashion a strap from a lace.

Selecting Fit

For greatest comfort, you should match a bit to the width and depth of your horse's mouth. Open your horse's mouth to check if it has a shallow or thick tongue. Many riders prefer a thicker, milder mouthpiece, but it would cause discomfort on a thick tongue.

Most important is the width of the mouthpiece. For a curb or Pelham bit, you can choose 4 1/2-, 4 3/4-, or 5-inch widths. Snaffles range in width from 4 to 5 1/2 inches, with the smallest size for a pony, and the largest for a large horse.

The wrong-sized bit will irritate your horse and affect its responses. One that is too narrow will pinch the corners of the horse's mouth. If the bit is too wide, it will rub the horse's lips as it sways from side to side. A snaffle that is too wide could also allow the horse to get its tongue over the bit, and the joint can hit the palate.

Hanging evenly in the horse's mouth, the bit should fit comfortably against the lips and follow the angle of the jaw. To measure for width, you can stretch a string across your horse's mouth. At the corners, tie a knot where the mouthpiece would exit.

Fit a curb bit snugly against the corners of the mouth, creating no wrinkles. (A curb bit may need the top of its shanks spread slightly so it won't rub the horse's cheeks.) Look for a snaffle to create one wrinkle at each corner. Too tight a snaffle will create more than one wrinkle of the skin and can deaden the lips and hit the premolars. Too low a snaffle will hit the horse's canines and incisors.

When using a double bridle, you should be sure that the snaffle fits above and behind the curb. Match the curb with the thin, lightweight snaffle. Look for rings no larger than 2 1/2 inches in diameter, with round edges that are unlikely to snag on the curb hooks. The snaffle should measure 1/2 to 1 inch wider than the curb to keep the two bits separate.

With a curb or Pelham, fit the shank length to your sport. The longer the cheek, the more leverage you can apply. Curbs range from a 5-inch cheek, used on hunters and dressage horses, to a 9-inch model, sometimes seen in Saddlebred classes. A Pelham cheek can measure from 4 inches, called the Tom Thumb, to 7 inches.

The curb chain lies flat under the chin, loose enough so that you can fit two fingers under it. When the reins are pulled, the chain presses tight when the bit reaches a 45-degree angle with the mouth. The curb hooks should rest on the outside of the shanks.

Attach the lip strap last. Connect the short strap to the offside bit loop. Wrap the long strap through the nearside loop, through the ring on the curb chain, and buckle it to the short strap. The strap should hang slack; when the curb chain tightens, the lip strap will slightly contact the horse's chin.

A bit's weight should be taken into consideration. Generally riders prefer a lightweight bit. For a thick but lightweight mouthpiece, pick a hollow-mouth curb or snaffle.

The most challenging aspect of bitting is to match the bit to your needs. Some trainers advocate using the mildest bit possible most of the time, feeling that a light bit lets the horse move forward confidently. Others move to more severe bits if the horse doesn't respond. Most trainers advise to increase control, when necessary, from a plain snaffle to a Pelham, rather than to go to a harsher snaffle such as the wire snaffle, which can result in permanent damage if used roughly.

This loose-ring snaffle hangs too low in the horse's mouth.

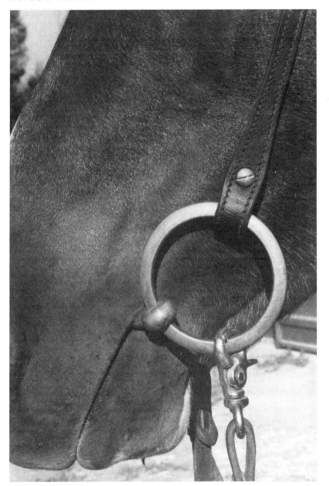

Some people continually experiment with a variety of bits, hoping to find the one that will be the key to a horse's mouth. If your horse responds well to the bit you are now using, consider yourself fortunate.

Features

Accessories can refine bit effects, or correct a horse's bad habit. To protect a bit from rubbing, you can slide a pair of rubber or leather bit guards onto the mouthpiece. This circular guard acts as a cushion between the bit and the horse's lips. Some guards have to be stretched over the snaffle bit rings. Others unlace to open, then lace onto the bit.

Similar in shape to the bit guard, the bit burr features short, stiff bristles on its inner side. The bit burr creates pressure to correct a one-sided horse. The burr discourages the horse from pressing harder on one side than the other.

Leather bit loops slide over the top ends of a full-cheek bit, attaching to the bridle's cheekpieces. These keep the bit in place and accentuate its nutcracker effect.

Quality Craftsmanship

Look for smoothness along all edges and joints. In a snaffle mouthpiece, feel the joint for a solid weld. Flex any moving parts and look for an even action. You should feel that the joints are well fitted, not jiggling or loose.

Look at the bit's finish. You should not see any pitting, dents, or lumps. Ask if the bit is hand finished. A quality bit will be hand-buffed and hand-polished. Because hand finishing demands time, it indicates better craftsmanship.

The two sides of a bit must match. Look for rings or shanks of the same size or angle. One shank must not appear longer or bend differently than the other.

Quality Recommendations

You can expect a handmade bit from an English or European saddler to be of the highest quality. Ask about the bit's guarantee. One of the best U.S. makers specializing in English-style bits for saddle-seat riding, is the Cash Lovell line from North Carolina. A large percentage of English bits are produced in Korean foundries. Experts disagree about the quality of these bits.

Insiders' Preferences

• "Any of Stubben's bits are very good. They're better finished and smooth, where some bits show rough edges. The metal and the weight seem uniform, and they are very well balanced and strong." (Saddle-shop owner)

• "Lemetex makes a nicely finished bit, somewhat better than some Korean bits. The Herman steel on some Korean models is also nicely finished." (Saddle-shop owner)

• "Cash Lovell bits are one of the few custom-made English bits, handmade in North Carolina." (Sales representative)

• "I like the weight of the Partrade bits, made in Korea. I've never found any poor craftsmanship on them. Their fit [width] is the true size, and they're well-balanced." (Riding-school manager)

Questions

• What is the brand name?
• Is the bit made of high-grade stainless steel?
• What is the country of origin?

Chapter 19

WESTERN BITS

Bits used in Western riding fall into the same three categories as English models: snaffle, curb, and combination.

The curb bit is considered standard for the trained Western horse. Trainers use the snaffle mainly as a schooling bit, and the Western Pelham as a variation of the curb.

Today's stock-seat riders rely on the curb bit primarily because of tradition. Cowhands who were in the saddle for long hours rode with a loose rein, guiding their horses by neck-reining instead of riding on contact.

With the curb bit, you apply pressure only to cue your horse to stop, turn, or collect itself. As you become more skilled, you control your horse by leg aids and neck-reining rather than with the reins.

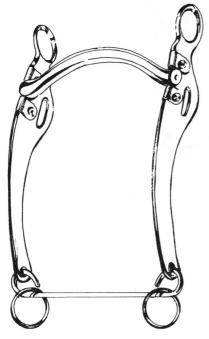
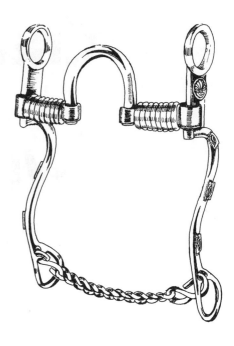

Two curbs: left, "Sweetwater" mouthpiece, loosejaw; right, correction or Billy Allen bit, with swivels at jaws and port.

Finding the right bit is a science. You must analyze your horse in order to locate a humane control device that allows you to communicate with light contact.

Basic Design

The traditional, old-time bit styles and the new, high-tech designs result in hundreds of styles of curbs. Each can vary in shank, mouthpiece, or weight.

Most curbs have distinctive curved shanks to prevent the horse from lipping the shanks. For example, shanks of the popular grazing bit bend far back from the mouthpiece, to prevent interference when the bitted horse feeds.

Shanks can be round or flat, short or long, wide or narrow. They can be fixed to the mouthpiece, or attached with a swivel, which is called a "loose-jaw" bit. Some trainers claim that this design allows you to communicate with only a slight movement of the bit and to use the bit as a lateral aid. Others fear that the movable shanks will pinch the horse's lips.

Curbs vary in severity. A curb with a long shank is usually more severe than a short-shanked one. Also important is the ratio of the bit, or the compared shank lengths above and below the mouthpiece. A bit with a 1:1 ratio has the same length of cheek at both ends. This short bit creates a gag action to force the horse's head up.

A bit with a 3:1 or 4:1 ratio is more likely to be effective with a horse that carries its head too high. Here the action cues the horse to drop its head and flex at the poll.

Look at a bit's purchase—the top of the shank above the mouthpiece as compared to the rest of the shank. The bit loops must be positioned on the correct purchase point to function correctly. One way to test this factor is to see if the curb strap rests naturally in the curb groove.

Curb mouthpieces can create pressure on any or all of four areas: the horse's lips, bars, tongue, and palate. Mild mouthpieces that you may select are the mullen, the straight bar, and the low port.

Some riders consider bits with larger ports to be more severe. With these bits, a more substantial port presses with a sharper action within the mouth, affecting the tongue and palate. These bits would include the "A" port, sometimes called a "whoa" bit, and the frog. The "A" port is a high port, with the mouthpiece shaped like the legs of the letter "A". The frog mouthpiece is a medium port, curved backward from the bit loops and fitted with a roller.

A bit with a wide, high port curves over the tongue. Some bitmakers feel that this creates a

good all-around bit that is easy on the horse's mouth and will not toughen it.

The Mona Lisa, half-breed, and Salinas bit styles feature a port fitted with a roller, also called a cricket. This small vertical or horizontal wheel rests on the horse's tongue. It is designed so that the horse can move it back and forth, enjoying the feel and the cricketlike noise it makes. Intended to calm the nervous horse, this roller can also distract the horse from concentrating on its work.

Two severe bits are the cathedral and the spade. Both are intended only for use by expert riders on well-schooled horses. The cathedral features a high port shaped somewhat like a steeple framed by two towers. The spade combines a straight mouthpiece with a half-breed port and roller. Braces connect a flat or spoon-shaped steel piece, measuring three or four inches long, to the mouthpiece.

Both the spade and the cathedral bit should rest comfortably in the horse's mouth. They create no pressure or pain when the reins are loose, but press against the sensitive roof of the mouth when you pull the reins. Proponents of the spade claim

Two curbs: left, loose jaw with braided nylon bottom connector; right, short-shanked "colt" bit with lifesaver mouthpiece.

that it can be used with great delicacy, allowing horse and rider to communicate through barely visible use of the reins.

A less often used bit is the ring bit. This severe style adds to the curb a metal ring that slips over the horse's lower jaw to apply extra pressure.

The shank snaffle, sometimes called a broken-mouth or cowboy snaffle, combines a snaffle mouthpiece with the shanks of the curb. This style can cause definite pain, since pressure on one rein pulls the mouthpiece directly against the bars of the horse's mouth. Two popular variations are the Tom Thumb or colt snaffle, which has short shanks, and the South Texas roper, which adds a wide port for tongue protection.

Do not confuse the shanked snaffle with the standard snaffle bit. Western trainers usually call the direct-action jointed bit a ring snaffle or an O-ring snaffle, and they use it for starting colts and for showing in snaffle-bit futurities. Many trainers school a young horse with the mild snaffle and later switch to the stronger curb bit.

Bitmakers have enhanced the standard snaffle. One version features a hinged mouthpiece, which pulls back toward your hands rather than up and down. This keeps it stable in the horse's mouth.

A different bit, the gag, is used for training. Based on its English counterpart, this bit has sliding cheeks that fit through the bit's slots. Rings allow two pairs of reins to be attached, for an effect similar to the double bridle.

A combination bit used by some trainers is the Western version of the English Pelham. In this bit two extra rein loops modify the basic curb. As with the English Pelham, the Western version allows you to add another pair of reins for both curb and snaffle effects.

The mouthpiece you pick will depend on your goals. For example, a seasoned horse may perform best with a ported bit, which produces leverage off the palate. A shanked snaffle can also help keep a horse light.

Whatever design you prefer, the bit's balance is critical. The balanced bit creates the desired response with the least amount of pressure and aggravation. It does not cause an unwanted response, as it does not apply pressure until you pull the reins.

Bitmakers suggest testing the balance of a bit by holding the mouthpiece on the tips of your forefinger and little finger to simulate the bars of the horse's mouth. Swing the bit back and forth. A well-balanced bit will swing for a long time, then return to its original position. A poorly balanced bit will rock and hang behind or ahead of its original position. However, realize that a bit's balance in the horse's mouth can be changed by the pressure of the headstall and reins.

Many fashionable bit styles, popular in the show ring, cannot be balanced due to their design. For example, the long-shanked bit with swept-back shanks can apply pressure continuously, even when the reins lie slack.

With any curb bit, look at the pitch, or curve, of the mouthpiece. A straight design will produce straight leverage when you pull the reins. A curve will allow the mouthpiece to fit over the tongue to give the tongue some relief. The angle of the curve can also encourage the horse to hold its head in a proper headset. You should also be sure that the port is formed in the dead center of the bit. A bit with an O-shaped mouthpiece, sometimes called the lifesaver due to its shape, functions by applying no pressure when the horse carries its head in the correct position.

In addition to being a part of the bit's design, the curb strap also affects its function. A mild low-port curb can become extremely painful when matched with a tight curb chain.

The flat curb strap attaches to one rein loop, rests under the horse's jaw in the chin groove, and connects to the opposite rein loop. Like the curb chain of an English bit, the Western curb chain acts as a fulcrum to the lever action of the bit. When you pull the reins, the strap tightens and also pulls the bridle's crownpiece down at the poll.

You will notice that some bits are designed with a special loop for the curb strap, next to the bridle loop. This prevents the strap from pinching the horse's lips. Don't confuse this loop with an extra slot on the shank, which is found on Pelham bits. Many novices mistakenly insert the curb strap through the rein slots, where it cannot lie against the curb groove.

A primarily Western device is the hackamore or jaquima, also known as a bitless bridle. It operates with a lever action similar to the curb bit.

The traditional hackamore consists of three parts: the bosal, the mecate, and the fiador. The bosal is a braided rawhide loop that fits around the horse's muzzle. Its ends are connected at the bottom by a heel knot. The bosal is thicker across the nose area, and it features two side buttons to hold the bridle cheekpieces in place.

The reins for a hackamore are called the mecate. This long rope knots around the bottom of the bosal to form a set of closed reins and a lead rope, which can be tied to the saddle to keep it out of the way.

The optional fiador is a rope throatlatch, which connects the headstall to the heel knot of the bosal. If you use your mecate to lead your horse, a fiador will help prevent the bosal from flipping upwards over the horse's muzzle.

Trainers use the hackamore in schooling colts, either in place of or alternating with the snaffle bit. However, a hackamore is not an especially mild training device, since it can exert strong leverage against the lower jawbone and nose. This device requires you to ride with a pull and slack motion, pulling only one rein at a time.

A variation on the bosal is the sidepull. This device consists of a noseband fitted with a curb strap or chain. It helps you place the horse's head by bringing its nose down and leading it to one side or the other.

A modification on the hackamore is the hackmore bit, also called the mechanical hackamore. This curb bit replaces the mouthpiece with a thick noseband. When you pull the reins, the shanks create pressure on the horse's nose and jaw, and the curb chain applies leverage against the chin groove.

While you are not allowed to ride with this hackamore in most regular shows, it is popular in rodeos, ropings, gymkhanas, and on the trail. Because it offers quick control through extreme pressure, use it with care. Many horsemen feel this hackamore is inhumane; others claim it is useful in reschooling a horse with a hard mouth.

A last variation on the hackamore features a mouthpiece added to the hackamore bit. One design, sometimes called a barrel control bit or a gag hackamore, increases the amount of control needed in such sports as barrel racing. With this bit, a twisted-wire snaffle slides up and down the rounded cheeks of the hackamore bit.

The gag/hackamore barrel-racer bit combines a sliding twisted-wire mouthpiece with a hackamore action.

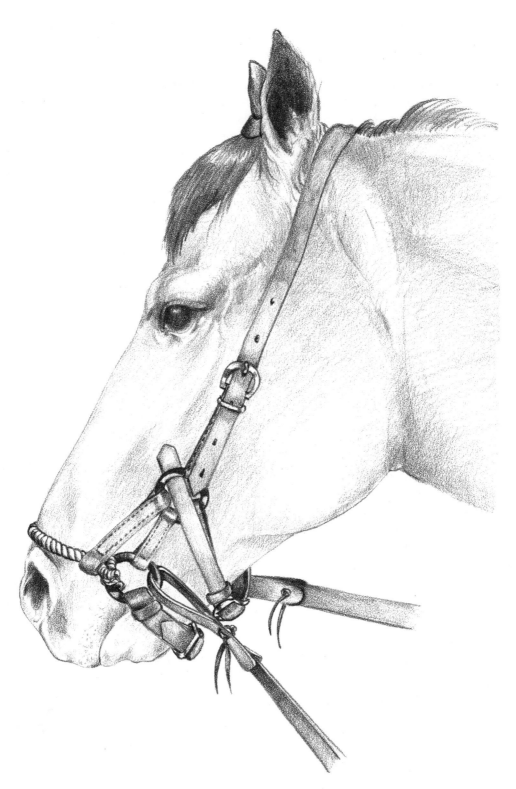

The sidepull applies lateral pressure on the
nose. Leather reins attach with thongs.

Two versions of the snaffle decorated with silver conchos.

Selecting Materials

Many of today's bits are cast of stainless steel, either in the harder 18-8 alloy or in the more flexible 17-4. Cheaper bits, cast or die-stamped of aluminum, nickel, and chrome-plated steel, are more likely to chip, bend, or crack. Quality stainless steel bits are crafted in the United States, with the Korean look-alikes generally considered to be inferior in materials and design.

The best quality bits are usually hand made of steel, iron, or an alloy. Popular alloys other than stainless steel are Monel and Dural.

Bitmakers utilize several techniques to manufacture bits including forging, brazing, and welding with a propane torch. They often temper steel for better shaping and greater hardness with resilience. Even when shaped in a narrow diameter, tempered steel will not bend out of shape.

In the handmade mouthpiece, sweet iron or sweet or mild steel is standard. Horses seem to prefer this metal to stainless steel. It helps maintain a moist mouth, which prevents injury to the bars or tongue. As the metal oxidizes with age, its taste improves.

Copper or copper-enhanced mouthpieces are popular because many trainers claim that this metal encourages a moist mouth. A solid copper mouthpiece will flex and contour to a horse's mouth over the years. You will see copper pieces added in many ways—a copper hood over a copper roller, loose copper rings encircling the mouthpiece, copper inlaid into the steel of the mouthpiece, or even as wire wrapped around the mouthpiece.

Some bitmakers avoid copper in their designs, or restrict it to a roller. They report that as copper oxidizes, it becomes bitter-tasting. If you do purchase a copper mouthpiece, avoid electroplated alloys. Look for true copper.

The shanks of handmade bits can be decorated with silver or copper pieces, or stained as blued steel. Silver serves to attract the judge's attention in the show ring, or even to improve the appearance of the horse's head. In general, silver today should be tasteful and subdued. Some riders claim that a larger silver bit creates the illusion of a smaller head, or that bigger shanks make a head look longer. Conchos on the shanks might mask part of the jaw, or even conceal an open mouth.

You can choose a bit with German silver or sterling silver overlaid—soldered in place—on shanks of blued iron, stainless steel, or Monel. Or, look for the higher-quality, more expensive silver inlaid bit, which features pure silver embedded into blued iron. The artisan chisels a line into the steel and then backcuts under the surface. He or she then hammers jeweler's sterling into the design, or brazes silver into the cut. A lesser-quality inlaid silver may be brazed into the cut design, with no backcutting to ensure its adhesion.

For the show ring, you may prefer a steel silver-mounted snaffle bit. With this bit the rings are inlaid with silver bands, and many bitmakers add conchos inside the rings, welding them in place by two braces. You should protect this hand-work by using a tie-on rein, because a metal snap or buckle could abrade the braces.

You can choose curb straps of several different materials. The mildest is the flat leather strap. Stronger versions add centers of rounded leather, textured rawhide, or chain. These increase pressure against the chin groove, and their use is restricted by some show associations.

Most curb straps feature buckles on each end, to attach to the bit rings and to permit adjustment. Some versions attach by leather laces instead of hardware.

The classic bosal is braided of rawhide strips over a rawhide core. This adds a resilient feel to the device, allowing it to shape to the horse's muzzle.

Most bosals today are plaited over a steel cable, which is shunned by traditionalists as being too rough and ungiving. You can tell the difference between the two cores by flexing first a steel core, then a rawhide core. The steel gives a feeling of resistance.

You can match your bosal with a mecate of natural or synthetic material. Again, the traditionalists prefer the vaquero's twisted hair mecate, braided of six-inch strands of mane hair. White mane hair is usually softer than black or brown. A coarser version consists of hairs from the tails of cattle, which the braider might wash in fabric softener to resemble the softer mane hair. (Wear gloves with the cowtail mecate.)

Other mecates, usually reserved for riding outside of the show ring, can be of cotton rope or braided rayon cord.

The sidepull can feature a noseband of iron, steel, natural rope, nylon rope, or braided rawhide. The rope style can be single or double, and the bottom may be a leather strap or a metal band.

Most hackamore bits combine stainless steel shanks and noseband with a padding over the noseband. You will see this padding made of leather, vinyl, fleece, or surgical rubber tubing. The noseband can be either flat or the more severe rounded style.

Selecting Fit

Fit is linked closely with the bit's design. Important factors for you to consider are the width and size of the mouthpiece. It should fit snugly into the corners of the horse's lips, creating no wrinkles. If it hangs slack, it can pinch.

Mouthpiece sizes range from pony to horse, usually 4 3/4 to 5 inches wide. Comfort is vital, so be sure that the bit is not too large or too narrow. The 5-inch size fits most horses; a horse with a small muzzle may require the next size down.

Besides determining the correct width of the mouthpiece, you should match its shape and diameter to your horse's mouth. Look at the width of your horse's jaw, the thickness of its tongue, the shape of its bars, and the stage of development of its teeth. Variations determine how your horse mouths the bit; a horse with a thick tongue may have difficulty closing its mouth over some mouthpieces. Most mouthpieces will measure about 1/2 inch in diameter.

Look at the bit's purchase. The bit loops must never rub the horse's jaw. They should bend slightly to the sides to allow adequate room for the jaw.

Place the curb strap to lie flat against your horse's chin groove. Adjust the strap's length so that it touches the chin groove when you pull the shanks to a 45-degree angle with the mouth.

You can choose a bosal from 3/8 to 1 inch in diameter, and a mecate from about 1/4 to 1 inch in diameter and 22 feet long. The bosal's inside length usually measures about 12 inches, before you tie the mecate around the bottom. If your horse has a smaller muzzle, you can buy a slightly shorter bosal, about 10 1/2 inches long. Look for a 1-inch gap between the horse's jaw and the bosal when there is no pressure.

A bosal should not fit too tightly, as it can pinch the tender skin of the muzzle. Adding or substracting a wrap of the mecate can adjust the bosal's depth. You can make a large bosal slightly smaller at the top and sides by wrapping the shanks or the nose button with pieces of soft cloth or sheepskin.

To operate properly, the top of the hackamore must rest on the bones of the nose, about one inch above the tip of the nasal bone. The weight of the heel knot and mecate allow the shanks to hang free until you pull a rein. Then the shanks should pull back to contact the bones of the jaw. The shanks drop forward when you release the rein.

You can choose either a pony- or horse-sized hackamore bit, in either a 7 or 9-inch shank. Adjust the bridle's cheekpieces so that the noseband rests on the nasal bones and the curb chain fits against the curb groove as it would with a curb bit.

A bit's weight affects its action. A curb bit like the popular grazing bit is lighter than the complex spade bit. Some trainers claim that a heavier bit helps to create a good headset. (Bits can weigh over 1 1/2 pounds.)

Features

Many loose-jaw bits feature a bottom bar, also called a slobber bar, which connects the two shanks. It can be made of solid metal, a chain, or a braided nylon tie. The bar holds together the shanks so that they do not flop. The added stability prevents narrow cheeks from bending. Also, a bar can improve a bit's balance by adding weight. With a ring snaffle, you may wish to add a hobble strap—a curb strap that attaches loosely under the chin to help keep the mouthpiece in place.

The decoration you select for the shanks is usually a combination of what appeals to you and what complements your horse. In general, women seem to favor more elegant designs, such as the

The rawhide bosal should not apply pressure until you shorten the reins.

heart-shaped motif. Men seem more likely to prefer the military-style, S-curved shank. Other stylish decorations include stars, eagles, and swirls.

Quality Craftsmanship

Craftsmanship is important in bit selection, because a bit must not break in the horse's mouth. The ones that do break are usually either of inferior materials or construction. Rider errors can also result in broken bits. (Never tie your horse by the reins.)

Look for a quality bit to appear uniform on both shanks. On a silver bit, feel the engraving. Compare both sides to verify that the design matches. Look at how the silver attaches to the shanks—conchos or overlaid silver may be riveted as well as brazed. You may see rivets in two places on each shank.

A handmade bit will be superior to a machine-made one. When a bitmaker crafts a steel bit mounted with silver, for example, he bends the steel, welds the mouthpiece to the shanks, polishes and blues the steel, engraves the silver, brazes the silver in place, and grinds and polishes any rough edges. All of these processes total at least four hours of handwork.

Look for a strong, solid weld at the cheek and mouthpiece. The joining should bind the sections, yet also yield. It can bend slightly to the pressure of the horse's jaws. If you try to bend the shanks, the metal should spring. They regain their original shape after you release pressure. Also test the rein end of the shank—it should bend but never break.

A hand-finished bit will feel smooth. Often an inexpensive cast bit will have rough edges or nubs that were formed during the molding process but not ground or polished to be removed. An uneven surface on the shank or mouthpiece will aggravate the horse's mouth.

When you look at a loose-jaw bit, check how the shanks join the mouthpiece. Usually the bitmaker fits either a hinge or pins through the shanks and onto each end of the mouthpiece. These moving parts can wear out after years of use, but an established firm will replace them.

Evaluate a hackamore bit by studying how the noseband covering attaches to the core. A better-quality bit will feature stitching; less-expensive models will be riveted.

On a bosal, study the plaiting. A quality model will feel smooth, with sixteen or eighteen plaits forming a finely textured surface. The finest bosals feature plaiting of twenty-four strands. Edges should be beveled to prevent rubbing the horse's jaw.

Verify that the bosal is plaited on a rawhide core by looking at the heel knot. The inner strands should appear finer than those covering the core, because they allow the bosal to be shaped to your horse.

Ask where a handmade bit was actually manufactured. Many bits from U.S. firms are actually crafted in Mexican shops, and the quality may vary. Bits made in the United States are often superior.

Finally, ask about the bit's guarantee. A quality-conscious bitmaker will offer a lifetime guarantee.

Quality Recommendations

Since Western tack is uniquely American, you can expect models made in the United States to be of the best quality. Look for production line or handmade bits by firms such as Quick, Dutton, Sliester, Trammel, and E.G.

Many foreign manufacturers market inexpensive casted copies of the above bitmakers' designs. These copies may not function the same as the originals, as fit, balance, and finishing are usually inferior.

Insiders' Preferences

• "Capriola sells the true Garcia bits—made by the finest craftsmen in the world. Also, the E.G. bits, made in Magdalena, Mexico, are functional and of good quality." (Bitmaker)

• "I look for better workmanship in an inexpensive bit—Madco is a good brand. My husband says Quick and Sliester are good products, but I think Sliesters are overpriced." (Saddle-shop owner)

• "In the handmade bits, Greg Darnall is as good as they come. I also recommend Tom Balding of Sheridan, Wyoming; in his bits and spurs, the craftsmanship and application are real good. In the more production-oriented bits, we like Don Hansen and Trammell. Trammell is the Chevrolet of the bit business, with middle-of-the-road prices, not too fancy a product. They're probably about the best manufactured bit." (Saddle-shop owner)

• "I carry American-made bits, like Sliester and Quick. There are some good bitmakers in the West—Don Hansen and Greg Dutton both make a good bit. Crockett made a good one, but they're out of business now." (Saddle-shop owner)

• "The E.G. bit is outstanding." (Saddle-shop owner)

• "Capriola was bought out, and the quality has gone.... They bought the Garcia name, but the bits are made in Mexico." (Saddle-shop owner)

Maintenance

Make sure that your bit remains comfortable for your horse to wear. Keep it clean and shiny by washing the entire bit with water and polishing the shanks. If your bit has a roller, check that no pieces of food are caught inside it.

Keep the mouthpiece tasting good to your horse. Do not wash it with soap. Dry a steel or iron mouthpiece after each use, and rub it with steel wool if it shows rust.

Questions

- Was this bit made by hand?
- Does it provide appropriate control for your horse?
- Do the angle of purchase and the bit ratio match your horse?
- If it contains silver, is it sterling or German?

Chapter 20

—

SCHOOLING EQUIPMENT

I f you seriously desire to improve your horse's way of going, specialized schooling devices can help you teach your horse to respond correctly to your aids. However, this tack is somewhat controversial. Some horsemen are convinced these tools produce quick, long-lasting results; others condemn them as inhumane gimmicks that force a horse into submission.

Basic Designs

On the ground, you can school your horse either on the longe line or with long lines (or reins). The difference between the two is that when you longe your horse, you use one rope and the horse circles you. With long lines, you hold two reins to guide the horse as you would from a cart.

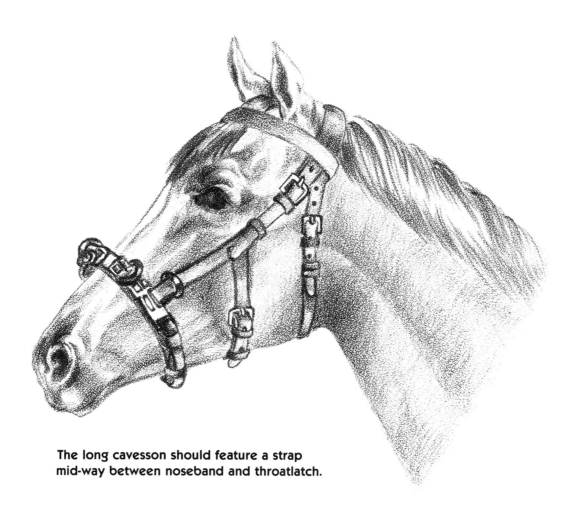

The long cavesson should feature a strap mid-way between noseband and throatlatch.

The aim of longeing is to teach the horse to move correctly. You control the horse's head by the pressure of the longe line, and its body by signals with the longe whip.

For precise control of the head, experts recommend outfitting the horse with a longeing cavesson. This headstall contains a heavy noseband to replace the bit. The best models feature a thickly padded noseband with a hinged nose plate across the top. You snap the longe line to one of three rings on the band, one on each side and one at the center. Each ring fits on a swivel; this allows you to reverse the horse on the longe line.

A crownpiece with browband and throatlatch holds the cavesson in position. The cavesson also has a jowl strap, an extra strap that fits under the horse's jaw between the throatlatch and the noseband. This secures the cavesson, as a throatlatch alone is not adequate. Some styles also have a strap running lengthwise down the horse's face, from browband to noseband.

The longe line is a longer version of the lead rope or shank. One end snaps to the longe cavesson and the other end is held in your hand (the line ends in a loop or a stop, a rounded section that prevents you from dropping the line.) For safety, never wrap the line around your hand—let the horse go rather than risk serious injury. It is

This bitting harness includes an overcheck an
side reins. Photo courtesy of Hartmeyer
Saddlery.

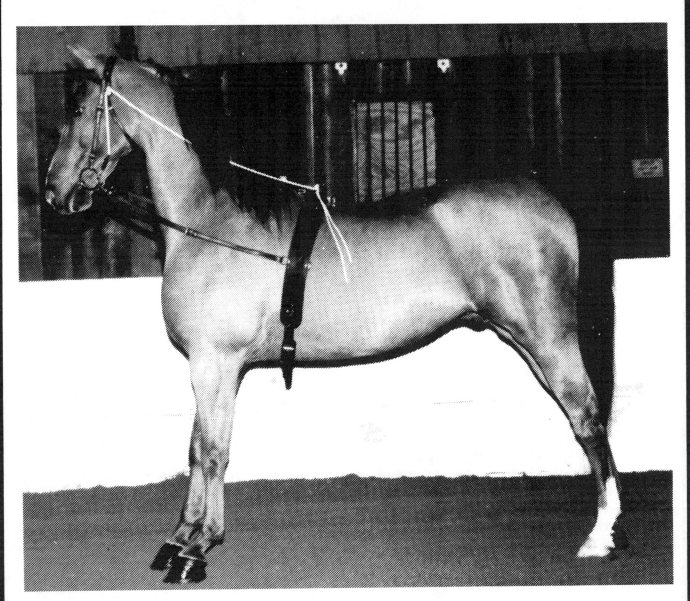

also advisable to wear gloves while longeing, to prevent rope burns.

At the tack shop, you may see longe lines equipped with a length of chain between the line and the snap. These are used by some trainers who longe with a halter or bridle, running the chain over the horse's nose. Obviously the classicists frown on this shortcut, but the chain does control a rambunctious horse.

Many trainers longe horses with a snaffle bridle in place of a cavesson. You can run the line through one bit ring and over the poll, and snap it to the opposite ring. When you change direction, you unsnap the line and reconnect it to the bit ring on the other side. Reins can be removed or left attached and secured behind the stirrup leathers so the horse won't trip over them.

The bitting harness or bitting rig teaches the horse to carry his head in a correct headset on both the longe line and long lines. The complete harness includes a snaffle bridle, surcingle, side reins, overcheck, and crupper.

Depending on the trainer's goals, harness components vary. The most basic element is the surcingle, which is also called a body roller. This padded cinchlike band encircles the horse's back and partway down its barrel. A girth fastens to the surcingle's billets to encircle the heartgirth.

Rings on the surcingle's top and sides help to guide the side reins, which are used to teach the horse to give to the bit and flex at the poll. Two terrets on each side of the surcingle, just below the horses' backbone, are used to guide a longe line or long lines. Some surcingles have additional rings to connect the overcheck (for a higher headset) and crupper (to hold the harness in place).

Side reins are a popular training aid with many trainers; they are used during longeing and under saddle. You can attach the pair of reins to the girth of a saddle as well as to a surcingle.

While longeing is common for horses of almost any age, long-reining is usually used for schooling a colt before it is ridden, or for reschooling an older horse. In the United States, it is often called ground-driving.

When long-reining most trainers outfit a colt in either a bitting harness or a bridle and surcingle, attaching the long lines to the rings of a snaffle bit. You can substitute a sturdy saddle for the surcingle, running the lines through the stirrups. (For safety, tie the stirrups together under the horse's belly.)

Selecting Materials

The leather cavesson features a noseplate of metal; nylon models usually offer fleece-padded nosebands. Nylon should not look like a reinforced halter; if it does it will be too flexible to exert pressure.

The longe line and long reins can be either long ropes or straps of nylon or cotton web. Cotton webbing feels softer and will not twist as much as nylon. On a longe line, look for leather reinforcement on both ends, and a leather hand grip. Long reins should have leather handholds, and the first four feet should be rounded to move freely through the surcingle terrets.

Bitting harnesses are available in leather, web, or plastic-coated nylon. A surcingle can be made of well-stuffed leather panels or a combination of leather and webbing.

Side reins appear in leather, leather with elastic inserts, all nylon, and nylon with elastic inserts. Some models feature a thick rubber insert between the rein and the elastic, to limit the amount of stretch.

Elastic simulates your hands better than the stiffer rubber. It will wear out faster, however, and some trainers consider that it encourages the horse to overflex and get behind the bit.

This cavesson's noseband includes a metal noseplate of brass, with swivelling D-rings for attachment of the longe line.

Long-reining requires a correctly-fitted surcingle.

This side rein of nylon web features elastic webbing inserts.

Selecting Fit

When you use any piece of schooling equipment, it is important that you adjust it properly. Too tight, tack can be inhumane and harmful. Tack that is too loose can be hazardous and ineffective. A cavesson or surcingle that slips during exercise will hinder your training.

Fit the cavesson with the throatlatch snug enough to hold the cheekpieces away from the horse's eyes. The noseband should not slide.

Any type of harness should fit snugly so that it stays in place, yet it should not press too tightly into the skin. When you put a cavesson or surcingle on your horse, check both sides of the horse to be sure that no straps are twisted or out of place. Try to adjust straps evenly, on the same holes on both sides.

A surcingle should allow for wide adjustment. To prevent abrasion, it should measure at least 4 inches wide.

Adjust side reins gradually. Start with them long and connected low on the girth or surcingle, and shorten them as the horse learns to flex to the pressure.

A longe line will run from 25 to 35 feet, with 30 feet considered ideal. Long lines measure from 20 to 24 feet, and both should be an inch wide for comfort. Learn to handle the lines safely, coiling your hand around, not through, extra loops to keep them from getting underfoot. Pay out the line to teach your horse to work freely.

Features

A surcingle should feature large rings so that the reins can slide easily through them. Extra rings will allow you to fine-tune your schooling by alternating rein adjustments.

Look for swivel rings or snaps on longeing equipment. This arrangement will prevent the line from twisting as the horse circle and reverses.

Quality Craftsmanship and Recommendations

Refer to Chapter 12.

Maintenance

Care for this tack in the same manner as you would any other strap goods.

Questions

- Can you handle this equipment safely?
- Are adjustments simple to make?
- Do hand parts feel comfortable in your hand?

Chapter 21

—

WHIPS

Whips augment the natural aids of your leg, hand, and voice. When you need to demand response, you heighten communication by applying this artificial aid.

A whip serves to extend your aids beyond your normal reach. The lash of a whip does punish the horse by causing pain; however, remember that horses are trained by a system of reward and punishment. You control the intensity—a whip can be used as lightly as a touch.

Basic Design

To touch your horse in the intended area, you need a whip that is stiff, yet resilient. Most whips consist of a shaft (the stiff length) with a handle, or stock, attached at one end and a lash or popper on the other.

Whip designs vary according to their intended use. On the ground, many horse-trainers like the schooling whip for schooling for halter and for trailer loading. Sometimes called a stock whip, the schooling whip features a short lash, which can be either a popper or a flat tab.

The longe whip cues your horse while you longe him in a circle around you. You rarely touch the horse with this whip; instead, you move it near the horse's hindquarters to signal for changes in gait, rhythm, or direction. Because you usually stand at least ten feet away from a horse you are longeing, the longe whip needs to have a long shaft and lash.

For riding, you can choose from a wide range of whips for the different disciplines. In dressage, hunt-seat, and saddle-seat riding these are called crops, bats, or sticks. If you ride Western, you'd probably choose a bat or a quirt.

An all-purpose whip is the crop, which consists of a stock holding either a short popper or a flat tab.

Riders of hunters and jumpers like the jumping bat, which resembles the jockey's racing bat. This flexible whip is short, with a wide tab so that you can swat your horse on the hip or rump if necessary. Besides causing pain, the tab creates a loud noise when it makes contact.

Some jumping bats are equipped with feathers, short thin lengths attached along the bottom of the stock. These models are considered to be less painful, since the feathers soften the blow somewhat. The noise of the feathers swishing can also increase the bat's psychological impact.

Two specialized riding whips are the dressage whip and the gaited whip. Dressage riders prefer a stiff whip, equipped with a thin tip or a string lash on the end. The stock is usually capped with a mushroom-shaped knob. This prevents the whip from slipping through your hand.

The gaited whip is used by saddle-seat riders to cue Saddlebreds, Arabians, Morgans, and Tennessee Walking Horses. This whip is stiff like the

A longe whip has a long stock and lash.

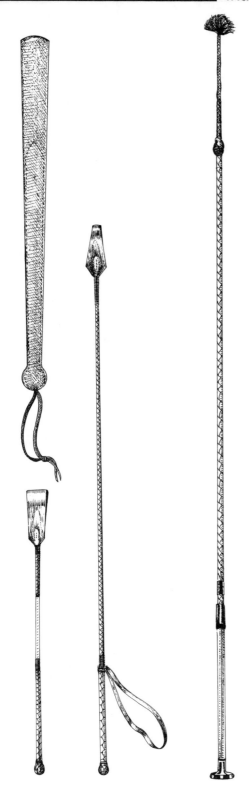

Clockwise, from left: dressage whip, crop, jumping bat, doggin' bat.

dressage whip, but does not have the wide knob.

Many Western riders use English-style crops and bats for schooling, although games contestants prefer to use Western bats or quirts to tell the horse to move faster. Some riders prefer a double-ended bat, a short stock with tabs on both ends.

One Western bat, the "doggin'" (as in "bull-dogging") bat is heavier than the styles preferred by hunt-seat riders. This flat whip is constructed of two wide sections of leather, stitched together over a spring steel core. It has no stock, and some models have a leather lash added on the end opposite the handle. The wide tab makes a noise to encourage forward motion.

The quirt is a flexible length of braided leather, with a handle on one end and a popper on the other. Because the quirt does not have a stock, you must use more wrist action to control it.

The driving or buggy whip consists of a long shaft with a short popper. Some horsemen use this in place of the schooling whip, since it is similar in design.

Selecting Materials

Traditionally whips were built around a whale-bone core. Today you can also choose cores made from fiberglass, plastic, steel, wire, wood, or rawhide. The popular fiberglass core is light-weight and usually firmer and better balanced than steel. Whips with carbon-fiber cores are also known for strength and lightness.

The core of the whip will not be visible, since it is always covered by plaited or wrapped material. The most expensive whips will be plaited with thin strips of calfskin. Cheaper ones will feature plaits of gut or nylon, or even plastic molded to imitate braided leather.

Dressage or gaited whips may be wrapped with heavy thread and usually have a leather-covered stock and metal cap. Other whip styles feature stocks wrapped or molded of rubber or vinyl.

To protect the end of the stock, some whips feature a metal tip. The knob of the dressage whip can be metal or leather.

The lash or popper is usually braided nylon, with loose fibers at the tip. Tabs are made of doubled leather, stitched onto and around the end of the stock. Wrapped threads may further secure the tab in place.

Western bats may be constructed of two wide leather pieces, stitched together over a spring steel core. The quirt is usually made of braided leather.

Selecting Fit

You can evaluate whips by their length, diameter, and how they feel in your hand.

Most schooling whips measure from 36 to 72 inches long. The longe whip can have a stock from 5 to 7 1/2 feet in length. The lash is usually slightly longer, up to eight feet long. Match the length of the longe whip to the radius of your usual longeing circle so that you can reach the horse at all times.

A crop or bat will run from 16 to 30 inches. The length you use is determined by personal preference,—or by the type of shows you attend. In hunter classes, you should carry a short bat, about 18 inches long, to look unobtrusive.

Dressage and gaited whips measure from 30 to 42 inches in length. A longer whip allows you to cue a large horse farther back. The driving whip can run from 45 to 72 inches, depending on the distance between horse and vehicle. In contrast, Western bats are short, ranging from 12 to 24 inches.

When you compare whips in the tack shop, handle each to feel its flexibility or stiffness. A "whippy" whip, especially a longer one, will be more difficult to control than a stiffer one. This is especially important in a longe whip, since the stock is so long.

It is traditional in hunt-seat riding that your whip matches the color of your boots. This rule doesn't seem to be observed often in today's show ring, but keep it in mind when you put together your show outfit.

In other forms of English-style riding, black is the traditional whip color. Riders of gaited horses sometimes choose brown, tan, white, gray, or navy. A major manufacturer offers some dressage and gaited whips with handles in the new shades of red and burgundy.

You will see bats and sticks in earth colors,— usually tan, brown, or black. A few models add red plastic or leather on the stock or handle.

Learn to use your whip in either hand, and apply it where it will evoke a positive response. Make sure your horse knows when you are applying it. Use the tool definitely, hard enough so that the horse knows it is not a fly, and use it only to reinforce your aid.

Features

Many crops and bats include an attached wrist loop. If you release your grip, the loop around your wrist prevents you from dropping the whip. Some experts consider this loop unnecessary and perhaps unsafe. If you do let go of the whip, it could flip and possibly hit you in the face.

Quality Craftsmanship and Recommendations

Look for strength and durability. A whip's stock should feel solid, with at least one layer of tightly wrapped covering. Check that the end cap is secure, and pull the lash to see how it is attached.

Quality brands are County, Stockmen's, and Wonder Whip.

Insiders' Preferences

• "Wonder makes a good, sturdy whip." (Saddle-shop owner)

• "Bullion whips are a high-quality brand made in England. The Great American and Mark VI whips are made in Massachusetts. The leather quality's not what the English is. If you use [the whips] hard, you can have the end fall off. With a high-quality English bat, it's rare to have the end break or the string unravel. Great American does a carbon-fiber whip—it's totally unbreakable, but that cheap end will come off eventually. Avoid the cheap Taiwan schooling whips; they don't hold up very long." (Saddle-shop owner)

Maintenance

Whips rarely break during use. However, you should avoid bending your whip in half to test its resilience. If the center snaps, the whip usually cannot be repaired.

Don't leave a plastic-wrapped whip out in the sun. Sunlight will deteriorate the plastic quickly in a hot climate.

Rewrap the stock with tape if the outer covering tears or peels. If your whip loses its lash, you can easily attach a new one. Buy a replacement popper at the tack shop, and tape it onto the stock with electrician's tape. On a longe whip, you can replace the lash with a long bootlace or two taped together.

Questions

• Is the whip the right length?
• Is the whip strong (test the whip by cracking the lash, or smack the tab on your thigh)?
• Does the whip's heft feel sufficient?
• For show use, when you hold the whip beside you in front of a mirror, does it look too long or short?

Chapter 22

—

SPURS

Spurs help you reinforce your leg aids by allowing you to touch the horse's barrel with less leg movement. These artificial aids refine your cues as you school your horse to move off your leg, to move forward, backward, or laterally.

Basic Design

Metal spurs fit around your boot heels and are held in place with straps. You can choose either English or Western styles.

In the English spur, the shank fits around your heel, and the neck is the long section that touches the horse. The shank usually features a loop on each end through which the spur straps thread. Some older models have buckles that attach to the straps.

The variation of the neck differentiates the styles of English spurs. Most common is the Prince of Wales, which features a slightly curved neck with a squared end.

The dummy spur is similar, except that the end is shaped like a rounded nub. This design is considered the most humane of all spurs.

More severe is the hammerhead, in which the nub of the neck is shaped like a downward-facing "L." The end of the "L" may be sharp, for a quicker and more painful response than the other styles previously described.

Many dressage riders prefer a spur with a rowel attached to the end. This movable, coin-shaped section is serrated with fine, blunt teeth. The rowel may be set vertically or horizontally. You can use a roweled spur lightly, gently rolling the rowel forward or backward to signal for such movements as the flying change of lead.

The necks of the above styles usually arch slightly downward, though some are straight from the shank. If you are a long-legged rider on a small horse, you might appreciate the gooseneck or raised spur. This features a neck that is somewhat S-shaped, so that the end reaches an inch or so higher than the shank.

If you feel it is awkward to make the spurs contact the horse's sides you might prefer the off-set spur. This style features a neck that is set on an angle, so that the right and left spurs differ. Both necks face inward, toward the horse's barrel, when you are in the saddle.

Spurs and straps are sold separately in pairs. Loop end straps consist of one piece of leather for other material to thread through the loop ends of spurs. If your spurs have buckle ends, you will need a set of two straps on each spur.

You can buy slip-on spurs in both English and Western styles. These slide onto your boots and remain in position through a slight pressure. They are not very popular, however, since they can be dislodged easily.

Western spurs are easily differentiated from English spurs. On a Western spur the shank, called the band, is usually wider. The spur's neck, called the shank, usually curves downward. All Western spurs have rowels, which are generally larger than those on English spurs.

The Western spur features two knobs, called buttons, on each side of the band. Buttons can be solid or swinging (these are also called "swingers"). The swinging buttons allow the spur

Two styles of Western spurs: left, stainless steel; right, cold rolled steel overlaid with silver trim, fitted with a chap guard.

strap to rest about one inch higher on your boot, then hold up the end of the spur so it cannot slip down.

Slots in the spur straps fit over the buttons. The strap itself is made of two parts, a short and a long piece, which connect with a buckle. Most strap styles are straight, although some riders prefer the curved design.

Western spurs are described according to the type of riding they are designed for: pleasure, cutting, show, roping, or rodeo. Actually, you can wear whichever spur you prefer, regardless of your riding style.

For safety's sake, pick a spur with dull rowels, with the points close together. Big rowels with long points may look flashy, but they can be dangerous if you fall.

Like bits, Western spurs can fall into two broad categories: Texas and California. The Texas spur is generally forged of one piece of metal, while the rarer California spur is usually made of sections connected by rivets or hinges.

Many spurs feature the traditional chap guard, a hooked projection on the top of the shank to keep your chaps from catching over the rowel. With close-fitting chaps, this is unlikely to happen, but wider chaps could easily snag.

Selecting Materials

All spurs are cast or forged of metal. Inexpensive Western styles are made from cast aluminum, nickel-plated steel, and chrome-plated steel. Spurs made from stainless steel will prove the more durable. The best spurs feature brass rowels and buttons.

Bit makers and spur-makers craft handmade spurs from cold rolled steel, cutting the sections with a band saw and welding them with a torch.

Western spurs are usually elaborately decorated, often with the steel blued. Some makers overlay plain or engraved silver, but the top artisans inlay

silver on the bands. When you order custom spurs, you can add your initials or brand to the outside bands.

The handmade steel spur is superior to the cast stainless steel spur, for you can request special modifications. It is difficult to alter a cast spur, for it can break if you attempt to bend the metal.

If you pick spurs for your English boots, you will probably choose stainless steel spurs. Some manufacturers offer less expensive models of chromed steel, brass, or Never-Rust. (The Never-Rust will bend to adjust to your boot.)

English spur straps are made from leather, vinyl, or braided nylon with leather straps most common in shows. Western-style spurs are usually made of wide leather, either single ply or doubled and stitched. Fancier versions are tooled in traditional designs.

Selecting Fit

You should not encounter problems finding the right size spurs. Unlike boots, spurs are manufactured in only three sizes: men's, ladies', and children's.

What will vary is the size of the neck (or the shank in Western models).

For example, you can choose a Prince of Wales that is as short as the 1/4-inch Tom Thumb, or that is up to 1 1/4 inches long. Dummy and hammerhead spurs average about 3/4 to 1 inch in length, while the roweled spurs add more length, compensating for the rowel's diameter to measure 1 1/4 inches.

Western spurs feature bands from 3/4 to 1 1/4 inch wide. The shanks range from 1 1/2 to 2 7/8 inches wide.

Rowels usually feature ten teeth, or points, although you may see from eight to sixteen points on various styles. The rowels measure from 3/4 to 2 inches in diameter. Today the 2-inch rowel is the most popular.

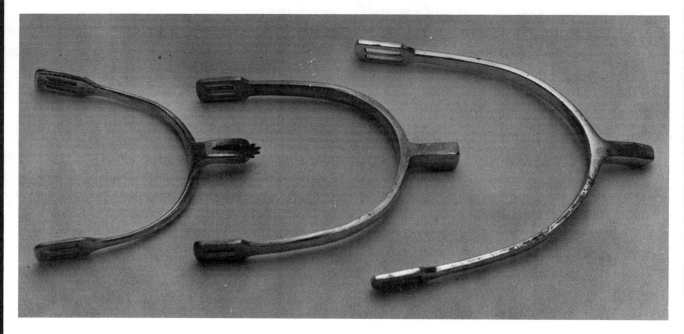

Three variations on the loop end English spur:
Left, a child-size brass spur with rowel; middle,
adult brass hammerhed spur; right, adult
chrome-plated spur, Prince of Wales style.

Experts recommend that a novice begin with a medium-length shank, then progress to a longer one. If you are a long-legged rider on a small horse, you will find a longer shank more effective. Try a shorter shank if you are a short rider on a large horse. A longer shank may be easier to use, as you will not need to twist your foot so far.

To be effective, spurs must be positioned correctly, generally at right angles to your heels. Most instructors recommend that you place your spur at the height of your boot's horizontal seams. A spur that is too low will be awkward to apply against the horse's barrel. Many English boots feature spur rests, leather knobs on the back seam to keep your spurs at the proper height.

Attach your spurs after putting on your boots. When the spurs are adjusted, the pressure of the straps will not allow you to get your feet into your boots or remove them while the spurs are on.

Place the spur so that the strap fits across your instep. Be sure that you match the spurs to your right or left foot. Without their straps, most styles are interchangeable, except for those featuring offset necks (English) or shanks (Western.)

Place English spur straps with the buckles on the middle of your foot. The strap ends should face to the outside, traditionally because they will not scrape the horse's flank. If your straps are too long, cut off the excess or tuck it under the strap or spur.

If you choose Western spurs, attach them with the strap's buckle toward the inside. The reason for this is that a buckle on the outside could easily catch on brush while trail riding.

Features

You can add heel chains to Western spurs. These fit under the sole of your boot, ahead of the heel, to keep the spur in place.

Currently popular are jinglebobs, dangling attachments on the rowels that add a jingling noise when you walk or ride. This old-time "cowboy jewelry" has made a comeback in the last five years.

Quality Craftsmanship and Recommendations

Evaluate a spur as you would a bit. Look for smooth edges and a hand-finished appearance.

Quality bitmakers also craft the best spurs. In Western spurs, three recommended firms are Elmer Miller, Ed Sims, and Kittleson's.

Quality English models include Stubben, Sprenger, and Imperial.

Insider's Preferences

• "You see [Western] spurs by Garcia—they aren't made by Les Garcia any more. Most are made in one plant in Mexico, and stamped Garcia, Fleming, or whatever. The ones marked 'EGARCIA' are made by Eduardo, south of Mexico City." (Saddle-shop owner)

• "I like the old-time Blanchard spurs, out of Yuma, Arizona. Today Kittleson's of Loveland, Colorado, makes the best copies of Blanchard spurs out of cold-rolled steel." (Saddle-shop owner)

• "Sprenger [English] spurs are German. They make a lot of models that aren't made in Korea. The Korean firms want to take on items they can produce in mass quantities, so you have to go to Germany for unusual models and sizes of spurs and bits. You pay more money, too. Sprenger makes a chrome-plated line that isn't as good as their stainless. The stainless are good quality." (Saddle-shop owner)

Maintenance

Care for spurs as you would a bit. Clean them with soap and water, and shine them with a silver polish. Spur straps often absorb mud and dirt, so clean them as necessary.

A broken spur might be repairable, but usually you will need to replace the pair. A skilled craftsman will be able to match a broken or missing handmade spur.

Questions

• Will the spurs remain in position?
• Do they feel comfortable?
• Can you control your leg position to apply the spurs efficiently?

Chapter 23

—

RESTRAINTS

Physical restraints enable you to control the horse's actions on the ground at times other than when schooling for performance. In the barn or paddock, these restraints influence the horse's behavior through pain, or negative reinforcement. They control two areas of the horse: the head and the legs. Because you can restrict or even immobilize the horse's movements with these restraints, you must use caution when using them.

Basic Designs

Several items are designed to restrain the horse's head: the control halter, the twitch, and the lip chain. The control halter exerts pressure on the horse's nose, jaw, and poll by tightening when you pull a rope attached to the halter. When the

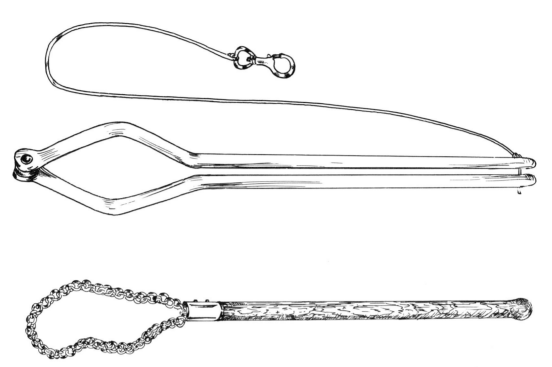

For effective restraint, choose between two twitch designs: Clamp (humane) or chain end.

horse responds correctly, yielding to the pressure by moving forward, the pressure instantly releases.

A twitch is a loop or clamp that restrains the horse by exerting pressure on its sensitive lip. One person holds the loop end twitch while another performs the grooming or veterinary procedure. Handle a twitch with care. If it flips loose, the stick could hit handler or groom.

The humane twitch is comparatively safer. You can attach it and leave it in place while you work on the horse. Some experts, however, feel that the humane twitch is less effective than the loop-end type.

You can choose between two twitch designs: top, clamp (humane); or bottom, chain end.

The chain shank can be used as a temporary restraint. You can run the chain under the horse's

upper lip, across its gums, as a powerful control.

Certain devices are designed to discourage the horse from biting. A muzzle is a cage or cover that fits over the horse's mouth and nose and is held in place by a headstall. The muzzle prevents the horse from biting its clothing, other horses or people, or eating its bedding.

The neck cradle and the bib also prevent the horse from chewing its clothing. The neck cradle is a device of wooden rods that encircles the horse's neck. The rods allow the horse to drop its head to eat, but not to bend its neck to chew its blanket or leg wraps.

The bib fits under the horse's chin, cupping its lower jaw. Shaped somewhat like a feed scoop, it snaps to the halter rings to prevent the horse from reaching its clothing.

The cribbing strap is a device aimed to discourage a horse from cribbing. Placed tightly around the throatlatch, it punishes the cribber.

The most popular cribbing strap creates a nutcracker effect against the horse's throat. A hinged metal plate squeezes the muscles of the throat as the horse expands its windpipe to crib. The more painful spiked strap features rough spikes that press into the horse's throat when it cribs. If the horse is not cribbing, the spikes remain retracted.

Leg restraints restrict movement. Never use these unless your horse is trained to accept these restraints, or it can panic and injure itself. Hobbles which force the horse to stand in place, consist of two cuffs that fit around the horse's forelegs. A strap attaches between the cuffs to keep the horse's feet close together. Because the horse must separate its legs to move, a hobbled horse stays in position.

Another style of hobble is the stake-out hobble. Here you fit a single cuff around one foreleg, attach a rope or chain to the cuff, and tie the rope to a stake driven into the ground.

The kicking chain is designed to discipline the kicking horse. A cuff fits around a hind ankle, and a short length of chain hangs from the cuff. When the horse kicks, the chain raps its leg.

Selecting Materials and Fit

The control halter is a network of polyester and dacron cords, held together with cast-bronze clamps. A strong plastic buckle can be adjusted so that the halter fits the horse's head.

You can buy or make a loop-end twitch. It is a round wooden handle, 18 inches long, which ends with a short loop of chain or cord. You adjust the severity of the restraint by loosening or tightening the loop.

The humane twitch is made from two aluminum or stainless steel clamps, 13 inches long, with a short cord and snap attached. Placing the twitch on the horse's lip, you wrap the attached cord around the handles of both clamps and clip the metal snap to the halter. This holds the twitch in place.

The muzzle is made of wire mesh, plastic, or aluminum; the neck cradle of wood; and the bib of leather, rubber, or plastic. All are available only in one size. Cribbing straps are made either of leather or nylon web, with metal or tough plastic plates to discourage wind-sucking. You can pad the strap over the poll with an optional fleece covering.

A strictly functional style of hobbles is a four-foot length of cotton rope that winds around the legs and is tied. You can fashion a similar version from a feed sack.

Many tack shops also sell manufactured hobbles, made in a figure-eight style of two leather cuffs connected by a strap. An adjustable buckle on one cuff closes the hobbles.

Most hobbles are made from flat webbing or flat or braided leather, 1 1/2 to 2 inches wide. Some models substitute a short chain for the center strap, and leather hobbles may be lined with fleece. The strongest design is made of links of chain, padded around the ankle area with vinyl.

Braided leather or rawhide hobbles, styled to match a show bridle, are intended for decoration only, not restraint. These doubled lengths of cord resemble reins, and are worn attached to the saddle in shows.

The kicking chain forms a cuff when snapped to itself. Thick vinyl padding protects the horse's pastern.

Questions

- Are you able to handle this piece of equipment safely?
- Can you remove the item quickly in an emergency?
- Will the item injure your horse?
- Will the item restrain your horse sufficiently?
- Can you use this restraint by yourself?

PART V:
CLOTHING

Chapter 24

WINTER BLANKETS

While most horses could easily dispense with horse clothing, most owners disagree. If you ride your horse in the winter, its heavy winter coat can be a health hazard. Exercise causes sweat, which cools and dries out slowly. A wet horse could catch a chill.

Blanketing can improve your horse's well-being in the cold season by reducing the density of its coat. A blanket flattens the horse's hairs and maximizes body heat, which can prevent the hairs from growing long and thick.

If you clip your horse's coat, you must replace the protective insulation with a well-fitted blanket. Depending on the climate, your horse's coat will remain smooth for several weeks, months, or perhaps the entire season.

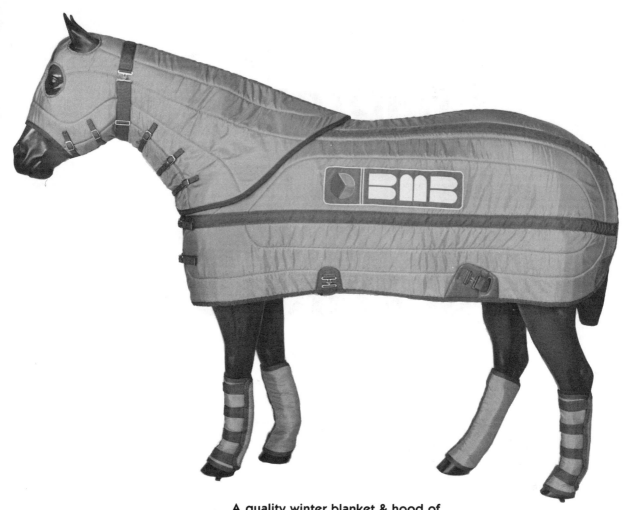

A quality winter blanket & hood of
durable nylon.

Basic Design

A blanket fits the horse by covering its chest
and sides, and sometimes wrapping around the
rump and the belly. All blankets create an opening
for the neck.

Blankets feature two or more layers of fabric.
The outside covering is a durable material designed for protection against the elements, while
the softer inside layer is designed to retain warmth
against the horse's body. Between these two layers

manufacturers sandwich one or more inner layers,
which increases the garment's insulation value.

You will see two categories of winter blankets:
stable blankets and turnout blankets. The primary
difference between them is based on their origins.
Turnout or storm blankets are based on the "New
Zealand rug," popular in Britain. This garment
drapes over the horse with the cloth hanging
straight down from the backbone, without cling-
ing to the contours of the horse's body. Most blankets of this type feature square corners over the
buttocks, and the fabric hangs below the horse's
barrel.

The stable blanket is form-fitted to hug the contours of the horse. It offers the advantages over the looser rug of a comfortable fit at the horse's shoulders, withers, and hips, with no rubbing. The blanket remains in place, regardless of the horse's actions.

When you look at a rug or blanket, you will notice that the pattern is formed of panels of fabric. A seam along the backbone joins the sections of a two-piece blanket, such as the New Zealand rug. On a blanket cut from three or four more panels, you will see extra seams on the sides, which join the pieces.

A rug or blanket may feature two darts sewn at the points of the horse's hips. These form a curved shape, adjusting the fabric to cup the rump. Without darts, the clothing will not reach as far back.

In a contoured blanket, the fabric lies along the backbone so that the blanket curves from withers to loins. Side seams allow the blanket to curve around the horse's hips and shoulders. Some contoured blankets feature darts lower than the point of the buttock, so that the blanket tucks at the rump.

When you look at a contoured blanket, you will notice that a form-fitting style will appear wider over the shoulders, tapered through the waist, and flared at the hips. This design helps the garment to remain close to the horse. If the blanket were looser, it might slip out of place and hang off center. The fabric's weight would pull it to one side, possibly entangling the horse.

Blanket contours are sometimes designed for specific breed conformations. You can choose a blanket tailored for a rangy Thoroughbred, a rounded Arabian, or a chunky stock horse.

Some stable blankets feature a cutback neck, in which the fabric curves back toward the withers at the neck opening. This design leaves the entire mane uncovered, preventing the blanket from rubbing mane hairs.

Styles also vary according to the attachments that secure the blanket onto the horse. At the neck, you can choose from two equally popular designs: the open or the closed front. Traditionally, the two sides of the blanket open and close at the horse's chest. You can fasten and unfasten the opening by buckling from one to four straps. This allows you to adjust the blanket to be wider or narrower, to cover the width of the horse's chest without rubbing.

Although the front-closing blanket allows you to remove the blanket conveniently, some horses learn to open the straps. Also, unbuckling and rebuckling straps adds extra time to your horse-keeping tasks. In addition, in a cold climate, your horse can become chilled if drafts blow through the blanket opening. You can provide extra protection with a front that overlaps, one section strapped over the other, or select a closed front.

The closed-front style solves the drawbacks of the open-front blanket. Instead of strapping the two front sides, you simply slide the blanket on over your horse's head. The closed-front blanket will hold better on a horse in a paddock or pasture.

Getting used to the closed-front blanket demands patience and dexterity. You will have to stretch to place it on a tall horse. The horse must stand still so that you can quickly guide the opening over its head. (You may need to spend some time schooling your horse to permit this procedure.) An easy method is to turn the blanket around so you only have to lift the smallest area (covering the chest) over the horse's head. You guide the horse's muzzle through the opening, slide the blanket down its neck, then turn the blanket around to position it on the horse's back.

Blankets are also held in place on the horse by one or more straps around the barrel. Traditional in Britain is the body roller, a separate wide padded girth that fits over the blanket to hold it in place. In the United States, most blankets feature attached surcingles.

On many blanket styles, a pair of long surcingles are stitched on the off side of the blanket. These connect to clasps on the near side. You will see them sewn in two ways: vertical at the shoulder and flank, or at an angle, on the bias. Bias straps cross each other under the belly, and they seem to hold the blanket in place better than straps with a vertical configuration. Bias straps divert pressure from the middle of the horse's back toward its withers and hips.

The bellyband surcingle features elastic webbing between the strap and buckles.

You can adjust the length of surcingles to fit your horse. For safety, keep the straps lightly touching the horse's belly, but not so tight that they rub the skin.

Many horse owners have found that lightweight surcingles do not withstand the horse's movement. Metal buckles can come apart, and the horse can easily wiggle free of the garment. Some manufacturers offer a more secure single surcingle. This short, hidden surcingle is sewn to the off-side edge. It reaches straight under the belly, threads through a slot near the blanket's bottom edge, and connects to a buckle above the slot.

Some horses still manage to undo the short surcingle. For these equine escape artists, you can try another style, the bellyband. This wide piece, attached to the off side of the blanket, wraps around the horse's belly and partway up the barrel. A series of straps secures the band. The bellyband also adds warmth by increasing the size of the blanket.

For better hold, many quality blankets feature leg straps, which are traditional on the New Zealand rug. These wrap above the insides of the gaskins to buckle onto the sides of the blanket. They help keep the garment in place over the rump.

To cover the horse's head and neck for extra warmth you can match your blanket with a hood. Contoured to shape the horse's head, the hood will protect the horse from its muzzle to its withers. The hood overlaps the neck of the blanket, and separate connector straps snap to rings on the blanket's shoulders to hold the hood in place.

A hood should curve over the poll and down the crest. Look for a flare at the bottom, to cup the withers. You should see large eye holes. Most models feature two separate cutouts for the ears, although some manufacturers prefer one ear hole for free ear movement with a strap separating this opening into two sections.

Selecting Materials

In selecting blanket materials, look for durability, warmth, and ease of care. In outer layer fabrics, you will see blankets of canvas duck, cotton drill, cotton/polyester blends, nylon, and acrylic.

Blanket linings can be burlap, wool, flannel, jersey, fleece, or nylon. As this fabric rests directly on the horse's coat, it should be soft, warm, and lightweight. The lining must never rub or chafe.

As a material for both the inside and outside of blankets, tough nylon predominates in today's market. Most popular is the quilted nylon exterior, of 200-, 400-, or 1000-denier smooth or packcloth nylon. Many styles add a urethane coating to resist snags. Blanket linings are usually a satiny nylon or polypropylene, although some manufacturers prefer the fluffier polyester or acrylic fleece.

Nylon's warmth, light weight, and easy care has made natural-fabric blankets almost obsolete. Old-timers may claim that cotton and wool better allow the horse's skin to breathe, but the manmade materials outlast any natural fabric. Nylon sheds dirt and is easy to wash, too. The nylon taffeta lining polishes the horse's hairs to produce a shinier coat.

The layering between the interior and the exterior of blankets is usually an insulating material. Manufacturers rely on two basic types: foam or fiberfill. Open- or closed-cell polyfoam, usually 1/2 to 3/4 inch thick, can improve the blanket's fit and keep it in place. Its main drawback is that it has a limited lifespan; foam tends to become stiff and eventually deteriorates.

Polyester fiberfill lasts longer than foam. Look for weights from seven to fifteen ounces. However, over its life, polyfill will lose its loft and flatten, reducing the puffiness of the blanket. A few blankets feature the more expensive Thinsulate filling. Others are double-insulated with both foam and lightweight seven-ounce polyfill.

Stitching patterns quilt the three or four layers. This prevents the insulation from shifting. In a diamond pattern, one tear will be confined within the neighboring diamond. However, some companies note that the excess stitching of the diamond design can compress the insulation and reduce the garment's warmth.

Some insulated nylon blankets can cause a horse to sweat underneath its clothing. The blanket may create too much warmth when the horse is kept indoors. Or, foam might inhibit air circulation and retain moisture. If foam absorbs sweat, it dries slowly and rots faster than the fluffier polyfill.

Manufacturers claim that polyfill self-regulates the horse's body temperature. It allows moisture to evaporate while still retaining body heat. This downlike material, popularized in ski clothing, provides good insulation and can be washed by machine.

When purchasing a nylon blanket, study the description of the type of nylon used. The higher the denier, the better the quality. The most expensive models are usually made from the toughest 1000 denier, although 200 and 400 denier give satisfactory performance.

Look for warmth and softness in the lining. A nylon taffeta, thick flannel, or polyester fleece will provide a snug interior. A few blankets still feature comfortable wool linings, which are warm but require extra care. Kersey linings were popular in years past, but this nonwoven material easily shreds and stretches out of shape. Once it tears, it must be patched to repair the lining.

Feel the weave of both inner and outer blanket fabrics. Better blankets will feature tightly woven material that resists tearing.

A quality blanket features sturdy webbing, bound on all edges and as reinforcements on outer seams. Look for textured nylon or polypropylene webbing, not a smooth finish.

One saddle-shop owner cautions you to check the quality of the binding. He mentions one manufacturer who sews poor binding onto a quality outer shell, thus compromising the garment's durability.

Surcingles must withstand pressure and abrasion. They should be made of nylon or polypropylene. Avoid cotton web, which is likely to rot or tear.

The best surcingles feature a section of heavy-duty cotton elastic webbing, stitched between the surcingle and the blanket. This provides additional comfort for the horse and helps protect the surcingle from stress.

Do not overlook the quality of a blanket's fasteners. Surcingles connect with a metal hook into a metal buckle end. When the strap is pulled tight, the hook can stretch or twist, allowing the strap to unfasten.

Zinc-plated-steel surcingle hooks are considered to be the most durable. Some manufacturers have tried to substitute high-tech plastic clasps; however, these do not withstand the pressures a horse will exert on them.

Any metal hardware that protrudes from the blanket's surface can snag on a wall or fence. Double-locked Velcro fasteners eliminate this possibility.

Hood materials should match the blanket. Most are made of quilted nylon. Look for a nylon rip-stop or taffeta lining, which will protect the horse's mane. Better hoods feature elastic inserts on the throat and connector straps.

The outer shell of most turnout blankets is treated for added protection from the weather. If you need a water-repellant nylon blanket, look for fabric that has been coated with a product such as two-ounce urethane. A rug of the New Zealand style will probably be a stiff, treated, twenty-one-ounce canvas.

Do not expect any fabric blanket to be totally waterproof.

On a canvas blanket, a hind leg strap threads through a slot to buckle above the binding. Although a vinyl patch reinforces the stress point, the strap's angle creates pressure on the buckle.

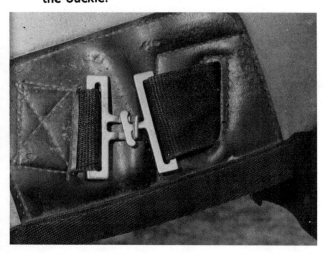

Selecting Fit

A blanket size should measure half the length of your horse. This totals the inches from the middle of your horse's chest, over the broadest part of its shoulder, and to the center of its tail. A properly fitted blanket should cover the top of the tail. If either the belly or the hip shows, the blanket is too small. Also, it will probably stretch too tightly at the chest, and it can restrict the horse from lying down comfortably.

Blanket sizes vary from 36 inches for a newborn foal to 84 inches for a very large horse. Ponies and yearlings generally require a size from 48 to 64. The average horse fits into a 72 to 76 size.

Estimate the length of the blanket from the withers to the chest. If it is too long, the blanket will slip. If it is too tight, it will rub the points of the horse's shoulders.

Compare the lengths of the neck opening and angle, or drop. The opening must be wide enough for the size of your horse's neck. The drop must not be too long or short, and both must be proportioned to your horse's forehand. Elastic added to the blanket front can help the horse to stretch its neck down to feed.

Can you adjust the surcingles for a snug fit? If they are too loose, they will catch on protrusions, and they can twist and weaken the fabric.

Look at the rear of the blanket. Does it form-fit the horse? The darts must fall in the proper location in order to fit closely.

Be sure that the blanket's sides reach down below the horse's belly. Ideally, you want the clothing to hang about four inches below the elbow and stifle. If a portion of the body is exposed to the weather, your horse might grow long hairs faster.

Also take into consideration the weight of the blanket. A heavier, noncontoured blanket may

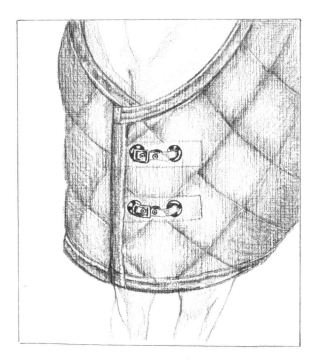

Two closure styles: top, removable straps thread through grommets; bottom, attached straps connect with buckles.

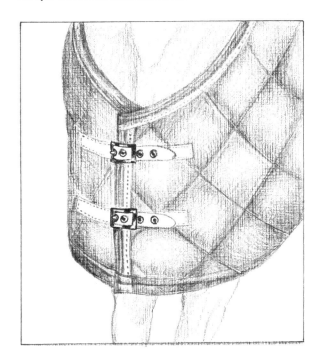

hang better. However, weight will not benefit a shaped-to-fit thermal style. More weight will also make the clothing harder for you to put on, take off, store, and clean.

Fit a hood by considering the horse's height. Manufacturers offer up to seven sizes, from extra small to extra large. A hood should adjust with four or five buckled straps, usually one or two at the jaw, one at the throat, and two on the neck. The throat adjustment should be a 2-inch wide surcingle, which can be fastened on the near side. All straps should feature adjustment buckles so that you can fit the hood snugly.

Plastic toggles close this open front.

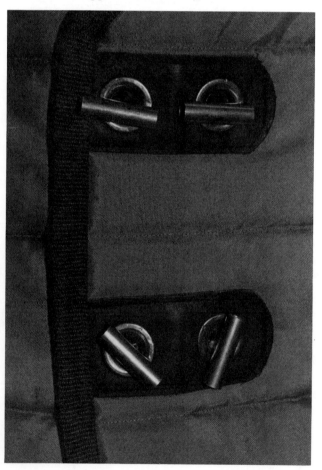

Features

Minor details can affect a blanket's durability. Before you buy, compare similar models for security and construction.

Study the closures if you prefer an open front. Lower-quality blankets feature a single detachable strap that slides through a pair of metal grommets. This strap can easily fail, either by unbuckling or by being chewed by the horse.

Two pairs of grommets allow for double straps. Or, a newer design substitutes a plastic toggle button. The toggle button slides through both grommets, and the ends twist to prevent it from slipping.

Another sturdy blanket design features two or even three straps at the front, securely sewn in place. Most will connect with tongue buckles, although some feature the surcingle clasps. Again, elastic inserts in the webbing will allow the closures to flex as the horse moves.

In addition to the style of closures, you can choose other features to increase the blanket's warmth. Leg straps, another legacy of the British rugs, prevent the garment from shifting. Sometimes called leg girths, these two adjustable web straps wrap around the inside of each hind leg. Each connects to a buckle at the bottom edge of the blanket, below the horse's flank.

Some leg straps feature snaps that connect to D-rings. The rings can be fastened to the blanket's exterior or interior. Elastic on the straps increases their resistance to stress.

If you are purchasing a blanket with a belly-band, you probably will not need leg straps. A blanket with a closed front, secured by a belly-band, simplifies the process of dressing and undressing your horse. You only have to secure two or three straps on the bellyband. Adding leg straps means four more fastenings and unfastenings each day which adds up to a lot of time with a barnful of blanketed horses.

Some turnout blankets feature a tail cover, also called a closed rear. This extra piece allows the garment to cover partway down the horses tail for greater warmth. It fits loosely to permit the horse to raise its tail. The tailpiece is usually either sewn in place or separate and designed to snap onto rings for easy removal from the blanket.

You might wish to add a tail cord to help keep your blanket on your horse. Many blankets feature two D-rings, sewn low on each side of the blanket's rear. You can stretch a narrow strap or piece of string from one ring to the other, underneath the horse's tail. Do not connect the cord too tightly or it will bind the tender skin of the horse's buttocks.

In extreme cold, you can add a separate fleece blanket liner. This can have an open or closed front, and some models add a surcingle. Or, try layering blankets on the horse. Running the tail cord through the rings on both blankets can help hold one blanket on top of another. Also, try connecting the surcingles of one blanket to the clasps of the other.

A turnout blanket may feature a reinforced neck opening. Some models have binding sewn around the opening for extra strength, and sheepskin lining padding the withers. Some cutback blankets add a plush collar to protect the mane.

Quality Craftsmanship

A blanket should look generally well made. A good blanket will feel soft yet strong. Feel the lining, which lies against your horse's skin. Look at the edges; they should not feel stiff or rough.

Stitching is crucial on a blanket. Look for straight, even stitches. The blanket should be lockstitched all over, with the stitching tight and the ends backtacked. Feel for smooth seams, with the stitches consistent in length.

On a quilted blanket, study the stitching for possible unravelling. Many are sewn in a zigzag pattern with varying distances between the quilted sections.

Find out what type of thread was used. Most reliable companies use a strong coated nylon thread, sewing blankets on an industrial sewing machine.

Tabs (or rings) at the rear permit you to attach a tail cord or tie two blankets together.

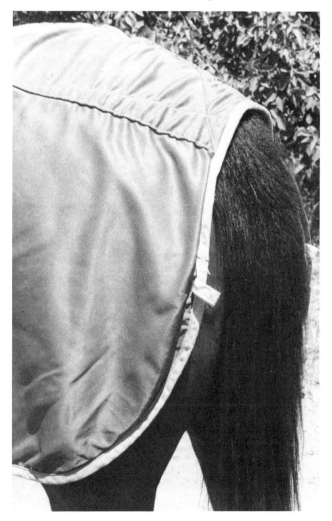

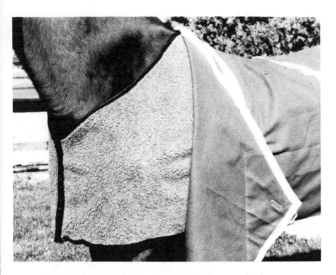

A polyester-fleece blanket liner will increase the warmth of horse clothing. This closed-front model is paired with a sheet. Photo courtesy of Hartmeyer Saddlery.

A quality blanket will feature edges that are stitched, or overseamed, before the binding is attached. The binding should appear even all along the edges, with a consistent width the entire perimeter of the blanket. Some companies double-stitch all bound edges. Look for webbing that is 1 1/2 inches wide. Binding can also strengthen seams, and quality blankets add a cover plate onto the length of each side.

Corners at the front and rear of the blanket should be rounded or mitered. Darts should be topstitched once on each side and twice at the point. Some designs feature darts stitched four times at the point.

The surcingles should be attached securely and close to the edge, with rows of stitching overlapped and sewn across the straps as well as along their length. Lockstitching will prevent unravelling. Most experts feel that surcingles should give

way in an emergency, to protect the garment's integrity. Restitching a surcingle is much simpler than reconstructing the entire side of a ripped blanket.

Look for reinforcements at stress points. Blankets are apt to fail at the shoulder, wither, and anywhere straps are attached. Some manufacturers stitch vinyl patches on the blanket to reinforce the edges where the straps connect. However, the pressure of the fastened strap can tear through the reinforcement and then rip the edge of the exposed fabric. A stronger material used to reinforce blankets is chrome-tanned leather, which usually outlasts vinyl and which resists drying out.

Check the placement of the reinforcement on leg straps. The webbing should insert or attach at a 45-degree angle. This will cause the strap to pull evenly, preventing excess stress. The strap's angle should contour to the direction of its fit, forming a straight line along its length.

Remember to test the hardware on a blanket. Check the snaps, rings, buckles, or Velcro for strength. Fasten and unfasten the closures to test their operation.

On a hood, look for large eye holes, bound with nonabrasive fabric. The inner fabric must feel satiny to protect the mane.

A quality blanket will be guaranteed by the manufacturer. The best feature a two-year up to a lifetime guarantee.

Quality Recommendations

For maximum durability, the new-style nylon blankets offer greatest value. Although their prices may seem steep, one nylon blanket will probably outlast two or three cheaper models. Ease of care and infrequent repairs are well worth the initial price tag.

A few recommended brands include Baker, Battle, Peakes, Triple Crown, and Winner's Circle.

Insiders' Preferences

• "Ayres Philadelphia, who made the original Baker blanket, has been gone for a while, but every other line offers a triple-weave plaid, which is basically the same fabric. The Baker blanket went to an acrylic in the seventies." (Saddle-shop owner)

• "Peakes makes blankets with a one- or two-year guarantee that we think is fantastic. The rate of return is nil; any that do come back, we repair in-house." (Saddle-shop owner)

• "Big D pioneered the lightweight, warm, foam-insulated blanket. Big D is the biggest seller." (Sales representative)

• "Triple Crown, Baker, and Big D are all sized uniformly." (Manufacturer)

• "Wilsun makes a nice-looking blanket. John Wilsun is the original designer of Triple Crown blankets, and we've been happy dealing with him." (Saddle-shop owner)

• "Peakes makes the best blankets and sheets you can find. The lining in the blankets is the same denier, 450, as on the outside of other firms. The four-piece design really fits." (Saddle-shop owner)

• "Big D rides on their laurels. They show no new innovations." (Saddle-shop owner)

• "Baker and Battle [Oklahoma City] are excellent blankets." (Manufacturer)

• "Every Big D leg strap tears out at the back. The webbing is not inserted at the proper angle and endures excess stress." (Saddle-repair specialist)

Maintenance

If you blanket your horse continuously, you would be wise to invest in two blankets. You can keep your horse blanketed consistently while you clean and air one blanket. This will reduce wear on both garments.

Care for your blanket by regularly brushing off loose hair. Follow the manufacturer's cleaning instructions. You can wash most models by machine; line-drying will prevent shrinkage.

A blanket can last a few months or several years, depending on the horse. Realize that when a horse snags any blanket on a nail, the fabric will tear.

Most blankets tear along the side. You should fix these rips immediately, either by sewing them yourself or by contacting a repair service through your local tack shop.

Questions

• Is this blanket suitable for the climate in my area?
• Will my horse wear the blanket indoors, outside, or both?
• Must the blanket be water-repellant?

Chapter 25

—

SHEETS
AND COOLERS

If blankets are considered to be like coats and sweaters, sheets and coolers could be considered jackets and wind-breakers. This clothing acts as lightweight barriers between the horse's body and the climate.

Use a stable sheet to cover your horse through the spring, summer, and early fall months. This one-layer garment protects your horse against dirt, dust, insects, and sunlight. In cooler weather, a sheet can provide some warmth for a horse stabled in a heated barn, and some grooms layer heavier blankets over a sheet.

Basic Design

Like a blanket, a sheet fits over the horse's back and hindquarters. Some models are cut back at the withers to prevent rubbing of the mane.

Most sheet styles open at the front, closing with one or two sets of straps. Two surcingles fasten the garment over the horse's body. Some brands also have leg straps to secure the sheet around the horse's hind legs.

For special occasions, you can outfit your horse in a dress sheet. An American variation on the British day rug, this garment covers the horse in style, adding some warmth while keeping the horse clean.

The dress sheet is fashioned like a looser-fitting version of the regular sheet. Its single surcingle is stitched to the sheet's underside, hiding it from view. Added to the rear is a fillet, or tail cord. This braided string rests loosely against the buttocks to hold the sheet in place.

The British day rug does not feature an attached surcingle. To secure the rug, you buckle a separate roller—a heavy surcingle—around the horse's heartgirth. Some rollers feature two contoured wither pads to help hold the roller in position.

A more practical style of sheet is the anti-sweat sheet. Made in the same pattern as the stable sheet, it is constructed of a meshed scrim. You can buy this design of sheet either with or without attached surcingles.

A cooler, also called a walking cover, is a large rectangle of fabric that drapes over most of the horse from its ears to its tail. A browband holds the cooler over the head; strings close it around the neck and chest, and a tail cord keeps it over the rump. The garment acts as insulation between the body of a warm horse and the possible chill of a brisk wind.

The "show robe" or show cooler is a shorter version of the cooler. Rather than draping from the poll, it is form-fitted at the neck.

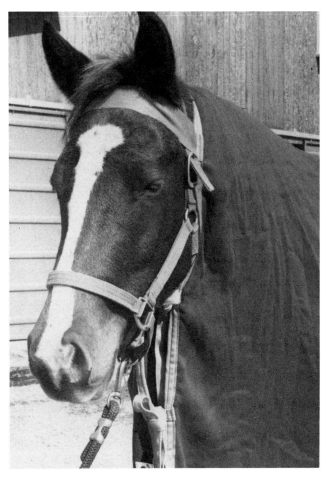

An acrylic cooler secures with a web browband and ties.

Some coolers are designed to fit more closely through the neck, shoulders, and hindquarters. A contoured back seam places the center of the garment over the horse's backbone, and a fitted neck allows the fabric to drape more evenly. Some models even have darts in the rear. The remaining fabric drapes like a regular cooler. Sometimes called a working cooler, a cooler with this design provides warmth as well as insulation.

Another British-designed sheet is the exercise rug, sometimes called the exercise sheet or quarter sheet. Popular with trainers of racehorses, this covering rests under the saddle and extends over the horse's quarters. In the brisk English climate, this rug provides protection and insulation for the clipped horse's back and loins.

A recent variation on the quarter sheet is one made of scrim cloth. Instead of providing insulation for the back and hindquarters, it protects these areas from insects during warm-weather riding.

The rain cover is another unique item of horse clothing. This water-repellant robe can be constructed like a cooler or a walking cover. You would not use this lightweight garment for protection in the paddock or pasture, but it is handy during the inclement weather common at many horse shows. While you are waiting to enter the ring, you can throw this cover over your horse to keep it somewhat dry from ears to tail (and to protect your saddle).

Selecting Materials

Study the quality of various fabrics, feeling their textures to evaluate durability. A sheet's material should feel flexible, not too stiff. The weave of a wool or wool-blend cooler should not be too loose, as it could snag and tear more easily.

In a sheet, the fabric should be lightweight, yet durable. Traditionally, the best quality is the 100 percent cotton hose duck, woven from ten-ounce cotton.

Cotton has been the preferred fabric for lightweight horse clothing because it breathes. Its major disadvantage is that it shrinks, so purchase a cotton sheet about four inches longer than the size of blanket your horse normally wears.

You can also choose a cotton blend, such as a cotton and linen sheet. Or, pick an easy-care synthetic blend—cotton blended with polyester, twill, or acrylic. Manufacturers also offer all nylon or acrylic sheets, and for the Western look, sheets constructed of cotton-denim fabric. In the pricey category are those constructed from either Cordura or Gore-Tex.

The edges of sheets are usually bound in a contrasting fabric. Nylon web, the most common material used, is also the most durable.

Dress sheets are made from soft, lightweight fabric, either acrylic or a wool blend. The authentic day rug is made from 100 percent wool.

Blanket firms will custom-make dress sheets in your stable colors. You can add options, such as grosgrain piping on the bound edges and elaborately stitched hip ornaments on each side. Your monogram, farm name, or horse's name can be sewn or embroidered on the rear corners.

The open weave of the mesh of the anti-sweat sheet allows air to circulate. The thermal air pockets insulate and cool off a hot or wet horse, without letting it become chilled. Some manufacturers claim that this garment simplifies grooming by its natural cooling, lessening the need to walk a hot horse.

The scrim fabric of the anti-sweat sheet may be jute, cotton, acrylic, or a cotton blend. One version, the Irish knit anti-sweat sheet, is made of a heavier, more textured mesh, often of a cotton/polyester or cotton/acrylic blend. Cotton absorbs water and helps the horse to dry off faster. The mesh allows air circulation and also helps prevent the horse from sunburn while you cool it out in hand or on the hot walker.

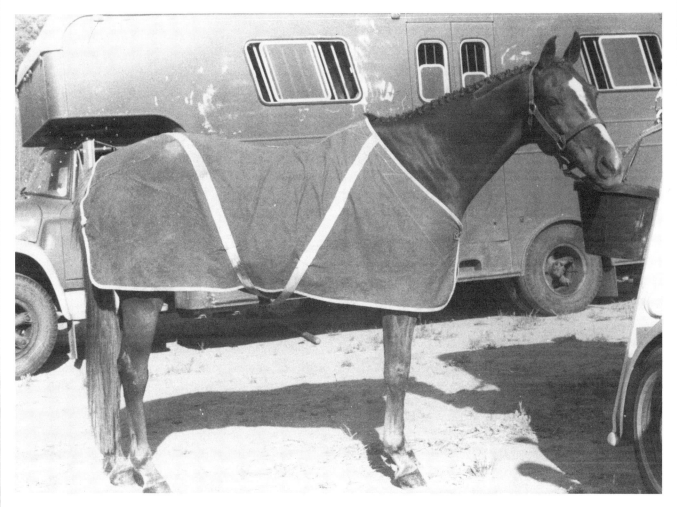

This cotton sheet features criss-cross surcingles.

The best quality coolers are made of 100 percent wool. Its absorbency will wick sweat from the horse and retain warmth in a chilly wind.

You can buy less expensive models of acrylic, acrylic blended with wool, or even a cotton/polyester terrycloth. Some grooms prefer a wool blend, claiming it is sturdier than 100 percent wool. Generally, the greater percentage of wool it has, the more expensive the cooler.

Some manufacturers offer a show cooler in a satin blend, a shiny synthetic fabric. The washable fabric polishes the coat while attracting attention to the show horse out of the ring. Some feature a flannel lining, or even an inner layer of polyester fiberfill.

Coolers feature wide binding, nylon web providing the greatest durability. The color of the ties, the tail cord, and the browband match the color of the binding.

You can buy coolers in solid colors or plaids. Or, you can have a cooler custom-made in almost any color combination. You can also add a monogram.

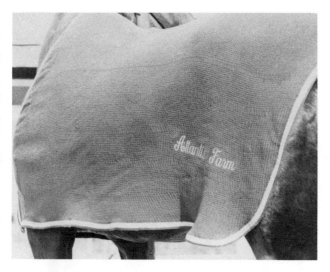

This anti-sweat sheet is made of a loosely-woven fabric.

This open-mesh anti-sweat sheet appears too small to cover the front of a large hunter. Also, the cotton fabric tends to shrink with use.

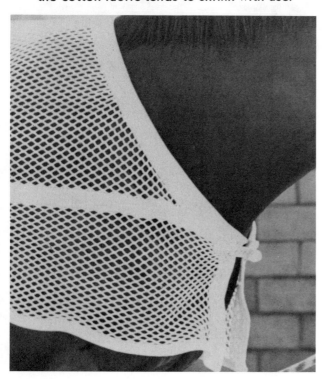

One model of cooler combines the insulation of wool with the evaporation of the anti-sweat sheet. Made of two layers, the inner lining is mesh and the outer fabric is wool.

Exercise rugs come in various weights of cloth to match the changes in season. A heavyweight 100 percent wool melton is considered the most effective fabric. Made in a variety of stable colors, exercise rugs can also be enhanced with piping and monograms.

The rain cover is made of a treated packcloth or nylon, coated with polyurethane. Some models feature a soft, absorbent cotton/polyester lining.

Selecting Fit

Once you know which type of sheet or cooler fits your needs, you can select the appropriate model. Most styles are offered in standard horse and pony sizes.

As with a blanket, a sheet should be the right size for your animal. Sheets range from 32 to 84 inches in length, with some manufacturers requiring the larger sizes to be special-ordered at extra cost. The dress sheet is usually available in a narrower range, from 48 to 80 inches, with most choices in the standard horse sizes of 72 to 80 inches. There is less selection among anti-sweat sheets; they usually are from 56 to 80 inches, or sometimes only small, medium, and large.

You can find coolers in a few standard sizes: small pony (60 by 66 inches), large pony (66 by 72), cob (84 by 90), and horse (90 by 96). Adjust a cooler according to the temperature. You can close the front by tying the attached strings, or you can fasten the edges with metal cooler clamps. In warmer weather, you may choose to leave the front open for greater circulation.

Fit the browband either in front of the ears or a few inches down the crest. The first method will cover the entire horse, while the latter concentrates heat around the body.

The exercise rug is made in one horse size, about 4 1/2 feet long. Some riders fold the front section of the rug up under the saddle, which doubles the fabric under the front panels. Slide the saddle's girth through slots on each side of the rug to hold it in place. The fillet drapes at the rear, over the gaskins, to help anchor the rug so that it does not flap in the breeze.

Features

Show stables usually choose sheets to match the barn's colors. Manufacturers note that recently there has been a desire for more color, both in the fabric and trim. This may be due to boredom with the conservative burgundy, gray, and silver, or new barns desiring distinctive colors. Recent examples include a turquoise sheet and a black sheet with hot pink trim.

Quality Craftsmanship

Better quality sheets and coolers will be stitched sturdily, with reinforcement at points of strain. On a sheet, look for mitered corners and reinforcement around the neck and chest, which help prevent the clothing from losing its shape.

Double or triple rows of stitching on edges and seams extend the life of the item. Wider binding allows greater protection along the edges; you may notice some sheets reinforced by a strip of webbing sewn along the length of each side.

Surcingles should be securely attached, with the same requirements as for winter blankets.

Choose certain details according to your preference. Some people like the convenience of permanently attached front closings. Others feel a removable strap is better because it can be replaced if damaged.

Quality Recommendations

See the recommendations listed in Chapter 24.

Insiders' Preferences

"Curvon is the oldest horse-blanket manufacturer in the United States, established 1891. They make beautiful coolers, nice cotton sheets, and Baker-style plaid sheets, but not the modern contoured blankets. Humphrys just changed hands last year and still make good quality sheets." (Saddle-shop owner)

"The best quality coolers are an 85 percent wool. Triple Crown's Pimlico is the top of their line. With the small percentage of acrylic, they can be washed in Woolite. Triple Crown does a lighter-weight wool, a 60–40, the Churchill Downs. The all-acrylic won't really cool a horse out—it's more of a trophy cooler." (Saddle-shop owner)

Maintenance

Most cotton and synthetic garments are washable. A sheet that is labeled "Tub Fast" can be washed, with little fading of the color. Be sure the garment is rinsed thoroughly after washing to avoid any skin irritation.

Unless recommended by the manufacturer, never take a chance and wash wool horse clothing. Most wool items should be dry cleaned.

Questions

- Will the fasteners keep the clothing on the horse?
- Will the cooler fabric absorb moisture?
- Does the fabric feel soft?

Chapter 26

—

BOOTS

Horse footwear and legwear provide protection and support. Boots and leg wraps guard against injury while your horse is performing, playing, or being shipped. Specific designs can protect lively youngsters, valuable competitors, or clumsy horses of any age or type.

Basic Design

Few horse boots actually enclose the foot. Most wrap around a portion of the lower leg, fitting snugly around the pastern, cannon, knee, or hock. A few styles enclose the entire leg, from the joint almost down to the toe.

A boot's design varies according to its function. Performance boots and wraps are shaped to allow the horse's joints to move freely. Some styles have support padding inside. Support and shipping boots usually cover a greater area of the leg, with no special provisions over the joints. All boot models fasten securely around the horse's leg or hoof.

Splint boots are the most common performance boots. These wrap around the horse's front cannon bones to protect the insides of the legs from being rapped. A cushion over the splint bones protects this vulnerable area, as many horses tend to knock one foreleg against the other. The padding absorbs the concussion.

Shin boots and ankle boots often appear identical to splint boots. Also called brushing boots, these boots cover the ankle and most of the cannon. They measure from eight to ten inches high and are shaped at the base to conform to the angle of the pastern.

Most brushing boots are padded to protect both the splint area and the inside of the horse's ankle. If your horse tends to brush, scraping one hoof against its other leg, these boots will protect a larger area than the splint boot.

Splint and skid boots protect contestants in speed classes.

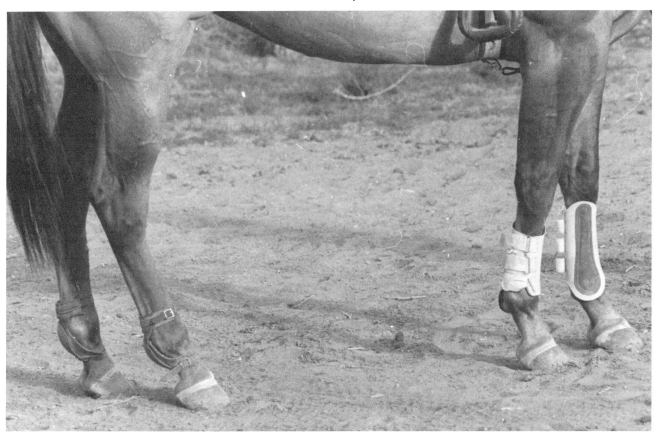

The ankle boot is a shorter version of the shin-and-ankle boot. It protects the insides of the horse's ankles from interference.

Any of these three styles of leg boots can be used on hind legs as well as forelegs.

The bell boot earns its name from its bell-like shape. Some people call this rounded dome an overreach boot. Covering the horse's front lower pastern and hoof, the bell boot guards against the horse stepping on the heels of its front feet.

If you own a cutting or reining horse, you

On a reining horse, skid boots prevent abrasions during long slides.

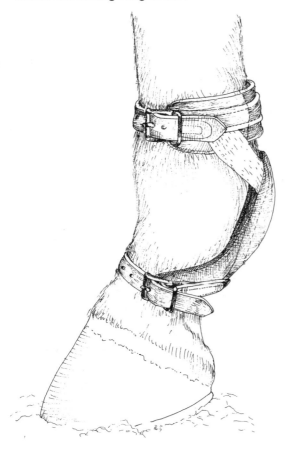

might want to use skid or sliding boots. During rollbacks and sliding stops, the horse can scrape the skin under its hind pasterns and fetlocks. These boots pad the area with a heel cup, preventing such injuries.

Manufacturers also design boots for other specialized sports. Quarter boots, also called overreach boots, are used on gaited horses, trotters, and pacers. They protect the quarter section of the front hoof from overreach injuries.

A recent innovation is a performance boot that encases the entire hoof. A ribbed sole adds traction, especially on ice. This style of boot can replace shoeing; it can be used when you wish to ride an unshod horse over uneven ground.

The Hufgrip boot also provides protection against ice and snow. Fabric-backed rubber shapes fit under the shoe to shape it to the foot.

Some boot styles combine protection and support. These fit snugly over the sesamoid area or tendons, and they aid the horse during hard work. The galloping boot resembles the shin and ankle boots, but it adds more padding inside to help support the horse's tendons.

The tendon boot features raised, shaped pads in its lining. These frame the tendons to create a supporting pressure during activity.

Tendon boots are made in both open-front and closed-front styles. Many jumper trainers prefer the open-front style. The design allows the horse to feel a pole when it raps it, which can increase the horse's respect for obstacles. Eventers, however, usually prefer the cushioning of the closed-front boot for protection over solid fences.

Another model of support boot is the sesamoid or rundown boot. These snugly fitted ankle boots help prevent stress on the sesamoid bones at the back of the fetlock, which may be fractured during hard work at speed.

Leg wraps also provide protection and support during performance. Polo wraps, designed for polo ponies, are also used in dressage schooling, reining, and cutting.

Shipping boots and standing bandages protect a horse's legs when it is in the van or stall. If you haul your horse frequently, or if it tends to scramble in the trailer, you should definitely use shipping boots every time you transport it. In a tight space, the horse is more likely to step on itself and possible become injured.

You can choose from lightweight boots for minimum protection or heavier models for greater coverage. Although shipping boots usually cover the length of the leg and the pasterns, many horsemen add bell boots when shipping to protect the hoof and coronet more fully.

Some bad haulers seem to enjoy kicking and striking in the trailer. If your horse does this, you may need to invest in knee or hock protectors. For the horse who kicks the tailgate, hock boots will guard against scrapes or capped hocks. Knee caps will protect the knees if the horse knocks its front legs while being trailered.

Most shipping boots don't add support. When your horse is vanned long distances, you might prefer to wrap stable bandages on all four legs for protection and support. Correctly applied, bandages can prevent swelling and ease the fatigue of traveling.

Bandaging is an art best learned by hands-on teaching. The bandage should be wound over layers of padding, usually sheet cotton or quilted pads, with even pressure. Improper bandaging — if bandages exert more pressure in certain areas of the leg — can damage the horse's tendons.

In the stall, some horses need to wear boots for protection. A horse who continually bruises its hocks or knees may need to wear boots full time.

Selecting Materials

You can pick boots of plastic, vinyl, leather, felt, suede, nylon, neoprene, or rubber. Many are separately lined with another material, usually felt, rubber, leather, plastic, or fleece, and some

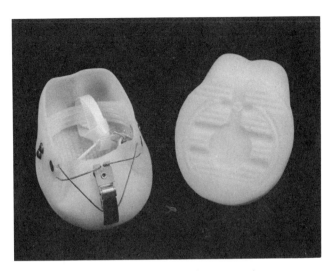

The sole of this vinyl boot provides traction while protecting the hoof. Courtesy Les-Kare Inc.

feature an inner layer of foam padding. Leg wraps are made from a variety of fabrics: cotton, polyester, and cotton/polyester blends.

In selecting materials, consider durability and comfort. Boots undergo a great deal of punishment, and they must withstand thousands of poundings, rubbings, and brushings. Padding must dissipate a blow over a broad area to lessen the chance of injury. Most splint boots add a outer leather splint guard to protect the sensitive splint area.

If your horse is going to wear boots for long periods of time, a soft, flexible wrap will feel better than a stiff leather one. Some durable materials don't breathe and will cause the horse to sweat underneath the boots.

Leather is a traditional, long-wearing material. Most leather boots are lined with a softer fabric. You can make leather boots more comfortable by softening them with saddle soap and leather treatment before your horse first wears them. Like shoes, leather boots will shape to the horse's leg after several uses. Cutters and reiners prefer the white leather or vinyl boots for competition use.

Easy-care synthetics have replaced leather in many styles of boot. You can choose soft, flexible fabrics such as neoprene or synthetic suede, or a stiffer plastic or vinyl. Some European boots have popularized a PVC foam lining, molded into a porous honeycomb texture. Plastics resist mold and bacteria, while retaining color, washability, and durable cushioning.

The open-front tendon boot supports the sides of the foreleg, leaving the front uncovered.

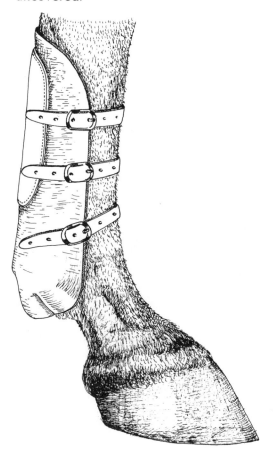

Fabrics such as felt, neoprene, and synthetic suede will snag loose vegetation and if you chose them, you may have to remove weeds and burrs from the edges of your boots after you ride through planted terrain.

Traditionally, boots fasten with straps and buckles, spaced along the boot's height. These can be made from leather or vinyl, to match the boot's material.

Handy Velcro straps have replaced buckled straps on many boots. Velcro closures exert even pressure over a broader area than straps. Although Velcro closures enable you to put boots on your horse more quickly, many horse-owners still prefer buckles. They claim that Velcro doesn't last long under hard use and that it gives way under stress. If you pick a boot or wrap with Velcro closures, look for wide, long sections.

Leather straps with buckles last a long time and can be maintained with proper care. They take longer to secure, but you can be confident that the boot will stay on your horse during your ride. Since each boot features at least two and even up to four straps, if one breaks, you can have it replaced later, and you will not lose the boot.

Some riders complain about boot buckles breaking and boots dislodging unexpectedly. However, before you blame your tack dealer, realize that the boot's materials must sustain a great deal of impact from the average horse. If kicked, a metal buckle may break or a leather strap tear. As one saddle-shop owner remarked, "You're dealing with a 1,000-pound animal that you can't reason with."

Bell boots secure either with Velcro or leather straps with buckles, or you can struggle with the pull-on type. The pull-on bell boots require expertise to slip over the hoof and onto the pastern. The first time you try it, you may question the possibility that they will stretch. Riders who prefer the pull-on style claim that because the bell boot is so close to the ground and is often stepped on, no closure will hold it onto the foot.

Selecting Fit

A boot must fit your horse snugly in order to remain effective. If it is too large, it will not stay in place. If it is too tight, it can interfere with circulation and the action of the horse's joints. A too-small boot may not even fit around your horse's foot or leg.

Sizes in boots are limited to small, medium, and large, and some come in only one standard size. You adjust the width to your horse's legs by the tension of the closures.

Fit depends on the horse's breed and the size of its leg and hoof. You will probably have to estimate which size to get, or you can ask the sales clerk for advice.

A new design in bell boots allows you to adjust one boot to fit all hooves. Plastic petals fasten together at the top to encircle the hoof. You can size the boot by adjusting how you fasten the petals. The separate petals flap up and down when the horse moves, however, which some people dislike.

Another innovation in bell boot fit is the no-turn bellboot, made of a tough vinyl. Its exterior shape, with four corners, resembles a cube more than a dome. Its felt lining features a nub at the heels, which keeps the back of the boot in place. The boot fits like a shoe. It does not spin, and the Velcro fasteners stay in front, over the horse's toe.

This "horse jogging shoe" has proven durable. Most bell boots fail when the horse steps on the Velcro fasteners and tears the stitching through the boot. When the Velcro remains in front, where it cannot be stepped on, it will resist wear much longer.

Also available in boot fasteners is a double-lock Velcro, with which you attach one loop section to a double-sided hook section and then fit the second loop strap over the top layer of the hook section. This design ensures a stronger fastener that is less likely to come apart under stress.

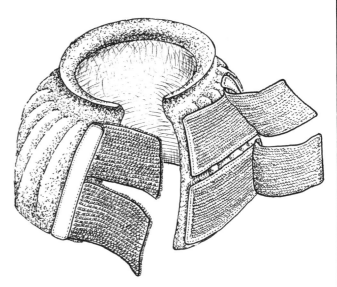

Rubber bell boots feature Velcro fasteners. Ribbed sides add strength.

An over-the-hoof boot must be sized correctly in order to remain in place. Courtesy Les-Kare Inc.

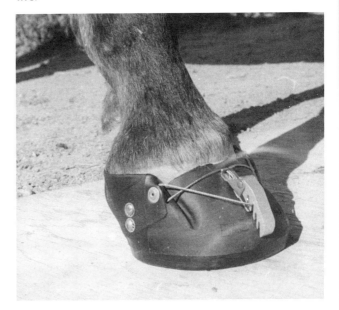

Inexpensive shipping boots of packcloth and polyester fleece feature three narrow Velcro fasteners for minimum protection.

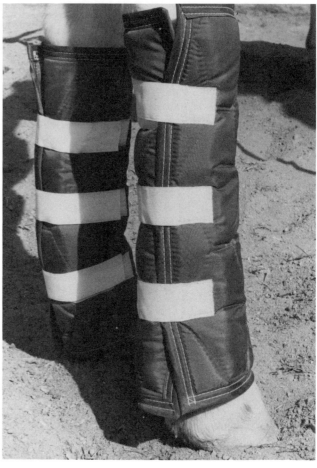

To protect the horse's legs, these nylon quilted shipping boots fit from the joint to mid-hoof.

When you put a pair of boots on your horse, make sure that you have the right and left boots on the correct legs. A performance boot that does not exactly fit will not remain in place. Buckled straps should always fit on the outside of the leg, with straps facing to the rear. Velcro straps usually wrap to the outside and rear also.

Boot height can vary, depending on whether the boot is designed to be used on the front or hind leg. Generally, boots intended for forelegs are slightly shorter than those meant for hind legs. Be sure that the top edge of a performance boot does not rub into a joint. Test the fit by bending your horse's knee or hock.

A shipping boot will measure about 16 inches high. The best ones feature four or five Velcro closures. The more closures, the less chance you take of the boot unfastening and slipping out of position. Closures should measure from 1 1/2 to 2 inches wide.

Quality shipping boots are contoured to fit each of the horse's four legs. Look for a boot sewn from two pieces, so that each side conforms to the shape of the leg. When you fit a set, determine which boot fits which leg. You might want to identify each one with a permanent felt-tip marker to save time in later uses.

Check the fit by trying to push the boot up and down and back and forth. You should be able to slide it up and down a little, but it shouldn't move sideways. Some riders adjust boots so that they can slide a finger between the boot and the back of the horse's leg.

Bandages and wraps measure from 4 to 6 inches wide. Most are 84 inches long, but some are as long as 108 inches. If the bandages are fitted with a Velcro strap on the end, look for a 2-inch width for greatest security.

Quality Craftsmanship

Look at how a boot's layers are joined. Stitching or bonding must resist abrasion and the constant stress of movement. Many fabric boots feature strong zigzag stitching over layers bonded together by adhesive.

If a performance boot features an overlaid cushion, check for sturdy topstitching. Because the padded area protrudes from the boot, it will receive most of the impact from the opposite hoof. Edges must be securely attached to prevent snags.

Compare two models by holding one in each hand. Feel the heft and the weight to calculate durability of craftsmanship, and the product that is probably stronger.

Quality Recommendations

You will find that many boots and bandages are not labeled with a brand name. Look for these

companies: Adams Equipment, Alprima, Hampa, Hinshaw, Josey, Kieffer, Ulster, and Woof.

Insiders' Preferences

• "People like the Ulster boots. Hampa is a good name, too. We buy a lot of boots from Champion Turf Equipment. Most are not marked, or marked with just a tiny stamp. The company doesn't do a lot of pushing of their brand." (Saddle-shop owner)

• "Wraps of Polarfleece insulate and maintain a steady body temperature. They measure 108 inches long, rather than the usual 84 inches." (Sales representative)

• "Ulster is the number-one brand. They have the best research and the best quality, and a good return policy. Everything I've seen from them is wonderful. It's high-priced, but worth it." (Saddle-shop owner)

• "I like the Legband polo wraps from Crump. They're a good Polarfleece fabric, wider than most. They stay flat and don't fray over time. The Miller's aren't as good—they don't give as good a wrap. When they fray at the ends, it causes an uneven pull." (Saddle-shop owner)

• "The Sympatex brand from DMS is moldproof, antibacterial, and cushiony, with four vinyl straps with buckle closures. They are shaped at the bottom to conform to the foot." (Sales representative)

• "Bar-F started the new no-turn design in bell boots. They fit so well, like a jogging shoe, and they're thick protection on a horse that hits itself. But, the straight bell-boot market can't accept the unusual shape. Hunt-seat riders won't accept them until Hampa makes one! They are better than the

Westropp—it's a gimmicky version of the bell boot that sold because it came in so many colors." (Saddle-shop owner)

• "Riders who like the natural boot next to the horse's legs choose the Euro-Protective, leather with a felt lining. They are a lot of work. You've got to oil the leather and brush the dried sweat off the felt. The felt absorbs water and the leather stretches, so they're not good for cross-country. I recommend to buy any leather boot small to start with, because they all stretch." (Saddle-shop owner)

• "Royal Riders are good middle-of-the-road neoprene splint boots." (Saddle-shop owner)

"I prefer the DMS boots to Hampa or Ulster. They all use the same materials. When the materials and stitching compare, I choose the heaviest boot for durability. DMS is heavier than the others. Also, I find Ulster higher priced." (Saddle-shop owner)

• "The Polarfleece wraps of Dacron cost more than Vac's, also a good product from a New Jersey mill. The Polarfleece are thicker, with nap on both sides. The choice depends on your application. But, for heavy use, get the heaviest fabric to withstand abuse better." (Saddle-shop owner)

• "We sell Ulster boots to lower level eventers. It's not going to absorb water cross-country. Once they get to three-day eventing, they go to the strap buckle, the leather boots. Those stay on better in rugged cross-country, where you might have to tape the Ulsters to make them stay on. Because the price on German boots has gone high, the neoprene boots have made a comeback, made in the United States for half the price." (Saddle-shop owner)

• "Wade no-turn bell boots strap in front with

Velcro. The vinyl exterior won't tear." (Sales representative)

• "Bar-F makes excellent black rubber bell boots with double Velcro." (Saddle-shop owner)

• "Dry Creek boots are a Cordura nylon with a brushed synthetic lining. They're very lightweight and don't absorb water. The ropers and reiners love them, but not the hunter/jumper and dressage people." (Saddle-shop owner)

Maintenance

Boots absorb a great deal of the terrain you cross, including mud, sand, water, and gravel. Sweat also soaks into the lining, so clean your boots often. You can wash most materials (with the exception of leather), either by soaking them in a bucket or by tossing them in the washing machine.

Treat leather surfaces the same as you would any other leather tack. Oil the boots to increase the protection of the exterior, and brush clean the inner linings.

The edges of boots must resist abrasion. Edges usually show wear first, by tearing or deteriorating. Repair rips as soon as you discover them, before the boot rips more. A tack or shoe-repair shop can usually stitch leather or fabric boots.

Questions

• Is the style suitable for your activity?
• Will the boot remain in place?
• Are the materials suitable for your riding environment?
• Can you put the boots on your horse easily and quickly?

Chapter 27

MISCELLANEOUS CLOTHING

In addition to blankets and boots, you can clothe your horse in other garments to maintain its beauty or protect it from injury. These include sweat wraps, mane tamers, tail wraps, and head bumpers.

Basic Design

Many show-horse trainers use the neck sweat and the jowl wrap, especially with breeds on which a thin neck and throatlatch are considered attractive. Although breeds such as the Arabian and Saddlebred popularized these wraps, they are also customary on many Morgans, Quarter Horses, Paints, and Appaloosas.

These heat-producing wraps function like the rubberized sweat suits worn by human athletes, retaining heat against the skin. During exercise, the wrap encourages heavy sweat and removes excess fluid from the skin's cells.

Sweating the neck and throatlatch benefits the appearance of stallions, which tend to develop thick necks. The neck sweat is also thought to help performance horses by slimming their throatlatches so they may breathe more easily and flex more at the poll.

A neck sweat covers the neck, beginning just behind the ears and ending at the withers. The jowl wrap covers a smaller area, usually just the throatlatch and the top of the neck behind the poll. This band builds a constant warmth rather than intense heat for a short period.

Depending on your goal, you can pick from a variety of other sweating garments. There are several sizes of neck wraps: ones to fit just the throatlatch, ones to fit the throatlatch and halfway down the neck, the full neck wrap, the neck and throat-

Waiting for a class, this filly wears a nylon show cooler with an attached mane tamer.

latch wrap, and ones to fit from the neck to the shoulders.

A larger jowl wrap, the Scotch hood, fits above the eyes and over the jawbones. The jowl hood covers the entire head except for the muzzle, eyes, and ears.

Other combination wraps are the full face and neck wrap and the head, neck, and shoulder wrap. Be aware that manufacturers will describe wraps differently, with no standard terminology. Verify the design by inspecting it before purchase.

If you wish to affect only the shoulders and chest, you can buy a shoulder wrap. Or, you can go for the full body wrap to encourage all-over slimming. Sweating off excess weight will result in clearly defined muscles that appear closest to the skin's surface. Because this can "bake" a horse into a lean, breedy look, most showpeople reserve full body wraps for halter horses.

A recent innovation is the electrified sweat wrap, which combines a neck wrap with a blow dryer. The dryer attaches above the horse's neck to blow hot air into the wrap. Experts note that this tool is effective in producing a fast (fifteen-minute) sweating, but that it can be hazardous. If you utilize this unit, be sure to monitor its operation constantly in order to avoid burning the horse's skin.

A neck wrap will help train a mane to lie flat on one side of the neck. Or, you can use a mane tamer, sometimes called a mane trainer. This lightweight wrap is attached to covers the entire mane, The slight pressure forces the mane hairs close against the neck.

The tail wrap is shaped to encase the top of the tail to encourage the hairs to lie flat. It also protects the tail from rubbing against a trailer or van's bar or chain during shipping. Tail wraps are also often placed over show horses' braided tails for protection when they not performing.

The head bumper is a "hard hat" for your horse to wear during shipping to protect its poll. It features slots, through which the halter crownpiece

threads to secure the helmet, and cutouts, through which the ears protrude. Use this protective device if your horse tends to carry its head high or if you must use a low-ceilinged transport.

Selecting Materials

Materials of wraps vary according to the purpose of the garment. The jowl wrap is fabricated from natural or manmade fabrics, with the most common style being a leather strap lined with sheepskin, polyester fleece, or felt. You can also select models made of wool knit, synthetic "hospital" felt, or nylon web lined with fleece over a foam layer.

Jowl wraps may allow the skin to breathe. However, garments that encourage heavier sweating, usually during exercise, are made from nonporous fabrics that create more intense heat.

Neoprene is the most common sweat-wrap material, although you will also see wraps from woven polyethylene and vinyl-coated nylon. Neoprene retains heat and conforms to the shape of the animal. It is usually laminated to a durable nylon exterior.

Neoprenes do vary, so look for a thicker, denser fabric if you desire more heat retention. The closed-cell neoprene will perform better, but it is more expensive than the more common open-cell construction. The neoprene wrap should stretch somewhat, to adjust to the movement of the horse, but it should not stretch out of shape after use.

Velcro straps are stitched along the edges of the wrap to fasten it onto the horse. A recent innovation, which eliminates the Velcro hook and loop sections, features neoprene laminated with a special fabric that fastens to Velcro hook sections. You can apply the Velcro sections anywhere on the wrap to get an exact custom fit—they are not stitched in place.

The mane tamer is made of nylon mesh, and usually has three Velcro straps. Some models add a longer strap at the withers, which secures around the girth.

Select a tail wrap of neoprene or vinyl. Be sure that the material does not irritate the sensitive skin under the tail.

Head bumpers are made of thick felt with a leather covering; 1/2-inch molded vinyl; or thick, high-impact foam with a vinyl coating.

Selecting Fit

A wrap must be the right size and shape to achieve the desired results. Manufacturers usually offer from three to five sizes, ranging through youngsters' sizes from extra-small to yearling, and horse sizes from average to extra-large.

Using the jowl wrap to control fatty tissue is a simple process. Fit the band over the jowl area and fasten it snugly so that it remains in place.

Test the fit by encouraging the horse to lower, raise, and stretch its neck. The wrap should not shift, yet it should bend enough to allow normal breathing, easy swallowing, and comfortable movement.

Fitting a sweat wrap involves more planning, as you will not leave this garment on continuously. Most users fit the wrap before exercise and remove it after the horse has cooled.

Most people who use sweat wraps enhance the wrap's effect by first applying a heat-producing lotion to the horse's skin. You can use a commercial product or mix your own liquid. Glycerin is a favorite of many grooms; others prefer a strong mouthwash, or alcohol mixed with glycerin.

Use a lotion that has been tested for possible skin irritation. Spray or rub it onto the skin, then adjust the wrap. A neck wrap should fit tightly at the base of the neck, without sliding to one side. When the horse drops its head, the wrap should not bend and flop forward.

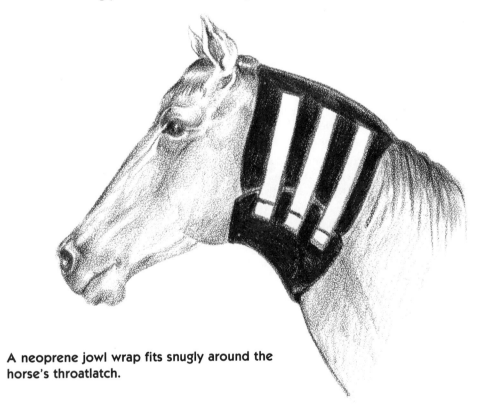

A neoprene jowl wrap fits snugly around the horse's throatlatch.

A sweat wrap should have at least four Velcro fasteners, a Scotch hood four or five, and a shoulder wrap six. Straps should be long enough to allow for a range of width adjustments, and they should measure at least 1 1/2 inches wide.

When you exercise your horse in a sweat wrap, watch that the reins or the longe line do not become caught under the Velcro fasteners. After the exercise, cool the horse out gradually and then blanket it and put it in its stall. Later, remove the blanket and wrap and rinse off the skin to prevent irritation.

Excessive sweating can be hazardous to your horse. Check its skin for dehydration by pinching it on the neck or shoulder. If it doesn't immediately retract into place, your horse may be dehydrated, and you must replace vital fluids (see a veterinary manual for additional information).

The mane tamer can be a frustrating device to keep in position. Manufacturers offer it in weanling, yearling, and horse sizes, but it always seems to slide forward or shift to the side. The girth strap helps remedy this problem.

A tail wrap should fit snugly, without exerting uneven pressure on the tail. You can use a cotton standing or track bandage, or you can buy a form-fitted wrap that fastens with Velcro. Look for the Velcro to be stitched in place vertically, which will resist accidental unfastening. The wrap should measure about 15 to 18 inches in length.

You will find only one size of head bumper. In most cases, young horses and ponies are not tall enough to need this protection.

Features

Some shoulder wraps feature a surcingle, which wraps around the horse's heartgirth to secure the garment. Because this surcingle could become snagged on a fence, you should look for one with a breakaway construction.

Another feature found on neck sweats is a short elastic strap that connects between the bottom of the sweat and either a surcingle, day sheet, or saddle pad. This 18-inch strap, fitted with a snap on both ends, will help keep the sweat in place during exercise or when the horse is in its stall.

You could also connect this strap between the top of a tail wrap and a sheet or blanket. The slight tautness will exert an upward pressure on the tail wrap, maintaining its position.

Quality Craftsmanship and Recommendations

Study the garment's construction. Flex the material to inspect how the stitches and fasteners absorb stress. Most garments fail when stitching tears.

Feel the density of the fabric, and look at how layers are joined. The more secure the bonding, the longer the item will last.

Some recommended brands are Slym-Line, SuperSweats, and Wrip Wrap.

Maintenance

Wash all fabric garments regularly, especially the sweat wraps. A dirty wrap can irritate the skin. After washing rinse the garment thoroughly to remove all traces of soap.

Questions

- Will the sweat wrap or mane tamer remain in place?
- Do you need to use lotions with the sweat wrap?
- How long should you leave the wrap in place?
- Is the head bumper thick enough to protect your horse?

PART VI:

BARN
EQUIPMENT

Chapter 28

GROOMING PRODUCTS

The grooming equipment you use falls into two broad categories: everyday cleaning supplies and special-event polishing equipment. Both categories include tools and horse-care products.

(For detailed information on using these products, refer to *Show Grooming: The Look of a Winner* [Breakthrough, 1987].

Tools

The most basic grooming tools are the standard combs and brushes seen in every tack room. The currycomb is probably the first tool you pick up to groom your horse. Its teeth rub the coat, usually against the lay of the hair, to loosen surface dirt and to rough up sweaty hair so that it can dry.

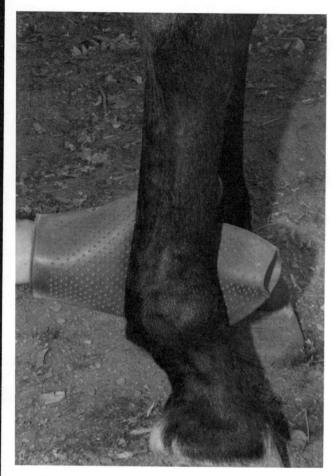

You can mold the rubber curry mitt around the contours of the leg.

Most currycombs are round or oval-shaped, designed to fit your hand. The flexible curry mitt is a rubber mitt with hundreds of raised nubs to massage your horse's skin that encases your entire hand. Some mitts feature a soft brush on one side.

Other currycombs are the square-shaped metal bar curry, and the rounded spring curry. A specialized metal style is the shedding blade, which is a flexible blade with teeth along one side. As you pull the tool across the horse's winter coat, the

teeth remove loose hair and accelerate the shedding process. One version of the shedding blade combines a blade with teeth as an inner row on a standard oval currycomb.

You can also use a cactus cloth or mitt as a flexible curry. You can wad the cloth into a ball, or fold it into a square. It will clean, shine, and massage the coat.

Brushes consist of a solid block with rows of bristles attached to one side. Most owners select at least two brushes, one firm and one soft. The dandy brush, often termed a mud brush, has stiff fibers for vigorous brushing. Some grooms use this tool instead of a currycomb.

Two other commonly used brushes are the all-purpose brush and the finishing brush. The all-purpose brush resembles the dandy brush, but has softer bristles. The finishing brush features very soft, flexible bristles. These sweep any remaining surface dirt from the coat's surface and help lay down the coat. With a sensitive horse, the finishing brush might be the only brush you would use on its face.

In another style of brush, the body brush, medium-firm bristles of a shorter length are set closely together on a flat base. This model is designed to be used after the curry or dandy brush. It massages the skin while you remove dirt and loose hair.

For a final shine, use the traditional stable rubber to wipe your horse's coat. Or, you can polish the coat with the cactus cloth.

Your basic hoof-cleaning tools are the hoof pick and a stiff brush. You can choose from the traditional one-piece model, combining pick and handle in one unit, a pick attached to a separate handle, or a compact folding pick.

A pick should be shaped so that you can pry loose any debris that is packed into the hoof. Look for a tip that is squared off, like a screwdriver. This shape will safely work under the packed dirt, manure, or rocks, without accidentally puncturing the horse's sole, frog, or heel.

Use a hoof brush to remove loose dirt and dried mud from both the sole and wall. One model of hoof pick features a pick on top and a brush underneath.

For other than basic cleaning, you need specialized items. When your horse is sweaty after exercise, you can wash him and then use a sweat scraper to scrape off the water and excess perspiration. This blade can look like a firm stick, with a channel running down one side, or it can be a flexible blade with a handle at each end. Many owners buy the combination shedding blade and sweat scraper, a blade that features one smooth edge and one with serrated teeth.

You should not need to buy too much equipment to bathe your horse. You can dedicate sponges for this purpose, either the natural or synthetic varieties. You can use a scrub-and-groom mitt for deep-down shampooing, or you can try a special wash curry. This model has an attachment on one end that allows you to connect a hose to the curry.

One final grooming item that you may need is the bot-egg scraper. During botfly season, tiny yellow eggs often appear on the hairs of your horse's legs, chest, and barrel. Unless you remove these eggs, your horse may ingest them and harbor the harmful bots internally.

To remove bot eggs, manufacturers have improved on the old standby, the single-edged razor blade. You can buy a special bot-egg knife, or use a grooming block, a rough-edged cube, to rub off the eggs. Both tools have proved safer than the razor blade; using them there will be less chance of your accidentally cutting yourself or your horse.

Many owners are satisfied with just cleaning their horses. For that out-of-the-ordinary look, you may want to take the time to add extra polish with further grooming.

To shape the mane, tail, and forelock, you can use a mane comb to separate the strands of hair. If the hairs are tangled, use a brush to handle snarls.

A metal pulling comb is a tool designed to remove a few hairs at a time. You can buy a combination comb and knot remover, which features multiple rows of teeth. Or, you can try a thinning knife or stripping comb, both of which feature sharp teeth to comb out and cut excess hairs.

Products

Manufacturers have developed a variety of equine beauty products. Some benefit the horse's well-being, while others are targeted to please the horsekeeper's pride of ownership.

For example, hoof-care products feature both useful moisturizers and beautifying polishes. Professionals debate the actual benefits of hoof moisturizers, with manufacturers' claims differing from medical opinion. Advocates affirm that the hoof will absorb topical applications. Others feel that moisture penetrates only at the coronary band, or that hoof health originates with the animal's diet.

Despite the controversy, most horse owners do apply hoof dressings. You can choose from ointments, salves, lotions, and oils. When selecting a brand, consult your farrier and veterinarian for recommendations. Read the labels to decide which type your horse needs. Some claim to moisturize by penetrating the hoof, seeping through soles, walls, and heel. Others promise to nourish the hoof and stimulate growth. More modest claims are made by those products purporting to aid the hoof in moisture retention.

Although you should clean your horse's hooves often, polishing is only for show. You brush on hoof polish for a glossy surface, which dresses up your horse's appearance. You can buy polish in black, brown, or clear tones. Black looks best on dark hooves, although many exhibitors also use it on white hooves. Usually a shade that matches the leg color will achieve a leggier look.

Another product category is skin preparations: shampoos, conditioners, and coat dressings. As in human cosmetics, there is quite an errray of brands and promises.

A quality shampoo should clean the skin and hair without drying the skin. It should remove surface dirt, stains, and any loose skin or dandruff.

Special conditioners and rinses will make your horse's mane and tail shiny and fluffy. Some coat dressings will help untangle a mane and tail, without shampooing.

For an all-over show-ring glow, you can apply a coat dressing, conditioner, or treatment. You can spray the lotion onto the coat or rub it in with a damp towel.

Materials and Craftsmanship of Tools

Currycomb are made from rubber or plastic, in either firm or flexible styles. Metal curries can be stiff or springy. Generally, the rubber and plastic currycombs are gentler on your horse's skin, but the teeth or nubs will wear smooth with use. The stronger metal teeth work better to break up caked mud. A rubber curry mitt will easily bend over the contours of the horse's body.

Check that a cactus cloth is the authentic maguey plant. Edges should be salvaged so that the loose weave does not unravel.

Brush fibers can be vegetable, animal hair, or synthetic strands. Some grooms claim that the vegetable bristles clean better than the synthetics. The horsehair brush is the softest, while pig bristles are strongest for deep-down cleaning.

Look at a brush's construction. Clumps of bristles should be firmly attached to the back of the brush. An open-backed model displays bristles looped through holes and wired into place. Other styles screw a two-part base into position, locking bristles between the parts.

The block of a brush will be either wood or a hard molded plastic. Look for a maple or hardwood back, coated with a finish to protect it from water. Without a finish, water can rot the wood so that it warps and eventually separates.

Choose a hoof pick cast from zinc or steel. For comfort, select one with a vinyl grip or a wooden handle. Avoid plastic picks, which break easily.

The aluminum mane comb will usually outlast one made of polypropylene. The plastic teeth will flex, but they can break off in tangles of hair. In a pulling comb, look for sharp edges at the base of the teeth so that you can easily remove unwanted hairs.

Selecting Appropriate Tools

Which tools you select does not affect your horse, as long as they feel comfortable on its skin. However, choosing the right utensil can affect your grooming efficiency. The easier you can handle a tool, the better and faster job you can do.

Because tools fit into your hand, look for a comfortable match. You will soon tire of stretching your fingers to grasp a too-large brush or curry. Some manufacturers offer child-sized tools.

Pick up a curry and feel how your hand cups its top. Most styles measure about 3 by 5 inches. If it has a hand strap, how is the strap attached? Riveted web straps will tear, and some plastic straps will crack and rip. Some plastic straps feature adjustments, so that you can fit the tool to your hand. A finger guard, a raised section on the comb's top, helps you hold the currycomb to exert pressure.

Look at the currycomb's teeth to check the shape, length, and the distance between teeth. You want the comb to collect dirt and hair, but you do not want the aggravation of having to pull collected hairs from the teeth after every stroke.

Brushes range from 2 1/2 to 5 inches wide, and from 5 1/2 to almost 10 inches long. The larger the brush, the greater the area you will clean in each stroke.

On most solid-backed brushes, each side contains depressions for your fingers. These allow you to hold the brush comfortably. A brush with a hand strap will usually feature a thinner base, without these depressions.

Bristles measure from 1 to 2 inches long. Look at the thickness of a single fiber when matching a brush to your grooming needs.

With other tools, consider if you prefer a one- or two-handed task. For example, you can buy a sweat scraper with a single handle, or the style that requires you to hold a hand on each end to control the flexible blade. Some flexible-blade models feature a strap on one end so that the ends can be attached for one-handed use.

Some mane combs feature an attached wooden handle, measuring about 4 inches long. You might find it easier to hold this tool than the comb without a handle. However, if the handle twists loose or your hand slips, you can hit yourself in the face with the comb's teeth.

Finally, when choosing a grooming mitt, test it by inserting your hand. The mitt will be difficult to use if your hand slides around inside the glove.

Quality Craftsmanship and Recommendations

Many grooming tools do not add brand names, so rely on your dealer's recommendations. Two reputable companies are Partrade and Wright-Bernet. For products, the following companies manufacture reliable items: Absorbine, Alto Lab, Exhibitor Labs, Farnam Company, and Ultra Grooming Products.

Maintenance

If you have acquired a collection of tools and products, store your stock in a cabinet or tack box. Use a plastic or wooden tote to carry your daily supplies.

Clean brushes and combs occasionally. Wash bristles in a bowl of warm water, with a teaspoon of salt added. Don't immerse wooden handles, as wood will rot from dampness. Dry brushes bristles down. Treat leather-backed brushes with saddle soap.

It is wise to disinfect your tools if you share equipment with other horses, or your horse suffers a skin irritation. You can saturate items with Lysol disinfectant, rinse them well, and air dry them in sunlight.

Questions

- Is a tool's texture compatible with your horse's coat?
- Are products nonallergenic?

Chapter 29

—

CLIPPERS

Even if you just ride for pleasure, you can utilize electric clippers for a quick, easy trim. Clippers are ideal for both trims and all-over clipping.

Basic Design

All clippers consist of a cylindrical body, designed to fit easily into the palm of your hand. The appliance contains a small motor, which converts electrical energy into mechanical energy to vibrate the steel cutting blades. The cord of the appliance plugs into a standard AC outlet, and you control it by turning the power switch on and off.

Clipper blades contain two elements: a top—or inner—blade and a bottom

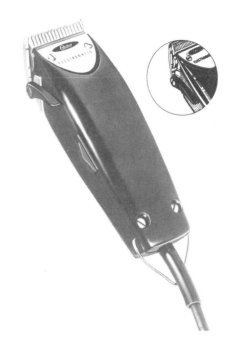

—or outer—blade. The cutting edge of each blade holds a row of steel teeth. When you maneuver the blades along the animal's coat, the teeth of the bottom blade act as a comb to hold hairs in place. The teeth of the top blade move back and forth across the bottom blade, cutting the tips of the hairs.

You can choose from among three sizes of animal clippers: small, medium, and large. The small and large models are intended for specific types of clipping, while the medium can be substituted for either.

Small clippers are often called trimmers or ear clippers. Primarily intended for use on the animal's face, these lightweight appliances feature less powerful motors than the other two sizes. A trimmer may also feature a magnetic or pivot motor. In the magnetic motor, the top blade is pulled from side to side by magnetic force and gravity. A pivot motor is more powerful, with the blade operating in a dual power stroke, or pushed and pulled across the bottom blade.

Although the trimmer cuts hairs more slowly than the other clipper types, its quiet motor is a definite advantage when you need to trim around a horse's eyes, ears, or muzzle.

Medium clippers are the most popular choice of many grooms. The best-known brand offers two models, both with a sturdy universal motor. This motor features an electromagnetic rotor (consisting of armature windings and a commutator) along with brushes to generate power, and its manufacturer claims it is the standard of the clipper industry. The motor powers the blades to run from 1,700 to 2,500 cycles per minute (CPM).

In addition to its durability, the medium-size clipper is versatile due to its interchangeable blades. You can choose from many sizes of blades, from those designed to clip a fast, coarse trim to those for a slower, surgically close shave.

Large animal clippers are built for heavy-duty cutting. These feature a large motor and blades, and a built-in fan helps cool the machine. You

Use a small clipper for face and leg trimming. Courtesy Oster.

The medium clipper is an all-purpose appliance.

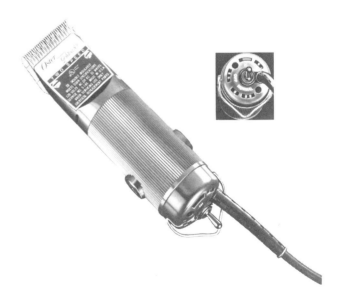

receive a standard pair of top and bottom blades with the machine.

The most expensive model features a variable speed switch. This allows you to control the clipping. For more precise work on a nervous horse, you can slow the speed to a quieter clip of 700 CPM. If you are in a hurry to complete the job, you can adjust the blades to cut as fast as 3,100 CPM.

A few recent developments have occurred in clippers. Some grooms like the flexibility of the cordless models. These are currently available only in the small trimmer style, so they are limited to facial touch-ups.

A recent design in body clippers is a model with a separate motor. The body of the clipper connects to the 1/8-horsepower motor with a twenty-foot cable. By being separate from the power source, the clipping unit stays cool and the motor's noise, even at 3,500 CPM, is less distracting to the horse. This machine uses the standard medium clipper blades.

Although electric clippers produce superior results, sometimes you may prefer to use a hand-operated clipping instrument. If you need to trim only a small section of hair, the fetlock clipper is an inexpensive alternative. This machine consists of two cutting blades that move back and forth as you squeeze the handle.

You can also try fetlock shears, a pair of scissors with blades that are curved to conform to the shape of the fetlock. However, you must have a steady hand and a quiet horse to use these safely, because you could easily puncture the horse's skin. Avoid using regular scissors, which are more difficult to control.

Some show grooms use a disposable razor for last-minute muzzle trimming. This tool is easy to use and cuts protruding whiskers efficiently. As with any razor, use it with care to avoid nicking your horse's skin.

Selecting Materials and Style

With a limited choice of clippers available from few manufacturers, you will encounter clippers made with only plastic and metal parts. Larger clippers feature metal bodies. Some medium and small machines have bodies of a tough plastic. This reduces weight, making the clippers easier to hold. Some grooms also feel that the plastic housing will not conduct heat as quickly as metal will.

A trimmer weighs from 19 to 24 ounces and will fit comfortably in the palm of your hand. Medium clippers can weigh from 20 to 24 ounces, measuring about 8 inches long and 2 inches in diameter.

Large animal clippers are the heavyweights, weighing almost five pounds. If you have weak wrists and small hands, you may need to hold this appliance with two hands. The machine is about 13 inches long and 3 inches in diameter.

Match a clipper's motor and blades to your task. When you choose the right tool, you will work more efficiently to complete a superior grooming job.

You can use a more powerful motor for a light-duty task, such as using a body clipper to trim a bridle path. However, you should not expect a lightweight trimmer to perform a body clip or to cut through a heavy winter coat.

Many people select certain clippers for their blade adjustments. Professional grooms are like photographers, who match specific lenses to each job, in that they prefer certain blade sizes for different cuts.

Small clippers are equipped with one set of blades, but many models feature a lever that adjusts the depth of the cut. Look for a blade that can be moved from close to medium trim, or from fine to coarse cutting. Although clipper blades cannot be interchanged with those of other size clippers, all clippers permit the removal of blades for sharpening or replacement.

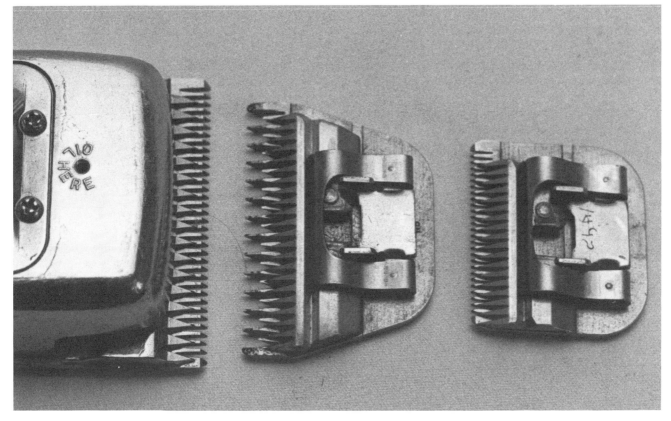

Three clipper blades: left, large animal clippers, middle, wide blade of medium clipper; right, regular blade of medium clipper.

Medium clippers offer the greatest range of blades. For the most popular model, you can select among eighteen different blades of fine-grain, high-carbon steel. Each is a one-piece unit that simply snaps in and out of the clipper head.

The interchangeable blades are made to fit into a specific clipper model. Each size is numbered, with the largest numbers containing the greatest number of teeth across the blade. These will produce the finest and closest cut. For instance, the size 40 blade is intended for surgical shaving, producing a cut of only 1/125 inch. One size bigger is the 30, for close cutting (1/100 inch) with-

out a shaved look. The 15 blade produces a medium-close length of 3/64 inch, which is recommended for trimming the animal's face, muzzle, and ears. This blade is considered the most versatile, because you can control the depth of the cut by angling the clipper blades against the skin.

A coarser blades is the 10, for medium-length (1/16-inch) hair. This blade will not affect the horse's color as much as the finer blades, since the hair is left slightly longer. The 8-1/2 blade leaves hair about 1/4 inch long and the 7 blade 1/8 inch. For longer coats, choose either the 4 or 5, which will result in hair from 3/8 to 1/4 inch long.

All of the above blades will cut with or against the grain of the hair. Realize that you cut closer when you aim the blade against the grain. Going with the grain can approximately double the above hair lengths, depending on the angle at which you hold the blades.

A recent innovation is the wider blade for the medium clipper. Measuring almost as large as the large clipper blades, this size allows you to clip a broader area in each stroke. It transforms a medium clipper into a body clipper, for medium or coarse clips.

The pair of blades on the large animal clippers produce a coarse cut equal to the 8-1/2 blade of the medium clippers. Two additional blade sets are available, one to produce a 3/8-inch clip, and the other to produce a surgical shave as close as .002 inch.

Quality Craftsmanship and Recommendations

Animal clippers are not fancy appliances. You will find that there is little choice among brands, with only four domestic manufacturers. Although all offer quality machines, most grooms choose the Oster or Sunbeam brands. These designs have been on the market for many years and will prove satisfactory for decades.

Maintenance

Clippers usually fail due to user error—either from ignorance, abuse, or forgetfulness. First, avoid clipping a dirty horse. Dust, hair, and encrusted mud will dull the edges of the teeth. The pressure of pushing through these obstructions will also cause the motor to overheat.

Always plug the cord into a grounded outlet. If you must use an extension cord, be sure it is a heavy-duty type in good condition.

Avoid overheating the machine. Do not press the clippers against the hair; allow the blades to slide through the hairs slowly while you guide the body of the machine. Holding the clippers level with a light, even pressure will result in a more even cut. Brush loose hair out of the way to avoid clogging the blades.

Any electric clipper's motor and blades will become hot over a period of time. Safeguard both the appliance and your horse's skin by cooling the machine. In a shallow can or dish, pour a small amount of commercial blade cleaner, kerosene, or a mixture of kerosene and oil. Periodically dip the whirring blades (not the body of the clippers) into this solution to cool them and flush out accumulated hairs; then switch off the appliance and wipe the residue from the blades. Carefully slide the two blades apart so you can lubricate between the bases. Apply a drop of oil on each end of the solid metal, not on the teeth.

You can also spray the blades with a commercial blade coolant. Or, take a break and let the clippers cool for at least fifteen minutes.

Don't forget to service your clippers. Follow the manufacturer's directions on lubricating the machine. Brush or blow out loose hairs after each use. If you use your clippers often, schedule a professional checkup at least once a year at an authorized service center (or contact a small-appliance repairman to clean and grease the machine).

Clean and oil the blades after you have finished clipping. You can wipe off all loose hairs with an oiled toothbrush. If blades seem to lose their cutting power, have them sharpened by a professional. With average use (once a month), blades should be sharpened every year or two.

Never hold the machine by its power cord, and be sure to disconnect it by pulling the plug, not the cord. Always switch off the motor before you unplug the clippers. If you wrap the cord around the body of the machine, leave a short loop near the base so that the cord is not pulled away from the motor.

Whenever you handle the machine, set it down carefully. If you drop it, the impact will probably break one or more teeth of the blades, which ruins the cutting action.

Small clippers feature a ring at the bottom, which allows you to hang the machine from a hook. When you hang the appliance with the blades pointing downward, the heated motor oil will drip out from the blades, not back into the motor.

Store clippers in a warm, dry location. You can buy a clipper tote bag to fit the large clippers, with separate pockets for the blades. Or, keep them in a hard-sided carrying case, with interior compartments for blades and cleaning gear. You can also use a small plastic tool box or art box.

Questions

- Is the motor's power sufficient?
- Are the blades matched to the task?
- How noisy is the appliance?
- Is the cord long enough?
- Do the clippers feel comfortable in your hand?

Chapter 30

—

MEDICAL SUPPLIES

Every horsekeeper should stock basic medical supplies to provide on-site treatment of minor problems. Although you should not attempt to replace your veterinarian, you can assist by combatting simple crises as they arise.

Remember that key medical guideline: "First, do no harm." Stock only those products that you know how to use, and that your equine practitioner recommends. Improper treatments could cause more damage to your horse than no treatment at all.

In general, you will treat four categories: wounds, irritation, lameness, or illness.

Wound Care

Here your task is to stop any bleeding and clean the wounded area. Unless the wound requires professional attention, you will apply topical medication.

A compress or pressure bandage is designed to be used directly on a wound site to stop bleeding. A pressure bandage can be several sterile gauze squares or Telfa pads wrapped securely in place with rolls of cotton or gauze, then taped. Or, you could wrap a pressure bandage with Vetrap or cotton standing bandages. For minor bleeding, a blood-stopping powder can sometimes be a substitute for pressure.

Clean the area of a wound by washing it well with water or hydrogen peroxide. Some experts recommend the antiseptic Betadine as a scrub. Wipe out all dirt and hair with sterile cotton balls soaked in water.

After cleaning a minor wound, select the right topical application. For a superficial cut, you can pick a drying agent to disinfect and encourage development of a scab. Useful products include gentian violent or gentle iodine, either in liquid or spray form, or a nitrofurazone powder. These products cover a minor wound with a protective film.

Treat a deeper, unsutured laceration differently. You must prevent a scab from forming too soon, because healing should occur from the inside out. Use a moisture-producing medication, such as scarlet oil or an antibacterial ointment. Lanolin is a popular ingredient, and some people like creams or ointments containing aloe vera.

Ointments are good for abrasions, too. Some salves and ointments also contain a fly-repelling ingredient to protect a wound from insects.

For a wound on a joint such as the fetlock or hock, apply a moisturizing ointment to keep the area flexible as it heals. Good choices would be lanolin-based salves or zinc-oxide lotions.

Prevent a wound from developing proud flesh by switching from a drying or moisturizing product to a caustic powder during the healing process. It is best to wait until the wound is fully filled in with new tissue before applying this powder.

A puncture caused by a nail or sharp object can be cleaned with hydrogen peroxide. Treat a sole punctured by a nail by pouring strong tincture of iodine into the hole after you pull the nail. (And be sure your horse is current with its tetanus shots.)

Treating Irritations

You may need to treat irritations of your horse's skin, hooves, or eyes. For skin problems, you can choose a fungicide or gall salve. A fungicide combats hair loss and restores skin condition. Gall salve heals sores caused by the rubbing of a girth or harness.

Thrush should be treated promptly and regularly until it is controlled. You can purchase lotions made specifically for this condition, or use a multi-purpose wound medication.

For a minor eye irritation, wash the horse's eye and apply a mild boric acid solution of one ounce mixed in a pint of water. Or, use a special eye solution.

Preventing and Treating Lameness

Horses that work hard or tend to have swollen legs may demand daily attention, depending on their medical history. Tools for nonemergency leg care include topical applications and bandages.

To maintain sound legs, you can use lotions that reduce inflammation by slowing down or speeding up the circulation of the blood: the brace or the liniment.

In general, a brace or "freeze" cools the legs. When you massage the liquid or gel into the skin, it reduces heat and minor swellings.

A liniment is a counterirritant, considered stronger than a brace in its effect. This product induces inflammation by creating heat. As circulation increases, soreness may be relieved. Liniment may also prevent a horse from stocking up, or becoming swollen while standing in its stall.

You can heighten each product's effect by brisk rubbing. The liquid should penetrate quickly and completely, without irritating the skin or causing hair loss.

Some leg-care products function as both a brace and a liniment—first acting to cool the leg, then heating it. Other brands include antiseptic and anesthetic ingredients to relieve soreness while reducing swelling.

You might notice other leg-care products at the tack shop, such as tighteners, paints, and blisters. Each is designed to treat a specific unsoundness, and you should use them only upon the advice of your horse-care professional.

For the most effective prevention of swelling, you may wish to wrap the horse's legs. You can wrap legs either after massaging them with liniment, soaking or hosing them with cold water, or without any prior treatment.

Stable bandages will function both as support and to retain the effect of a liquid. You will apply two items to each leg: a padding and a securing bandage.

The padding inside the bandage retains cold or warmth, absorbs medication, and protects the leg from injury, chafing, or pressure of the bandage. You can buy sheet cotton; quilted cotton or polyester pads; or wraps of felt, fleece, polyester, elastic foam, or tricot and foam.

Many horsemen feel that sheet cotton remains the superior choice for padding. These are thin folded sheets of cotton or gauze-wrapped cotton, which are not washable. You can only reuse them once or twice. However, you can buy reinforced cottons, which are washable, for a longer-lasting wrap.

Quilted cottons can be washed and reused indefinitely. Crisscross stitching holds the inner layer of padding in place, and bound edges make the pads durable. Some quilted cottons contain a double layer of polyester-fiber fill for maximum protection.

Newer synthetics may provide greater durability and more cushioning than any cotton wraps. Whichever material you choose, check that it measures about 14 inches wide, or long enough to reach from the horse's knee or hock down over the heels. Its length should allow for it to wind almost twice around the legs.

The bandage itself is a long strip of fabric, which winds over the wrap. Traditional stable bandages are also of cotton, cut from flannel bandage cloth. You can purchase three yards of this napped fabric and tear strips of 4 to 6 inches wide.

Cotton flannel will not stretch, so it cannot bind the leg to cause tendon problems. If you must apply a cold-water bandage, cotton will hold water better than a polyester material. Cotton may shrink, however, and thus must be used with caution.

Some horsekeepers prefer track bandages, made from a closely knitted fabric with a slight stretch. These are available either in a flat knit or a short pile, with either string ties or Velcro closings. Most users pick Velcro closings, because the ties may slip if they are too loose, or hurt the leg if too tight. Most styles measure 4 to 6 inches wide and 9 feet long.

Elastic bandages can be harmful if they exert too much pressure. If you are advised to apply them, wash them a few times first so that the stretch relaxes.

Bandaging is a horse-care skill that is best learned by watching an expert demonstrate the technique. Briefly, you place the inner wrap around the leg at the front of the cannon bone, wrapping from front to back without creating any wrinkles against the skin.

Start the outer bandage just below the top of the padding. You might tuck the end of the bandage under the wrap's edge, to hold the wrap snug. Wind the bandage down the leg, almost to the edge of padding, and back up to the top, maintaining consistent pressure all along.

Secure the bandage so that it remains in place without constricting the horse's leg. Tradition demands that you secure the bandage on the outside of each leg. This was developed as a safety precaution by grooms who pin bandages.

Some horse-owners complain that the popular Velcro straps don't hold as well as the old safety pins, ties, or adhesive tape. If you are concerned with Velcro, tape is a good compromise, because it is durable and equalizes the pressure around the leg.

Test a bandage for even pressure by inserting two fingers at the top and bottom. If you can feel any area pinching the leg, remove and reapply the bandage.

When your horse is lame, you must judge the severity of the problem before making the decision to begin treatment. Often a bruise or strain has caused inflammation, and you may choose to treat the swelling yourself.

First apply cold to the area to slow the circulation and stop the swelling. You can choose soaking or a compress. Soaking can be done with a hose, streaming cold water over the leg, or by standing the horse in a bucket, soaking tub, or whirlpool.

The compress maintains cold for a longer period, sometimes without the need to restrain the horse. You can apply cold-water bandages or fit the horse with ice boots. Manufacturers offer 18-inch tall ice boots, made of tough neoprene or vinyl with nylon lining. In the lining are pockets that hold pieces of ice or frozen packs of "blue ice." You slide the ice into the pockets and secure it by folding flaps over the pockets. Straps above the knees hold the boots in position.

In an emergency, you can fabricate your own ice boots by freezing blue ice around a cylindrical object. To put on the boot place the pack on the horse's leg and secure it with Vetrap, tape, or a special ice wrap. These wraps are molded to fit near or off shin, hock, or knee; they stay in place with Velcro fasteners.

After applying cold, next you apply heat to draw out the swelling. You can mix a medicated poultice from commercially available pastes and powders, then wrap it against the leg under a bandage.

Soak a hoof in a rubber or leather poultice boot. Models fit over hoof, ankle, or even up to the knee. Or, you can substitute a rubber or vinyl exercise boot to hold medication.

Standing bandages of cotton flannel are wrapped over quilted wraps, then taped.

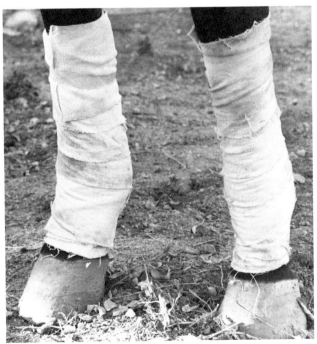

If you own a barnful of active horses, you might want to invest in one of the recently developed racetrack products. Called by various brand names, these wraps and shoes fit onto leg or hoof to promote healing through pulsing electromagnetic stimulation. Manufacturers claim these products will accelerate the body's natural healing process.

Detecting and Treating Illness

To detect illness, you need a veterinary thermometer, about 5 to 7 inches long. The rectal type you should buy will have a loop at one end for securing a string. When you insert the thermometer, let the string dangle so that you can remove the thermometer easily. Some people attach a small alligator clamp to the end of the string, to clamp to a few tail hairs.

Consult your veterinarian before stocking other medications, such as antibiotics and cough remedies. Some products require a prescription, as the Food and Drug Administration controls many substances. If you feel comfortable administering medications yourself, you will want to stock tools such as a pill crusher, balling gun, oral dose syringe, and syringes and needles.

Quality Recommendations

Unless you're advised differently, you can rely on major health-care brands such as Absorbine, Bickmore, Corona Products, Cutter Animal Health, Farnam Company, Franklin, or Horseman's Dream.

Maintenance

Store your medical kit in a box or cabinet designated for these supplies. A good size would be about 15 to 18 inches wide, 9 to 12 inches deep, and 24 to 30 inches high. This should adequately house the bottles, tools, and supplies you will keep on hand.

Place the kit in an accessible location, yet not out in the open. You want to keep supplies as clean and dry as possible. Protect the kit from pets, children, and horses.

Keep your kit maintained so that the necessary supplies are always ready for use. When a bottle is almost empty, make a note to purchase another. If you slam the box lid on your thermometer, buy a new one right away. And in winter months, store liquids indoors to prevent them from freezing.

Don't buy large economy sizes of products unless you own several horses. Shelf life may be limited and you would discard unused medications. Also, remember that in an emergency, you will want to locate items quickly. Searching through a trunkful of bottles and jars will slow down your response time.

Clean bandages regularly. Reroll them after you remove them, unless they need to be washed first. Roll them with the outer edge on the inside, so that they are ready for the next use.

Questions

- Do you know how to use supplies safely?
- Do your supplies match your horse's condition?
- Should you provide special storage for medicines?

Chapter 31

STABLE EQUIPMENT

Keeping your own horse will require more purchases than just grooming equipment. Around the barn, you will need a variety of items to care for your horse properly.

Most of this "barn stuff" is not glamourous, but it means more to your horse than a fancy bridle or silver-mounted stirrups. Because your horse spends almost all its days in a stall, corral, or pasture, it is important to provide for its basic needs.

Feeding Equipment

You can choose from several feeders designed to contain hay, grain, or both types of feed. Hay feeders feature bars through which the horse picks the hay stems.

Most common is a hay rack, built from iron, steel, or durable plastic rods or tubing. It can attach to a wall, fit into a corner, and hold from twenty-five to thirty pounds of hay.

Many horse owners prefer the hay net, a bag fashioned of knotted rope or plastic strands. It opens to hold several sections of hay.

Always hang your rack or net at a height appropriate to the level of the horse or pony's head. One that is too high can cause the dust or bits of hay to fall into the horse's face and eyes. If the rack or net is too low, accident-prone animals are likely to get a hoof trapped.

If your horse lives in a corral or pasture, you can mount a hayrack or net on the wall of a building or on the fence. (Be aware that some horses will quickly chew through the ropes of a hay net, however.) With a group of horses, you might pick a freestanding hayrack of steel or aluminum. Various sizes allow from four to twelve horses to feed at once; they hold about a day's feed per animal. For stability, the top of the rack should measure from 1 to 2 feet higher than the horses' withers.

To feed pellets, grain, and supplements, you can buy a manufactured bowl of iron, polyethylene, steel, or rubber. Most horsekeepers consider these more sanitary than the traditional wooden manger. Uneaten feed often collects at the bottom of a manger, and years of damp grain can cause the wood to rot and smell sour and moldy. Also, unless the wooden feeder is edged with metal, your horse can chew the top and even the sides.

You can choose a round, rectangular, or corner feeder. Many feature metal eye bolts to suspend the feeder from a wall or fence, approximately 38 to 42 inches from the ground. Snap the feeder's bolts to screw eyes mounted on the wall so that you can remove the feeder for cleaning.

Feeders can contain different amounts of feed, usually from 18 to 24 quarts. You can also buy small-sized foal feeders, equipped with divider bars to prevent the mare from eating her foal's grain. The bars can be adjusted or removed to accommodate the size of the foal's muzzle.

Many horses seem to enjoy burrowing to the bottom of their feed and tossing out the food on top. To thwart this type of eater, you can use a "feed-saver ring" or buy a feeder with a lip, an overhanging edge.

The ring is a metal framework that fits over the top of the feeder. It forces the horse to eat only by dipping its muzzle directly into the feed, preventing the animal from throwing out food.

The second solution features a lip that is molded onto the feeder. This lip protrudes either inside or outside the container, or both, and helps keep grain or pellets within the bowl.

To provide a constant supply of salt, you can put a mineral box beside the feeder for loose salt, or mount a holder for a five-pound salt block. Holders are made of metal wire, coated with vinyl. In a corral or pasture, you can set a large-sized salt block onto a section of pipe sunk into the ground.

You can choose one feeding container for both hay and concentrates. The combination unit can be a large tub or box, or a bowl or tray attached to a hayrack. With the latter design, loosened stems and leaves of hay fall into the tray instead of on the ground. If you mount this model outside, add a lid on the top to protect hay from rain.

When you position a feeder in a stall, corral, or pasture, consider efficiency and safety. The ideal location is one where you can feed without entering the horse's domain. Many horses become excited at feeding time, and you will be safer on the other side of the fence or door.

In a stall or small corral, a corner is the best location for a feeder. Try to avoid placing a feeder near a door or gate, where your horse might crash into it. The worst location would be one where you would have to walk behind the horse to feed it. Even a gentle horse is rarely able to resist grabbing a mouthful as you pass, and a rambunctious one could easily bite, kick, or step on you.

Watering Equipment

Watering equipment also needs to provide your horse with a safe, healthy source of nourishment. Horsepeople disagree on the superiority of water buckets and tanks versus automatic waterers.

Automatic waterers do save a lot of time. Attached to the water supply, they refill themselves according to the animal's thirst. Some include automatic heaters to prevent water from freezing.

However, realize that the convenience of automatic waterers costs more than those you refill by hand. Like any plumbing, you pay initial installation costs, and then maintain the lines to sustain the water flow in all weather.

Filling a bucket or tank with a hose is time-consuming, and carrying water buckets to your horse is even worse. But, you may prefer these chores to attempting to maintain automatic waterers. Also, you can monitor the amount of water your horse drinks.

Traditionally, horse owners provide water in a variety of containers: the bucket, a metal or plastic trash can in a corral, or a livestock tank in a pasture. Old standbys are laundry tubs or bathtubs, with smooth corners to prevent injury.

Buckets are good waterers, especially if water needs to be carried by hand. Also used as feeders, buckets are constructed from steel, rubber, or polyethylene. (Most people avoid metal buckets, which are more likely to cause injury.) Plastic is easier to clean, with the rotational molded bucket stronger than one formed through injection molding.

You can choose from sizes holding from eight to twenty quarts. Although all are shaped in the traditional wide-topped design, the flat backed or square cornered types fit better against a wall or into a corner.

If you prefer the automatic waterer, you can select from wall-mounted or freestanding models.

These refill to provide a constant water supply either through the pressure of a float or by the horse pressing a paddle.

Look for durability in an automatic waterer. Cast iron seems to last longer than plastic. If your horse is the playful type, pick a waterer with a well-protected mechanism and a metal pipe connection, rather than a hose.

Position your waterer so the horse cannot move it. Locate it away from feed, if possible, so the horse is not as likely to dunk hay. A good height is from 38 to 42 inches high. For a fresh water supply, drain and clean the waterer at least weekly.

Barn Equipment

To clean your horse's stall, corral, or pasture, you will need tools and containers. Although the shovel is the traditional scooping tool, the manure rake is more efficient. You can use it to pick up manure while leaving bedding material.

A typical manure rake has twenty metal or plastic tines, about a foot long and spaced 3/4 inches apart. The tines are shaped so that you can scoop under the waste material. You can use some models to rake or spread bedding as well as sifting straw or shavings from waste.

You can transport manure to your compost pile or garden in a wheelbarrow, cart, or manure basket. Look for an easy-rolling transport, with a large capacity and oversized wheels. If you choose the manure basket, you should pick a lightweight, durable plastic model with a capacity as large as 2 1/2 bushels.

Some baskets have molded handles; others feature rope handles. If you are cleaning only one or two stalls, a manure basket is less expensive and sometimes easier to handle than a wheeled transport. A basket can ease your aggravation if you must maneuver through a narrow aisle or walk down steps to your manure pit.

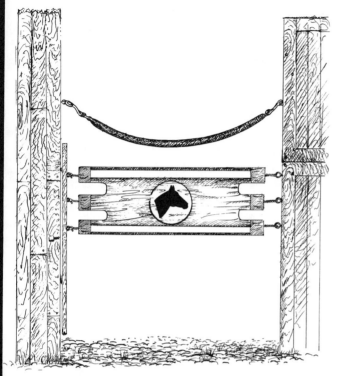

Cover an open stall door with a vinyl stall guard. You can add a separate vinyl-covered chain strap.

You can make horse-keeping more efficient with storage and convenience equipment. Protect feed inside grain bins. Some barns feature metal-lined wooden bins. Slanted tops will prevent a horse from figuring out how to lift the lid.

You can buy metal or tough plastic bins to hold 500 to 700 pounds of grain, or 500 pounds of pellets. Some models are divided to store two types of feed in one container.

If you have only a one- or two-horse stable, metal trash cans are good containers. Horses are able to lift lids on these, however, so tie them down as necessary. Lids of plastic cans can be locked on, but rodents might gnaw through the plastic.

Measure feed with metal or plastic scoops. A scale in the feed room will help you verify that you dispense the correct amount.

Organize your tack on saddle, bridle, and halter racks, either portable or permanently mounted models. Each saddle should rest on a separate rack, which are usually made of metal tubing, iron rods, or wood.

A saddle cover or carrying case will protect your saddle in the tackroom and during transit. Avoid vinyl covers, which do not permit leather to breathe. The best choice is a 12-ounce cotton-duck fabric, with a fleece or flannel lining. The loosely-woven duck breathes, and the soft lining prevents scratches. If you pick a case that covers your entire saddle, look for one with a sturdy wraparound zipper.

Rounded brackets of metal or plastic are best for hanging bridles and halters. When you hang the crownpiece over this shape, the leather sustains an even pressure. Bridles hung on hooks can bend and eventually crack in the center of the crown.

Store frequently worn blankets on blanket racks. You can buy one rack—made of four metal rods joined by chains—that holds four blankets. Or, you can attach a separate blanket bar to the front of each stall.

A tack trunk may seem like a fancy piece of

equipment, but it will help you organize equipment at home or on the road. Though you can use any type of trunk of 6- to 11-cubic-feet capacity, the styles designed for horsemen are best.

Some trunks are constructed of wood; others are molded fiberglass or plywood laminated with a vinyl or Plexiglas exterior, with a steel top for durability. You can order these in your stable colors. Fancier models feature monograms, chrome or brass trim and hardware, and nylon covers to protect them in transit.

Look for a large trunk—one that will hold a saddle—to measure at least 2 feet high, 3 feet wide, and almost 2 feet deep. It should be equipped with one or two trays inside, to organize smaller items.

Match your show trunk with additional storage boxes. You can buy a medicine box, bandage box, and braiding box, all of which store specialized items.

You can equip your stall doors with stall guards or screens, which allow you to leave the door open for ventilation and still keep the horse inside. Stalled horses usually enjoy being able to watch other horses and the outside activity.

With a gentle horse, a stall guard can be a single strap hung at chest height. This is usually a chain or cable covered with vinyl, which snaps across the average doorway, 3 to 4 feet wide. Or, three straps of webbing can form a grid across the stall opening.

Showier stall guards are made of solid sections of rubberized vinyl, reinforced with cable for strength. You can buy these in your stable colors, adding your monogram for extra style.

Removable stall screens fit across the upper half of a stall doorway, allowing ventilation of the stall with the top and bottom doors open or removed. These durable wire mesh screens are manufactured in square styles, which cover the entire opening, and yoke styles. The yoke style is U-shaped so that the horse can put its head over the screen, but not swing from side to side.

A wire stall gate permits good air circulation. The yoke style discourages the horse which weaves from side to side.

For security, mark your tack, or photograph your saddle's serial number.

Finally, secure your valuable tack by locking it in the tackroom, trailer compartment, or a heavy trunk bolted in place. Law-enforcement officials recommend labeling saddlery with permanent identification. You can use an engraving tool or miniature branding iron to permanently mark your tack. For insurance purposes, photograph equipment and keep the bills of sale. Store the photographs and bills in a safe place, away from the barn.

Questions

- How difficult is installation of the equipment?
- Does the product prevent waste and remain sanitary?

Chapter 32

—

INSECT-CONTROL PRODUCTS

Flies, gnats, mosquitoes, ticks, mites, and lice can attack horses year round. You can prevent irritating pain and the spread of disease by reducing their numbers. When you establish an ongoing program to kill or repel insects, fewer will torment you and your horse.

Insect-control products fall into three broad categories: devices, chemical methods, and natural reduction. Most horse owners battle the insect invasion by a combination of efforts.

Devices

These products shield the horse from insects by directly protecting the horse or by deterring pests from the barn or paddock. First, you can purchase protec-

Protect your horse's face from irritating insects by fitting a mesh fly mask.

tive clothing to cover the horse's body. A fly sheet fits over your horse like a regular stable sheet. Made from a lightweight mesh, it both ventilates and guards against fly bites.

To protect your horse's face, you can outfit the horse with a special bonnet. Choose either a browband with leather or vinyl fringes, which dangle over the horse's eyes, or a mask of nylon mesh fabric that shields most of the face. The ear net, a small bonnet with ear-shaped pockets, ties under the chin.

When you groom or ride your horse, carry a fly whisk to swish off the flies. This instrument looks like a crop with a "duster" instead of a tab or popper.

You can outfit your barn with protective devices. Some stall screens help shield the horse from flies. Some barn owners install electrified fly screens in place of door grills.

Adhesive flypaper is a old-fashioned, low-cost remedy. You can buy coiled strips about 18 inches long, or larger, fly-attracting sticks.

An electrical insect killer produces immediate results. Hang this appliance in a location safe from your horse, plug it in, and watch winged insects buzz into the trap. Attracted by the ultraviolet light, flies and mosquitoes will enter through the screen and be killed instantly.

Chemical Methods

Certain chemicals repel or kill pests around the barn and on your horse. These products are poisons, so always follow the manufacturer's directions.

Agricultural scientists base most insecticides on pyrethrin, a component of pyrethrum. This natural substance is derived from the dried flowers of various species of the chrysanthemum. Over the years, it has proven to be the most effective insecticide and the least hazardous one to animals and humans. Other compounds used in insecticides include dichlorvos (also an ingredient in some wormers), Permectin, Permethrin, Ectrin, and Resmethrin.

Spraying a prepared insecticide in a barn will repel insects. You can either apply the product to surfaces or introduce it into the air. The surface or residual spray coats walls, fences, and even trees —all areas where flies are likely to land. Its effect lasts from two to four weeks.

Space sprays are diffused into the atmosphere through a mister or fogger. Misting releases a finer, lighter spray, which does not require evacuation of the area. The fogger permeates the atmosphere with a penetrating cloud.

Many stable managers install an automatic spraying system. A large canister (thirty to fifty-five gallon capacity) holds a quantity of premixed liquid, which is piped through a layout of tubing and nozzles placed at intervals along the barn's ceiling. A timer activates a pump, which forces the insecticide through the tubing to mist from the nozzles.

A less expensive automatic spray system, useful in a two- to four-stall barn, substitutes an aerosol spray can for the larger barrel. Batteries activate the spray.

Chemicals can also attract and kill pests. You can hang a fly strip containing a pyrethrin-based insecticide. When the insect lands, it absorbs the pesticide. Or, you can distribute poisoned bait granules. The granules' high sugar content lures flies to their death.

Nonpoisonous baits also can be used to kill flies. Purchase a commercial solution, or brew your own concoction of yeast dissolved in water. Place it in a trap to entice insects to enter. The trap might be a glass jar, with insects flying through a screen or maze to reach a strong-smell-

ing bait. Another design is a pyramid constructed in a screen box. Flies seek the bait and become trapped inside the box. When one fly begins buzzing inside a trap, the sound attracts hordes of others. Death occurs due to dehydration, which is accelerated on a hot day.

The most common chemicals used for insect control on horses are topical applications that make your horse's coat repel flying and crawling pests. These nontoxic ectoparaciticides include sprays, wipes, powders, ointments, and roll-ons that you apply directly to the hairs of the coat. Again, pyrethrin is the predominate active ingredient. Always follow the manufacturer's directions, for some products can irritate the horse's skin. Discontinue use if you observe any adverse reaction.

Many wipe-on products should be rubbed onto the hairs with a moistened cloth, sponge, or fleece mitt, which aids in smooth application. Spraying a liquid is simpler, although many horses resent the noise of this procedure. You can reduce the noise by using a pump sprayer with the nozzle adjusted to a fine mist. The slight hiss is much quieter than the sound of most aerosol sprayers. Avoid spraying your horse's face; use an ointment, wipe-on, or roll-on product around eyes, ears, and muzzle.

Many repellants seem to provide longer-lasting effectiveness when you wipe them onto the coat. You can rub both with and against the hairs to cover more of the shaft; spraying only applies the solution to the exposed tips of the hairs.

If you show your horse, avoid oily formulas, which attract dust. You can use a combination hair polish and fly repellant. Also, some wound ointments contain pyrethrin to prevent insects from landing on the area.

Powdered insecticides will treat certain insect pests. For combatting lice and mites, specially formulated powders can be rubbed into the horse's coat or mixed with water to create a paste that can be applied to the coat.

Another protection is to attach to your horse

special tags or strips, which release consta.it low levels of insecticide. Choose from a collar-browband for the face, tags for halter or forelock, and strips tied to the tail.

You can also rely on internal, feed-through, insect killers. Now on the market is a supplement impregnated with a larvicide. This product passes through your horse's body without harm, but it remains active in the manure. The larvicide kills fly larvae when flies lay eggs in the manure.

Natural Reduction

The natural, nonpoisonous method of insect control reduces the population of flies by breaking their life cycle. You introduce additional insects into your environment that actually lower the number of external parasites.

Several laboratories around the country market fly predators, pupae of species that prey upon fly larvae. You distribute the not-yet-hatched insects throughout your area, especially in and around the manure pile. As the fly larvae hatch, your tiny helpers consume the pests.

Unfortunately, science has not yet developed the fly predator that reproduces itself automatically. You must contract for a series of laboratory shipments, usually spaced at three-week intervals throughout the season. An effective program requires that you disperse additional predators on schedule.

Recommendations

Product results vary greatly, depending on your specific insect problem. You will need to experiment among products as you wage your war against insects. Usually you will rely on a combination of products. Consult your equine practitioner and other local horseowners for environment-specific brands.

Questions

- Does this method pose any health hazards?
- Which method requires the least time for effective results?

PART VII:

MISCELLANEOUS

Chapter 33

—

LEATHER
CARE

You can increase the longevity of your leather by cleaning and treating it with the appropriate products. By cleaning the hide, you remove harmful substances, and by conditioning, you replenish the leather's original fat content.

Leather needs to be nourished to retain its pliability. Enemies of leather are heat and water, both of which cause dryness. Water dries leather by melting the fat that seeps from the fibers. When leather becomes too dry, it is brittle and likely to break.

Cleaning Products

Although conditioning leather is important, first you must clean it. Remove dirt and sweat before they start to dry the leather.

Saddle soap is the traditional cleanser. Most people choose a glycerine soap. Others claim that glycerine washes out natural oils; they prefer castile, lanolin, or vegetable-oil soap. You can buy glycerine soap in bar, spray, liquid, or paste form.

Apply soap to a dampened sponge or cloth, using just enough soap to work up a fairly dry lather. Rub the soap into the leather with a back and forth motion on strap goods, a circular one on larger pieces.

Clean both sides of the leather. You will probably need to scrub longer and more briskly to erase the black marks that metal rubs into leather. Remember to rinse your sponge or cloth frequently and to reapply soap. Don't keep using a dirty sponge, since all you will do is rearrange the dirt on your leather.

As you clean, inspect the condition of the leather. Note any worn areas that might develop cracks. Places likely to show wear are billets, stirrup leathers, ends of cheekpieces (where the bit rests), and leather girths.

Do not soap suede seats or flaps. Use a stiff bristle brush (not a wire one) or fine sandpaper to remove dirt and most spots. Then wipe gently with a damp sponge. For stubborn dirt, try rubbing with an artgum eraser.

Keeping leather in good condition prolongs its life. This stirrup leather shows wear from the eye of the iron, but regular care maintains its strength.

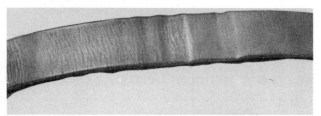

New on the market is a unique suede cleaning liquid, made by Dyo of Dallas, Texas. The product is formulated for use on any suede or roughout leather. You can apply it with a damp sponge to work up a lather, rub it against the grain to raise the nap, and brush the grain when it dries.

After soaping, rub leather with a soft cloth to polish the grain side to a soft luster. The saddle soap adds a waxy finish that helps protect the leather.

Conditioning Products

Although you should clean leather after each use, it does not need to be nourished that often. Avoid over- or under-conditioning leather. You should not wait until the leather feels dry or hard, and you should not overfeed your leather so that it feels limp, flabby, and greasy. In a dry climate, treat leather more often, as often as every two weeks.

Leather that is used heavily and soaked with water or sweat may need conditioning once a week. For lightly used leather, conditioning once a month or even once every six months may be sufficient, depending on the leather's texture.

Two traditional standbys for conditioning leather are dubbin and neatsfoot oil. Dubbin, a lanolin product, is a creamy lotion that can be rubbed into the flesh side of the leather. Neatsfoot oil is a fluid fat obtained from boiled ox feet; it tends to darken leather. Some experts claim that neatsfoot oil opens leather's pores and makes it too soft; however, it is the conditioner of choice for many others.

Always choose 100 percent pure neatsfoot oil, never the neatsfoot-oil compound. The pure oil is entirely animal fat, which is a more natural product that leather can absorb. The less-expensive compound will not soak in as well, and it leaves a sticky residue.

You can brush or wipe neatsfoot oil on your tack. Allow it to soak in, and then wipe off any excess before storing your tack. Try not to over-oil a saddle, as excess oil might seep into your breeches or chaps.

At the tack shop you will also see leather dressings, preservatives, and restorers. Many are oil-based products, with neatsfoot oil as an ingredient, and others are creams. Reserve a leather restorer only for leather that is dry, hard, or very dirty.

Look for an oil that penetrates the leather, yet does not soak onto your clothing. Some recommended products are Lederfit saddle oil, Bienenwachs leather balsam, Ledersbalsam, IPS liquid cleaner, and Hydrophane. All are European products, especially recommended for leather goods produced in Europe.

Another standby is Lexol and Lexol PH. Neither version will darken leather, and many saddlers recommend this brand for Western equipment.

Avoid oiling a saddle with a product not intended for that purpose. Saddlers discourage riders from soaking saddles in olive, vegetable, or peanut oils. Each product will create a sticky condition that will probably ooze oil onto your clothing.

Some new leather products combine both cleaning and conditioning agents. In a cream or liquid form, these save time since you can perform both procedures in one application.

Some of the oil-based conditioners act as waterproofing agents as well as nourishing leather. For greater water repellancy, you can also treat leather with mink oil or wax. However, mink oil does not soak into all leathers and sometimes leaves a gooey film on the tack. Try it first on a small, inconspicuous area.

Well-cared-for leather should gleam softly. Oiled leather will not have an undesirable shine. Never use a polish on leather tack, as it can seal the pores, and the leather will dry and crack.

Check the condition of Western stirrup leathers, and oil leather that appears this dry.

However, for show harness, you can choose a special dressing that does add a glossy, patent-leather-like finish that will not harm the leather.

When breaking in new tack, use the same conditioning products as for older tack. The conditioning process takes time with stiff leather; be patient and don't try to substitute a heavy dose of oil for weeks of use. Applying thin coats of dressing over a period of time is the best method.

If you buy English strap goods in a light London tan color, you can accelerate the darkening process. Rather than applying heavy coats of oil, which can make the leather limp, you can dye the tack with leather dye or stain.

Dying leather is similar to dying hair, except that the color remains permanent. Results vary according to the leather's thickness and the tanning agent used, which can affect the density and speed of penetration. Do not attempt dyeing unless you follow manufacturer's instructions carefully. You will not be able to correct a mistake.

Choose a liquid product for dyeing leather. Two reputable firms are Fiebing's and the Dyo Chemical Company.

When dyeing leather, first clean it thoroughly, and be sure you scrub off any wax on the leather's grain side. Daub some dye on a test piece of leather, or the flesh side of the piece you plan to darken. Watch how the dye penetrates, and decide if the test meets your requirements.

Working in a well-lighted area, spread the dye over the piece with a brush, cloth, or dauber furnished with the bottle. Let the tack dry, and then rub off any excess dye from the leather's surface.

Do not try to touch up any spots you have missed. If you see streaks or you desire a deeper tone, apply a second coat of dye.

After the leather has dried thoroughly, apply a finish of conditioner or wax. You can choose from a carnauba cream, or a liquid or solid wax. Some people rub on a thin coat of Vaseline and let it stand for twenty minutes before wiping it off.

Tools

In addition to leather-care products, you may wish to purchase a few basic craftsmen's tools. You probably will not want to repair your own tack, but you can make minor adjustments.

A revolving leather punch will cut round holes in six different sizes, through leather up to 1/4 inch thick. When you need to add extra holes to stirrup leathers or bridle straps, the gadget will punch them quickly. Buy a heavy-duty model, with sharp tubes that cut clean edges without tearing the leather.

To use a punch, calculate the size of the new hole by fitting the tubes into an adjacent hole, the same size as the new one you plan. On the leather's grain side, center the tube in place, holding the punch so that the tube presses straight into the leather, not at an angle.

Squeeze the handles of the punch. (If the leather is thick, use both hands.) Rotate the leather while the punch is still in place to burnish the edges of the hole.

Use a leather knife or shears to trim ends of loose straps, which can detract from your appearance in the show ring. For minor repairs, you can buy an automatic awl for hand sewing of leather. Some people prefer repairing with rivets, which can be applied with a rivet setter.

Chapter 34

—

SPECIALTY GEAR

For certain types of equestrian sport, manufacturers have developed specialized equipment. This chapter discusses three popular pursuits: trail riding, roping, and vaulting.

Trail Riding

Whether your journey lasts minutes, hours, or days, it is an expedition that often calls for specialized equipment to assist you and your horse. For a pleasure ride, plan your equipment according to the climate and the length of the ride. If you plan a brief tour with no stops, your tack can be whatever is comfortable—saddle, bareback pad, or even no saddle. New on the market is a saddle pad or bareback pad with built-in pockets on the back, stationed behind your thighs.

Here you can stash small items, such as a wallet, sunglasses, or a camera.

Also, you might try a new, two-piece bareback pad. A molded plastic pommel with a built-in handhold attaches to a girth and fits over a separate pad.

You might improve your saddle's comfort by adding a seat saver. This polyester fleece pad straps over the seat and cantle of either a Western or English saddle, providing extra cushion under your seat bones.

During an extended ride, take along a halter and lead rope for tying your horse at rest stops. An innovative design combines both halter and bridle into one unit. An extra cheekpiece is stitched onto a halter's cheeks, with snaps to connect to the bit. Simply unsnap the bit and connect a lead rope to the halter ring. A variation is a pair of bridle cheeks with snaps on the ends; these connect to the rings of any halter to convert it into a bridle.

You will probably add extra luggage on extended rides. How much you carry on your horse depends on the type of saddle you use.

Most English saddles are equipped with two rings on the off-side panel to buckle a small sandwich case or saddle pouch of leather or vinyl. A gusseted pouch can expand to provide enough space for a lunch, a jacket or raincoat, and possibly a set of binoculars.

For a Western saddle, you can choose a cantle bag to hold a day's lunch, a camera, and a jacket. This zippered pouch of nylon, vinyl, or leather usually measures about 20 inches long, 6 inches wide, and 5 inches deep. You tie it behind the cantle by threading the saddle strings through the metal D-rings sewn to each end of the bag.

Alternatively, with a Western saddle, you can use horn bags, a pair of two bags that slip over the pommel. The horn fits through a cutout in the yoke between the two bags. Each measures about 8 inches square, with room for a camera, binoculars, or a first-aid kit.

When you plan to carry more items, you can hang saddle bags behind the cantle. Two large bags are connected by a wide yoke, which lies across the saddle's rear skirts. Saddle strings thread through eyelets on the yoke. These bags are constructed with gussets so that they can expand to hold a large load. They usually measure about 11 by 12 inches, or 14 inches square, with gussets from 2 to 5 inches across. The top of each bag closes with a flap to secure contents.

One design, called the packing saddlebag, combines the cantle pouch and the gusseted bags. With this bag, a zippered pouch is added onto the yoke.

Saddlebags are made from a variety of materials. Leather is the most traditional, although it requires regular care. You can also choose bags of durable fabric, such as canvas, nylon, or PVC.

Lined saddlebags allow you to pack specific items. For greater protection of fragile gear, choose bags of quilted nylon padded with a foam center. You can also buy insulated nylon saddlebags, which cover a polystyrene shell that will keep ice frozen for almost a day.

On an overnight trek, you can add a bedroll pack above your saddlebags. Stuff a foam pad and sleeping bag into this spacious pack, and strap it in place.

Fasten single items to your saddle with other specialty containers. You can find cases designed for pliers, wire cutters, or a hoof pick. On a Western saddle, a hoof pick case might strap around the flank cinch.

You can pack beverages in plain or fancy cases. Water canteens are available in several styles, from the drab military type to a leather-covered model suitable in the hunt field. For spicier liquids in the hunt field, pick the traditional flask. This cylindrical metal flask, large enough for several nips worth of liquor, slips into a leather case.

The well-equipped fox hunter also carries a leather sandwich case, strapped to the rings of the saddle. Inside is an aluminum (or silver) box to protect sandwiches from being squished during the morning's gallops.

In a more casual situation, you might choose a trekking canteen. Made of vinyl, this pouch holds a plastic sandwich case and a drinking cup, fitted with a lid.

If you pack a rifle on your Western saddle, carry it in a scabbard. This leather case will protect most rifles or carbines, with or without a scope. It straps to the rear cinch ring and latigo of the front cinch and holds the gun at a diagonal angle.

An expedition might require more equipment than you can carry on your saddle. If so, load your extra gear in panniers, one on each side of the back of a pack animal. Tie or strap panniers in place onto a Western or pack saddle.

Saddle panniers look like oversized canvas or nylon saddle bags, with a wide strap fitting over a regular Western saddle. Slots fit over the fork and cantle, and two tie-down straps fit over the seat and behind the cantle. A front and a rear cinch fasten over the saddle's regular cinches, and a web breeching strap keeps the panniers from shifting.

If you plan to carry more than sixty pounds, fit your beast of burden with a pack saddle. This combination of harness and saddle tree allows the most secure arrangement of the greatest load of gear.

The most common type of pack saddle is the sawbuck, sometimes called the crossbuck. Two pairs of wooden crosspieces, called "bucks," fit over the horse's withers and back to allow the load to be tied in place. This design is said to have originated with Native Americans, who tied deer or elk horns together to arch over their horse's backs.

The bucks fit onto two bars of the wooden tree, lined with wool, which rest on each side of the horse's back. The tree secures with two cinches, front and rear, over an oversized saddle pad or blanket.

A recent development in the pack saddle is a double cinch, with both front and rear cinches connected by a large center diamond. This style of cinch provides better security.

To prevent the tree from shifting, straps and rigging form a harness that connects the tree to a breast collar and breeching, pronounced "britchen." A crupper, which is optional, can be used to keep the saddle from sliding forward as the horse moves downhill.

A recent development is a pack saddle designed for either riding or packing. This consists of a fiberglass tree, complete with pommel, horn, cantle, and stirrups. It is fitted with a standard pack harness.

The pack saddle and harness must be in top condition. The farther in you pack, the more important it becomes that you check your equipment. Remember, you are depending upon your horse to transport you and your gear during the expedition. Faulty equipment could jeopardize the horse's safety.

You can strap either hard or soft panniers to your pack saddle. Hard styles include panniers made of wood, aluminum, steel, or molded plastic. Soft panniers are made of canvas or a tough synthetic.

Horse packing is an art, best learned from an expert. Sloppy packs can cause problems ranging from a minor gall to a major disaster on the trail. Briefly, the panniers hang from the near and off sides of the pack saddle's tree. They strap or tie onto the tree securely, so that the load does not shift. Each pannier should weigh the same and hang at an equal height.

Roping

The sport of roping utilizes specially crafted ropes, measured, cut, and tied on each end. On the rope's back end is a rosebud knot. On the front is the hondo, securely tied around and through the rope to prevent slipping. A burner of

Successful team roping requires proper ropes for heading and and heeling.

leather or rawhide aids the rope to slide through the loop quickly.

Each roping specialty requires appropriate equipment. For calf roping, you will pick a polyethylene, or poly, rope, or a hemp rope with a polyethylene core, called a poly-grass rope. The traditional grass ropes have almost disappeared, as contemporary hemp cannot sustain the extreme pressure of roping a 400-pound calf. Some ropers pick a newer, more expensive blend, a combination of polyethylene, nylon, and dacron.

With speed so crucial, calf ropers usually prefer a rawhide burner to a leather one. The slick surface lets the rope slide more rapidly through the loop, and this helps the rope tighten its slack while the loop remains on the calf's head. Many team ropers have also switched to rawhide burners.

Team ropers use nylon or nylon and polyethylene ropes. These synthetics will dally better around the saddle horn, adhering to the rubber the ropers wrap around the horn's post. A polyethylene or poly-grass rope will not hold in place, and a sliding rope can burn your hand or even amputate a finger.

Aged nylon is the traditional rope material for team ropers. To make this material, the manufacturer seasons lengths of nylon outdoors for up to twelve months. Fresh nylon rope contains a great deal of wax, which the sun's heat and dirt's abrasion removes. Six-hundred-foot coils are stretched across a field for weathering.

A team roper's green rope is a mixture of nylon and poly. Because this blend will stay straight, not kinking as all-nylon would, the machine-spun strands are tied without any stretching.

Steer ropers, who tie their ropes to the saddle horn, can select ropes made of either nylon or polyethylene. Most use nylon ropes, although some stick with the polyethylene. Most steer ropers continue with the ropes they have used before in calf or team roping.

Calf ropers generally use ropes from 28 to 30 feet long. Team ropers choose ropes from 30 to 35 feet long.

The rope's diameter affects its swing, with sizing usually a personal preference. Polyethylene ropes range in diameter from 1/4 to 7/16 inches, increasing in 1/16-inch increments. Poly-grass can be measured by millimeters or by number of threads—from sixty to sixty-nine threads.

Nylon ropes run from 5/16 to 7/16 inches in diameter. Most ropers choose the 3/8-inch size.

Because ropers demand more gradations, manufacturers offer ropes in several in-between sizes. For example, you will see a nylon rope in three versions of one size: scant, true, and full. A 7/16 true rope measures exactly that diameter. A scant rope is slightly smaller, with just a few strands removed. Full is slightly larger. Neither is smaller or larger enough to fall into the next dimension.

These sizes have been created due to ropers' requests for smaller ropes. In competition, you can throw a slightly smaller rope more quickly. The smaller rope feels lighter, which gives you a psychological advantage. Its only disadvantage would be its lightness when you try to throw it into a wind, which would hinder your throw.

Ropes are tied two ways, for either right- or left-handed ropers. The right-handed rope twists to the right, the left-handed one to the left.

The left-handed ropes developed because a left-handed roper cannot use a right-handed rope efficiently. The machine has spun the strands to the right, and when tossed from the left, the rope kinks. If you are one of the 10 percent of ropers who are left-handed, you will find yourself at a disadvantage. Few coaches can instruct you, and you will not be able to head steers due to the logistics of team roping.

Nylon ropes add another choice: texture, graded as soft, medium, or hard. Again, gradations add medium-soft and medium-hard, to allow for the roper's personal preference.

Headers swing a softer rope, with a smaller loop. This will pull down, not off, the horns. A harder rope could flip off before the roper pulls the slack.

A heeler would choose a medium-to-hard rope and wants a bigger loop, to stand up around the steer's legs. Many heelers throw a loop ahead of the steer and tighten it when the animal steps into the loop.

Calf and team ropers use piggin strings to tie their animals. Almost all choose strings of three-ply nylon, measuring 6 1/2 feet for calves, 7 feet for steers. The strings range from 1/8 to 5/16 inches in diameter; team ropers prefer the thicker, heavier models.

Like ropes, piggin strings come in soft, medium, and hard textures. Beginners usually start with the soft texture, which is easier to twist around the animal's legs. A skilled roper finds the harder string faster to tie.

Another version of calf and steer roping is breakaway. Here a special connector allows the rope to fall free of the animal's neck after the loop tightens. The roper does not dismount to tie a piggin string.

Breakaways are made in plastic or Velcro

The vaulter uses the surcingle's handholds
to perform required movements.

models. Two halves of a plastic clamp separate under pressure; the Velcro detaches.

Calf ropers often use a neck rope, a short rope fitted midway down the horse's neck. The catch rope is threaded through the neck rope, then tied to the saddle horn. When the roper catches the calf, the neck rope holds the catch rope in front of the horse, under its chin. This helps guide the horse to back straight away.

Calf ropers may also add a jerkline to their equipment to aid the horse's stop. Here a rope runs from the bit shank or bottom bar, through the neck rope, around the saddle horn, and ties to the catch rope. Pressure from the roped calf shortens the jerkline to cue the horse.

Serious ropers store their coiled ropes in round cans or bags. A polyethylene rope could be stowed in either style of container, requiring no special care. Team ropers store their nylon ropes in cloth bags. With a poly-grass rope, you must choose an airtight plastic can. Weather affects the grass core, which can become limp on a hot, dry day, and stiff in a humid climate. The can allows you to control the rope's feel. You can stiffen it by storing it with a wet rag, or seal it from humidity in the protective can.

Many ropers also treat ropes for a slicker feel. You can rub talcum or baby powder on the rope for several feet along the areas your hands will contact.

Vaulting

This sport requires simple longeing equipment and a special surcingle. The vaulting surcingle is a wide, padded leather band featuring two iron handles, padded with leather, on each side of the withers. The large handles and additional straps permit the vaulter to hold onto the surcingle for the various movements.

Pad the surcingle with a thick Western saddle pad. Because the pad provides a cushion and traction for the vaulter, avoid a slippery fleece pad. Experts recommend a cotton duck cover on the top side of the pad to add a secure footing.

PART VIII:

WORKING YOUR WAY THROUGH THE MARKETPLACE

Chapter 35

—

BUYING STRATEGIES

Once you know how to select quality, you can begin to purchase equipment wisely. In order to gain the most value for your dollars, plan your shopping according to your needs, buying style, and retail outlets.

Collection Development

Buying separate pieces of horse equipment eventually results in a collection. Although you evaluate each item within its type, your individual buying decisions can total a sizeable amount of products.

Your collection reflects you. Are you the down-to-earth type, who chooses plain, stripped-down models with no frills? Or would you define yourself as a connoisseur, who chooses only a few quality items that last for decades?

Retailers relish the visits of the "tack nut," who enjoys buying a variety of different styles. If you fit this category, your tack room is packed with filled trunks and jammed shelves. (One tack nut confesses to owning eight saddles for one horse.)

You might be a follower of fashion, always searching for the newest designs to keep up with trends. Maybe you consider yourself a high-tech buyer, attracted by flash, color; interested in the latest developments and improvements.

To improve your horsemanship, your practical goal is the acquisition of appropriate equipment. Develop a well-balanced collection by planning your purchases. If you are entering the sport, you will want to build a collection of basics. This implies breadth—one item each of the important horsekeeping tools, supplies, and tack.

If you board your horse, a checklist of the necessary items would include the following items: saddle, bridle, saddle pad, halter and lead, currycomb, dandy brush, body brush, hoof pick, hoof dressing and applicator, large and small sponges, sweat scraper, fly repellant, disinfectants, veterinary thermometer, saddle soap, leather conditioner, and a bucket.

Add these products if you keep your horse at home: feeder, grain storage, feed scoop, waterer, wheelbarrow or manure basket, and manure rake or pitchfork.

Once you have the basics, you can begin to develop your collection's depth, selecting items specific to your riding discipline. When considering purchasing any additional item, you should first decide how it will interrelate with the equipment you already own. For example, if you show, you should aim to match a new saddle pad, bridle, or bit to your other show tack. Purchasing a new bit also requires you to measure the diameter of the bit rings and the width of the intended bridle's cheekpieces to be sure the cheeks will fit inside the bit rings.

Seeking Advice

You will want to expand upon this book's guidelines by asking specific questions of experts you can speak with directly. Choose your advisors carefully, for you will encounter a wide range of knowledge among experts. In speaking with over 100 people during the research for this book, I estimate that approximately one-fourth did not possess a thorough knowledge of the available products, or were unwilling to share their knowledge.

Don't be embarrassed about asking questions, and realize that any expert is opinionated. Compare opinions, and when one differs from another, ask for the reasons.

Usually, you have no way of certifying your advisor's background. For example, many riders trust their trainers. Even though the trainer may be an expert rider or instructor, he or she can be a poor source of equipment advice.

All segments of the industry agree that trainers commonly mislead their customers about saddlery. Few trainers can be experts in all areas of horsemanship. A trainer must understand equine behavior, equitation, and human psychology in order to educate horse and rider. Equipment knowledge is probably limited to those items frequently used.

You could compare the professional trainer to a race car driver. A driver concentrates on excelling in one area of the sport. Yet, when specific advice on the construction or operation of the car is needed, a mechanic is consulted. Likewise, top horse trainers do not pretend to specialize in saddlery. They consult experts in the tack industry.

Because there are no absolutes in equipment, each rider may succeed with different tack. Trainers, like all riders, may tend to recommend the products they purchase, since those are ones with which they are most familiar.

Keep your tack collection organized and
account for all equipment, so you can locate
needed items quickly.

What frustrates the knowledgeable retailer is when you ask about a product using the phrase, "My trainer says..." What if your trainer sent you to buy a pair of five-eighths-inch-wide harness-leather reins? The tack-shop owner knows that this rein will be too wide and thick for your hands. Can the owner convince you to purchase a more appropriate rein size, against your trainer's instructions?

This scenario occurs in all riding disciplines, with instructors at all levels. Retailers urge trainers to communicate more closely with them, to accompany the student or to call first to discuss the student's specific needs. Retailers are eager to share their knowledge with fellow professionals.

Find out if your trainer has an open mind about product choices. You will gain the most valuable advice from someone who willingly investigates all options.

Unfortunately, manufacturers may not be reliable sources, either. Product loyalty, jealousy, ego, and lack of knowledge can limit the validity of their advice. Look for a manufacturer who is a practicing horseperson, and who has been in the business for a while. Find out if the firm holds membership in WAEMA—an indicator of professionalism—and ask for references from local customers. You can consult sales representatives on product-specific questions, but do not expect unbiased opinions. You must separate facts from salesmanship.

Saddle-repair professionals often offer buyers assistance. A proprietor of an established shop will have seen the proof of quality over the years, and that experience can validate your estimates. Remember that a proprietor also will hold definite opinions.

Often a good source can be a fellow rider, who knows you and your horse. An amateur can be just as well-informed as a professional, and often holds fewer prejudices.

Finally, consult local retailers. A reliable shop can offer useful advice. Many shop owners will give honest help; others are concerned only with making a sale. Like a ski shop, a good saddle shop will be concerned with your needs, and still be familiar with the attributes of all brands in order to advise you.

Working Your Way through the Marketplace

You can buy horse equipment at a variety of locations, each offering advantages and disadvantages. The location you choose depends on your buying style. If you consider yourself a cautious buyer, you will probably prefer comparative shopping at retail outlets. On the other hand, if you tend to buy impulsively, you may receive better value by shopping by mail, where you can survey goods without succumbing to clever sales ploys. You should avoid auctions and show exhibits, where you might tend to make a quick decision you would later regret.

The most accessible market is often the local retail outlet, either a tack shop, a feed store, a Western wear shop, or a department store. Its prime advantages are service and on-site display of goods. To remain in business, a local store must please its customers by answering questions about every product, offering advice, and displaying a well-stocked inventory.

Evaluate a shop's service commitment by observation and inquiry. First, listen to how the owner and staff interact with customers. Are they knowledgeable about the products they stock? Are they too aggressive, approaching you as soon as you step inside? Can you never locate someone to assist you when you have a question?

As you deal with the sales staff, listen carefully to their marketing techniques. Many clever salespeople can adjust their pitch to your expressed needs.

Realize that any salesperson needs to interview

you to respond to your needs. You may have a preconceived idea of what you want, which may not be what you really need. A knowledgeable clerk will query you to find out how much you know. If the salesperson perceives that you are unsure or have been misinformed, a product's actual features can be tactfully pointed out.

Do not purchase products by relying solely on brand-name identification. Many shops offer quality items that are not advertised in any magazines. Often an item that is comparable to a famous-name one will prove a better buy, and a knowledgeable sales clerk will explain the pros and cons of two similar products. Hearing each item's advantages and disadvantages should help you to evaluate the design, materials, fit, and craftsmanship of competing goods.

When you look at a product without a brand name, ask the sales clerk which national firm distributes it. You can rely on the following respected distributors: Colt-Cromwell, Inc.; B. T. Crump; Champion Turf Equipment; St. Lawrence Sales; Midwest Saddlery Company; and MacPherson Leather Company.

If you are buying a saddle, you should either bring your advisor with you to the shop or seek out the most knowledgeable person in the shop. Look for the person who has the most background in various models' construction details. Often this is the owner.

In some posh shops, the staff sells products through snob appeal. They may use esoteric jargon or recommend an item through its connection to a famous name. Don't let this atmosphere sway you into buying a product that you don't need. Continue inquiring for specific information, asking for definitions of unfamiliar terms. Remember that Bruce Davidson or Roy Cooper are not personally coaching you when you buy a saddle that they endorse.

You can also evaluate a shop by surveying the quality of the displays. A service-oriented shop will display its goods in an organized fashion,

even in a limited floor space. You should be able to locate a certain product within its type.

A shop's product lines will vary depending on the locale and its specialty, which is usually the owner's riding style. Ideally, a well-stocked shop will offer a range of prices within each product type. This shows you that the owner does not favor or discriminate against any level of horsemanship. A shop that offers only the most inexpensive lines indicates that the owner caters to popular demand, probably pleasure riders concerned primarily with an item's cost, or that the owner doesn't care about stocking quality products.

Inquire about the shop's selling policies. Can you take a saddle home to test its fit on your horse? Can you return or exchange an item for another item or for credit? Is there a time limit on returns? Does the shop offer guarantees? The best shops stand behind their merchandise with an unconditional guarantee on every item in stock.

Also, ask if the owner belongs to the trade organization Western and English Retailers of America. Such membership can indicate a professional orientation and commitment to the industry.

During this inquiry, you will get a feel for the quality of the shop's service commitment. You should sense whether the shop is primarily interested in quick sales, or providing service with expertise and developing long-term customers.

Some shops claim that they offer discount pricing. Compare their goods and prices with competing shops to evaluate the truth of this claim. And realize that in the long run, service after the sale can be more important than a lower initial price.

The custom shop offers the ultimate in individualized service. Often you deal directly with the craftsman himself. Such personalized service will result in exactly the product you desire; however, you must maintain an open mind. The expert craftsperson needs to confirm your expectations in order to produce the equipment. Tact or diplomacy may not be displayed in responding to your questions. If you are frank, explaining your desire and requesting advice, you should be able to establish a comfortable communication.

Be aware that custom work may take longer. Many one-person shops have waiting lists, because the product often depends on a single craftsperson. Remember that you cannot hurry an artist, and assure yourself that the product will be worth the wait.

Horse shows and fairs often feature commercial exhibits, some duplicating the stock of a retail shop. The attractive displays and festive show atmosphere can lure you into buying high-priced items. Some dealers do offer discount prices; if you know what the regular prices are, you can sometimes save money and take home a souvenir. Investigate the dealer's integrity by finding out if he or she represents a reputable shop or mail-order establishment. Ask about returns or exchanges if you purchase an unsatisfactory item. Before you buy, scan prices of similar products in surrounding exhibits.

Mail order catalogs have become popular sources for all types of consumer goods. According to the most recent statistics, 14 percent of retail purchases are made through mail order.

Mail order offers convenience and comparison shopping. If you acquire a stack of catalogs, you have access to almost every type of horse equipment manufactured. Make a quick, toll-free call, and a delivery truck will bring it to your mailbox or doorstep. Mail order may cost you less. Some firms price name-brand items lower than your local retail shop. However, be sure you add any shipping and handling costs to the item's price.

Another advantage of U.S.-based mail order is that if you order from an out-of-state firm, you will not pay your state sales tax. On a major purchase, you can save quite a bit of money. Be aware that a 1987 bill introduced in the House of Representatives may eliminate this savings, however.

You can even import quality items into this country through shopping mail-order firms located abroad. For English saddlery, one recommended source is W. & H. Gidden, Ltd., 112/122 Tabernacle Street, London, EC2A 4LE, England. (This firm has been in business since 1806.)

The primary disadvantage of mail order is the distance between you and the goods. You must evaluate a possible purchase from catalog copy or a photograph. How do you know the item will meet the firm's promise?

Again, check the firm's background before making any purchases. Do they maintain a customer service department, which you can call to ask specific questions about a product's origin or size? Do you receive exactly what you bought?

Finally, you can buy goods through an auction or private party. Here you must use caution, as the seller may lack any knowledge of the product.

Consumer Rights

"Let the buyer beware.... They have to wade in and get stuck, and that is the way men are educated." (Attributed to Henry T. Havemeyer, 1804–1874, former Mayor of New York.)

Today you do have rights as a U.S. consumer. Primarily, you have the implicit right to expect satisfactory service from goods, even without a written warranty. Businesses operate within the free enterprise system. You support a business by purchasing its product, so the seller must please you by delivering the goods you buy.

Manufacturers and merchants vie for your disposable dollars. This competition can lead to improved goods and lower prices—or it can create confusion for the unsophisticated buyer.

Be skeptical. Watch out for deceptive selling practices, which may fall outside laws enforced by state consumer agencies. First, beware of advertising claims. Businesses try to bedazzle and beguile the gullible buyer with glamourous adjectives and celebrity endorsements. Study an advertisement closely, and inquire about the product's description and expected function.

Try not to judge products by the amount of advertisements you see, or an ad's surface appeal. One company may promote its brand of horse boot in full-page, full-color ads in national horse magazines. Its competitor, which may actually manufacture a superior product, might place a small, unillustrated ad in the same magazine.

Second, inquire about a product's warranty. If a saddle offers a five-year guarantee, what parts are covered? If you encounter problems, who will repair or replace the product—the manufacturer or the retailer?

Investigate a merchant's record on backing his goods with your local Better Business Bureau. (This agency may only list those firms that have been the source of complaints, however.)

If you do not receive satisfaction, contact your state's consumer agency. It may be a separate governmental section, or one affiliated with the state attorney general.

When you order by mail, follow recommended guidelines. Keep a record of the order. Buy a small item on your first order, to test how the company fulfills its promises. Pay by credit card or C.O.D., as either method allows you to stop payment for fraud or nondelivery. You can have the charge removed from your credit card, or stop payment on a check if you pay C.O.D.

When you charge an order on your credit card, find out if the firm applies a surcharge. Also, ask if the account is billed before or after the company ships the item.

If you order an item over the telephone, ask for the salesperson's name. Find out if the item is in stock for immediate delivery, and ask for a definite shipment date.

Check references of a mail-order firm by telephoning the company. Get names of local customers you can call to ask if they were satisfied with the firm.

If you do encounter mail-order problems, you can contact the Federal Trade Commission. This agency sets legal guidelines for all U.S. mail-order firms. Also contact the Better Business Bureau, the Direct Marketing Association Mail Order Action Line, and the regional office of the U.S. Postal Inspection Service.

Chapter 36

MONEY-SAVING TIPS

Generally, when you purchase tack you get what you pay for. A quality product will cost more than one of inferior materials or craftsmanship.

Experts do note that a low price does not always imply poor quality. If you can't afford to buy top quality goods, you can still receive satisfactory value by careful shopping.

Also, realize that a top-of-the-line model may not be worth the price, which can be double that of a medium-priced version. For example, is a $1,500 saddle really twice as good as the $700 one? You will have to decide if that extra $850 for a renowned brand name is really worth it.

You can save money and receive maximum value by careful shopping, evaluating what level of quality you require in certain products.

This sample chart will help you determine your quality requirements:

Best Quality (Do not scrimp on safety.)

Saddle	Girth
Bridle	Halter and lead
Bit	Brushes
Stirrup leathers	Hoof pick
Stirrups	Pad
	Winter blanket

Medium Quality

Sheet	Boots
Martingale	Noseband
Breastplate	Longe line

Average Quality (These items receive hard wear and don't vary in quality that much.)

Whip	Sweat scraper
Curry	Mane comb

You can also resort to a wide variety of alternative acquisition methods. The most popular way to save money is to buy used equipment.

You can buy used tack from a variety of vendors, with the safest choice being a tack shop that sells used items on consignment. A reputable shop will accept only those items in salable condition. A knowledgeable tack-shop owner would not market a saddle with a broken tree, or a bridle with rotted leather.

Buying a used item through a tack shop involves paying a markup, however. You can locate better bargains from private parties, either through advertisements or word of mouth. However, you must inspect these items carefully. Also do not expect to receive any sort of guarantee, as the seller does not operate a business. You must also gauge the honesty of the seller, if you do not already know the person. How do you know the tack you buy really belonged to the seller, and wasn't stolen from someone's tackroom? If you buy stolen goods, you may be forced to return them to the rightful owner if law enforcement agencies trace you as the buyer.

Experts recommend to avoid buying tack at a flea market or swap meet. Again, the tack may be stolen, and usually the quality is poor. Saddles sold at these locations are usually damaged inexpensive models or worn-out antiques.

You should purchase tack at a tack auction with the same caution as you would a horse at a horse auction. Evaluate the quality of the goods and the reputation of the auction sponsors. If you attend a complete dispersal of a well-known barn or farm, you can usually assume that the goods will be of acceptable quality. A fly-by-night operation, in your town for "One Night Only," could be dumping illegal or no-name goods.

Saddles are probably the number one item purchased used. With your saddle being your major tack investment, a preowned model might save you considerable cash compared to a new one. You can also avoid the uncomfortable breaking-in period.

One disadvantage about buying a used saddle is that your choices will be limited as compared to new models. Also, you must be sure that the saddle matches your needs; if not, a bargain model might turn out to be worthless. An English saddle will have molded its seat and flaps to the previous owner's conformation. Realize that buying a used saddle is like buying someone else's shoes.

Inspect a used saddle carefully. Saddle-repair experts advise you to check the tree's solidity first. A craftsperson can repair a broken tree, but the cost can equal the price of a new saddle.

Test for a broken tree by grasping the cantle and attempting to bend it back and forth. On a Western saddle, try to rock the seat. If the tree

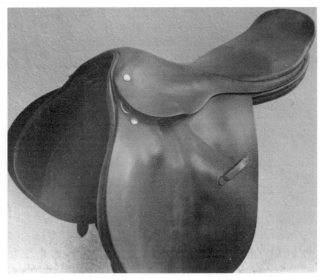

A used all-purpose saddle shows wear on the flaps, where the rider's leg pressure has imprinted stirrup leathers.

Test a used saddle for a broken tree.

feels wobbly where cantle meets the seat, the tree is probably broken. Ask for an expert's opinion if you feel unsure about a tree's condition.

Check the Western saddle's tree to see if it is rawhide-covered or a molded synthetic model. Pull up the stirrup leathers, where they hang over the bars of the tree, and look for a smooth surface and the yellowish-clear color of rawhide. Feel for the lacing that secures the stretched rawhide over the wooden tree. A Ralide tree will look and feel like plastic, and a fiberglass tree's surface feels like a rough-textured cloth.

The saddle's brand name may be stamped on the top side of the near-side sweat flap, or on the Western saddle's latigo carrier. If you do not see a manufacturer's name on a Western saddle, inspect it carefully. In the Southwest, many "no-name" inexpensive saddles are made in Mexico. These imports are often inferior in materials and craftsmanship. Mexican hardware, especially the rigging's D-rings, is more likely to fracture under stress.

Next, look for signs of wear. The flaps and seat of an English saddle will show the most wear from the rider's weight. Is the stitching solid? Do billets appear strong? Does it appear that the previous owner conditioned the leather regularly?

Avoid a saddle that has dried or mildewed leather. Expert care can rejuvenate these conditions, but the effort will require careful reconditioning.

Check a Western saddle's leather on all portions, especially underneath the jockeys and fenders. Pull down the stirrup leathers to see if they appear secure.

Certain conditions require simple repairs, the most obvious being a loose horn cap, which is usually the result of torn or frayed stitching. A saddler can reglue and stitch the leather, or fit a new cap. The saddler can also install a new seat.

You can replace a worn cinch, stirrups, or latigos yourself. If a saddle appears fine except for a missing fender or torn jockey, a craftsperson can build a replacement section to match the rest of the saddle. An expert can even take apart a saddle completely and rebuild it to look like new. Expect to pay a stiff price for such renovations, however.

Many older Western saddles, made by respected firms, are still excellent buys. The following saddlemakers, many now out of business, built good saddles during the last fifty years: S. D. Myres, Forrest Knott, Pick Pickering, Hamley's, Porter's, Miles City Saddlery, Jedlicka's, Visalia, and Olsen-Nolte. If you find a well-kept saddle bearing the stamp of one of these makers, buy it.

When you are in the market for a specific piece of tack, you might explore the bartering method. Here you do not pay the seller in cash—you exchange goods or services for the tack you want. For example, you could trade stereo equipment, a VCR, or even a used car for a saddle. If you don't mind hard work, maybe you could trade a certain number of hours of mucking stalls for a bridle.

Similar to the barter method is swapping. Here you would exchange two similar items. For example, if you wanted to switch to cutting from barrel racing, you could propose a swap to the owner of a cutting saddle.

A successful barter or swap requires a mutual agreement between you and the seller. It usually turns out to be a one-sided benefit, as the person who is most anxious to negotiate gives more than the other. If you suggest a barter, the item's owner may not agree immediately—or will have to consider, "What's in it for me?" The ideal situation is when that person mentions wanting to get rid of that extra saddle in the tackroom. If you lack the cash, you could casually suggest a swap.

On the other hand, you can resell tack that you no longer need. As the seller, you will offer goods to suspicious buyers. Prove your good faith by displaying the original bill of sale for your saddle, and by showing photographs of you in the saddle. You don't have to point out the equipment's weak points, but buyers appreciate any honesty.

You can explore various alternatives in selling your tack. You can consign goods to a tack shop, advertise in the classifieds or on bulletin boards, hold a barn sale, or tell your fellow riders. Decide if you will consider any barter or swap proposals.

You can also buy major pieces of equipment cooperatively, an arrangement in which two or more horse owners own a fair share of an item. Sharing the purchase of an infrequently used item usually proves most satisfactory. For example, four owners can purchase a set of body clippers. Each contributes about $30 and therefore can use the machine as needed. If you enter into this type of agreement, it is wise to describe the purchase and use terms in a written contract. You don't have to have this contract drafted by an attorney or notarized, but it will clarify each person's benefits and obligations. Then if one person moves to another barn, you can solicit another owner or pay off the one who withdraws from the agreement.

Renting or leasing tack are other options. If you only need an item occasionally, you might be able to rent it from a tack shop or an individual. Again, you may have to convince the owner of your good faith, and probably you will be required to leave some type of deposit.

Finally, you can extend the value of your tack collection by repairing and recycling goods. If you sew, you can repair fabric items by hand or machine. Save parts from irreparable items to use as replacements on others. You can recycle straps, buckles, and clamps to create new blanket straps or lead ropes.

Bibliography

The following books and periodicals provide additional information on saddlery design and use.

Baker, Jennifer. *Saddlery and Horse Equipment*. Arco, New York: 1985. (British slant; emphasis on English style.)

Beatie, Russell. *Saddles*. Norman, Oklahoma: University of Oklahoma Press, 1981. (History, types, and fit of Western saddles.)

Edwards, E. Hartley, and Price, Stephen. eds., *Complete Book of Horse and Saddle Equipment*. Los Angeles, California: Exeter, 1981.

Edwards, E. Hartley. *Saddlery*. San Diego, California: A.S. Barnes, 1963. (British slant; history and types of English tack.)

Pastene, H. Alexander, *Riding Contact*. Hilton Head, South Carolina; Cooper Clark Company, 1987. (Fitting English saddles.)

Richardson, Julie, ed. *Horse Tack: The Complete Equipment Guide for Riding and Driving*. New York: Morrow, 1981.

Sherer, Richard. *Horseman's Handbook of Western Saddles*. Franktown, Colorado: Sherer Custom Saddles, 1988. (Update of 1977 title, *Buyer's Guide to Western Saddles*.)

Tack 'n Togs Merchandising, *Tack 'n Togs*. (Monthly trade magazine.)

Tack 'n Togs Merchandising, *Tack 'n Togs Book: Annual Buyers' Guide Issue*. Minnetonka, Minnesota (Industry directory by manufacturer and product.)

Taylor, Louis. *Bits: Their History, Use, and Misuse*. North Hollywood, California; Wilshire Book Company, 1977. (Types and uses of English and Western bits.)

Tuke, Dianna. *Bit by Bit: A Guide to Equine Bits*. New York; Arco, 1978. (British slant; English bits types and uses.)

Tuke, Dianna. *Stitch by Stitch: A Guide to Equine Saddles*. London: J.A. Allen, 1970. (British slant; English saddlemaking, styles, and fitting.)

SOURCE LIST

—

The following North American firms contributed information to this book. Each listing includes contact address and primary product. Be aware that some companies sell only through dealers.

Adams Equipment Company
PO Box 489, Cookeville, TN 38503 (Western pads, boots, bits)

Armstrong Supply Company
PO Box 22267, Chattanooga, TN 37422 (Western bits, spurs)

Australian Stock Saddle Company
PO Box 987, Malibu, CA 90265 (Australian saddles, accessories)

Avent's Saddlery
PO Box 325, Meriden, NH 03770 (English saddlery)

BMB
1935 Walker, Wichita, KS 67213 (Horse clothing, halters)

Bar-F Products, Inc.
1955 Airport Boulevard, Red Bluff, CA 96080 (Boots, sweats)

Big D Products
705 Soscol Avenue, Napa, CA 94559 (Horse clothing)

Blue Ribbon
737 Madison Street, Shelbyville, TN 37160 (English saddlery)

Bork of Pendleton
Route 8, Box 284-A, Caldwell, ID 83805 (Western cinches)

D.R. Brittain Custom Saddlery
PO Box 697, Hays, KS 67601 (Western saddlery)

Brown's Performance Saddles
Rt. 2, Box 132, Nevada, MO 64772 (Endurance saddles)

Canterbury, Ltd.
PO Box 585, Quakertown, PA 18951 (English Saddle pads)

Cashel Enterprises
717 Schoen Road, Silver Creek, WA 98585 (Saddle pads)

Champion Turf Equipment
330 S. Mission Road, Los Angeles, CA 90033 (Western saddlery)

Circle Y of Yoakum, Inc.
PO Box 797, Yoakum, TX 77995 (Western saddlery)

Colorado Saddlery Company
1631 15th Street, Denver, CO 80202 (Western saddlery)

Courbette Saddlery Company, Inc.
PO Box 2131, Heath, OH 43056 (English saddlery)

Court's Saddlery Company
403 N. Main Street, Bryan, TX 77801 (Western saddles)

Cowboy Products
PO Box 396, Sheridan, WY 82801 (Western strap goods)

Crates Leather Company
515 Holtzclaw Avenue, Chattanooga, TN 37404 (Western saddlery)

B. T. Crump Company
PO Box 1597, Richmond, VA 23213 (English saddlery)

Custom Metal Crafters, Inc.
815 N. Mountain Road, Newington, CT 06111 (Saddlery hardware)

D J Enterprises
PO Box 13976, Sacramento, CA 95083 (Boots, control halter)

Dan's Saddlery Corporation
65 Mahan Street, W. Babylon, NY 11704 (English saddlery)

Diablo Manufacturing Company
PO Box 1108, Grass Valley, CA 95945 (Silver trim)

Double R Leather Company
PO Box 72965, Chattanooga, TN 37407 (Western saddlery, bits)

Dressage Extensions
23550 San Juan Drive, Tehachapi, CA 93561 (English saddlery)

Greg Dutton Bits
2043 Don Pasqual Road, Los Lunas, NM 87031 (Western bits)

Eiser's
1204 N. Broad Street, Hillside, NJ 07205 (English saddlery)

Foxwood
19 Main Street, Laurel, MD 20707 (English & Western saddlery)

Frontier Saddle Pads
PO Box K, Nogales, AZ 85628 (Western pads)

Garcia Bit and Spur Company
500 Commercial Street, Elko, NV 89801 (Western bits, spurs)

Gardiner Imports
854 Albany Post Road, Gardiner, NY 12525 (English saddles)

Gateway Products
825 W. Colorado, Holly, CO 81047 (Barn equipment)

Hartmeyer Saddlery
7111 W. Bethel, Muncie, IN 47304 (English saddlery)

Hergon Saddle Cinch Factory, Inc.
1311 S. Broadway, Denver, CO 80210 (Western cinches)

Hermann Oak Leather Company
4050 N. 1st Street, St. Louis, MO 63147 (Leather tannery)

Hinshaw Manufacturing Company, Inc.
PO Box 2539, Burlington, NC 27215 (Boots, saddle pads)

Horse of Course
6395 Gunpark Drive H, Boulder, CO 80301 (Horse clothing)

Horseworld Emporium
4129 E. Bell Road, Phoenix, AZ 85032 (Australian saddles)

Hoyt and Worthen Tanning Corporation
60 Railroad Street, Haverhill, MA 01830 (Leather tannery)

Hulling Saddlery
376 Ogden, Denver, CO 80218 (Western saddlery)

Humphrys Manufacturing Company
1241 Carpenter Street, Philadelphia, PA 19147 (Horse clothing)

Jimmy's 20th Century Saddlery
Box 354, Prescott, AZ 86301 (English saddlery)

Kathy's Show Equipment, Inc.,
1674 Rincon Avenue, Escondido, CA 92026 (Western saddlery)

Keyston Brothers
1848 Deming Way, Sparks, NV 89431 (Western saddlery)

M. L. Leddy
2455 N. Main, Fort Worth, TX 76106 (Western saddlery)

Les-Kare, Inc.
PO Box AAA, Pojoaque Station, Santa Fe, NM 87501 (Boots)

Libertyville Saddle Shop, Inc.
PO Box M, Libertyville, IL 60048 (English and Western saddlery)

MacPherson Leather Company
PO Box 390, Los Angeles, CA 90053 (Western saddlery)

John G. Mahler Company
9012 Chancellor Row, Dallas, TX 75247 (Leather tannery)

Midwest Saddlery
4415 "B" Drive South, Battlecreek, MI 49017 (English saddlery)

Elmer Miller
Rt. 6, Box 6319, Nampa, ID 83651 (Western bits, spurs)

Joe Miller Saddlery, Inc.
PO Box 601, Rosebud, TX 76570 (Western saddlery)

Miller's Harness Company
235 Murray Hill Parkway, E. Rutherford, NJ 07075 (English saddlery)

Dennis Moreland Enterprises
PO Box 330, Goldthwaite, TX 76844 (Western strap goods)

National Bridle Shop
PO Box 292, Lewisburg, TN 37091 (English saddlery)

Oster
5055 N. Lydell Avenue, Milwaukee, WI 53217 (Clippers)

Ronie Peakes and Son
5 Sibley Street, Auburn, MA 01501 (Horse clothing)

Perforated Pad Company
PO Box 159, Woonsocket, RI 02895 (Horse clothing)

Potts Longhorn Leather
3141 Oak Grove Street, Dallas, TX 75204 (Western saddlery)

Frank Principe
2939 208th Street, Langley, B.C. (Canada) V3A 4P5 (Western bits)

Quick Bits
PO Box 485, San Jacinto, CA 92383 (Western bits)

Ralide, Inc.
PO Box 131, Athens, TN 37303 (Saddle trees)

Rawhide Manufacturing
683 Marsat Court, Suite B, Chula Vista, CA 92011 (Western braided goods)

Ronmar Industries, Inc.
4781 Woodstock Road, Roswell, GA 30075 (Western strap goods)

Ropers' Supply Company
PO Box 1886, McAlester, OK 94501 (Roping gear)

Royal Riders Manufacturing Company
529 S. Second Street, San Jose, CA 95112 (Horse clothing)

Sharon Saare Saddles
1267 Clover Drive, Santa Rosa, CA 95401 (Endurance saddles)

Saddle Barn Tack Distributors
415 E. Second Street, Roswell, NM 88201 (Western saddlery)

Saddle King of Texas
PO Box 947, Waco, TX 76703 (Western saddlery)

Saddlery Trade Associates, Ltd.
PO Box 29446, Richmond, VA 23233 (English saddlery)

Saint Lawrence Sales
12 W. Flint Street, Lake Orion, MI 48035 (English saddlery)

Schneider Saddlery Company, Inc.
1609 Golden Gate Plaza, Cleveland, OH 44122 (English and Western saddlery)

Sherer Custom Saddles, Inc.
PO Box 385, Franktown, CO 80116 (Western saddlery)

Dale Shoemaker
2861 Lakeshore Road, Manistee, MI 49660 (Arabian show halters)

The Side-Saddlery
PO Box 4076, Mt. Holly, NJ 08060 (Sidesaddles)

Ed Sims Spur Company
Drawer A. Uvalde, TX 78802 (Western bits, spurs)

Smith Brothers Roping Supplies, Inc.
I-35 and Ropers Road, Denton, TX 76201 (Roping gear)

Spanish Silver Bit Enterprises
16506 Wilton Place, Torrance, CA 90504 (Western bits)

Sporthorse Equipment
400 Seavey Lane, Petaluma, CA 94952 (English strap goods)

Stonewall Saddles
27180 Citrus Avenue, Perris, CA 92370 (Endurance saddles)

Sunburst Bits and Spurs
Rt. 1, Box 96M, Mt. Vernon, MO 65712 (Western bits, spurs)

Super Sweats
5112 Viceroy, Norco, CA 91760 (Sweat wraps)

Tex Tan Western Leather Company
708 Highway 77A, Yoakum, TX 77995 (Western saddlery)

Harry Thurston's Saddle Shop
3144 E. Bell Road, Phoenix, AZ 85032 (Western saddlery)

Toklat Originals, Inc.
PO Box 1257, Lake Oswego, OR 97034 (Pads, boots, bits)

Triple C Leather Company
Rt. 3, Box 604, Morgantown, KY 42261 (Leather tannery)

Triple Crown Blanket
PO Box 484, Alpharetta, GA 30201 (Horse clothing)

Victor Leather Goods
3678 Roseview Avenue, Los Angeles, CA 90065 (Western saddlery)

Victor Supreme
2507 E. Bell Road, Phoenix, AZ 85032 (English and Western saddlery)

Vigil's Saddle Shop
8008 Rio Grande Boulevard NW, Albuquerque, NM 87114 (Western saddles)

Vogt Western Silver, Ltd.
PO Box 2309, Turlock, CA 95380 (Silver trim)

Walsall Hardware Corporation
7831 E. Greenway Road, Scottsdale, AZ 85260 (Hardware)

Winner's Circle Horse-Wear
16007 Chastain Road, Odessa, FL 33556 (Horse clothing)

Wonder Whip Company
Box D, Fostoria, IA 51340 (Whips)

Wrip-Wrap
PO Box 816, Norco, CA 91760 (Sweat wraps)

ACKNOWLEDGMENTS

The following contributors have generously shared their expertise as primary source material in my research:

Carla McReynolds, Black Horse, Ltd., Albuquerque, New Mexico

Ricardo Vigil; Vigil's Saddle Shop, Albuquerque, New Mexico

Bill Hill, Hill's Saddle Repair, Albuquerque, New Mexico.

George and Joyce Lamb, The Horse of Course, Boulder, Colorado.

Sue Burkman, Arabian and Andalusian trainer, Perisian Park, Sun Valley, California.

Annie McCutcheon, Dressage Extensions, Tehachapi, California.

Patricia Kinnaman, Traditional Equitation School, Los Angeles, California.

Brian Carters, Kensington Leather Company, Attleboro Falls, Massachusetts.

Martha Kasser, European Equestrian Supply, Santa Monica, California.

Jimmy Wiebe, Jimmy's 20th Century Saddlery, Prescott, Arizona.

Verne Albright, founder and past president of the American Association of Owners and Breeders of Peruvian Paso Horses.

Barbara Currie, President, International Andalusian Horse Association.

Julie Bergman, equestrian journalist, Los Angeles, California.

Greg Dutton, Dutton Bits, Los Lunas, New Mexico.

Cole Smith, Smith Brothers Roping Supplies, Inc., Denton, Texas.

Arnold Weiner, Eiser's, Hillside, New Jersey.

Karen Bell, Foxwood, Laurel, Maryland.

Leanna Noble, Miller Harness Company, East Rutherford, New Jersey.

Jane Guthrie, Hartmeyer Saddlery, Munice, Indiana.

Susan Foster, Avent's Saddlery, Meriden, New Hampshire.

Donald F. Ritterbusch, Knightwood Saddlers, Aurora, Colorado.

Virginia Newkirch, The Stitching Bench, Ridgefield, Connecticut.

Ken Kimberley, Kimberley's Supply Barn, Lebanon, New Jersey.

Dianne Fay, Certified Riding Instructor, Los Lunas, New Mexico.

Harry Thurston, Harry Thurston's Saddle Shop, Phoenix, Arizona.

Jane Hickey, Greenway Saddlery, Phoenix, Arizona.

Tahna Curtis, Rancher's Feed and Saddlery Company, Scottsdale, Arizona.

Derek Miller, Horseworld Emporium, Phoenix, Arizona.

Bob Hunter, M. L. Leddy, Fort Worth, Texas.

Bob Mezin, Kathy's Show Equipment, Escondido, California.

Colin Dangaard, Australian Stock Saddle Co., Malibu, California.

Trevor James, Trevor James Saddlery, Australia.

Robert Beech, National Bridle Shop, Lewisburg, Tennessee.
Deborah Kopman, Gardiner Imports, Gardiner, New York.
Richard Sherer, Sherer Custom Saddles, Inc., Franktown, Colorado.
Dale Shoemaker, Arabian halter designer, Manistee, Michigan.
Charlotte Kneeland, The Side-Saddlery, Mount Holly, New Jersey.
Jack Martin, Libertyville Saddle Shop, Libertyville, Illinois.
Henry Gleisner, Saint Lawrence Sales, Lake Orion, Michigan.
Joe Miller, Joe Miller Saddlery, Inc., Rosebud, Texas.
Bob Owen, BMB, Wichita, Kansas.
Ronie Peakes, Ronie Peakes and Son, Auburn, Massachusetts.
Sharon Saare, Sharon Saare Saddles, Santa Rosa, California.
Barbara Weatherwax, The Saddle Tree, Sunland, California.
Jan Haugen, Saddlery Trade Associates, Ltd., Richmond, Virginia.
Bryant Holman, Saddle Barn Tack Distributors, Rosewell, New Mexico.
Harold Lamb, Potts Longhorn Leather, Dallas, Texas.
Michael Quick, Quick Bits, San Jacinto, California.
Juan Ortiz, Rawhide Manufacturing, Chula Vista, California.
Teri Kingsford, Bork of Pendleton, Caldwell, Idaho.
Barbara Harwick, Canterbury, Ltd., Quakertown, Pennsylvania.
Helen King, Cashel Enterprises, Silver Creek, Washington.
Harry Hauser, Courbette Saddlery Co., Heath, Ohio.
Susan Phillips, Victor Supreme, Phoenix, Arizona.
Janet Munchak, Triple Crown Blanket, Alpharetta, Georgia.
Daniel Crates, Crates Leather Co., Chattanooga, Tennessee.
Wendy Dowling, Sporthorse Equipment, Petaluma, California.
E. L. Butterworth, B. T. Crump Co., Richmond, Virginia.
Sandy Allinson, Dan's Saddlery Corp. West Babylon, New York.
Eugene O'Neill, Wonder Whip Company, Fostoria, Iowa.
Jim Strait, Sunburst Bits and Spurs, Mount Vernon, Missouri.
Joy Borchers, Super Sweats, Norco, California.
David Tissenbaum, Deluxe Saddlery, Baltimore, Maryland.
Manny Ortiz, Frontier Saddle Pads, Nogales, Arizona.
Al Herr, Hergon Saddle-Cinch Factory, Denver, Colorado.
John Mahler, John G. Mahler Co., Dallas, Texas.
Richard Kerwin, Oster, Milwaukee, Wisconsin.
Frank Rocha, Spanish Silver Bit Enterprises, Torrance, California.
Jerry Stoner, Stonewall Saddles, Perris, California.
Char Rueschenberg, Wrip-Wrap, Norco, California.
D. R. Brittain, Brittain Custom Saddlery, Hays, Kansas.
Lucille Glass, Les-Kare, Inc., Santa Fe, New Mexico.
Nicki Parkhill, Hulling Saddlery, Denver, Colorado.
Peter Runyon, Victor Leather Goods, Los Angeles, California.
Betty Kjera, Winner's Circle Horse-Wear, Odessa, Florida.
Elmer Miller, Miller Bit and Spur, Nampa, Idaho.
Gary Parsons, Court's Saddlery, Bryan, Texas.

I also appreciated receiving information from the following firms:

Adams Equipment, Inc.; Armstrong Supply Company; Bar-F Products, Inc.; Big D Products; Blue Ribbon; Champion Turf Equipment; Circle Y of Yoakum, Inc.; Colorado Saddlery Co.; Cooper Clark Co.; County Saddlery; Cowboy Products; Custom Metal Crafters, Inc.; Diablo Manufacturing Co.; D J Enterprises; Double R Leather Co.; Garcia Bit and Spur Co.; Gateway Products; Hermann Oak Leather Co.; Hinshaw Manufacturing Co., Inc.; Hoyt and Worthen Tanning Corp.; Humphrys Manufacturing Co.; Keyston Brothers; Neil Love Ropes; MacPherson Leather Co.; Midwest Saddlery; Dennis Moreland Enterprises; Perforated Pad Co.; Frank Principe, Silversmith; Ralide, Inc.; Ronmar Industries, Inc.; Ropers' Supply Co.; Royal Riders Manufacturing Co.; Saddle King of Texas; Schneider Saddlery Co., Inc.; Ed Sims Spur Co.; Tex Tan Western Leather Co.; Toklat Originals, Inc.; Triple C Leather Co.; Vogt Western Silver, Ltd.; Walsall Hardware Corp.

Also, special thanks to Carl Norberg, Executive Director, and Glenda Chipps, Services Coordinator, Western and English Manufacturers Association, Denver, Colorado; Susie Hare, Mountain States Men's, Boy's, and Western Apparel Club, Denver, Colorado; Ralph Beatty, Western and English Retailers Association; and the Public Relations Department, American Quarter Horse Association.

INDEX

Tack Shops

Following is a list of tack shops that sell equipment discussed in this book.

24 KARAT SADDLERY
3325 ALLDAY RD
HUNTINGTON MD 20639

3L TACK & SADDLERY
5525 MISSION RD
BONSALL CA 92003

A J SADDLERY
39 HILLIARDS BRIDGE RD
VINCENTON NJ 08088

A-1 ANIMAL CENTER
7280 E. BROADWAY
TUCSON AZ 85710

AA CALLISTER CO
3615 S REDWOOD RD
SALT LAKE CITY UT 84119

ACREDALE SADDLERY
5248 INDIAN RIVER RD
VIRGINIA BCH VA 23464

ADAMS WESTERN STORE
1415 WESTERN AVENUE
LAS VEGAS NV 89102

AGWAY FEEDS
24 MAPLE STREET
SOUTH CHELMSFORD MA 01824

AGWAY INC.
RD 6 BOX 620
ALLENTOWN PA 18106

AIKEN SADDLERY
111 E PINE ROG
AIKEN SC 29801

AL BAR RANCH
55345 FIR ROAD
MISHAWAKA IN 46545

AL-DAHNA STUD
13185 NE COUNTY LINE RD
LONGMONT CO 80501

ALASKA MILL & FEED CO
114 N ORCA
ANCHORAGE AK 99501

ALBERS OF NEVADA
PO BOX 10430
755 TIMBER WAY PUR#02656
RENO NV 89510

ALDERGROVE SADDLERY
27153 FRASER HWY
ALDERGROVE BC CANADA 99999

ALFRED'S TACK SHOP
RT. 3, BOX 274
CARTHAGE NC 28327

ALL THE KINGS HORSES
199 ETHAN ALLEN HWY
RIDGEFIELD CT 06877

ALLIES TACK SHOP
RT 2
N KINGSTON RI 02852

ALLTAKER ACRES TACK SHOP
RT 516 & WATERSDORF ROAD
SPRING GROVE PA 17362

ALMELUND EMPORIUM
37455 PARK TRAIL
ALMELUND MN 55002

ALMONT SADDLERY
780 NORTH VAN DYKE
ALMONT MI 48003

AMBERBROOK TACK SHOP
RT 4 BOX 190
AIKEN SC 29801

AMERICAN FEED & FARM
PO BOX 92219
WORLDWAY STATION
LOS ANGELES CA 90009

AMERICAN FEED & FARM
870 REDWOOD HWY
GRANT PASS OR 97527

AMERICAN MORGAN HORSE
PO BOX 960
SHELBURNE VT 05482

AMERICAN SADDLE HORSE MUSEUM
4093 IRON WORKS PIKE
LEXINGTON KY 40511

ANDRES'S BOOT & SADDLE
13356 HWY 88
PO BOX 753
LOCKEFORD CA 95237

ANIMAL CLINIC OF BAKER
2490 TENTH ST
BAKER OR 97814

ANIMAL HEALTH & VET SUPPLY
966 BEAUMONT AVENUE
BEAUMONT CA 92223

ANIMAS VALLEY ARBARIST
613 COUNTY ROAD 213
DURANGO CO 81301

ANNAPOLIS RIDGE FEED FARM
4 PACIFIC WOODS
GUALALA CA 95445

APACHE SADDLERY & HORSE SUPP
1441 AMBOY ROAD
AMBOY IL 61310

APALOOSA HORSE CLUB
ATTN:CHERYL STARKE
PO BOX 8403
MORCOW ID 83843

APPLE SADDLERY
2536 INNESS ROAD
GLOUCHESTER
ONTARIO CANADA K1B 4C5

ARABIAN HORSE EXPRESS
8TH & MAPLE, COLUMBIA BLDG
PO BOX 845
COFFEYVILLE KS 67337

ARABIAN HORSE TRUST
12000 ZUNI STREET
WESTMINSTER CO 80234

ARCOLA FEED HRDWRE
13814 HWY 6
ROSHARON TX 77583

ARENA, THE
3219 BECHELLI LANE
REDDING CA 96002

ARIZONA SADDLERY
1687 SOUTH WOODWARD
BIRMINGHAM MI 48009

ARIZONA SADDLERY
315 MAIN ST
ROCHESTER MI 48063

ARROWHEAD FEED & SADDLERY CO
3200 NORTH HARRISON STREET
SHAWNEE OK 74801

ASHBERRY ACRES
4658 SEEMEN STREET SW
NOWAREE OH 44662

ASHLAND SADDLERY
1539 CLEVELAND AVE
ASHLAND OH 44805

ATLANTA SADDLERY
1670-C HWY 9 S
ALPHARETTA GA 30201

AUSTIN'S SADDLERY
209 E ELM
UNIT 14
O'FALLON MO 63366

B & E FEED & SUPPLIES
1414 6TH ST
NORCO CA 91760

B & L TACK & FEED
2190 SKYTOP TRAIL
DOVER PA 17315

B BAR Z'S
556 PALMER BLVD
SARASOTA FL 34232

B.J.'S TACK & SADDLE
RT. 1, BOX 253H
COTTAGEVILLE SC 29435

BACK ACRES SADDLERY
4550 LAPEER RD
PORT HURON MI 48060

BACK PORCH, THE
HWY 70
LENOIR CITY TN 37771

BAG 40 SUPPLY
3120 MEMORIAL BLVD.
KERRVILLE TX 78028

BAHR SADDLERY LTD
STEELES AVENUE WEST
HORNBY,ONTARO CANADA L0P1E0

BAIRD ISD
BOX 1147
BAIRD TX 79504

BALSAM QUARTER TACK
RT1 LONG SHOALS RD.
ARDEN NC 28704

BANCROFT SADDLERY LTD
734 E MAIN RD
PT SMITH RI 02871

BARBER'S TACK & HORSE SUPPLY
7907 HWY 72 WEST
MADISON AL 35758

BARRINGTON SADDLERY
420 WEST NORTHWEST HIGHWAY
BARRINGTON IL 60010

BAYBROOK TACK SHOP
90 BAYVIEW AVE
BERKLEY MA 02779

BEAR CREEK WESTERN STORE
RT 1 BOX M HWY 16 W
AMITA LA 70442

BEDFORD SADDLERY
56 BABBITT RD
BEDFORD HILLS NY 10507

BELANGER'S TACK SHOP
RD 4 BOX 4570
CARIBOU ME 04736

BELLAMY CREEK FARM
1045 NORTH BELLAMY
SONIA MI 48846

BENNIGHT TRAINING STABLES
7007 MILLSTREAM
SAN ANTONIO TX 78238

BERWICK LTD
1669 WESTERN AVE
ALBANY NY 12203

BETTY JO TACK SHOP
RT 2 BOX 678
GALAX VA 24333

BETTYS REST SADDLERY
1718 CHAPEL RD
HAVRE DE GRACE MD 21076

BEVAL SADDLERY
PARK AVENUE
GLADSTONE NJ 07934

BIG BEND SADDLERY
EAST HIGHWAY 90
ALPINE TX 79831

BIG OAK TACK & GROOMING
RT 14 BOX 60
COX RD
ANDERSON SC 29621

BIG R STORES
BOX 548
KLAMATH FALLS OR 97601

BIRT SADDLERY CO
468-474 MAIN STREET
WINNIPEG MANIT CANADA R3B1B6

BISHIPS TACK SHOP
181 RT 202 H
HEMMINGFORD
QUEBEC CANADA J0L1H0

BIT & BRIDLE TACK&TOGS SHOP
2720 NEW HARTFORD RD
OWENSBORO KY 42301

BIT OF BRITAIN
400 OLD ELM RD
NORTHEAST MD 21901

BITS & BRIDLES SADDLERY
10176 BALITMORE NAT PIKE
ELLICOTT CITY MD 21043

BITS AND PIECES
1250 HWY 74
SUITE B 130
EVERGREEM CP 80439

BLACK HORSE LTD INC
1715 SAN PEDRO NE
ALBUQUERQUE NM 87110

BLACK HORSE SADDLE SHOP
2103 MAPLE AVE
ZANESVILLE OH 43701

BLACK SMITH TACK SHOP
RT 1 BOX 110
GLADE SPGS VA 24340

BLACKENEY FEED & LIVESTK
CORNER INDUSTRIAL DR.
ZEBULON GA 30295

BLACKWELL NORTH AMERICA
1001 FRIES MILL RD
BLACKWOOD NJ 08012

BLUEBERRY MARE HILL
262 FOSFARM HILL RD
N BERWICK ME 03906

BOBS SADDLE SHOP INC
RT 206
MOUNT HOLLY NJ 08060

BOOT AND SADDLE SHOP
300 SOUTH GILLETTE AVENUE
GILLETTE WY 82716

BOOT HILL TACK AND REPAIR
933 10TH AVE
SIDNEY NE 69162

BOOTS-N-SADDLES
PUBLIC SQUARE
LAURENS SC 29360

BOTHELL FEED CENTER
20809 BOTHELL EVERETT HWY
BOTHELL WA 98021

BRACKNEY'S WESTERN STORE
RR 1 BOX 1
GREENCASTLE IN 46135

BRANDING IRON WESTERN CORRAL
10831 WOODEDGE
HOUSTON TX 77070

BRANDYWINE SADDLERY
RT 7 BOX 6008
STANTON
WILMINGTON DE 19804

BRASS TACK SHOP
FAY RD - ANASAR FRM
ABINGDON CT 06230

BRENNANS BIT & BRIDLE SHOP
SNAKE HOLLOW RD
BRIDGEHAMPTON NY 11932

BRIDLE PATH
460 ADA DRIVE
ADA MI 49301

BRIDLES & BRITCHES
2308 ELGIN AVE
GRANDE OR 97850

BRIDLES N BRITCHES
630 GENTRY WAY
RENO NV 89502

BRIGHTON FEED & FARM SUPPLY
370 N. MAIN
BRIGHTON CO 80601

BRIGHTON HARNESS & SADDLE
11364 BUNO RD
BRIGHTON MI 48116

BRINDLE LEDGE TACK SHOP
153 PAIGE HILL RD
GOFFSTOWN NH 03045

BROOKSIDE TACK SHOP
MINERAL SPRINGS RD
W PERU ME 04290

BROWN ROAD HAY & GRAIN
7601 BROWN ROAD
INYORKEN CA 93527

BUCKEYE RANCH & SADDLE SHOP
7638 MERIDIAN RD N
VACAVILLE CA 95688

BUCKLE DOWN LIMITED
385 LANCASTER AVENUE
FRAZIER PA 19355

BUCKS COUNTY SADDLERY
RT 202 & 263
4765 YORK RD
BUCKINGHAM PA 18912

BURBANK PET & EQUESTRIAN
1830 RIVERSIDE DRIVE
GLENDALE CA 91201

BURDIC FEED INC
301 N RR STREET
KENT WA 98032

BURDIC HOMESTEAD
18422 CASCADE VIEW DRIVE
MONROE WA 98272

BURGESS STABLES RIDING
RT. 4, BOX 188A
VICTORIA TX 77904

BURGUNDY'S WESTERN WEAR & SAD
107 NORTH MAY ST
THUNDER BAY ON CANADA P7C3N8

BURNS FEED STORE
29215 SE ORIENT DR
GRESHAM OR 97080

C & A FARM AND RANCH
1944 ROUTE 68 NORTH
XENIA OH 45385

C & L UNICORN RANCH
1306 99 ST E
TACOMA WA 98445

C & M HORSESHOE SALES
201 PORTER RD
CONROE TX 77301

C BAR C ARABIANS
19336 HILLSIDE DRIVE
SONORA CA 95370

C C SADDLERY
105 N MAIN ST
WATFORD CITY ND 58854

C M TACK
17100 W 53 ST
SHAWNEE KS 66217

C T TACK AND FEED
PO BOX 624
RT 626
GASBERG VA 23857

CABALINE SADDLE SHOP
11101 STATE ROUTE 1
PO BOX 398
PT REYES STATION CA 94956

CABIN BRANCH SHOPPE
231 PENN AVE
SOUTHERN PINES NC 28387

CAHABA SADDLERY
5090 CAHABA VALLEY ROAD
BIRMINGHAM AL 35243

CAHABA TACK
370 NW BROAD STREET
SOUTHERN PINES NC 28387

CALABASAS SADDLERY
23998 CRAFTMAN ROAD
CALABASAS CA 91302

CALADON'S TACK LOFT
RD 1 ENGLE ROAD
INDUSTRY PA 15052

CALIFORNIA THOUROUGH SALE
201 COLORADO PLACE
ARCADIA CA 91006

CAMELOT TACK SHOP
6594 FISHER RD
WILLIAMSON NY 14589

CAMELOT TACK SHOP
349 STAGE COACH RD
TRINIDAD CA 95570

CAMERTON HALL SADDLERY
34128 STATE RD 54 W
ZEPHYRHILLS FL 34249

CANTEBURY MANOR TACK SHOP
605 STARKEY RD
ZIONSVILLE IN 46077

CANVASBACK TRAINING
BOX 398 SELKIRK
MANITOBA CANADA R1A2B3

CAPISTRANO TACK & FEED
32124 PASEO ADELANTO E
SAN JUAN CAPISTRANO CA 92675

CARDEN SADDLE SHOP
WOODEN SHOE RD
NEENAH WI 54946

CARDINAL HILL SADDLERY
7008 WOLF RUN SHOALS RD
FAIRFAX STATION VA 22039

CARDINAL PETS AND SADDLES
1208 FM 78
SCHERTZ TX 78154

CAROL CRITTERS
206 E MAIN ST
LOWELL MI 49331

CAROUSEL TACK SHOP
1771 PRINCESS ANNE
VIRGINIA BCH VA 23456

CARR'S WESTERN WORLD
316 WEST HOBSONWAY
BLYTHE CA 92225

CARRIAGE SADDLERY
1584 NEWPORT BLVD
COSTA MESA CA 92627

CASPIAN FARMS SADDLERY
825 COLLEGE AVENUE
SANTA ROSA CA 95404

CASTLE ROCK CARRIAGE & HORSE
2499 WITZER RD
PENRYN CA 95663

CATAMOUNT FARM
RR 1 BOX 795, MOUNTAIN RD.
PITTSFIELD NH 03263

CATERINO & SONS
127 NORTH MAIN
STANTON PA 18504

CENTAUR FORGE LTD
PO BOX 340
117 N SPRING STREET
BURLINGTON WI 53105

CENTAUR SADDLERY SHOP, THE
238 11TH AVENUE SE
ALBERTA CANADA T2G0X8

CENTAUR TACK SHOP
RT. 9 BOX 490
LUCEDALE MS 39452

CHAMPION STABLES AND SDL
RT 1 BOX 280
DOSERLL VA 23047

CHAMPIONS ROW TACK
9800 SCHERIDAN RD
BURT MI 48417

CHAP SHOP
110 NORTH INDEPENDENCE STREET
HARRISONVILLE MO 64701

CHARLIE HORSE
2100 CAPE HORN RD
HAMPSTEAD MD 21074

CHARLIE'S TACK SHACK
14005 MIDLAND RD
POWAY CA 92064

CHARLOTTE SADDLERY INC
11301 KATY HWY
HOUSTON TX 77079

CHICK HARNESS & SUPPLY
US RTE 13
HARRINGTON DE 19952

310

CHINOOK BOOKSHOP, THE
210 N. TEJON ST
COLORADO SPRING CO 80903

CHOCOLATE DROP TACK SHOP
2976 LONGBRANCH RD
UNION KY 41091

CHRISTENSEN SADDLE SHOP
1471 SOUTH SARATOGA SUNNYVALE
CUPERTINO CA 95014

CHRISTIANSONS
BOX 467
72052 CHURCH ST
BERWYN CA 95663

CIRCLE J SADDLERY
201 CENTER ST
PO BOX 1089 ASSINIBOIA
SASKATCHEWAN CANADA

CIRCLE JR WESTERN SUPPLY
RT 3 BOX 2935
HILLSBORO OR 97124

CIRCLE S WESTERN STORE
14329 JOHN CLARK RD
GULFPOINT MS 39503

CIRCUS FEED & SUPPLY
3106 WHITFIELD AVE E
SARASOTA FL 34243

CITY COUNTRY SADDLE SHOP
612 DOOR STREET
ANTEGO WI 54409

CLAISSICAL HORSEMAN
117 1/2 E BRANCH
ARROYO GRANDE CA 93420

CLASSIC SADDLERY
15 CATLIN RD
BROOKLINE MA 02146

CLASSIC SADDLERY
90 EAST MICHIGAN BOX 656
GALESBURG MI 49053

CLASSIC SADDLERY
387 BOSTON POST RD
PO BOX 537
SUDBURY MA 01776

CLASSIC TACK LTD
27153 FRASER HWY BOX 1288
ANDERGROVE BC CANADA V0X1A0

CLAYTON SADDLERY
6200 CENTER ST
CLAYTON CA 94517

CLEARWATER SADDLERY
299 PINE DR
ALTOONA PA 54720

CLEMONS BOOT COMPANY
439 SE JACKSON
ROSEBURG OR 97470

CLINTON FEED & SADDLERY
8914 SIMPSON LN
CLINTON MD 20735

CLIPPETY CLOPPETY SHOPPE
38 E MAIN ST
MILAN MI 48160

COACH STOP SADDLERY
LAMINGTON ROAD BOX 244
BEDMINSTER NJ 07924

COLONIAL SADDLE SHOP
897 FREEWAY DR
NAPA CA 94558

COMPETITIVE EDGE SDL, THE
2 WEST STREET
NEWTOWN CT 06470

COREY'S COWBOY CENTER
1419 WEST AVENUE NORTH
CROSSVILLE TN 38555

CORINTHIAN HORSE SPORT, THE
225 INDUSTRIAL PKWY SOUTH
PO BOX 670 AURORA
ONTARIO CANADA L4G4J9

CORRAL, THE
AL HODGES
1711-15TH STREET
BOULDER CO 80302

COTTON'S COWBOY CORRAL
320 5 ST
MARYSVILLE CA 95901

COUNTRY FEED BARN
PO BOX 492
1345 3RD ST
INYOKERN CA 93527

COUNTRY FEED STORE
2111 E VISTAWAY
VISTA CA 92084

COUNTRY PALACE TACK SHOP, THE
26614 TELEGRAPH RD
FLAT ROCK MI 48134

COUNTRY SADDLERY
52 WATER ST
3
PT PERRY ONTAR CANADA

COUNTRY SUPPLY
1305 E MARY ST
OTTUMWA IA 52501

COUNTRY TACK
US RT 7
LANESBORO MA 01237

COUNTRY TACK & OUTFITTERS
ATTN: ANNE GROSSMAN
91 E. BROAD STREET
PATASKALA OH 43062

COURBETTE SADDLERY CO INC
585 INDUSTRIAL PKWY
HEATH OH 43056

COW PUNCHERS PALACE
4683 COVINGTON HWY
DECATUR GA 30035

COWAN SELECT HORSES INC.
BOX 1270
HAVRE MT 59501

COWBOY COUNTRY
3390 W 11
EUGENE OR 97402

COWHAND, THE
200 W. MIDLAND AVNEUE
WOODLAND PARK CO 80863

COYOTE CREEK TACK
2435 FEATHER RIVER BLVD
OROVILLE CA 95965

CRAZY CAROUSEL
3211 HARWOOD RD.
HUDSON HEIGHTS
QUEBEC CANADA J0P 1J0

CREATIVE MIND PRODUCTS
PO BOX 724
MENDOCINO CA 95460

CRITTERS CHOICE
10804 FAY ROAD
CARNATION WA 98014

CROSS TIES SADDLERY
2470 WISTERIA ST
SARASOTA FL 34239

CROWLEY FEED & SUPPLY
1621 N CROWLEY RD
CROWLEY TX 76036

CRYSTAL SPRINGS RANCH SADLRY
0946 STATE HWY 133
CARBONDALE CO 81623

CULTURED COWBOY
1521 72 BYPASS NE
GREENWOOD SC 29646

CULVER MILITARY ACADEMY
THE CULVER EDUCATIONAL FOUND
CULVER IN 46511

CUMBERLAND GENERAL
RT 3, BOX 81
CROSSVILLE TN 38555

CUSTOM BREEDING
9320 SOUTH OLD STATE ROAD
WESTERVILLE OH 43081

CUSTOM MADE TACK SHOP
1120 COLE STREET
ENUMCLAW WA 98022

D A MC CRAY SADDLERY
1232 MATTHEWS-MINT HILL RD
MATTHEWS NC 28106

D BAR M WESTERN STORE
1020 E 4TH ST
RENO NV 89512

D D'S LEATHER LOFT
OLD PINE HILL RD
BERWICK ME 03901

D & D FARM RANCH SUPERMRKT
PO DRWR 1309
516 1H 10 E
SEGUIN TX 78156

D'AMOURS
107 CHEMIN LAKESIDE
KNOWLTON
QUEBEC CANADA J0E 1V0

DAN'S BOOTS & SADDLES
6903 4 NW
ALBUQUERQUE NM 87107

DANAMARK EQUINE ENTERPRISES
49025 COUNTY RD 129
PO BOX 2942
STEAMBOAT SPGS CO 80477

DANS FRONTIER SHOP
558 MAIN ST S
WOODBURY CT 06798

DARK HORSE SADDLERY
2117 HILLSBORO RD
FRANKLIN TN 37064

DAVES SADDLERY
491 MAIN ST
FERNDALE CA 95536

DAYDREAM FARM TACK SHOP
5204 OLD A & P RD
RIPLEY OH 45167

DEER MEADOW FARMS
LAKE HURON DRIVE
DESBARATS ONT CANADA P0R1E0

DEL'S FARM SUPPLY
7720 OLD HWY 99 SE
OLYMPIA WA 98501

DELICATE FOX, THE
3979 W MARKET
AKRON OH 44313

DELS FARM SUPPLY
16533 HWY 507 SE
YELM WA 98597

DELTA SADDLERY
339 E KETTLEMAN LN
LODI CA 95240

DEXTER MILL
3515 CENTRAL ST
DEXTER MI 48130

DIAMOND CUSTOM TACK
2125 GALE ROAD
PUEBLO CO 81006

DIAMOND H TACK SHOP
4631 O'MALLEY RD
ANCHORAGE AK 99516

DIAMOND OAKS CDC
6375 HARRISON AVENUE
CINCINNATI OH 45247

DISCOUNT FEED & TACK
28418 FELIX VALDEZ
TEMECULA CA 92390

DISCOUNT TACK
GENERAL DELIVER
PORTHILL ID 83853

DISCOVERY TRAIL
1629 POLLASKI
SUITE 105
CLOVIS CA 93612

DOMINION SADDLERY
2502 CRAIN HWY
BOWIE MD 20716

DOMINION SADDLERY
RTE 1 BOX 84
CHANTILLY VA 22021

DOMINION SDL
480 RIVERSIDE DR
BURBANK CA 91506

DON HARTS WESTERN SHOP
819 W MAIN AV
W FARGO ND 58787

DONOVAN SADDLE & WESTERN WEAR
RT 1 BOX 54 A
OAKLAND MN 55912

DOONAREE FARMS TACK SHOP
RR 2
COOKSTOWN ONT CANADA L0L1L0

DOUBLE "J" SADDLERY
2087 EAST RIVER RD
CORTLAND NY 13045

DOUBLE D WESTERN STORE
7524 CHAPMAN HWY
KNOXVILLE TN 37920

DOUBLE J TACK
1912 NE 179TH STREET
RIDGEFIELD WA 98642

DOUBLE L TACK SHOP
177 CHAPEL GREEN ROAD
FREDERICKSBURG VA 22405

DOUBLE M SADDLERY
PO BOX 693 STAGE RD
MOULTONBOCO
CENTER HARBOR NH 03254

DOUBLE M WESTERN STORE
678 RT 67
BALSTON SPRINGS NY 12020

DOUBLE R TACK SHOP
11794 WILKES RD
YALE MI 48097

DOUBLE S TACK SHOP
ATTN: MARY ANN SORBER
RD 1 BOX 334
SOMERSET PA 15501

DOUBLE TREE TACK SHOP
1005 HIGH SCHOOL RD
SEBASTOPOL CA 95472

DOUBLE WW WESTERN STORE
1709 THONOTOSASSA ROAD
PLANT CITY FL 33566

DOVER SADDLERY
1644 WASHINGTON STREET
HOLLISTON MA 01746

DRESSAGE EXTENSION
23550 SAN JUAN DRIVE
TEHACHAPI CA 93561

E.R.'S SADDLERY
117 N LAFAYETTE
SOUTH LYON MI 48178

EAGLE ROCK STABLES INC
9785 ROSE WAYNE CTR RD
CLYDE NY 14433

EAGLE SADDLERY & TACK
2650 N MERIDAN RD
EAGLE ID 83616

EDEN FARMS SADDLERY
4723 HWY 66
ASHLAND OR 97520

EISER'S
VALMONT INDUSTRIAL PARK
KIWANIS BLVD PO BOX T
HAZLETON PA 18201

EMERY-PRATT CO.
1966 W MAIN ST
OWOSSO MI 48867

END OF THE TRAIL
200 ANN ST
PICKENS SC 29671

EQUERRY
203 SO RANCHO
SANTA FE RD
ENCINITAS CA 92024

EQUERRY EQUESTRIAN CENTER
7125 BLENHEIM ST
VANCOUVER ONTA CANADA V6N162

EQUERRY EQUESTRIAN, THE
1390 N MC DOWELL
PETALUMA CA 94975

EQUESTRIAN CENTRE INC, THE
31 OLD AVON VILLAGE
PO BOX 798
AVON CT 06001

EQUESTRIAN CENTRE TACK SHOP
2435 CHEROKEE RD
ATHENS GA 30605

EQUESTRIAN SHOP INC
1812 TURNPIKE ST
RT 114
NORTH ANDOVER MA 01745

EQUI SPORT
8440 UMERTON RD
LARGO FL 34641

EQUI-MED
24 LINCOLN ST
N EASTON MA 02356

EQUIDAE FINE SADDLERY
RR 2, KING CITY
ONTARIO CANADA L0G 1K0

EQUIN-LINE
349 W 100 S
VALPARAISO IN 46383

EQUINE COUNTRY CLUB
RD 1 BOX 225A
AVONMORE PA 15618

EQUINE QUARTERMASTER TLD
15 HWY 27 UNIT 5
NOBLETON ONT CANADA L0G1N0

EQUINE RESEARCH
PO BOX 9001
3909 TIMS
TYLER TX 75711

EQUINE SHOPPE,THE
20416 VIKING AVE NW
POULSBO WA 98370

EQUUS
656 QUINCE ORCHARD RD
GAITHERSBURG MD 20760

EQUUSPORT
7550 BLACK FOREST
COLORADO SPGS CO 80908

ESCONDIDO SADDLERY
903 E VALLEY PKWY
ESCONDIDO CA 92025

ESENGARD'S
RD 1 POPPLETON RD
BOX 50
DUNHAMVILLE NY 13054

ESTHER FURNACE TACK SHOP
229 MONTOUR BLVD
BLOOMSBURG PA 17815

EUROPEAN EQUESTRAIN SUPP
1187 COAST VILLAGE RD
SANTA BARBARA CA 93108

EUROPEAN EQUESTRIAN
ATTN: MARTHA CASSER
225 26TH ST
SANTA MONICA CA 90402

F M BROWN & SONS
205 WOODROW AVE
SINKING SPRINGS PA 19608

FAIRPLAY STORES LTD
2604 KENSINGTON RD
CALGARY ALBETA CANADA T2N3S5

FARM & RANCH
PO BOX 1329
516 1H 10 EAST
SEQUIN TX 78156

FARM CITY
440 SOUTH PARK AVE
APOPKA FL 32703

FARM GRO SUPPLY
214 WEST HANCOCK
NEWBURGH OR 97132

FARM HOUSE, THE
22341 ASHVILLE HWY
LANDRUM SC 29356

FARMERS FEED RANCH SUPP
26500 SCOTT RD
SUN CITY CA 92381

FARMERS MARKET FEED & TACK
1989 LANDSTOWN ROAD
VIRGINIA BEACH VA 23456

FEED BARN, THE
25 BUENA VISTA AVENUE
GILROY CA 95020

FEED CORAL
7571 HWY 35
BIG FORK MT 59911

FEED SEED AND TACK
1726 RT 30
NO VERSAILLES PA 15137

FIELDCREST TACK SHOP
10 SIPPEWISSETT
FALMOUTH MA 02574

FIELDSTONE PRK TACK SHOP
RT 3 35J
MANSFIELD TX 76063

FISHERS WESTERN SHOP
2666 N US 23
DELAWARE OH 43015

FIVE FILLYS TACK SHOP
105 N CLINTON
STOCKBRIDGE MI 49285

FLEET STREET-EQUISMAG
656 QUINCE ORCHARD RD
GAITHERSBURG MD 20878

FLORADALE TACK
LEES HILL ROAD
BROOKSIDE NJ 07960

FLYNN'S SADDLE SHOP
8633 W STATE ST
BOISE ID 83703

FOOTHILL SADDLERY
7161 MONTEREY STREET
GILROY CA 95020

FORT TACK, THE
5601 SO 56TH ST
ALAMO 4
LINCOLN NE 68516

FOUR SEASONS FARM
ATTN: RENEE FARNUM
120 S DEWITT RD
DEWITT MI 48820

FOUR WINDS, THE
2504 N SHIELDS
FT COLLINS CO 80524

FOX RUN SADDLERY
7345 HIGHWAY 329
CRESTWOOD KY 40014

FOX-HALL ARABIANS
126 FOX HALL RD
SAN ANTONIO TX 78213

FOXCROFT FARMS TACK
ROUTE 16 BOX 160
FEISE RD
O.FALLON MO 63366

FOXTROT
161 W 61 ST
RM 9C
NEW YORK NY 10023

FRANKLIN SADDLER
4100 TELEGRAPH ROAD
BLOOMFIELD HILLS MI 48013

FRANKTOWN FEED & RANCH SUPPLY
2129 NORTH STATE HIGHWAY 83
FRANKTOWN CO 80116

FRAZIER PARK FEED
PO BOX 580
FRAZIER PRK CA 93225

FRENCH'S HITCHING POST
1323 2ND STREET
SAN RAFAEL CA 94901

FRIENDLY MEADOWS TACK
625 ZINNS MILL ROAD
LEBANON PA 17042

FRONTIER FEED & SUPPLY
3490 DESHUTES ROAD
ANDERSON CA 96007

FRONTIER SADDLERY
RR4 STOUFFVILLE
ONTARIO CANADA L4A 7X5

FRONTIER STABLES SUPPLY
4506 FRONTIER
HOUSTON TX 77041

FYING CHANGES TACK
617 W 8 AV
EUGENE OR 97402

GANDRIDGE SADDLERY
2892 BLVD. HARWOOD
SAN LAZAR QUEC CANADA J0P1H0

GAYER'S SADDLERY
309 MAIN STREET
LAUREL MD 20707

GENESEE VALLEY TACK
131 MAIN ST
GENESEO NY 14454

GLASTONBURY TACK SHOP
2671 MAIN STREET
GLASTONBURY CT 06033

GLEN VIEW TACK
936 OLD DOLINGTON RD
WASHINGTON CROSSING PA 18977

GOLD BEACH VET CLINIC
240 STEWART ST
GOLD BEACH OR 7444

GOLDEN ROYAL
PO BOX 5917
ACTON IN 46259

GOLDEN ROYAL WESTERN/ENGLISH
12603 SOUTHEASTERN AVENUE
INDIANAPOLIS IN 46259

GOOD HORSE TACK SHOP
103 N SOUTH ST
FARMVILLE VA 23901

GOOD HORSEMAN TACK SHOP, THE
2545 LAWRENCEVILLE HWY
DECATUR GA 30033

GOODELL WESTERN STORE
501 O ST
FORTUNA CA 95540

GOODLANDERS TACK SHOP
PO BOX 178
125 PLEASANT HILL RD
LEWISBERRY PA 17339

GORDON BROS
2488 PALM AVE
HIALEAH FL 33010

GRAHAM THOROUGHBRED FARMS
RT. 6, BOX 365
PARIS TX 75460

GRAND CHAMPION TACK
9701 N. MICHIGAN RD
CARMEL IN 46032

GRAND PRIX SADDLERY
29 W 130 ST
HINCKLEY OH 44233

GRAND PRIX SADDLERY
14777 PEARL ROAD
STRONGSVILLE OH 44136

GRANITE BAY EQUESTRIANS
3998 DOUGLAS BLVD. #E
ROSEVILLE CA 95661

GRAY FARM CENTER
RT. 11, BOX 61A
GRAY TN 37615

GRAY PONY SADDLERY, THE
13418 RT. 108
HIGHLAND MD 20777

GREAT AMERICAN HORSE STORE
213 PUMPKINTOWN HWY
PICKENS SC 29671

GREAT LAKES FEED&SADDLE INC
900 WOODMERE
TRAVERSE CITY MI 49684

GREAT WEST STOCKMAN
1771 MC ARA ST
REGINA
GREENVILLE SC 29613

GREATER SOUTH FLA TACK & FEED
172 COUNTRY RD 577
ZEPHYR HILLS FL 34249

GREENWAY SADDLERY
2902 E GRENWAY RD
PHOENIX AZ 85032

GREY FOX, THE
MAIN ST
MILLERTON NY 12546

GRIFS WESTERN
6211 SW 45TH STREET
DAVIE FL 33314

GROOM CLOSET TACK SHOP
2005 W CHESTNUT
ENID OK 73703

H & H TACK SHOP
NORTH RAILROAD ST
ANNVILLE PA 17003

H BAR H FEED & SADDLERY
725 SOUTH MOLLISON STREET
EL CAJON CA 92020

H KAUFMAN & SONS
139 E 24TH ST
NEW YORK NY 10010

HACKNEY ENGLISH SADDLERY, THE
18627D TOMBALL PKY
HOUSTON TX 77070

HALLS SADDLE AND HORSE SUPP
2989 HORSELEG CREEK RD
ROME GA 30161

HANCOCK FARM & SUPPLY
8026 AQUARIUS RD
MOHAVE VALLEY AZ 86440

HAND-C HARNESS SHOP
612 SOTH MATIN ROAD
HASTINGS MI 49058

HANDY HUNTER
1319 W BROADWAY
OVIEDO FL 32765

HANGING TREE, THE
SOUTH 275 PLAZA
WEST POINT NE 68788

HANSON CENTER FARM CLUB
5901 GARFIELD AVENUE
HINSDALE IL 60521

HAPPY APPY SADDLE SHOP
STATE HWY 345
ALLENWOOD NJ 08720

HAPPY AT HILL HORSERY
STAR RT 1 BOX 44
MCHENRY MD 21541

HAPPY HORSE LIMITED
18431 SE 400
ENUMCLAW WA 98022

HARROWSMITH SADDLERY
HWY 38 PO BOX 40
HARROWSMITH
ONTARIO CANADA KOH 1V0 99999

HARTEYERS SADDLERY
7111 W BETHEL AVE
MUNCIE IN 47304

HATCH'S DISTRIBUTORS
15677 E 17TH ST
AURORA CO 80011

HAWK SHADOW SADDLERY
BOX 79B RD#2
NEW RINGGOLD PA 17960

HEARNS GROOMINGG & PET SUPPLY
504 W LEE BLVD
LAWTON OK 73501

HEAVENLY HREEDS
PO BOX 724
MENDOCINO CA 95460

HENDERSON & PARK
501 W. MAIN
GREENWOOD MO 64034

HERITAGE CARR, (TINKHAM)
103 EVERETT ST
TINKHAM DIVISION
MIDDLEBORO MA 02346

HERITAGE SADDLERY
1340 POTTSTOWN PIKE (RT 100)
WEST CHESTER PA 19380

HERTELS FEED & TACK
350 OLD WOMANSPRINGS RD
YUCCA VALLEY CA 92284

HESPERIA VET SUPPLY
11960 HESPERIA RD
HESPERIA CA 92345

HIDE-A-WAY FARM & FEED
PO BOX 457
CHULUOTA FL 32766

HIGH BROOK HORSE & HARN.
PO BOX 325
RT 106
S WOODSTOCK, WY 05071

HILL TOP TACK
5822 172ND STREET SE
BOTHELL WA 98012

HILLTOP FEED & RANCH STORE
2727 E HILLCREST DR
THOUSAND OAKS CA 91362

HILLTOP SADDLE SHOP
244 EAST MAIN STREET
EAST ISLIP NY 11730

HILLTOP TACK
RT 2 BOX 761
TALBOTT TN 37877

HINKLES
P.O. BOX 2109
WINSTON SALEM NC 27102

HINSDALE TACK SHOP
430 W 75TH ST
DOWNERS GROVE IL 60516

HITCHIN POST
416 NO PORTER ST
ECKLEY CO 80727

HITCHIN POST, THE
54 MANHATTAN RD
MONEE IL 60449

HITCHING POST SADDLE SHOP
11403 MAIN SST
MIDDLETOWN KY 40243

HOBBY HORSE
RD 2 GLENFIELD RD
SEWICKLEY PA 15143

HOBBY HORSE
8352 PLATZ RD
FAIRVIEW PA 16415

HOBBY HORSE FARM TACK
RT 1 BOX 239
BANKS OR 97106

HOBBY HORSE SADDLERY
371 W JERICHO TURNPIKE
HUNTINGTON NY 11743

HOBBY HORSE TACK SHOP
29495 WILDLIFE LN
BROOKSVILLE FL 33512

HOBBY HORSE, THE
1201 CECELIA DR
NEWPORT RITCHIE FL 34653

HOOFBEATS
RFD 2 BOX 17A
ALBURG VT 05440

HOOFBEATS INC
304 E MAIN
BURLEY ID 83318

HOOFBEATS INC
1271 COMMISSIONERS RD
W LONDON ONT CANADA N6K1C9

HOOKS SADDLERY
2150 HWY 35
KALISPELL MT 59901

HORSE & BUGGY SADDLERY, THE
10 LITTLE NECK RD
CENTERPORT NY 11743

HORSE & HOUND
142 WEST GRAND RIVER
WILLIAMSTOWN MI 48895

HORSE & HOUND
5958 SOUTH HOLLY
ENGLEWOOD CO 80111

HORSE & HOUND SADDLERY
COUNTRY PLAZA
RTE. 5, HWY HN
LAKE GENEVA WI 53147

HORSE & RIDER
188 COW HILL RD
CLINTON CT 06413

HORSE & RIDER INC, THE
5605 W FRIENDLY AVE
QUAKER VLG SHOP CTR
GREENSBORO NC 27410

HORSE AND COUNTRY
RT 1 BOX 56 1 AA
PERRY AR 72125

HORSE COUNTRY LEDYARD INC
1 COLBY DR
LEDYARD CT 06339

HORSE EMPORIUM
805 CLINTON ST
WAUKESHA WI 53186

HORSE EMPORIUM
PO BOX 781
ELMA WA 98541

HORSE HAVEN SADDLERY
505 PARKER RD
SARVER PA 16055

HORSE HAVEN SADDLERY
ATTN: DONNALEE RELYEA
FRANKLINVILLE RD
LAUREL NY 11948

HORSE LOVERS HAVEN TACK SHOP
MAIN STREET - PO BOX 789
MILLERTON NY 12546

HORSE N AROUND
1859 N DECATUR
LAS VEGAS NV 89108

HORSE N AROUND STUFF
10411 N 23 PL
PHOENIX AZ 85028

HORSE N HABIT, THE
530 MAIN ST
PO BOX 475
MEDFIELD MA 02215

HORSE NOTIONS
3709-11 W 140TH ST
CLEVELAND OH 44111

HORSE OF A DIFFERENT COLOR
14769 RT. 226
ALBION PA 16401

HORSE OF A DIFFERENT COLOR
6959 KINGSBURY
ST LOUIS MO 63130

HORSE OF COURSE
2434 DICKNEY POINT RD
SARASOTA FL 34231

HORSE PLACE, THE
2640 HWY 139
MONROE LA 71203

HORSE STORE, THE
RT. 1, BOX 298
CARBONDALE IL 62901

HORSE STUFF
70 E. PROSPECT
WALDWICK NJ 07463

HORSE WORKS, THE
PINEWOOD PLAZA - RTE 117
ESSEX JUNCTION VT 05452

HORSE'N TACK SHOP
RR1 BOX 391
MT PLEASANT RD
SEWELL NJ 08080

HORSEMAN SOURCE, THE
11435 HUNGATE
COLORADO SPRINGS CO 80908

HORSEMAN'S EXCHANGE
5945 OMAHA BLVD
COLORADO SPGS CO 80915

HORSEMAN'S LTD
10 WINTHROP ST
REHOBOTH MA 02769

HORSEMANS CORNER
CAMDEN PLAZA
CAMDEN SC 29020

HORSEMANS HANG UP, THE
5735 A HOLLIFTER
GOLETA CA 93117

HORSEMANS SOURCE, THE
6295 LEHMAN DR
SUITE 204B
COLORADO SPRINGS CO 80918

HORSEMANS TACK & TOGS
5985 GLENWOOD
BOISE ID 83704

HORSEPLAY
7104 GREENWOOD RD
SHREVEPORT LA 71119

HORSEPOWER
BOX 467 RT 14
S RANDOLPH VT 05061

HORSES AND TACK
129 PENNSYLVANIA AV
MEDFORD NY 11763

HORSES DECOR
110 MONTEREY NORTH
LOS ALAMOS NM 87544

HORSES STUFF SADDLERY
40965 14 MILE RD
NOVI MI 48377

HORSESHOE TRAIL SUPPLY
940 SHNECIK RD
C/O HORTON KENNELS
EPHRATA PA 17522

HORSETHREADS
PO BOX 5 RAILROAD BLVD
MIZPAH NJ 08342

HORSETOWN WESTERN STORE
1231 SHALLOWFORD RD NE
MARRIETTA GA 30066

HORSEWEAR
2332 S. 9TH PLACE
MILWAUKEE WI 53215

HORSIN AROUND
511 W GUADALUPE RD
GILBERT AZ 85234

HORSIN AROUND TACK & GIFT
RT 302
PO BOX 346
RAYMOND ME 04071

HOUCK & SADDLERY LIMTED
5504 SOUTHERN BLVD
YOUNGSTOWN OH 44512

HOUSE OF TACK & SADDLERY
RTE 5
KIRKLAND NY 13323

HUGHES HORSE AND RIDER SUP.
151 RANDOLPH ST
CANTON MS 02021

HUNTER & HUNTRESS
18 E NELSON ST
LEXINGTON VA 24450

HUNTING HORN, THE
120 VILLAGE LANDING
FAIRPORT NY 14450

HUNTING HORN, THE
PETERBOROUGH PLAZA
PETERBOROUGH NH 03458

HUSKEY'S
HWY 21 YEAGER RD PO BOX 591
HILSBORO MO 6350

HUTCH'S TACK SHOE
PO BOX 204
LOWELL FL 32663

INDIANA HARNESS & SADDLERY
E 3030 SPRAGUE AVE
SPOKANE WA 99202

IRON BELL TACK SHOP
2 WRIGHT RD
HOLLIS NH 03049

IRON MTN SADDLERY
16869 SW 65TH
LAKE OSWEGO OR 97035

J & L LEE BOOK CO
281 E PARK PLAZA
66 & O ST
LINCOLN NE 68505

J B TACK SHOP
W 6559 KIESLING RD
JEFFERSON WI 53549

J BAR M SADDLERY
1101 S LEBANON ST
LEBANON IN 46052

J&B SADDLERY & HARNESS
121 COUNTER ST
KINGSTON
ONTARIO CANADA K7N1B5

J.L. BLAIR SADDLERY
312 CENTER
DOUGLAS WY 82633

JACOBS BOOTS & SADDLES
11105 QUIRK RD
BELLEVILLE MI 48111

JEDLICKA'S
2605 DE LA VINA ST
SANTA BARBARA CA 93105

JOHNSON SADDLE SHOP
4518 HWY 53
SAGINAW MN 55779

JOHNSTOWN FEED SADDLE
RT 18 BOX 3250
CONROE TX 77302

JOLLEYS WESTERN STORE
WOLCOTT HOLLOW RD
ATHENS PA 18810

JP WESTERN WEAR
12 CHAPIN RD
PINEBROOK NJ 07058

JR'S COUNTRY STORE
311 NO HOSPITAL DR
PAOLA KS 66071

JUDY'S CITY PARK TACK SHOP
4300 DUMAINE
NEW ORLEANS LA 70119

JUSTIN CARRIAGE WORKS
7615 ASSYRIA ROAD
NASHVILLE MI 49073

K & S SADDLERY
228 162 ST
SPANAWAY WA 98387

K AND E LEATHER CO
17311 62ND AVE W
LYNNWOOD WA 98037

KALEVA FEED STORE
14645 KANGAS RD
KALEVA MI 49645

KAMOOK WESTERN STORE
219 LAUREL ST
PT ANGELES WA 98362

KATHYS TRADING POST
PO BOX 373
SUN CITY CA 92381

KEITH SADDLE SHOP
12751 WORTHINGTON RD
PATASKALA OH 43062

KELLEMS SADDLE SHOP
222 MAIN BOX 40
GARDINER MT 59030

KENT SADDLERY
462 WINTHROP STREET
REHOBOTH NA 02769

KENTUCKY HORSE PARK
4089 IRON WORKS PIKE
LEXINGTON KY 40511

KENTUCKY HORSE SUPPLIES
OUTLET MALL LTD.
11501 BLUE GRASS HWY.
LUISVILLE KY 40299

KENTUCKY TACK SHOP
3380 PARIS PARK
LEXINGTON KY 40511

KESSLER TACK SHOP
PO BOX 73 RT 224 E
NEW HAVEN OH 44850

KIMBERELY EQUINE DIVISION
PO BOX 460
RYE CO 81069

KIMBERLY SUPPLY BARN
RD 3 RT 22 WESTBOUND
LEBANON NJ 08833

KIMMEL'S SADDLE SHOP
462 MATHEWS ROAD
YOUNGSTOWN OH 44512

KINGS PADDOCK TACK & SADDLERY
RT 1 BOX 109A
CLYDE TX 79510

KINGS SADDLERY INC
184 NO MAIN
SHERIDAN WY 82801

KINNETTS LEATHER & TACK
2037 BRUSH CREEK RD
PO BOX 176
EAGLE CO 81631

KLOVER LEAF TACK
701 SW 7 AV
WILLISTON FL 32696

KNIGGE TACK SHOP
22636 VERMONT ST
HAYWARD CA 94541

L BAR M EQUESTRIAN SHOP
3518 E SANTA FE
FLAGSTAFF AZ 86004

L G SALES CO
6611 DOWER HOUSE ROAD
UPPER MARLBORO MD 20772

L M EQUESTRIAN SPORT
6500 N HWY 89
FLAGSTAFF AZ 86001

LAKE LOS ANGELES TACK
17424 1/2 E AVE O
PALMDALE CA 93550

LAKELAND VET EQUINE
14101 W 62ND ST
EDEN PRAIRIE MN 55344

LAKEVIEW STABLES & TACK
8712 NOTESTINE
FT WAYNE IN 46815

LAS COLINAS(DALLAS CTY)
600 ROYAL LN
IRVING TX 75039

LAUDERDALE COUNTY FARM
49TH AVENUE S
MERIDIAN MS 39301

LAURDEN FEED & SUPPLY
5 MILL RD
BELEN NM 87002

LEADING REIN TACK SHOP
11400 LADRA VISTA
AUSTIN TX 78575

LEADING REIN TACK SHOP, THE
5750 BALCONE DR STE 102
AUSTIN TX 78731

LEATHER SHOP
115 SO FOURTH
CROKETT TX 75835

LEBMANS CORRAL
8701 PERRIN BEITEL RD
SAN ANTONIO TX 78217

LEEWARD TACK
95124 KAUAMEA PLACE
MILIANI HI 96786

LEWIS FEED & TACK STORE
2421 S YORK RD
GASTONIA NC 28052

LIBERTYVILLE SADDLE SHOP
306 PETERSON RD
LIBERTYVILLE IL 60048

LIGHT HORSE, THE
1 POLK
SAN JUAN BATISTA CA 95045

LIGHTNING G HORSEMAN SHOP
CLAPP HILL RD
LAGRANGEVILLE NY 12540

LIMERICK HORSE & TACK
RR 2 BOX 723
LIMERICK ME 04048

LINCOLN HILL SADDLERY
ROUTE 5 BOX 339
LEXINGTON VA 24450

LINDEN ACRES
997 LAKEFIELD RD
GRAFTON WI 53024

LINE CREEK FEED/TACK
HWY 16
BROOKS, GA 30205

LITTLE HOSS FEED & SUPPLY
18281 LEMON DR
YORBA LINDA CA 92686

LIVERY CO.
2073 N TA MIAMI ST
NAPLES SHOPPING CTR
NAPLES FL 33941

LIVERY STABLE
10432 WATTERSON TRAIL
JEFFERSONTOWN KY 40299

LIVERY STABLES
RT 4, BOX 317A
MARION SC 29571

LLOYD RANCH SUPPLY
510 N MAIN
KING FISHER OK 73750

LOCK STOCK & BARREL
621 BROADWAY
ROCK SPRINGS WY 82901

LOFT TACK SHOP, THE
RT. 6, BOX 110
MANKATO MN 56001

LOMBARDO EQUINE SUPPLY
216 VILLAGE GREEN
WILTON CT 06897

LONG HARNESS SHOP
72 MAIN STREET BOX 697
CANADA N0L1S0

LOS OSOS VALLEY EQUINE FARM
1869 LOS OSOS VALLEY RD
LOS OSOS CA 93402

LUCKY HORSESHOE
102 N. MOLALLA AVENUE
MOLALLA OR 97038

LUSTERS SADDLERY
RD 1 LUTZ RD
ZELIENOPLE PA 16063

LYNNE'S PLACE
4812 PALM BCH BLVD
FT MYERS FL 33905

M BAR C TACK PET SUPPLY
PO BOX 599
LAKESIDE AZ 85929

M BAR D FEED & TACK SHOP
8791 CAMERON
ANCHORAGE AK 99507

M J KNOUD
716 MADISON AV
NEW YORK NY 10021

MAIN STREET TACK
622 WEST MAIN ST
MONROE WA 98272

MAINE COUNTRY TACK
RD 2 BOX 292
GARDINER ME 04345

MALES' TACK & SADDLE
205 E. PACIFIC
SALINA KS 67401

MALLARD COVE DISC. TACK
RD 4, BOX 231
CHESTERTOWN MD 21620

MARIN TACK & FEED
1599 SIR FRANCIS DRAKE
FAIRFAX CA 94930

MARLBORO FEED & SUPPLY
918 HIGHWAY 33
FREEHOLD NJ 07723

MARSHALL'S
2504 13 ST
GULFPORT MS 39501

MARSTON'S WHOLESALE DISTR
483 MAIN ST PO BOX 789
PRESQUE ISLE ME 04769

MARTIN RANCH SUPPLY
522 MARTIN AV
ROHNERT PARK CA 94928

MARTINS SADDLERY
2709 IRIS AVE
BOULDER CO 80302

MARY F HARCOURT
10537 CARRIAGE RD
SPOTSYLVANIA VA 22553

MARY'S TACK SHOP
3675 VIA DE LA VALLE
DEL MAR CA 92014

MASSEYS CORRAL INC
2421 SECOND AVE N
BIRMINGHAM AL 35203

MAYNARD'S
3249 W 51ST AVE
VANCOUVER BC CANADA V6N3V8

MAYVILLE SUPPLY CO.
7300 FOSTORIA ROAD
MAYVILLE MI 48744

MC CAULEY & CO.
463 WARDSCORNER RD
LOVELAND OH 45140

MCCRACKEN FARMS
660 WHITE RD
BROCKPORT NY 14420

MCLELLAND'S SADDLERY
317 NO DIXIE HWY
LAKE WORTH FL 33460

MEETING STREET TACK SHOP
975 SAVANNAH HWY
CHARLESTON SC 29407

MERIDIAN SADDLE SHOP
126 E BROADWAY AVE
MERIDIAN ID 83642

MERIPOSA SADDLERY
5025 HWY. 140
P.O. BOX 730
MERIPOSA CA 95338

MERRIMACK FARM & COUNTY STORE
MIAN ST
BRADFORD NH 03221

METROPOL PET & TACK SADDLERY
36745 GROESBECK
MT CLEMENS MI 48043

MID WESTERN SHOP
499 E VILLAUME
S ST PALM MN 55505

MIDWEST BRIDLE & BIT
BOX 156
WYNOT NE 68792

MIDWEST FARM & HOME SUPPLY
221 W ATKINSON PLAZA
MIDWEST CITY OK 73110

MIDWEST SADDLERY
4415 B DR SOUTH
BATTLE CREEK MI 49017

MILLER STOCKMAN
3350 YOUNGFIELD
WHEATRIDGE CO 80033

MILLER STOCKMAN
215 FOOTHILLS PKWY.
FT. COLLINS CO 80525

MILLER STOCKMAN
PO BOX 5407 TA
DENVER CO 80217

MILLER STOCKMAN
8500 ZUNI ST
DENVER CO 80221

MILLS LEATHER SHOP
13620 NE 20TH ST
BELLEVUE WA 98005

MITCHELL'S WESTERN STORE
RD 6 POTTER RD
AUBURN NY 13021

MOUNTAIN SPRINGS TACK
412 W SIERRA HWY
PALMDALE CA 93550

MOUNTAIN TACK EXCHANGE
BOX 467
7205 CHURCH STREET
PENRYN CA 95663

MOUNTAIN VIEW FARMS
RT 1 BOX 380
BECHERD TN 37324

MUELLER'S TACK & TOG SHOPPE
1400 PINE RIDGE RD
NAPLES FL 33940

MURRAUY FEED
407 WEST 9000 SOUTH
SANDY UT 84070

MURRAY FEED
5250 SOUTH STATE
MURRAY UT 84107

NANCY AMBERSIANO
595 SHELLEY ST
LIVERMORE CO

NATIONAL SADDLERY CO INC
1307 S AGNEW AVE
OKLAHOMA CITY OK 73108

NAYLORS FARM & RANCH SUP
102 OLD ROBSTOWN RD
CORPUS CHRISTI TX 78408

NECHAKO TACK & GIFTWARE
5496 SALT LANE
LANGLEY BC CANADA V3A5C7

NEDROW TACK SADDLERY
6500 SO SALINA ST
NEDROW NY 13120

NELSON'S TACK SHOP
MAIN ST
BOX 201
DOWNSVILLE NY 13755

NEW ENGLAND HORSE SUPPLY INC
HASKELL HILL RD
RFD 1   BOX 1008
HARRISON ME 04040

NEWFOUNDLAND SADDLERY LEATH
383 DUCKWORTH STREET
ST JOHNS NEWFOUNDL A1C5R6

NIGHTWINDS TACK SHOP
315 MT. AVENUE
P.O. BOX 146
BERTHOUD CO 80513

NIGRO'S WESTERN STORE
10509 WEST 63RD STREET
SHAWNEE KS 66203

NINA'S TACK SHOP
12 KINGMAN ST
ST ALBANT VT 05478

NORCO RANGE OUTFEDDERS
969 6TH STREET
NORCO CA 91760

NORTH SHORE SADDLERY
6308 NORTHERN BLVD
EAST NORWICH NY 11732

NORTHVILLE SADDLERY
200 S MAIN ST
NORTHVILLE MI 48167

O W SADDLES
734 E 2 AV
DURANGO CO 81301

OAKHURST FEED SUPPLY
49214 RD 426
OAKHURST CA 93644

OAKLEY'S
3015 MT PINOS WY
STE 201
FRAZIER PARK CA 93225

OCEANSIDE TACK SHOP
325 B 15 AV S
JACKSONVILLE BEACH FL 32250

OFFUTS ENGLISH WEAR
201 EASTMAN LN
PETALUMA CA 94952

OK FEED STORE
1594 SOUTH DIXIE HWY
MIAMI FL 33146

OLD FRONTIER
211 ROBINSON AV
GROVERTON GA 30813

OLD RIDGE TACK SHOP
2816 RIDGE RD
WILLIAMSON NY 14589

OLD STORE LTD.
5800 SUTH MIDWAY RD
BROKEN ARROW OK 74014

OLDE HICKORY SADDLE SHOP
RR8 Box 1352
HICKORY NC 28602

OLSENS CHINO VALLEY GRAIN
HWY 89
PO BOX 427
CHINO VALLEY AZ 86323

OLSON'S TACK SHOP
11408 NE 2ND PLACE
BELLEVUE WA 98004

OMAHA VACCINE CO., INC.
4658 SEEMEN ST SW
NAVAREE OH 44662

ORTEGA TACK
3165 RANCHO VIEJO RD
SUITE G SAN JUAN
CAPISTRANO CA 92675

OUTFITTERS SUPPLY
7373 HWY 2 E
COLUMBIA FALLS MT 59912

OUTPOST, THE
438 N WASHINGTON STREET
BERKLEY SPGS WV 25411

P.J'S COUNTRY FEED & BIRD
1516 E LOS ANGELES AVE
SIMI VALLEY CA 93065

PADDOCK ROOM, THE
226 E SILVERSPGS BLVD
OCALA FL 32670

PADDOCK SADDLERY
15605 CHILLICOTHE RD
PO BOX 631
CHAGRIN FALLS OH 44022

PADDOCK TACK SHOP INC
600 ROUTE 22
DELMONT PA 15626

PAINTED PONY
4575 B PALM BEACH BLVD
FORT MEYERS FL 33905

PAKULIS OUTDOOR PRODUCTS
RT 44 PO BOX 31
PUTNAM CT 06260

PALMER SADDLE SHOP
37 COUNTY RD 232
DURANGO CO 81301

PARADE ACRES
54 GARVIN FALLS RD
CONCORD NH 03301

PARAGON HORSE SUPP
RT 14 BOX 155
CANTON GA 30114

PARD'S WESTERN SHOP
306 NO MAPLE ST
URBANA IL 61801

PARTNERS TACK SHOP
108 ELM DR
NEWPORT NEWS VA 23602

PASTIMES
97 WEST FIRST ST
LOYALTON CA 96118

PAT'S TACK SHOP
RR 2
PAISLEY ONTARO CANADA N0G2N0

PEDLEY VETERINARY SUPPLY
8978 LIMONITE
PEDLEY CA 92509

PEGASOS PRESS
535 CORDOVA RD SUITE 163
SANTA FE NM 87501

PET EMPORIUM
5112 FREDERICKSBURG RD.
SAN ANTONIO TX 78229

PETERSON'S WESTERN WEAR
336 MAIN STREET
TWIN FALLS ID 83301

PIASA LEATHER & SADDLE
5442 NO 2ND ST
ROCKFORD IL 61111

PINE TREE SADDLE SHOP
RT. 1
WEILAND ROAD
NEW LONDON WI 54961

PONY EXPRESS
1440 OXBOTTOM ROAD
TALAHASEE FL 32312

PONY EXPRESS & SADDLERY
156 W SADDLE RIVER RD
SADDLE RIVER NJ 07458

PORTAGE HORSE AND RIDER SHOPE
4242 STATE RT 44
RPPTSTPWM PA 44272

POTOMAC HORSE TACK
14211 QUINCE ORCHARD ROAD
GAITHERSBURG MD 20878

PRESTIGE SADDLE & HARNESS
322 W END BLVD
QUAKERTOWN PA 18951

PRINTED HORSE, THE
PO BOX 1908
FT. COLLINS CO 80522

PURDUE VET SUPPLIES
PURDUE UNIVERSITY
SCHOOL VET MED-LYNN HALL
W. LAFAYETTE IN 47907

QUAIL HOLLOW FARM&TACK
767 WILSON TERRACE CT
CARMEL IN 46032

QUAIL HOLLOW TACK
FLOWER MOUND TX 75028

QUIET SHOPPE SADDLERY
3935 POPLAR HILL ROAD
CHESAPEAKE VA 23321

RAFTER 6 STABLE SUPPLY
RT 1 BOX 122
HUGHESVILLE MO 65334

RAINBOW CITY WESTERN STORE
3354 RAINBOW DR
GADSEN AL 35901

RAINBOWS END TACK SHOP
RT. 4, BOX 380
SEAFORD DE 19973

RAMAPO SADDLERY & TACK SHOP
171 LAKE ST
RAMSEY NJ 07446

RAMS WESTERN STORE
4845 S. DURFEE AV
PICO RIVERA CA 90660

RANCH MART-SADDLE TREE
8452 FREDERICKSBIRG
SAN ANTONIO TX 78229

RANCHER'S FEED & SADDLERY
10439 N SCOTTSDALE ROAD
SCOTTSDALE AZ 85253

RANCHER, THE
4821 NW 6 ST
GAINESVILLE FL 32609

RANCHERS WAREHOUSE
10624 N 71ST PLACE
SCOTTSDALE AZ 85254

RANCHLAND WESTERN STORE
209 N MAIN ST
AINESWORTH NE 69210

RANCHO FEED & MERCANTILE
41065 FIRST STREET
TEMECULA CA 92390

RASCAL'S ROOST
SADDLER NORTH
RT 1 BOX 301
HECTOR AK 72843

RASMUSSEN'S
96 BRIARWOOD
ATTN: RAY
IRVINE CA 92714

RATTY'S TACK SHOP
RR 1, BOX 159
YME NH 03768

RAWHIDE TACK SHOP
12622 BUSH ST
S EL MONTE CA 91733

READING RIDGE SERVICE, THE
C/O PENNY DENTON
1 MOONLIGHT M
WECKENBURG AZ 85358

RED BARN SADDLE
4913 COLLEYVILLE BLVD
COLLEYVILLE TX 76034

RED RIVER VALLEY HAY CO.
3007 SKYWAY CIR N
IRVING TX 75038

RENEGADE OF WESTERN WEAR, THE
14335 OLD HWY 80
EL CAJON CA 92021

REVELSTONE TACK SHOP
RR 2
BALTIMORE ONTO CANADA K0K1C0

RHINEBECK TACK & LEATHER
ROUTE 9 P.O. BOX 321
RHINEBECK NY 12572

RICH'S TACK SHOP
297 LITCHFIELD RD
NEW MILFORD CT 06776

RICHMOND HARNESS & SADDLE
213 W. BROAD
RICHMOND VA 23220

RICK'S SADDLE SHOP
9 WATER STREET
ENGLISHTOWN NJ 07726

RIDGE RANGE WEST. WEAR
3313 34 ST
LUBBOCK TX 79410

RIDING CONNECTION, THE
2043 PALOS VERDES DR NO
LOMITA CA 90717

RIDING HABIT
ROUTE 8 BOX 5410
LUFKIN TX 75901

RIDING HABIT/RIDGEBURY INN
RD 1 BOX 342 RIDGEBURY ROAD
SLATE HILL NY 10973

RIDING STORE
2816 W. 75TH STREET
WOODRIDGE IL 60517

RINGSIDE SADDLERY
600 MAIN STREET
SOUTH BRITAIN CT 06487

RIVERSIDE BOOT & SADDLE
742 W HWY 39
BLACKFOOT ID 83221

RJ'S FARM & FEED
390 DARATMOUTH
WYCKOFF NJ 07481

RLB SADDLERY
2550 BROWNSVILLE RD
LIBRARY PA 15129

RLB SADDLERY INC
ATTN: R BONENBERGER
3166 LAUREL RIDGE
BRIDGEVILLE PA 15017

ROBESON SADDLERY
1338 PITTSFORD
MENDON RD
MENDON NY 14506

ROBINSON'S
461 N MAIN
OVERTON NV 89040

ROCKIN G LEATHER WORKS
9888 S BERNARD RD
CANBY OR 97013

ROCKIN H QUARTER HORSE
RT. 3, BOX 190
MAGNOLIA MS 39652

ROCKING HORSE SADDLERY
6707 AYLESBURY RD
TOPEKA KS 66610

ROCKING HORSE SUPPLY
RT. 2, BOX 183 F
SALEM AL 36874

ROCKINGHAM BAG CANVAS CO
18 W JOHNSON
PO BOX 54
HARRISONBURG VA 22801

ROD'S WESTERN PALACE
3099 SILVER DR
COLUMBUS OH 43224

ROHRER'S TACK CORRAL
701 SOUTH SPRING GARDEN
CARLISLE PA 17013

RON RICHARDS SADDLRY
2510 TELEGRAPH AVE
OAKLAND CA 94612

ROSERIDGE SADDLERY & HARNESS
24242 275 SE
MAPLE VALLEY WA 98038

ROSSLYN TACK SHOP
RR 5 ROSSLYN RD
THUNDER BAYONA CANADA P765M9

ROWES WESTERN STORE
1034 E MAIN ST
DANVILLE IL 61832

ROWLEY HARNESS SHOP
115 CENTRAL STREET
ROWLEY MA 01969

RUARK STABLES TACK BOX
10777 E HWY 160
ALAMOSA CO 81101

RUTHIES TACK SHOP
105 OLDWICK RD
WHITEHOUSE STA NJ 08889

S (N) C TACK SHOP
STAR ROUTE BOX 52201
PAKRUMP NV 89401

S AND R TACK SHOP
1133 NO STINE RD
CHARLOTTE MI 48813

S DIERINGER SADDLERY
GENERAL CROOKS TRL
CAMP VERDE AZ 86322

SADDLE & LEATHER SHOP INC
48 16TH AVE SW
CEDAR RAPIDS IA 52404

SADDLE BROOK TACK SHOP
442 GLEBE RD
WESTMORELAND NH 03467

SADDLE KNOLL TACK SHOE
PO BOX 427
BAHAMA NC 27503

SADDLE PAD TACK SHOP, THE
3334 WEST PALMETTO ST/HWY 76
FLORENCE SC 29501

SADDLE RACK
5335 LEXINGTON RD
ATHENS GA 30605

SADDLE RACK, THE
109 MC NULTY STREET
BLYTHEWOOD SC 29016

SADDLE SHED, THE
237 PROVIDENCE ROAD
S GRAFTON MA 01560

SADDLE SHOP, THE
741 WEST JERCHO TURNPIKE
HUNTINGTON NY 11743

SADDLE SHOP, THE
5008 E SPEEDWAY
TUCSON AZ 85712

SADDLE SMITH, THE
RR1 ALTON
ONTARIO CANADA

SADDLE TRAMPS
RT 2 BOX 282
FLETCHER NC 28732

SADDLE-UP
PO BOX 39
216 NAJOLES
MILLERSVILLE MD 21108

SADDLEMAKERS
18422 CASCADE VIEW DRIVE
MONROE WA 98272

SADDLER TACK SHOP
815 EAST MAIN STREET
ST CHARLES IL 60174

SADDLER, THE
13 DANBURY ROAD
WILTON CT 06897

SADDLER, THE
9342 56TH STREET
TEMPLE TERRACE FL 33617

SADDLERY IN GREAT FALLS, THE
PO BOX 57
731 EL WALKER RD
GREAT FALLS VA 22066

SADDLERY, THE
6894 W STERRETTANIA ROAD
FAIRVIEW PA 16415

SADDLES & SUCH
2135 GERMANTOWN RD SOUTH
GERMANTOWN TN 38138

SAGEBRUSH SADDLERY
103 1/2 MOUNTAIN VIEW
ELLENSBURG WA 98926

SAM'S HORSE SUPPLY
307 SHAMROCK CENTER
DUBLIN GA 31021

SAM'S WESTERN WEAR
8930 LIMONITE
RIVERSIDE CA 92508

SAN DIMAS EQUESTRIAN CTR
299 EAST FOOTHILL BLVD
SAN DIMAS CA 91773

SAN MARCOS FEED
RT. 2, BOX 150M
SANTA FE NM 87505

SAN-ZAM KENNELS AND STABLS
5206 N GRIMES
HOBBS NM 88240

SANDRIDGE SADDLERY
2892 HARWOOD BLVD
PO BOX 589
HUDSON QUEBEC CANADA J0P1HC

SANTA ANA FEED & SADDLERY
1421 EAST FIRST STREET
SANTA ANA CA 92701

SANTA ROSA SADDLERY
5338 HWY 12 W
SANTA ROSE CA 95407

SCHNEIDER SADDLERY CO.,INC
1609 GOLDEN GATE PLAZA
CLEVELAND OH 44124

SCHRIER SUPPLY CO.
RURAL ROUTE 1
BOX 135
CUMBERLAND IA 50843

SCOTT COLBURNS SADDLERY
20411 FARMINGTON ROAD
LIVONIA MI 48152

SCRAPPY'S PET CORRAL
503 FOURTH ST
CLOVIS CA 93612

SERENDIPITY
95 EAST MAIN
PRICE VT 84501

SEVEN ACRES TACK SHOP
3420 YOUNGSRIDGE RD
LAKELAND FL 33809

SHADE TREE EQUINE SHOWCAS
1716 W MAIN
BOZEMAN MT 59715

SHANKS SADDLERY
764 RODERICK ST
CN V8X2R3

SHATZLEIN SADDLE SHOP INC
413 W LAKE ST
MINNEAPOLIS MN 55408

SHERI'S WESTERN COLLECTION
570 BLUE LAKES BLVD. N.
TWIN FALLS ID 83301

SHERWOOD STOCKMAN SUPPLY
ROUTE 5 BOX 235-D
SHERWOOD OR 97140

SHOW & TRAIL
3216 BELUE ROAD
WICHITA FALLS TX 76305

SIGN OF THE HORSE
134 SILK FARM ROAD
CONCORD NH 03301

SIGNATURE ARABIANS
24107 NE 180TH ST
WOODINVILLE WA 98072

SILLA VILLA STABLES
RT 2 BOX 173
ELKHORN NE 68022

SILVER SADDLE
HWY 62-65 NORTH VAIL MALL
HARRISON AR 72601

SILVER SPUR SADDLE&LEATHER
2509 FIRST AVENUE
HIBBING MN 55746

SIMONS TACK'N TOGS
9210 SO TACOMA WAY
TACOMA WA 98499

SKAGIT GRANGE
115 E FIR
MT VERNON WA 98273

SKIP-NAN LEATHER & TACK
ATTN: C F ENGELHARDT
CATNIPACRES ASHLEY RD
WEST CHAZY NY 12992

SMITH & EDWARDS
3936 N HWY 84
OGDEN UT 84404

SMUCKER'S HARNESS SHOP
2014 MAIN STREET
(RT #23 CHURCHTOW)
NARVON PA 17555

SNAFFLES TACK SHOP
738 HOPWELL RD
MARYVILLE TN 37801

SNOWY RIVER FEED
3084 N NELLIS
LAS VEGAS NV 89115

SOLDAN'S CASHWAY FEEDS
1800 W GRAND RIVER
OKEMOS MI 48864

SOLDANS FEED & SUPPLIES
5200 SO LOGAN
LANSING MI 48911

SOLDANS FEED&PET SUPPLIES
12286 US 27
DEWITT MI 48820

SOPERS LEATHER GOODS
27 W MAIN ST
WALLA WALLA WA 99362

SOUTH HAMPTON SADDLERY
1110 SOUTH HAMPTON ROAD
WESTFIELD MA 01085

SOUTH MERIDAN FEED & FODDER
15105 MERIDIAN S
PUYALLUP WA 98373

SOUTH WIND EQUESTRIAN
RD 1 LEBANON ROAD
MILLVILLE NJ 08332

SOUTHERN SADDLERY, INC.
765 MID-BROADWELL ROAD
ALPHARETTA GA 30201

SOUTHWIND NORTH
BOX 111B
CHELSEA VT 05038

SPECTRUM SADDLE SHOP
6750 N. STATE RD. 7
COCONUT CREEK FL 33073

SPORTHORSE INC, THE
6511 132ND AVE NE
KIRKLAND WA 98033

SPRING LAKE SADDLERY
MIDDLE COUNTRY RD RT 2 BOX A3
MIDDLE ISLAND NY 11953

SPRING VALLEY TACK N TOGS
PAULINSKILL LAKE ROAD
RD 5 BOX 865
NEWTON NJ 07860

SPRINGFIELD SADDLERY
ROUTE 1 BOX 80
MARTINS CHAPEL ROAD
SPRINGFIELD TN 37172

SPRINGHOUSE TACK SHOP INC
RD 9 BOX 148
GREENSBURG PA 15601

SPRUCE FARM SADDLERY
PO BOX 127
BRISTOL ME 04539

ST CROIX SADDLERY
4858 BANNING AVE
WHITE BEAR LAKE MN 55110

STABLE DOOR, THE
11 MAIN STREET
WARRENTON VA 22186

STABLE SHEET
PO BOX 157
OSCEOLA WI 54020

STABLE SHEET
11909 LARLE INDUSTRIAL
BURNSVILLE MN 55337

STABLE TACK SHOP
172 N TRANSIT ST
ROCKPORT NY 14094

STABLEYARD TACK SHOP
17 CIRCLE DRIVE
HUDSON NH 03051

STAGECOACH WEST
RT 5 N RT 20
IRVING NY 14081

STATE LINE TACK
RT. 121
PLAISTOW NH 03865

STEINBERG TACK & FEED
2929 W EDINGER
SASNTA ANA CA 92704

STITCHING HORSE
RT 1 BOX 36
SMITHFIELD KY 40068

STITCHING HORSE LEATHER
77 MAIN ST
KINGSTON NJ 08528

STOCK SHOP
13813 N 51ST AVENUE
GLENDALE AZ 85306

STOCKMAN'S HARNESS & SADDLE
1820 LEE RD
ATTN:LINDA
ORLANDO FL 32810

STOCKMENS RANCH SUPPLY
BOX 2160 E HWY 10
DICKINSON ND 58601

STOMBOCK SADDLERY
16123 SHADY GROVE ROAD
GAITHERSBURG MD 20877

STONEBROKE SADDLERY
RT 6 BOX 678 STIDHAM RD
CONROE TX 77302

STONY HILL STABLES
TOWNLANE
AMAGANSETT NY 11930

STONY RIDGE TACK SHOP
9970 LIBERT ROAD
CHELSA MI 48118

SUNRISE FEED
1104 NORTH NELLIS BLVD
ATTN:SUZANA
LAS VEGAS NV 89110

SUNSET ENGLISH & WESTERN WEAR
16300 SW 296TH STREET
HOMESTEAD FL 33030

SUNSET FEED & SUPPLY
7650 SW 117TH AVE
MIAMI FL 33183

SUNSET SADDLE SHOP
WILLOW RD
RT 1
PLYMOUTH WI 53073

SUNSHINE TACK SHOP
1122 FIR AVE BLDG A
BLAINE WA 98230

SUNSHINE TACK SHOP
10500 59TH AVE
DELTA BC CANADA V4K3N3

SUNYBROOK STABLES
STAR RTE. 62 - BOX 375
GUNTERSVILLE AL 35976

SURREY, THE
10107 RIVER RD
POTOMAC MD 20854

SWANS NEST FARM
STAR RT. 1
THE SWAN CENTER
MARBLE HILL GA 30148

SWEENYS SADDLE SHOP
902 S 8 ST
MANITOWAC WI 54220

T & N INC.
815 HWY T
FORISTELL MO 63348

T & T
20 ROUNDTREE ST
KINGS PARK NY 11754

T.E.F. TACK
RT 2 BOX 81
MINE RUN VA 22568

T.H.E. TACK SHOP
6814 MAIN STREET
WILLIAMSVILLE NY 14221

TABORTON DRAFT SUPPLY
RD 3
TABORTON RD
AVERILL PARK NY 12018

TACK & LEATHER OF PT ORCHARD
9494 GRAVELY LN SW
PT ORCHARD WA 98366

TACK AND ANTIQUE EMPORIUM
511 W JACKSON AVENUE
SPEARFISH SD 57783

TACK ATTACK
221-A WEST CENTER STREET
WESTBRIDGE MA 02379

TACK BOX
5845 W PARK BLVD
PO BOX 864045
PLANO TX 75075

TACK BOX, THE
120 W DONITA AVE
SAN DIMAS CA 91773

TACK BOX, THE
9453 HARMSA RD
ATTN MARGO LAVALLE
MORTON GROVE IL 60053

TACK BOX, THE
ATTN: BETTY HARMON
3 B WEST FEDERAL ST
MIDDLEBURG VA 22117

TACK ETC
5233 LOWER RICHLAND BLVD
HOPKINS SC 29061

TACK IN THE BOX
2413 82ND STREET
SALEM OR 97301

TACK LOFT, THE
3665 EAST ENON ROAD
YELLOW SPRINGS OH 45387

TACK N STUFF
73725 MC KAY
ROMEO MI 48065

TACK ROOM
153 POST ROAD EAST
WESTPORT CT 06880

TACK ROOM
2421 FALLS AV
WATERLOO IA 50701

TACK ROOM
2929 ROLLING HILLS RD
TORRENCE CA 90505

TACK ROOM & SUPPLY
308 S TOWER
CENTRALIA WA 98531

TACK ROOM SADDLERY
10325 LYLEWOOD
ST LOUIS MO 63131

TACK ROOM, THE
3808 S DIVISION
GRAND RAPIDS MI 49508

TACK ROOM, THE
MAIN ST
PITTSTOWN NJ 08867

TACK ROOM, THE
7717 WILLIAMSON RD NW
ROANOKE VA 24019

TACK ROOM, THE
2202 N BROAD STREET
CAMDEN SC 29020

TACK SHACK
13400 NE 175TH
WOODINVILLE WA 98072

TACK SHED, THE
5019 HANNON
ERIE PA 16510

TACK SHOP AT CARDINE HORSE
1840 GIBBS SHOALS ROAD
GREER SC 39650

TACK SHOP, THE
215 SO BALSAM ST
MOSES LAKE WA 98837

TACK SHOP, THE
2407 INDUSTRIAL DR
JEFERSON CITY MO 65109

TACK SHOP, THE
RT 11 BOX 441-L SCHILLINGER R
MOBILE AL 36609

TACK TOWN INC
HIGHWAY 46
BALDWIN ONTAR CANADA 10E1A0

TACK TRUNK
EAST 11517 TRENT
SPOKANE WA 99206

TACK TRUNK
17589 PLUM CREEK TRL
CHAGRIN FALLS OH 44022

TACK TRUNK INC, THE
13 SOUTH CHERRY STREET
LEBANON OH 45036

TACK TRUNK, THE
1111TH 10TH 1
PEN ROSE CO 81240

TACK UNLIMITED
117 E ILLINOIS AV
SPEARFISH SD 57783

TACK WORKS, THE
4468 LOWER RT RD
PO BOX 533
BUCKINGHAM PA 18912

TACK'N GIRFT
149-HWY 27 N
BOX 958 N NOBLETON
N NOBLETON ONT CANADA 99999

TACKERIA, THE
13667 E CITRUS DR
LOXOHATCHEE FL 33470

TACKMAKER RANCH, INC.
21701 E BRITTON RD
HARRAH OK 73045

TADAGIES TACK
108 N. MAIN STREET
GALENA MA 21635

TAL-Y-TARA
2103 O'FARRELL
SAN FRANCISCO CA 94115

TALLY HO TACK SHOP
61 HOUSATONIC STREET
LENOS MA 01240

TANGLEWOOD SADDLERY
916 GRAND AVE
W DES MOINES IA 50265

TANNERY SADDLE SHOP
11 CHRISTIAN LN
WHATLEY MA 01039

TARA HILL TACK
151 OLIVE SPRINGS
SOQUEL CA 95073

TARA HILL TACK
ATTN: BARBARA BRECHEL
151 OLIVE SPRINGS RD
SANTA CRUZ CA 95065

TAYLOR'S INC.
10495 OLYMPIC DR
DALLAS TX 75220

TAYLORS PET CENTER
607 E LEE RD
TAYLOR SC 29687

TELEPHONE TACK SHOP, THE
RT 4 BOX 316
LEXINGTON VA 24450

TENPENNY TACK
5245 SW TOPEKA
TOPEKA KS 66609

TERWILLIGER'S
MARKET STREET
BOX 147
MACKINAC ISLAND MI 49757

TES WESTERN ROUNDUP
2727 HIGHWAY 101 EAST
PORT ANGELES WA 98362

THREE PONIES TACK
4786 EAST CENTER ROAD
HASTINGS MI 49058

THREE SADDLES TACK SHOP
815 EAST MAIN STREET
ST CHARLES IL 60174

TINY TACK SHOPPE
RD 1, BOX 70
LANCASTER ROAD
FOMBELL PA 16123

TOLL BOOTH SADDLE SHOP, THE
RT 541 BOX 205
MEDFORD NJ 08055

TOMAGS
104 MAIN ST
KLAMATH FALLS OR 97601

TOMS FEED SERVICE INC
415 E WINONA AVE
WARSAW IN 46580

TONY'S BOOT REP
111 E TRAIL
DODGE CITY KS 67801

TONY'S SADDLE SHOP
365 W U S HWY 30
VALPARAISO IN 46383

TONY'S TACK FACTORY
6078 STATE RT. 128
MIAMITOWN OH 45041

TOP BRASS
24816 ADIN AVE
NEWHALL CA 91321

TOP LINE TURF SUPPLIES
5772 CAMINO DEL REY
BONSALL CA 92003

TRAILS END TAC & FEED
440 W. YELLOWSTONE
CODY WY 82414

TRAVELING TACK BOX, THE
CAROLYN HAYNES
8214 BOJACK
HOUSTON TX 77040

TRIPLE CROWN WESTERN WEAR
296 CHURCH ST
ROYSTON GA 30662

TRIPLE J TACK SHOP
RFD 1
KENLY NC 27542

TROPHY TACK CO.
13329 SOUTH MEMORIAL
BIXBY OK 74008

TWO QUARTER FARM
7508 E COUNTY RD 100
MIDLAND TX 79701

UNCOMMON MARKET
707 W. MAIN STREET
LEXINGTON KY 40508

UNZICKER STABLES & TACK
RT. 2, BOX 156
CHAMPAIGN IL 61821

UTE PASS COUNTRY STORE
HCR 2272
WOODLAND PARK CO 80862

V BAR V WESTERN SHOP
17500 SE MC LOUGHLIN
MILWAUKEE OR 97267

VALLEY FARM CENTER
235 1
MT VERNON WA 98273

VALLEY FEED COMPANY
1486 FREEDOM BLVD
WATSONVILLE CA 95076

VALLEY TACK SHOP
6780 CENTER RD
VALLEY CITY OH 44280

VENCELS MVP CLUB, INC.
1704 WOOD SMALL RD
TERRE HAUTE IN 47802

VENCELS WESTERN STORE
R R 24
TERRE HAUTE IN 47803

VENTURA FEED & PET SUPP
PO BOX 1806
ACCOUNTS PAYABLE
VENTURA CA 93002

VENTURE FARMS SADDLE LEATHER
UNIT 6 BOX 10
WRIGHTWOOD CA 92397

VET & FARM SUPPLY (PUEBLO)
254 E HWY 246
UNIT C
BUELLTON CA 93427

VIC BENNETT SADDLE CO LTD
5809 103 STREET
EDMONTON ALBER CANADA T6H2H3

VICKERS WESTERN STORE
1460 YELLOWSTONE AV
POCATELLO ID 83201

VICTOR SUPREME SHOP
17011 NORTH 54TH STREET
SCOTTSDALE AZ 85254

VICTORY PASS, THE
121 W BROADWAY
DERRY NH 03038

VICTORY SADDLE CO
614 SO VICTORY BLVD
BURBANK CA 91502

VILLAGE HARDWARE & TACK SHOP
PO BOX 419 HIGHWAY 21 N
ONTARIO CANADA N0P2K0

VILLAGE PET SHOP
1505 MAC CORKLE SW
ST. ALBANS WV 24177

VILLAGE SADDLERY, THE
50 S. MAIN STREET
CATTARAUGUS NY 14719

VIRGINIA BEACH SADDLERY #904
3161 NEW BRIDGE RD
VIRGINIA BEACH VA 23456

VISION QUEST FARM
300 MOOTY BRIDGE ROAD
SUITE 204 - C/O ESA
LA GRANGE GA 30240

VISTA MADERA FEED & TACK
13560 SKYLINE BLVD
OAKLAND CA 94619

W W WESTERN WEAR
190 MARKUSON DR
PRINEVILLE OR 97754

WACHTER HAY & GRAIN
114 SO MONTGOMERY
OJAI CA 93023

WAGON WHEEL TACK & REPAIR
381 ATLANTIC AV W
DASSEL MN 55325

WALCO INTERNATIONAL
1703 E CHICAGO
CALDWELL IL 83605

WALNUT HILL SADDLERY
7701 CRILE ROAD
PAINESVILLE OH 44077

WATSON LEATHER PRODUCTS
2726 RIVER VIEW DRIVE
KALAMAZOO MI 49004

WEATHERVANE TACK SHOP
532 MAIN ROAD
TIVERTON RI 02878

WELL DRESSED HORSE, THE
151 GODDARD RD RR3
FREEPORT ME 04032

WENIGER'S
364 JEFFERSON RD
ROCHESTER NY 14623

WEST BRANCH TACK SHOP
RFD BOX 1826
HAMDEN ME 04444

WESTCHESTER LEATHER WORKS
28 W MAIN
STATESBORO GA 30458

WESTERN CREATIONS SADDLERY
1138 EAST FILLMORE
COLORADO SPRINGS CO 80907

WESTERN RANCH SUPPLY
PO BOX 1497
303 N 13TH ST
BILLINGS MT 59103

WESTERN WAYS
RT 5 BOX 1160
FOREST VA 24551

WESTERN WORLD
2473 WEST 200 SOUTH
OGDEN UT 84404

WESTERN WORLD
249 BLANDING BLVD
ORANGE PARK FL 32073

WESTERN WORLD
660 CALIFORNIA WAY
LONGVIEW WA 98632

WHARF, THE
980 EAST FRONT ST
VENTURA CA 93001

WHEATLEY FARMS FEED & TACK
RT 3 BOX 168
LA PLATA MD 20646

WHISPERING PINES TACK SHOP
11 PORTLAND NORTH BUSINESS
PARK - RTE. 100
FALMOUTH ME 04105

WHISTLE FIELD FARMS
RT. 1, BOX 53
AFTON VA 22920

WHITE HORSE TACK & VET SUPPLY
98 B MAIN STREET
TEMPLETON CA 93465

WHITE'S TACK SHOP INC
7716 VICTOR-MENDON RD
VICTOR NY 14564

WICHITA SHOE SUPPLY
1404 S SENECA
WICHITA KS 67213

WIESCAMP FARMS TACK
10505 RD 102 SOUTH
ALAMOSA CO 81101

WIESE VET SUPPLY
210 S MAPLE
ELDON MO 65026

WIGWAM TACK SHOP, THE
397 INDIAN HOLLOW RD
WINDHAMD CT 06280

WILD ROSE WESTERN
589 MILLER ROAD
BARNUM MN 55707

WILD SUNDAY FARM
5112 FREDERICKSBURG RD
SAN ANTONIO TX 78229

WILDWOOD TACK SHOP
163 F.M. 1830 W
ARGYLE TX 76226

WILSON WESTERN WEAR
604 SOUTH MARKET
WATERLOO IL 62298

WINCHESTER WESTERN WEAR
920 ABBOTT
SALINA CA 93901

WINCHESTER WESTERN WEAR
3291 STEVEN CREEK BLVD
SAN JOSE CA 95117

WINDCHASE FARM
930 MARYLAND AVE
PHOENIX AZ 85013

WINDWALKER TACK
1102 W HUNTZINGER
SELAH WA 98942

WINDY WILLOW FARM
1504 SOUTH PAK
NEENAH WI 54956

WINNER CIRCLE, THE
3289 ERWIN DR
WENTZVILLE MD 63385

WINNER'S CIRCLE
1703 E FORT LOWELL
TUCSON AZ 85719
WINNER'S CIRCLE, THE
1411 EDMOND RD NW
PIEDMONT OK 73078

WINNERS CUP IND. HILLS
EQUESTRIAN CENTER
16000 TEMPLE ST
CITY OF INDUSTRY C4

WISCONSIN SADDLERY
4637 MILLTOWN RD
GREENBAY WI 54313

WITT'S TACK SHOP
3781 HAPPY VALLEY CIRCLE
NEWMAN GA 30263

WONDERLAND FARMS
RD 5
WEST CHESTER PA 19382

WOODLAWN SADDLERY LTD
8405-J RICHMOND HWY
ALEXANDRIA VA 22309

WOODPECKER FARM TACK ROOM
RT 3 BOX 140
ATT ART LUBAN
WOODFORD VA 22580

WOODS FEED-SADDLERY
RT 202 BOX 135
MANCHESTER ME 04351

WOODSEDGE EQUESTRIAN
RT 2 BOX 396J
TALAHASSEE FL 32301

WOODSTOCK FARM & LAWN CTR
2020 S RT 47
WOODSTOCK IL 60098

WOODWARDS FEED SPLY
JEANNE BICK
969 MAIN ST
RAMONA CA 92065

WORKHORSE, THE
147 N 1ST
MONTROSE CO 81401

WORLD CHAMPION HORSE EQPT
730 MADISON ST PO BOX 278
SHELBYVILLE TN 37160

WXICOF
914 RISKE LN
WENTZVILLE MO 63385

WYNONA TACK SHOP
4109 E NORTH ST
SALINA KS 67401

WYOMING HONOR FARM
BOX 32
RIVERTON WY 82501

YOUNG ACRES TACK & APPAREL
3601 YOUNG ACRES FARM RD
WINSTON SALEM NC 27106

ZAMZOW'S
6313 FAIRVIEW AVENUE
BOISE ID 83704